Rediscovering
America

Books by Roger G. Kennedy

MINNESOTA HOUSES

MEN ON A MOVING FRONTIER

AMERICAN CHURCHES

ARCHITECTURE, MEN, WOMEN, AND MONEY

ORDERS FROM FRANCE

GREEK REVIVAL AMERICA

THE SMITHSONIAN GUIDE TO HISTORIC AMERICA
(12 volumes — Editorial Director)

ROGER G. KENNEDY

....

Rediscovering America

A National Trust
for Historic Preservation Book

HOUGHTON MIFFLIN COMPANY
BOSTON·1990

Color photography by Robert Lautman,
Jack Kotz, and Dick Bancroft

Copyright © 1990 by Roger G. Kennedy

ALL RIGHTS RESERVED

For information about permission to reproduce selections from this book,
write to Permissions, Houghton Mifflin Company,
2 Park Street, Boston, Massachusetts 02108.

Library of Congress Cataloging-in-Publication Data
Kennedy, Roger G.
Rediscovering America / Roger G. Kennedy.
p.   cm.
Includes index.
ISBN 0-395-55109-9
1. United States—History, Local.   2. Architecture—United States.
3. United States—Description and travel—1981—Views.   I. Title.
E180.K45 1990 90-40751
973—dc20   CIP

Printed in the United States of America

DOH 10 9 8 7 6 5 4 3 2 1

The maps on pages 5, 8, 13, 48, 56, 75, 77, 94, 138, 163, 185, 195, 257,
and 297 were executed by Mapping Specialists, Ltd., of Madison,
Wisconsin. The map of Savannah is based on a plan by William de
Brahm.

Charts on pages 168 and 310 are by Mary Reilly

Book design by Robert Overholtzer

For Elisabeth Dean Kennedy

Acknowledgments

While most of this book is new, some bits of it have appeared in print over the last five decades in eighteen books and I have forgotten how many articles and speeches. Along the way hundreds of people — friends, family, colleagues, critics, street corner disputants, symposiating contestants, talk-show humiliators, librarians, and students — have caught errors, admonished, exhorted, inspirited, and called to duty. As I reflect on the experience of these years, I grow increasingly grateful to three classes of people. First are the inspirators, whose influence I felt first. Next are those generous spirits who give focused attention to the writing of others, though not bound to them by any claim of common citizenship in a university, or even of friendship. And finally, the editors.

For me, the first inspirator was my mother, to whom this book is dedicated. She read to us, rereading lines she liked, to give us a sense of the succulence of language. Then came school teachers Kenneth Hunter and John Briggs at the St. Paul Academy. Being there in the Depression years to receive their wisdom seemed a miracle to me, and it was, a miracle hard bought by my parents. After that, gratitude is due to the anonymous authors of the GI Bill, and to Norman Holmes Pierson at Yale, who told me I might be a writer. He said so on the strength of an essay on Scott Fitzgerald, which reappeared in *Men on a Moving Frontier* twenty years later.

After the inspirators come the colleagues, cosufferers in composition, members of the brotherhood and sisterhood of the bruised. Acknowledgments of aid by them have appeared repeatedly in each of my earlier books because repeatedly they have been willing to read and think and gently admonish, and again I thank them for help — they will know when they come upon the corrected passages for how much.

Now as to editors. It is one thing to take time away from one's own submissions to immortality; that is kind enough. But to help someone else toward even a modest fame while remaining resolutely anonymous — that is abjuration as saintly as coaching high school track.

I have been the beneficiary of miles of red and blue lines, acres of sticky tabs of yellow and green, of canyon walls of admonitory graffiti, expletives undeleted on margins. Tom Watkins, now the editor of *Wilderness* magazine, with the backing of Wallace Stegner and David Lavender, encouraged me to enlarge my focus from *Minnesota Houses* to the general history of the Old Northwest, and brought forth *Men on a Moving Frontier.* Hugh Galusha, president of the Federal Reserve Bank of Minneapolis, assured me that it was not presumptuous for a banker to read and to write, and Tyrone Guthrie emboldened me to think of the stage when writing (to the bafflement of the *New York Times,* it seems, much later). When Lady Guthrie asked me to speak of and for Tyrone at the Abbey Theatre in Dublin, it was a great chance to put to work what he had tried to teach several of us about writing as reading. My mother had been right about language.

Gentle reader, if you are a writer too, you know how fearfully we entrust our work, the children of our spirit and the fragile artifacts of our craft, to others. But already I know, as these words are written, that this child, *Rediscovering America,* is going forth into the world healthier than it was when it was only mine, and handsomer too, thanks to its publisher, Jonathan Latimer, its editor, Karen Stray Nolting, and editors Gerry Morse, Luise Erdmann, and Peg Anderson.

I offer thanks to Naomi Glass, who refused to tell callers where I was when I was writing, and managed my office so that I might keep doing so, and to Joyce Ramey, who stood firm upon the second line of defense and brought order to the confusions of many unintelligible drafts. Elsie Mosqueda did crucial research, found pictures and maps, and offered good-humored advice at critical moments. Frances Kennedy found time away from saving Civil War battlefields to do many things that, in my most fervent bachelor aspirations of thirty-five years ago, I could not have imagined anyone being gracious and ingenious enough to do.

And when she was forced to attend to her own manuscript, she provided Mesa, our greyhound, to rest a head upon my foot.

Contents

x

Preface

A Way of Looking at History

IN SCIENCE, securities analysis, or the writing of history, we begin
with curiosity, proceed into skepticism, and in the end must draw
conclusions in the presence of much that remains unknown. This
progression appears to be natural, recapitulating as it does many
biographies. Curiosity seems as appropriate to youth as skepticism to
middle age, and one of the qualities we admire in a wise old age is a kind
of redemptive diffidence.

It is easy to observe these stages in the career of Thomas Jefferson,
historian. One of his earliest pleasures was inquiring about the origin of
human habitation in America. He questioned all the received wisdom of
his day on the subject. He called it hearsay, and hearsay much of it
remains, a clutter of unexamined prejudices, partial truths, and hunches,
still confusing us, despite his efforts, more than one hundred sixty years
after his death.

Jefferson had heard many theories about the "monuments" left by
the first settlers of his region. Dissatisfied with all he had heard, he did
his own digging, commencing with archaeological work upon the only
Native American architecture of which he was aware, the barrow graves
of piedmont Virginia. "I wished to satisfy myself whether any, and
which of these opinions were just." The opinions against which he
wished to test himself, in this and in so many other instances, were
French, especially the patronizing gossip passed along about Native
Americans by Georges-Louis Leclerc, comte de Buffon, the zoologist
and chemist.

So with pick and shovel (in truth, probably the picks and shovels
of his slaves) Jefferson undertook an exploration of a conical earthen

building about forty feet in diameter on a site beside the Rivanna River "opposite to some hills, on which there had been an Indian town." But when all his cuts and crosscuts, pits and ditches, were complete, he was still dissatisfied. Though he could estimate that the barrow held a thousand or more skeletons, it told him nothing more. He was left with little solid evidence with which to dispute Buffon.

This story from Jefferson's *Notes on the State of Virginia*, written initially to be distributed privately to a small audience of French savants, tells us as much about eighteenth-century science as it does about him. Changing reactions to this story, voiced at intervals between his time and ours, show how we — the reactors — have changed. Once this self-told tale of the youth of our scientist-historian-president seemed merely an incident in the rising trajectory of his amazing life. Now it seems equally a tale of the brash youth of European-American science. Admiration for his scientific fervor has been increasingly accompanied by embarrassment at his failure to sense that he was trespassing.

Jefferson was a genius, but a genius of his own time. It took European-Americans nearly a century and a half after he laid down his pick to learn how to shrink from promiscuous excavation among the bones of other peoples' departed.

"The sculls were so tender, that they generally fell to pieces on being touched."

We read his words and wonder how Jefferson's descendants would have felt had they been written by a Powhatan or Nottoway scientist reporting a "dig" in the family graveyard of the Jeffersons or Randolphs.

Retrospective reverence comes easily after two hundred years. What is more remarkable is the progression of Jefferson himself toward awe in the presence of the unknown. Indeed, there is in the rhythm of his account something more, something that suggests that between the experience and the account he came to feel the remorse of someone who knows he has pressed curiosity too far. This is especially remarkable because the audience for which he was writing was ferociously skeptical; they could be as derisive of "softness" or sentimentality in anthropology as they were in religious matters. But as his account goes forward there is a change of tone:

> A party passing, about thirty years ago, through the part of the country where this barrow is, went through the woods directly to it, without any instructions or inquiry, and having staid about it some time, with expressions which were construed to be those of sorrow, they returned to the high road, which they had left half a dozen miles to pay this visit, and pursued their journey.

Curiosity had done its job as a propellant to disciplined inquiry. Skepticism had done its job clearing away impediments. But after thirty years and more, Jefferson continued to recall the crumbling of the skull of a child in the hand of a scientist and the silent vigil of the descendants of the survivors of whatever holocaust had caused that child to die. And now it was not so much irritation at the failure of an archaeological "dry hole" that occupied his mind but a sense that the largest questions in life might not yield to science at all. This side of Jefferson's character, though rarely revealed, is important in giving us guidance when we come to the edge of evidence and look into the abyss beyond. He helps us to be comfortable in saying "We have come this far and can go no farther." Or more simply: "We do not know and are unlikely to learn." Or more simply still: "This is a mystery."

After making his own scissors-and-paste anthology of the Bible and brooding about religious matters for forty years, Jefferson wrote:

> When I was young, I was fond of speculations which seemed to promise some insight into that hidden country, but observing at length that they left me in the same ignorance in which they had found me, I have for many years ceased to read or to think concerning them, and have reposed my head on that pillow of ignorance which a benevolent Creator has made so soft for us, knowing how much we should be forced to use it.[2]

Mr. Jefferson's candor can embolden the rest of us to state our own positions on such matters, and on history as well. A mystery, about which research is unlikely to diminish our ignorance, is at the center of our lives. I set out my thoughts about the architectural consequences of that proposition in *American Churches* nearly a decade ago.[3] But Jefferson urges us *not* to rest upon a principle of diffidence where it is *not* appropriate. Though the center is mysterious, it is surrounded by the sector of the known, along the periphery of which there is always something more to be learned. That we do not know everything does not mean that we have learned nothing. Claiming too little is as bad as claiming too much.

Along that frontier, spreading confusion, there is always hearsay. In his *Notes* Jefferson did battle against the French variety. Had he read German as well (and failed to be elected president, leaving him able to pursue his archaeological researches), he might have tackled with equal fervor German hearsay about Native American architecture, even that passed along by the magnifico of German erudition, Johann Wolfgang von Goethe.

Goethe and Jefferson were contemporaries who had much in common, though neither appreciated the architecture of the country of the other. Jefferson's Rhine journey in 1787–1788, in the footsteps of Goethe, yielded the dullest of his travel notes; he did not like the Gothic and could not recognize the Romanesque. Goethe was guilty of worse, for in verse he reinforced among Americans the pernicious notion that they had no medieval architecture of their own. This misconception was common in his time, though Spanish historians had written widely of their discoveries in Mexico and Peru, and there were already many reports of the earthen architecture of the Ohio and Mississippi valleys. Still, many accepted the tangle of misconceptions embedded in Goethe's lines:

> America, you're better off
> Than our own continent that's old.
> At tumble-down castles you scoff,
> You lack basalt, I'm told. . . .
> No memory haunts you.

North America is, of course, very "old" in human habitation, full of "tumble-down castles" — some of the best, in Mexico, built of basalt. In the area now included in the United States, there are places shadowed by a deep antiquity, often accompanied by vestiges of the cathedral building of Europeans themselves.

Pecos, New Mexico, comes to mind. There, not far from Santa Fe, near a major freeway, one can find on a grassy flat ruins of ninth-century houses and remnants of a walled town of the fourteenth and fifteenth centuries that may have housed twenty-five hundred people. Beside the town is the foundation for a cruciform church with a nave 170 feet long, 90 feet wide at the transept. It was not a cathedral, for it had no resident bishop in its short half century of life, but it was the largest church north of Mexico City (probably — our knowledge of Mexican architecture is so incomplete that we may be ignorant of others). Had it not been burned during the Pueblo revolt of 1680, it would have remained the largest in the United States, I believe, until Saint Patrick's Cathedral in New York was completed in the 1880s.*

Pecos has been a place of apparently continuous human habitation since the time of Charlemagne and Alfred the Great. People were living there and creating architecture before the invention of algebra or of multiplication by ten using zero, before the founding of Saint Mark's in Venice or of the acropolis at Zimbabwe, before the sacking of Canterbury by the Danes, and before the mutual excommunication of the pope and the patriarch of Byzantium. That is true antiquity!

Even with a great deal more curiosity, Goethe could not have known of the great church at Pecos; it was rediscovered only in 1967. But there may still be some European authorities who are unaware of it and think of this as a "New World" and their own, by comparison, as "Old."

Acknowledging what remains unknown, even now, about our old continent and the story of humankind upon it, we can begin to probe toward some understanding of our history. Jefferson showed the way. Having learned of Captain Cook's exploration of the Bering Strait

*Saint Patrick's cornerstone was laid in 1858, but the structure was not completed until 1888. Benjamin Henry Latrobe's Baltimore Cathedral of 1818 (though extended in 1890) was slightly smaller than the church at Pecos.

and of the similarity between Native Americans and many peoples of northern Asia, Jefferson made the connection between the two groups. He also had the good sense to reserve judgment as to whether the former were descended from the latter or vice versa.

He did not know what has been learned since his time about the writing of history in North America. Though we lack knowledge of exactly when the first historians arrived or were born here, we do know that they were here as early as the time the Venerable Bede commenced his chronicles of Britain. They facilitated the systematic accumulation of written records by the Aztec and Maya, among others. We have not yet found historical writing north of the Mexican border, though we have, of course, found plenty of what might be called historical "illustration" on rocks and ceramics.

In deference to those first historians, it is no longer possible to begin an exploration of American history with the relatively recent accounts of American events by Europeans — those compliments to the beauty of the Caribbean people recorded by Columbus in 1492. (It is remarkable, though true, that in a few places history courses still begin with the "first settlement" by those tiny bands of Europeans who found themselves among the well-settled urban Indians of Mexico or the agriculturalists of New England.) If we readers follow our natural instinct to look for early writing, we are likeliest to find it to the south in Mexico and in other parts of Latin America. But since this book is meant to confine its observations upon history within the United States, I will merely let that instinct set the compass needle, looking for antiquity first along our southern borders.

Thereafter we will swing about the country, exploring each of its major regions. The sequence in which these explorations are presented is intended to offer a set of impressions that may, at the end, arrange themselves chronologically in the reader's memory. Then, in a second group of essays, the focus is brought down from the regional and general to the lives of individuals. My intention is to use biography, with its hard specificity, to make some test holes in the thick overlay of hearsay that lies with unusual depth upon the history of the American Middle West. While this might be done for any region, I have chosen to suggest the process in two areas with which I have deep personal associations, the northern half of the Mississippi Valley and the Cumberland Plateau.

We are all moved to return home. Writers are moved, in addition, to return to their work, especially if they are dissatisfied with it. Historians have more reason than most for dissatisfaction, because they keep learning new things that challenge what they thought was true when they first wrote about a subject. Critics help in this; they send us back to remedy our errors and add what we missed.

So, in putting these essays together, I have revisited subjects about which I have been writing for nearly forty years, going back again to people and places. Mostly this is a book about the history of places. Even when it presents a hero — when the center point is a person — that person is in a place, asking us to look about, to smell the air, look to the horizon, measure the trees, scuff the ground, listen for animals. That is the way with homecomings; the people we find in home places seem to belong there, especially when, in Gertrude Stein's terms, there is a there there.

The short biographies are of people who, in one way or another, are heroes for me. They chose themselves not because they were "representative" or "typical." I have never met a typical person. No, they are here because in life they were magnetic enough to draw into their stories a good deal of the collective experience of their times.

These heroes all inhabited places that still exist; we can visit them there, feel their presence, as one can sense the spirit of Thomas Jefferson at Monticello, George Washington at Mount Vernon, and — why not? — Alexander Hamilton at the Grange or Aaron Burr at the site of his dream city near El Dorado, Arkansas. That does not mean that we will spend much time with architectural history, though in the past I have written a half-dozen books on that subject. There is, it is true, an essay on Franco-American neoclassicism in the United States and another on the Greek Revival.[4] They are included because from these first two of our national styles we can learn more about life in America between the wars (Revolutionary and Civil) than we might learn from literary sources or landscape alone.

We move about from region to region, though this is not a guidebook like the twelve volumes of *The Smithsonian Guide to Historic America*. Some of these essays were adapted from the ones introducing each of those volumes, but here I have enlarged them to provide more room for rumination. That expansiveness may be useful to people contemplating a sojourn somewhere in the United States for a few days or to management migrants assigned somewhere or another and wishing to know more about either.

I am grateful to those who wrote the body of each of the guides for the opportunity to read their work and learn from them. That process, over two years' time, gave me occasion to think about each section of the country, about what is conventionally said of it, and about how true that "hearsay" might be. As a professional lender (banker) and investor for thirty years or more, I have been trained in skepticism. Historians, too, are trained that way, but they are not rewarded professionally for acting on opinions at variance with the consensus, as some bankers, and more venture capitalists, are. So skepticism about "hearsay" has been quite natural to me since the 1950s, when I first wrote for *The New Republic* and *Law and Contemporary Problems*.

Regional history has been important to me, first as a release and later as an adventure. While living in Minnesota and trying to build the business of a bank, I found that weekends of exploration were relief from routine, and walks about small towns provided escape routes from motels. One of two books written as a result, *Men on a Moving Frontier,* was in the form of a series of paired biographies.[5] Three halves of these pairs reappear, much revised, as Chapters 15, 16, and 17, offered as gifts of gratitude to my heroes, Giacomo Beltrami, Henry Hastings Sibley, and Ignatius Donnelly. Now, nearly thirty years after I met these people for the first time, we have become reacquainted through their letters and journals. They have led me to think and write about other men and women on other kinds of frontiers.

While another hero, Thomas Jefferson, has urged us toward skepticism, this book is not deliberately "revisionist." The shelf life of revisionism is short. Even children in kindergarten have little respect for too much showing off at the expense of the teacher. Instead, my endeavor is merely to search for truth.

Life changes history, and new sides of truth are exposed by digging around it. When that occurs, it is a joy to be able to call one's friends and show them what has been revealed, though it be an incomplete discovery.

I offer this book in the hope that it communicates that joy.

1

··

The Oldest South

Alabama, Florida, Georgia, Louisiana,
and Mississippi

T HE SOUTHERN SHORES of what are now the United States were settled ten thousand or more years before the first Europeans arrived. Even then it was the French and Spanish, not the English, who first established themselves in the Old South. The Spaniards, in fact, had insinuated their forts, missions, and villages well into the Alabama and Florida interior long before the British made their first attempts at colonization in either New England or Virginia.

Having asked the Pilgrim Fathers to wait, holding back 1620, Thanksgiving, and all that, I should acknowledge that chronology requires us to request that even Jamestown and 1607 stand by as well. This is not merely because the pageant of Captain John Smith and Pocahontas comes along rather late in our parade, with Sir Walter Raleigh and the "lost colony" only a little before it, but because Captain John and Sir Walter have no pride of primacy even among the English. The relatively chilly climate of Virginia and North Carolina became acceptable only after the failure of earlier British attempts to settle considerably farther south.

The salubrious Gulf first beckoned the British; their expeditions sought to seize the entryways to the Mississippi and to make a beachhead at Pensacola in a region they called Carolana after their first King Charles (the one they later beheaded), not Carolina after their second. They failed — but we are already several thousand years ahead of our story.

The most impressive site remaining from the prehistory of the Old South — Poverty Point — is not impressively named nor is it easy to

1

A lithograph giving a nineteenth-century European view of the marriage of Pocahontas and John Rolfe in a moment of truce between the English settlers of Virginia and the Native Americans they displaced. *Courtesy of the Library of Congress*

find. It lies along a back road near the hamlet of Monticello, twelve miles north of the midpoint of the throughway between Monroe, Louisiana, and Vicksburg, Mississippi.

This location far from the seaboard conjures us to look outward from the center of our continent, not inward from any stern and rockbound coast. It also tells us to be at least as respectful of *our* predecessors on *this* continent as were the fathers and grandfathers of the Pilgrim Fathers of *their* predecessors on their own. The citizens of Old England regarded with appropriate awe the ancient Britons who built Stonehenge, a work better known, but neither more ancient nor more ambitious, than Poverty Point.

At the same time that the English were laboring slabs of stone into a circle one hundred feet in diameter upon Salisbury Plain and surrounding them with an earthwork three hundred feet wide, the ancient people of Louisiana were moving thirty million fifty-pound loads of earth into a composition of six concentric ridges, the widest of which is four thousand feet in diameter.

Three thousand winters and spring rains have washed over this achievement; the Bayou Macon has cut deeply into it and left it vulnerable to plows, pillage, and that indifference which arises in the presence of a history we do not feel to be our own. As a result, this monument to the

American past is beyond restoration, but not beyond recognition and respect.

Poverty Point is a magnificent puzzle; eight miles of its rings can still be discerned, still 10 feet high, 75 feet wide, and 100 to 150 feet apart. At the time of the spring and fall equinoxes, if one climbs by its earthen ramp to the top of a mound to the west of the rings, one can still have a clear view of the sun rising over the central thirty-seven-acre plaza, a view like that found at similar conjunctions of earth and sun at Stonehenge.

But the Old South is even older than Poverty Point. Near Little Salt Springs in central Florida, archaeologists are exploring the traces of "hardy pioneers"* who hunted giant tortoises, mastodons, giant sloths, and bison twelve thousand years ago. Ten thousand years later some southerners had become agriculturists — considerably earlier than the people of the British Islands left any evidence of doing so in Ireland.

By the time the Dorian Greeks invaded the Aegean Basin and conquered Troy, centers of trade and ritual observance like Poverty Point were established throughout the lower Mississippi Valley. By A.D. 1300 the culture of the Old South had developed large towns, some housing more people than would come together in Baltimore, New Orleans, or Cincinnati by A.D. 1800.

Later, in the age of Froissart and Boccaccio, of the Hundred Years War and Giotto, the good citizens of whatever they called what is now Moundville, Alabama (about fourteen miles south of Tuscaloosa), created a four-hundred-acre ceremonial cluster of twenty mounds, some over sixty feet in height. Most of them remain, and below the bluffs the Black Warrior River can still be fished.

There are intriguing "barrow pit" indentations in the surface of the plateau that were probably fishponds, where the people of "Moundville," like the priests and priestesses of Astarte or the monks at Fountains Abbey in Yorkshire, may have kept fish for sacred meals.

History is the universal solvent for biography, but it does not obligate us to abstain from peopling these places with individuals who, like ourselves, may have felt the persuasion of politicians and evangelists, going on pilgrimages, as we do, to consult with shamans and hermits and curators of curious objects kept discreetly in reliquaries.

Around A.D. 1200 there may have been about three thousand inhabitants at "Moundville," as many as populated Baltimore on the eve of the American Revolution. It was, however, not as large a city as Cahokia, opposite modern St. Louis, the metropolis of the Mississippian culture

---

Pioneer means "a person on foot who explores new territory." It is derived from the Old French word for an infantry scout and ultimately from the Latin *pedes*, from which we also get *pedestrian*. There is no reason to think that the Indians of Florida had horses until they got them from the Spaniards ten thousand years later.

An imaginative depiction of the Mississippian Indian complex near Cahokia, Illinois, built before European explorers and diseases arrived in the New World. The central mound was more extensive than the Great Pyramid in Egypt. *William R. Iseminger, Cahokia Mounds State Historical Site*

of which "Moundville" was a second city, like Chicago or Los Angeles. Cahokia had a larger population than any European community built in America until the middle of the eighteenth century.

Archaeologists have observed that the decline of these large complexes at Cahokia and "Moundville" had begun even before European diseases cut some native populations to a tenth of their numbers. Nevertheless, as late as 1650 only ten thousand or so of the two to three hundred thousand inhabitants of the Old South were descendants of Europeans. And few of those ten thousand spoke English. The Spanish and French languages and architecture were dominant even after Europeans had been at work in the Old South for fully two hundred fifty years.

This is not New England. Despite the lack of subtlety in that remark, we may imagine a winter migrant from Dedham to Palm Beach who, believing it all started at Plymouth Rock, might be surprised to chance upon the huge keep of Fort Matanzas, thrusting its arrogant bulk out of the swamp fifteen miles south of St. Augustine. It was built in 1736, but it

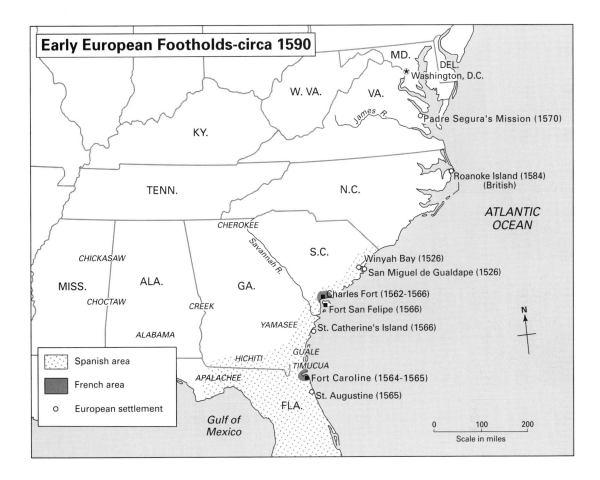

Early European Footholds-circa 1590

MD.

DEL.

*Washington, D.C.

W. VA.

VA.

James R.

Padre Segura's Mission (1570)

KY.

Roanoke Island (1584)
(British)

TENN.

N.C.

ATLANTIC
OCEAN

CHEROKEE

Savannah R.

S.C.

CHICKASAW

Winyah Bay (1526)

San Miguel de Gualdape (1526)

MISS.

ALA.

GA.

Charles Fort (1562-1566)

CHOCTAW

CREEK

Fort San Felipe (1566)

N

YAMASEE

St. Catherine's Island (1566)

ALABAMA

GUALE

HICHITI

TIMUCUA

APALACHEE

Fort Caroline (1564-1565)

Spanish area

FLA.

St. Augustine (1565)

French area

Gulf of
Mexico

0   100   200

o   European settlement

Scale in miles

looks two centuries older, as if it were one of the vanished Spanish forts
that once occupied every major strategic point on that coast. Or older
still — in the twilight it has the aspect of an outpost of Aigues-Mortes,
the Crusaders' port in the marshes of the south of France, or a strong-
point intended to protect Seville from pirates ascending the meanders of
the Guadalquivir.

Let our imaginary Yankee traveler next come upon the pinnacle of
Spanish military architecture in North America, the Castillo San Marcos
guarding St. Augustine itself. In 1675, when its walls were nearly complete, it was considerably more impressive than anything the English
had managed to erect upon their precarious footholds on the continent.
This enormous structure, with its four stone bastions and backward-
sloping walls, was built to withstand cannon fire, as it did on three occasions when the British sought to take it and failed. It was the culmination of Spanish technical advances achieved through building eight
previous forts upon the site since Juan Ponce de León claimed the area

Construction of the Castillo San Marcos began in 1672, and additions were made over the next three hundred years. It guarded the sea approach to St. Augustine. *Florida State Archives*

for the king of Spain in 1513. The first of these was in place a century before the Pilgrims set foot in America.

There was, as well, a massive Spanish fort in Pensacola, and the brick citadel of the French at Mobile, Fort Condé, was once as formidable as the Castillo at St. Augustine. These brooding, baleful crystals of hostility look to the sea — reminding us to persist in our southward reorientation. These were outposts of the Caribbean system. The organizing reality in this region from the onset of the Europeans until 1820 or so was the Caribbean, not the American landmass.

As one stands before the Castillo observing ceremonies in which English, French, Spanish, Confederate, and American flags are hauled up and down to the accompaniment of their respective national anthems (when available), it is well to recall the West Indian origin of the first European and African settlement in North America north of Mexico (Blacks, both slave and free, were present). Established in July 1526 by Lucas Vázquez Ayllón and called San Miguel de Gualdape, it was near a town today called Winyah Bay in Georgetown County, South Carolina.

Ayllón was accompanied by five hundred followers — slaves, three Dominican friars, eighty-nine horses, silkworms, a doctor, a surgeon, and an apothecary. There must have been at least one shipwright, for

The onset of the Renaissance in North America is marked by the Vitruvian engaged columns of the Governor's House in St. Augustine. This view is dated 1764. *Florida State Archives*

Ayllón was forced to replace one of his fleet, lost in a gale, with the first oceangoing vessel built by Europeans on American shores.

Gales were (and are) frequent, and navigation perilous amid the confusions of the southeastern shore, where cypress swamps merge by imperceptible degrees from boggy ground into shallow sea. And the mosquito thrives. San Miguel was a failure; after only six months, it collapsed. Ayllón and many of his followers succumbed to a local disease that may have been malaria (meanwhile transmitting their own microbes to the natives).

St. Augustine was founded by Pedro Menendez de Avilés in 1565. By 1706 the Spaniards had brought their version of the Renaissance to North America. The engaged classical columns of their Governor's House anticipated others placed upon the façade of the Mission at Santa Barbara, California, in the nineteenth century, and those of the Texas Alamo. Nothing in New York or Philadelphia was so far advanced.

St. Augustine contains many buildings marking it as Spanish. Menendez attempted to make it so, and to assure that it would also be Roman Catholic, he massacred his French Protestant competitors who had settled near present-day Jacksonville. He also began laying the foundations for a series of missions, which lasted until the end of the seventeenth

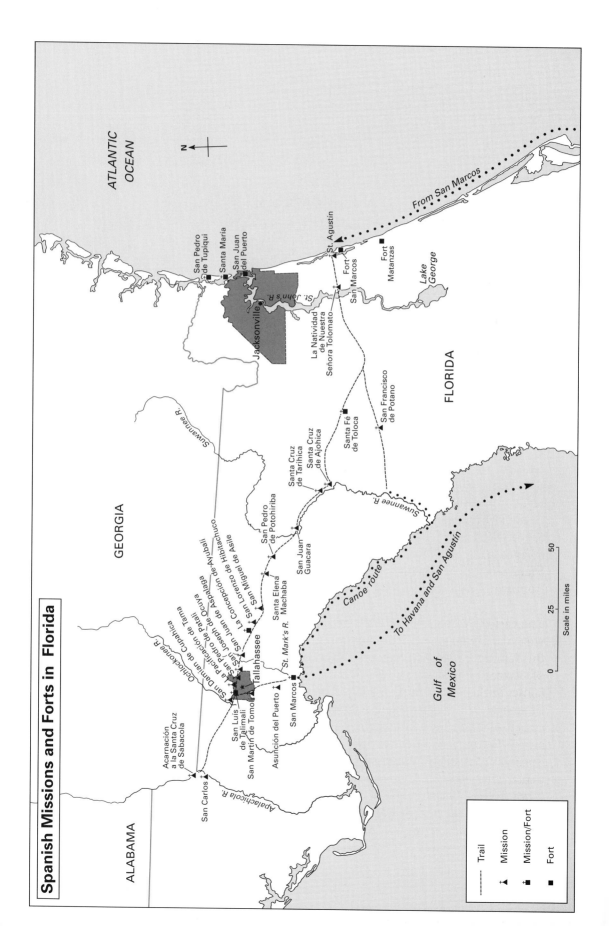

Spanish Missions and Forts in Florida

ATLANTIC OCEAN

FLORIDA

GEORGIA

ALABAMA

Gulf of Mexico

Lake George

St. John's R.

Suwannee R.

Suwannee R.

Ochlockonee R.

Apalachicola R.

St. Mark's R.

Jacksonville

Tallahassee

St. Agustín

San Pedro de Tupiqui

Santa María

San Juan del Puerto

La Natividad de Nuestra Señora Tolomato

Fort San Marcos

Fort Matanzas

San Francisco de Potano

Santa Fé de Toloca

Santa Cruz de Ajohica

Santa Cruz de Tarihica

San Pedro de Potohiriba

San Juan Guacara

Santa Elena de Machaba

San Miguel de Asile

La Concepción de Hibitachuco

San Lorenzo de Asile

San Juan de Aspalaga

San Joseph de Ocuya

San Pedro de Patale

La Pacificación de Tama

San Damián de Cupaihica

Ocuya

Acarnación a la Santa Cruz de Sabacola

San Carlos

San Luis de Talimali

San Martín de Tomole

Asunción del Puerto

San Marcos

From San Marcos

To Havana and San Agustín

Canoe route

Scale in miles

0   25   50

Trail

Mission

Mission/Fort

Fort

N

The Renaissance put its imprint upon California: the Santa Barbara Mission as it was in 1903. *Santa Barbara Historical Society*

century, when they were destroyed by the English and their steadfast allies the Creek, a confederacy of several Indian tribes inhabiting parts of Georgia, Alabama, and northern Florida.

By 1715 the island missions and eighteen more along the fertile bottomlands of the Apalachee and Ocilla rivers, well into Alabama, were ravaged and abandoned. We are lamentably uninformed of the life of the friars, Free Blacks, and "mission Indians" who lived in them. But St. Augustine and Matanzas can set our imaginations turning.

The earliest views of New Orleans show a village quite different from what we might expect from surviving buildings, all of which are from the Spanish period (after 1763) or later. At the outset there were no signs of piazzas or balconies, though the Spanish in St. Augustine had balconies in the seventeenth century. There are drawings of little houses of French New Orleans in about 1725, half-timbered or of palisaded construction, squat, with the walls filled in with brick or mud mixed with straw. We may assume that the older French settlements like Ocean Springs (Old Biloxi, Mississippi, 1699), Fort Louis (near Mobile, Alabama, 1711), Natchitoches, Louisiana (1714), and Natchez, Mississippi (1716), looked like this, too, for New Orleans was a latecomer (1718), and these were the ways Frenchmen had built for generations.

Soon things came to be grander and breezier; the breeziness appeared after 1730 or so with the spread of the piazza, and later the

10

A French *bastide*, or fortress town, in the New World, built around a parade ground. New Orleans in 1803. *Courtesy of The Historic New Orleans Collection, Museum/Research Center*

veranda. The grandeur arose after the intermingling of French and Spanish imperialism throughout the entire region from St. Augustine to the Texas border. The recently restored Ursuline Convent at New Orleans (1749–1753) is exceedingly French, even if we imagine it without the mansard roof imposed in the 1850s. The nearby Cabildo (1795) is, however, a Mexican-Spanish building, almost a duplicate of the Casa Reales built in Antiquera, Mexico, a decade earlier.

The subjects of Bourbon kings of France and Spain not only built these splendid buildings, they also assured the success of our Revolutionary War. This point is underscored by plaques and earthworks in Yorktown, Virginia, and Pensacola, Florida, which tell of the two great sieges of 1781. The capture of the British expeditionary force led by Lord Cornwallis at Yorktown was made possible by the participation of three times as many French fighting men as Americans. At Pensacola a Spanish force of four thousand captured another British army, of fifteen hundred men, together with four hundred Choctaw and one hundred of the faithful Creek.

From Spanish garrisons came money and supplies for the Americans as George Washington strove to keep his army together. At Valley Forge in 1779 he was jubilant at the news that the French and Spanish governments had crossed the line from lend-lease to formal declarations of war on Great Britain; he expected "that this formidable junction of the

The Cabildo in New Orleans: Hispanic classicism in the northern provinces of the Spanish Empire. *Courtesy of The Historic New Orleans Collection, Museum/Research Center*

House of Bourbon will not fail of establishing the Independence of America in a short time."

The Spanish forces in the Old South were led by a military hero of Washington's dimensions, Bernardo de Gálvez, veteran of wars against the Portuguese, Algerians, and Apache. As governor of Louisiana, he had already opened the port of New Orleans to the Americans, confiscated British shipping there, and sent supplies to George Rogers Clark, who was campaigning in the Ohio Valley. In the summer of 1779 Gálvez assembled an expeditionary force of Spaniards and Canary Islanders, Free Blacks and Native American recruits, and swept up the Mississippi, collecting British outposts and prisoners as he went. Fort Bute went first, then Baton Rouge, and Fort Pammure in Natchez. One flying column took Thomson's Creek and Amité, farther west, while another settled down for a siege of Pensacola.

The British attempted a counterstroke against St. Louis but were repulsed, and the Spanish under Pourre, one of Gálvez's officers, pursued

Bernardo de Gálvez, leader of the expeditionary force that captured Pensacola.
Mississippi Department of Archives and History

12

them all the way to Fort St. Joseph near the present Michigan border, which they then captured. Washington wrote the Spanish that among the beneficial effects "upon the Southern states" was a forced diversion of British forces that would otherwise combine against him. Gálvez, who was by no means exhausted, however, sent another army of Blacks and Whites to take Mobile, then press on against the citadel at Pensacola.

The twin victories of Yorktown and Pensacola, brilliantly led by Washington and Gálvez, drove the British to the conclusion for which Washington had hoped since 1779. (Histories of the American Revolution written as recently as the 1970s emphasized anxieties in Madrid about a possible domino effect of American independence and reluctance to enter into a formal alliance with the rebels in the British colonies. It may be true that what Gálvez had done was viewed in Spain

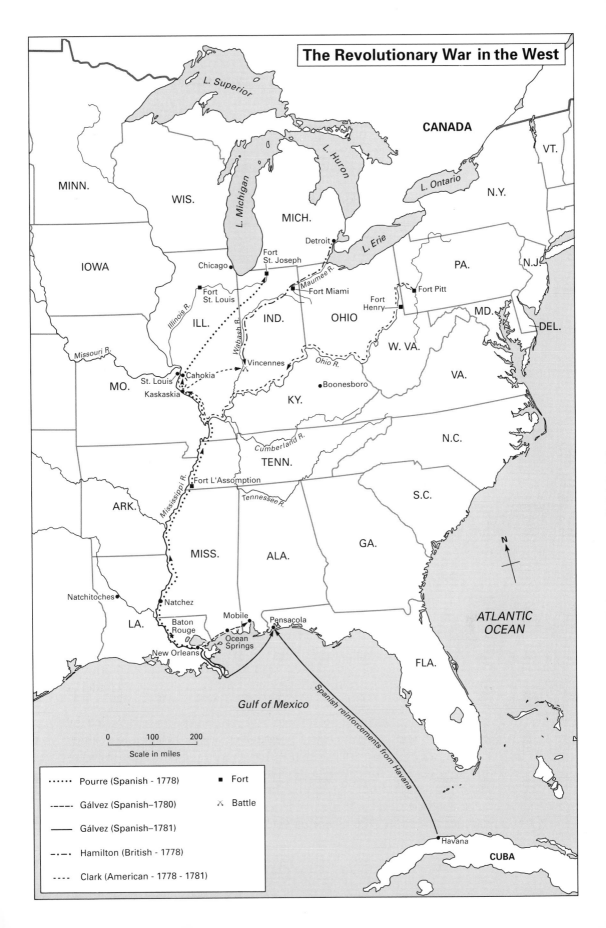

The Revolutionary War in the West

CANADA

VT.

N.Y.

MINN.

WIS.

MICH.

L. Superior

L. Michigan

L. Huron

L. Ontario

PA.

N.J.

IOWA

Detroit

Fort St. Joseph

Chicago

L. Erie

Maumee R.

Fort Miami

MD.

DEL.

Fort St. Louis

Illinois R.

ILL.

IND.

OHIO

Fort Henry

Fort Pitt

W. VA.

Missouri R.

Wabash R.

Vincennes

Ohio R.

VA.

St. Louis

Cahokia

Kaskaskia

MO.

Boonesboro

KY.

N.C.

Cumberland R.

TENN.

S.C.

Mississippi R.

Fort L'Assomption

Tennessee R.

ARK.

GA.

MISS.

ALA.

Natchitoches

Natchez

Mobile

Pensacola

LA.

Baton Rouge

Ocean Springs

New Orleans

FLA.

ATLANTIC OCEAN

N

Gulf of Mexico

Spanish reinforcements from Havana

| 0 | 100 | 200 |
Scale in miles

Havana

CUBA

····· Pourre (Spanish - 1778)   ■ Fort

--- Gálvez (Spanish–1780)   ✗ Battle

— Gálvez (Spanish–1781)

–·–· Hamilton (British - 1778)

---- Clark (American - 1778 - 1781)

primarily as an attack on the English, and strengthened the Americans only by happenstance. I have been unable to ascertain what Gálvez himself thought at the time.)

This does not carry us very far into the history of the Old South, but local historical societies and house museums await with full expositions of the nineteenth century and its central event, the Civil War. It is well to be wary of any preconceptions, however, for there are many surprises in store for the curious traveler. The largest, perhaps, is the persistence of Native Americans throughout the region and the profusion of dialects among them — and among Whites and Blacks as well.

Then, too, there are the complexities of the Civil War story; we learn that the Confederate flag never flew over Natchez, in part because the builders of many of its wonderful white-columned houses were opposed to secession, as were the Yankee merchants who were largely responsible for the construction of the Garden District of New Orleans. We learn that Major General William Tecumseh Sherman's bodyguard during his March to the Sea was composed of southerners, the Alabama Cavalry. We also learn that the chief political problem for Jefferson Davis was the propensity of state governments within the South to act as independent sovereignties. They behaved as if they were members of the *first* Confederacy, that governed by the Articles of Confederation and Perpetual Union (1777–1787), rather than of the second (1861–1865).

The surprises of natural history are equally great: the great Cohutta Wilderness within an hour and a half of Atlanta, with virgin timber and mountainous terrain up to five thousand feet, the stands of loblollies in the Sipsey Wilderness in Alabama and Bienville Forest in Mississippi.

Everywhere, however, it is the brooding presence of great age that one feels once one is relieved of the limitations of Eurocentric hearsay and free to experience how very old the Old South really is. Poverty Point and Moundville are merely two places where this presence is especially numinous. Of European antiquities, Fort Matanzas is at once a magnificent anachronism and a reminder of certain constants — the associations of piracy and architecture, for example. Matanzas was created to make it difficult for British or Dutch pirates to slide up brackish estuaries behind St. Augustine and take it from the rear, while Castillo San Marcos stood ready to withstand the assaults of the formally constituted fleets of the enemies of Spain.

This most medieval of European constructions south of Quebec and north of San Juan is not far down the coast from Amelia Island, where "Sir" Gregor MacGregor, a Scot claiming to be a hereditary baronet, held forth, threatening to extend his island kingdom to include all Spanish Florida, until he was stamped out by Andrew Jackson. MacGregor's architectural connection, Dr. William Thornton, was the designer of the United States Capitol, Tudor Place (a most elegant villa), and Octagon House, the headquarters of the American Institute of Architects, all in Washington. Thornton was MacGregor's sponsor with the United States government and among the veterans of Waterloo who, Thornton hoped, would turn their military prowess on the Spanish empire, with MacGregor providing their fleet.

This story is told in *Orders from France;* it may be enough to note here that Jackson wiped out MacGregor as a geopolitical force, not because of any aversion to piracy or invasions of Spain, but because Jackson's friends among the slave merchants of Savannah desired the elimination of MacGregor's competition in this trade, one of his sidelines and their chief though illegal source of revenue.

Finally, there is another island, Galveston, where the Napoleonic veterans, having ignored the blandishments of Thornton and MacGregor, did in fact make their assault upon the Spanish possessions. There they met Jean Laffite, another pirate, and Barthélemy Lafon, another architect. Laffite was wont to distribute to his literate victims Lord Byron's "Corsair," in which he had been admiringly depicted. How many poetic pirates can any other region boast? Or, for that matter, how many piratic architects like Lafon, who laid out most of the Garden District and the town of Donaldsonville and designed Laffite's Red House, where he practiced architecture and piracy and studied hieroglyphics and corollary, coded messages.

Pirates had been drawn to these coasts since the beginning of the sixteenth century, attracted by the opportunity to participate in the transfer of the immense riches of America to Europe. They were distinguished from the captains and admirals licensed by the crowns of England, France, and Holland chiefly by the color of legality given the predations of the latter by a slip of paper bearing a sovereign's signature. Piratic squadrons and imperial navies went after the same booty — metals refined in Mexico and Peru that were first sweated out of the ground by Native American laborers and later by slaves imported from Africa.

The earliest European settlements arose from a desire either to attack or to defend the routes taken by Spanish fleets carrying American treasures. The British and Dutch outposts in the West Indies and on the North American shore, seen without sentiment and absent the benediction of lawyers, were the roosts of state-chartered pirates. The Spanish fortresses were intended to give shelter from their raids.

European architecture in the Old South began to become elegant during the next stage in the development of the Caribbean system, when cotton and sugar joined silver and gold as a source of great wealth. The French, British, and Dutch had not been able to deprive the Spaniards of their hold on the lucrative mainland; the inland mines of San Luis Potosí and Peru were beyond the reach even of Sir Francis Drake and Sir John

Hawkins. So the islands of the West Indies were stripped of their trees and became vast sugar plantations. To supply those plantations with food and draft animals, Barbadian planters shifted capital and younger sons to Georgia, Florida, and the Carolinas and, indeed, organized northern supply points as distant as Shelter Island, off the north coast of Long Island, and Rhode Island.

As late as 1803 Napoleon thought of Louisiana primarily as a supplier of foodstuffs to provide for the sugar plantations of Saint Domingue, the early name of Haiti, the richest island in the world. He was willing to sell this mainland colony to the United States only after it was clear that rebellion and wholesale destruction had reduced the value of the island, always the centerpiece in his plan. Many refugees fled to the United States from the hideous consequences of his effort to reclaim its sugar plantations. After a decade of massacre and burning, the armies of France, Spain, and Britain reduced Saint Domingue to its present impoverished and devastated condition.

The refugees from Saint Domingue transferred three important contributions to the antebellum South: the technology of sugar production; certain attitudes toward the use of African slaves that differed, in their utter, unrepentant ferocity, from those prevailing before their arrival; and, commensurately, a terror of slave rebellion. Any uprising in the Caribbean was immediately felt to be a threat to the Gulf States. Reciprocally, until 1865 there was constant agitation to include Cuba and the West Indies within the expansionary ambitions of the slave-and-plantation system of the Old South.

The modern visitor can see vestiges of this interaction in the architectural unity of the shores of the Gulf. Everywhere the pirates roamed, everywhere the slave system penetrated, cottages raised on stilts (or posts or high basements) appeared. After 1730 or so, from Brazil to Wilmington, North Carolina, piazzas or verandas were added. After 1830, thousands of creole cottages were given the classical touches bringing them within the ambit of what we chose to call, sometimes, the Greek Revival. But the old hip-roofed cottage form, with extended eaves, reminded all those visitors who had traveled the old pirate routes that they were still within the Caribbean system.

By that time, however, most people had ceased to think about pirates so much as they did about Greeks and Goths. This was the time of Tara, white columns, chivalry of a sort, and names for plantation houses drawn from the romances of Sir Walter Scott. We will come to a somewhat more extended discussion of these matters and of the origin of the American front porch in Chapter 14.

2

···

On Privacy and Space
Arizona, Nevada, New Mexico, and Utah

S ITTING AT THE CLOSE OF DAY upon a rock in Arizona, watching the shadows move out from the walls of a very old adobe
building. They turn the gray-brown earth darker until it is
almost blue. Things do not seem the same as they did in a garden
on the Potomac.

Nostrils and mouth are much in need of another run on the canteen.
Hands are gritty. Has it ever rained here? I don't recall a blade of grass,
much less a tendril of vine, in the last five miles. Later the moon crawls
up the bowl of an indigo sky uncomplicated by clouds but punctured by
the dry light of the desert stars.

Dry. This climate preserves ruins very neatly. Perhaps our feeling
that civilization is especially old in places with little rainfall, such as
Arizona, the Nile Delta, or Mesopotamia, is simply the result of the
longevity of their architecture. Civilization may be much older in the
Amazon or the Congo, or the lower Mississippi Valley, but the evidence
has been decomposed by quick-growing vegetation that enshrouds,
splits, crumbles, and finally dissolves it; cities and strongholds, gardens
and fortresses, become mud downstream in a delta. Not here.

Dry. The delta of the Colorado, unlike that of the Nile, has no water
in it much of the time. That is our fault; we have so overgrazed and over-
built in the valley of the Colorado that what rain there is sluices and
burns out all at once. We have given our great river flash floods or
cracked and baked-out oven plains. And somehow our own desolation
has diminished our esteem for the people who preceded us and made a
civilization upon that ground before we laid it waste. Perhaps that dimin-

Anasazi stonework in the ruins of Pueblo Bonito, Chaco Canyon, New Mexico. *Photograph by Jack Kotz*

ishing may lighten our burden of responsibility for what we have done and for what we are doing.

We Euro-Americans do not seem to feel antiquity in the American Southwest as we do in the Nile Delta. Nor do we feel grandeur in Canyon de Chelly (pronounced "Shay") as we do at Persepolis or Palmyra or Leptis Magna. This cannot be something so simple as European-American ethnic impermeability to Native American accomplishment; the ancient Egyptians are as foreign to white- or pink-skinned northern Europeans as the Hopi or Navaho.

Something in the modern American sense of the past stands between us and the architectural legacy of our own country. It is as if we were dyslexic to our own masonry literature. The dry Southwest has presented us with a profusion of ruined villages, watchtowers atop mesas, cliffside sanctuaries and fortresses, and the markings of an extensive medieval road system. Yet we travel into the fastnesses of central Asia for a few tumbled towers and embrace with fervor the hill towns of Apulia from which Frederick II of the Hohenstaufen ("Stupor Mundi") has been gone so long. Some of us even venture into the hostile valleys of Syria for the sight of a red-rock carving. But we reject the immense presence of the hill towns of the Anasazi.* It remains difficult in our European-schooled minds to register that these were built long before the Genoese got as far into the North Atlantic as the Canary Islands, long before the birth of Columbus, Cortés, or certainly Captain John Smith.

Must we go for another set of generations prating about an "empty continent" and thinking about woodland, prairie, rain forest, mountain, and desert people as if they could have been all the same, about agricultural people living in the same villages for hundreds of years as if they were "hunter-gatherers"? It is not enough to say that anthropologists have known all these fine distinctions for a long time; the popular historical consciousness has not absorbed many anthropological certitudes, nor has fiction, drama, or, goodness knows, the repertory of presidential speechwriters.

One example may suffice: if an assembly hall full of college seniors were asked when cotton culture commenced in the United States, some hands might rise to indicate knowledge of the growing of some of the long-fibered, silky, "sea island" variety along the coast of South Carolina and Georgia in colonial days, with black seeds easily ginned by a device long employed in India, whence the first of those seeds had been imported. More hands might rise to acknowledge the expansion of cotton production after Eli Whitney developed a new kind of gin in 1793, which could remove mechanically the stickier green seeds of the hardier upland variety, which ultimately created the piedmont realm of King Cotton.

But how many college seniors would think first of the cotton culture originated a thousand years earlier in New Mexico? Or of the cotton textiles produced and used there while the ancestors of Eli Whitney were still wrapping themselves in the pelts of animals?

Mainstream American culture has been very slow to accommodate to the reality that there was an agricultural, settled, and architecturally sophisticated medieval people within our own borders. We do not have the historical imagination to animate the grandeur they left behind, though the two powerful religious groups, very much alive in the American Southwest, might enlighten us. The Mormons and Native Americans have very different stories to tell, proceeding from radically dissimilar experiences. But each of their belief systems has deep roots in the ancient American past.

The Native Americans do not evangelize; the Mormons do. As a result, part — though only part — of what the Mormons have to say

*Anasazi means "ancient ones" or, more precisely, "ancient enemies" in the Navaho language.

about that past is made available to "gentiles" (non-Mormons) in written form. The writing of history is at the core of their evangelism, and they draw upon scriptures believed to antedate European settlement.

Though they are different in this way, the Latter-day Saints and the Native Americans have in common a tenacious sense of the privacy of the central mysteries of their religion. Accordingly, they do not make available to outsiders the rituals that reinforce their views of history. One does not climb the steep ascent to Acoma uninvited, and nose about where one has not been asked to enter, without quickly learning how private is the Southwest. The lessons of Acoma, or of any pueblo, are there, and a welcome, too, at certain times, but only with the explicit invitation of the elders. Nor is it wise to blunder into a Mormon temple. A tabernacle, yes. But temples are not for gentiles. Likewise, the people of the pueblos and the Hopi of the mesas guard their traditions from profanation, courteously but firmly turning away the idly curious.

So we go to the landscape they have constructed for elucidation, venturing sometimes a little out of the way in order to see the Mormon and Pueblo landscapes directly juxtaposed, where they reveal some things that neither might disclose if taken separately. The most striking revelation made manifest by seeing their works together is that these two cultures were the most proficient irrigators in American history. The most staggering accomplishment of the Anasazi, of the Hohokam of the Gila Valley, and of the Salado of the upper Salt River Valley was not *on* the ground but *in* it: their irrigated agriculture. Remnants of their canal systems still carry water in Arizona. After them no one managed so well until the Mormons, who were the first Anglo-Americans to use irrigation for farming.

The Mormons were, of course, latecomers. Tens of thousands of masonry dwellings were built in this region a half thousand years before they came. Some are still occupied by the descendants of those who built them. Villages such as those atop the mesas at Acoma and Oraibi and in the pueblos near Santa Fe are full of life, though much of that life is hidden from outsiders.

Why were other cliffside villages abandoned — Betatakin, Inscription House, or Keet Seel, east of Lake Powell in Arizona? It is apparent that the Anasazi had lived there for a thousand years, developing an ever more complex culture and architecture. Then they were there no longer. Other Native Americans have taken their place. The Navaho are still farming near Keet Seel in Canyon del Muerto, having arrived about 1650 — from whence we know not — to replace the Anasazi who had departed — we know not why or whence — three centuries earlier. These ancient ones had occupied that valley and Canyon de Chelly since a time well before the unruly folk of Athens permitted their customs to be put into writing by Solon.

An Anasazi reservoir: the purposeful use of a scarce resource by a sophisticated people. *The University of Utah Archaeological Center*

It is possible that Acoma, with a thousand years of unrecorded history, is the oldest continuously occupied town in the United States. Perhaps Oraibi is older. The Hopi came there sometime before Petrarch composed his first verses, before the completion of the Arena frescoes by Giotto or *The Divine Comedy* by Dante. We do not know precisely when. The records are architectural, not literary, and architectural records do not date easily among people who build in the same way over hundreds of years.

In the nineteenth century people permitted their historic imagination to run beyond the documentary evidence to try to understand these events. Those who had read the Bible, *Le Morte d'Arthur,* the Chronicles of Charlemagne, or the Norse eddas naturally thought of great battles as explanations for the disappearance of peoples. Did some American Armageddon account for the abandonment of one set of buildings or another, or a whole valley full of buildings, such as those along the Ohio, the Colorado, and the Salt? Tiresome twentieth-century scholarship, nourished not in the library but in the databank, speaking in unrhymed and unmetered "bits," has belittled such large explanations, yet it has offered nothing satisfactory in their stead.

A portrait by Adrian Lamb of Joseph Smith painted more than a century after his death; there are no accurate images of him drawn from life. *National Portrait Gallery, Smithsonian Institution, Washington, D.C.*

Religion has always responded to mystery, because it is about mystery. In the 1830s Joseph Smith offered an explanation for the abandonment of Native American habitations. He had grown to manhood amid the ruins and remnants of prehistoric civilization around Palmyra, New York. This experience was full of mighty stimuli to a questing spirit like his, though it was based on evidence far less distinct than the southwestern ruins around which so many of his Mormon followers live today. In a fervent apprehension of American antiquity, Smith was called to prophesy.

As a result the Book of Mormon is the only major religious tract of the European tradition to place Native Americans at the center of its story. It is unique in requiring Euro-Americans to consider soberly their relationship to those who preceded them upon this continent.

Mormon, according to Joseph Smith, was the name of a non-Indian who died in a great battle, leaving behind a record of the early history of his people. That record he committed to his son Moroni, who set down the rest of the story. Mormons believe that this was the record discovered in the 1830s by Smith. Was Smith correct in his history? The remains of fortresses and mounds and the density of arrow and spear points found around Palmyra may, indeed, indicate that great battles were fought among Indian nations there about the time of the possibly historic King Arthur of Britain. Skeptics cannot prove the contrary and, as Winston Churchill said of Arthur, "It is all true, or it ought to be; and more and better besides."

Keeping in mind the theological basis of the respectful relationship that later evolved between these two irrigating desert cultures, one may travel sixty miles beyond the Arizona border, into the Mexican state of Chihuahua, to visit a remarkably intact pueblo complex, known as Casas Grandes, within sight of the thriving Mormon town of Nuevos Casas Grandes. Blue-eyed, blond-haired people, speaking Spanish or English, often with Scandinavian accents, are found here, as they are in similar Mormon habitats shadowed by the Sierra Madre, the Wasatch, the Sawtooths, and the Kaibab or thriving beside the Mazatzals.

The "new town" of Casas Grandes lies in an irrigated oasis first created by the canal system of the departed people of the pueblo. The Mormon community, laid out as are many of their other villages throughout the Great Basin, is set in wide open configurations quite unlike villages of the Midwest. White-painted houses are set back twenty-five feet from streets that seem as wide as the boulevards of Paris, allowing room for irrigation ditches to run alongside. There is more space around the dwellings than is customary among the gentiles — space much needed, for behind the houses in the center of town are farm buildings and farm machinery. Mormons have a saying that nothing should be thrown away; they are remarkable for their abhorrence of waste.

The Mormon landscape: a characteristic hay derrick.
Utah State Historical Society

There are other Mormon signs and symbols: against the sky is the spindly crotchet known as the Mormon hay derrick, a means to pile hay that seems to work but looks like the skeleton of a windmill without blades, made of wood where wood can be found. Where a little more wood was found and saved, it was often used to make a "Mormon fence" of vertical slats. Along such a fence, if there is water enough, one sees a few "Mormon poplars," though insects and drought have done in most of them.

Early on, Mormon settlers learned how to use adobe from their Pueblo neighbors. The people of Casas Grandes, for example, baked their bricks in units three feet long and twenty inches wide. Mormon adobe is still to be found as far north as Idaho, along with stonework almost as fine as the Anasazi construction — about eight hundred years older — on Pueblo Bonito in Chaco Canyon. Mormon teaching and practice emphasized masonry construction; the Mormons recruited masons and deployed them to sustain until the end of the nineteenth century building patterns largely abandoned elsewhere in the United States.

"Mormon poplars" in Utah. *Utah State Historical Society*

In the Mormon village of Willard in the Cache Valley, in Alpine and Spring City, Utah, or in Snowflake, Arizona, there are many houses with four rooms over four, under gable roofs, like those of New England towns of the 1750s. These tend to be of masonry, whereas in New England they would more likely be wooden. The Mormons adapted well to arid western conditions, building fine adobe center-hall houses in St. George and Santa Clara in the Virgin River country of southwest Utah. When one approaches a white frame meetinghouse such as that in Pine Valley, only the tiny brackets under the eaves and the hillsides beyond — blue-green with sage and juniper — tell us that we are not in some New Hampshire dale. It is all very peaceful.

But it was not so at the beginning. Joseph Smith and his family were driven out of Palmyra to Kirtland, Ohio, in 1833–1836. There he devised the first of the curious admixtures of traditional New England meeting-house forms with Carpenter Gothic elements that reappeared in Utah to the end of the century. Another curious admixture — social and psycho-logical rather than architectural — was the Mormons' economic system. It combined the communitarian ideals of several sects such as the

The Ward Chapel in Pine Valley, Utah, a New England or upstate New York meetinghouse form transported to the intermountain West by the Mormons. *Utah State Historical Society*

Rappites, Shakers, and Fourierists with the need to assimilate poor newcomers into the church. A number of social experiments began at Kirtland and developed in Utah, such as the United Order of Enoch, about which there is much scholarly debate. Some say it was a military order, but all seem agreed that its chief function was community building among disparate converts.

Kirtland was no more secure than Palmyra had been. Smith, who was tarred and feathered by a lynch mob, took his flock west to Missouri, where an advance guard of Mormons had settled in 1831. A second temple was commenced at Independence, but it was never completed. Mutual hostility, murder, barn burnings, and harassment recurred between the Mormons and their neighbors. Moving from county to county, Smith responded to attacks by threatening vengeance.

Whatever each of us may conclude after reading what Joseph Smith left to us as a history of the American Middle Ages, and whatever each of us may feel about his theology, all historians agree on certain consequences of his history and theology. The Mormons consistently strove to convert the Indians to join them, one reason for their unpopularity with the frontiersmen of Missouri. There was ample reason to fear a Mormon alliance with the Sacs and Foxes, who had been herded into the neighborhood after the Black Hawk War had shown how effective they were in battle.

For consorting with the Indians and other misdemeanors, eighteen Mormons were killed and fifteen wounded at Haun's Mill in September 1838. A surrender to the militia barely prevented a much larger massacre. Smith was taken hostage and his people retreated eastward out of Missouri, retracing their steps to establish themselves in Illinois. This First Mormon War set neighbor against neighbor in Missouri and provided guerrilla training to many who were led after 1854 to other purposes in Bleeding Kansas by John Brown and the Quantrills.

Fifteen thousand strong, the Mormons became a political force welcomed by Abraham Lincoln in Illinois. Their neat, masonry town of Nauvoo became the largest in the state. To this day people in Utah, Arizona, New Mexico, and Idaho apply the architectural lessons learned there in the 1840s; those center-hall, four-over-four dwellings are their "Nauvoo houses."

Once again, however, there was no peace. Smith and his brother were killed by a lynch mob with the complicity of jailers in Carthage, Illinois. The Mormons commenced another long march under the leadership of Brigham Young, this time across Iowa and the great plains to Utah, following advice from John C. Frémont. Frémont had published a report on Utah's Bear River Valley and the eastern shores of Great Salt Lake: "water excellent, timber sufficient, soil good and well adapted to grains and grasses . . . will sustain any amount of cattle." The missionaries and trappers interviewed by Young confirmed Frémont's description and so did the evidence of the Mormons' delighted eyes when they gazed upon their new Zion in the summer of 1847.

Utah was Indian territory, only nominally governed by Mexico. Young continued to be solicitous of the Indians and recruited tribesmen to fight battles with those who threatened his flock. The running battles of New York, Ohio, Missouri, and Illinois broke out again, with Mormons and non-Mormons deploying Indians against each other. One hundred twenty men, women, and children making for California across Mormon territory were massacred in September 1857 at Mountain Meadows in southern Utah. By a miracle of last-minute negotiation and a tacit agreement to narrow responsibility for the Mountain Meadows massacre to the Mormon leader actually on the scene, a second Mormon war was averted.

This was the one diplomatic triumph of James Buchanan's administration as it blundered into the Civil War. In the midst of that war Abraham Lincoln spoke to an emissary from Utah: "When I was a boy . . . in

The Mormons move west across Iowa from Nauvoo, Illinois.
Courtesy of the Library of Congress

Illinois there was a great deal of timber on the farms which we had to clear away. Occasionally we would come to a log . . . too hard to split, too wet to burn, and too heavy to move, so we plowed around it. That's what I intend to do with the Mormons. You go back and tell Brigham Young that if he will leave me alone, I will let him alone."

The Mormon landscape recapitulates the history of the sect as the settlers renewed the architecture of lost Zions: Palmyra, New York; Kirtland, Ohio; Independence, Missouri; and Nauvoo, Illinois. The ordered, hierarchic landscape they imposed upon the western land is the direct projection of the persistence of a patriarchy that commenced with their prophet, Joseph Smith, and their Moses, Brigham Young. Smith and Young were builders in the precise, vocational sense: one was a glazier-carpenter, the other a carpenter-builder by trade. Perhaps that is why they were such effective builders in the metaphorical and institutional realms. They had a full consciousness of the interaction of buildings and people and knew how the constructed environment shapes behavior.

They envisaged an agricultural community, a holy experiment like that of the Pilgrim Fathers. Young made the necessary adjustments to the desert West, but he could not anticipate the harsher adjustments of such a rural society to the rush of mining and industrialization that overwhelmed the Mormon heartland in the twentieth century. It came so quickly that the Old West continued to persist side by side with the new.

The Mormon cityscape: St. George, Utah. *Utah State Historical Society*

The year 1923 is within many living memories. In 1923 the old came into a series of violent abrasions with the new. The U.S. Smelting and Refining Company's copper smelting plant was under construction in Midvale, on the east bank of the Jordan River on the outskirts of Salt Lake City. This was the consummate expression of the aggregate skills of John D. Rockefeller, Samuel Newhouse, and Spencer Penrose. Samuel Untermyer, their lawyer, had achieved the consolidation of the Utah smelters and refineries. For alleviating the irritations of competition in the production of copper, he received the largest legal fee paid to that date, $750,000 — about $8 million in 1990 purchasing power.

The land around the smelter was once a mountain, part of a blue-green, sage-covered range called by the Paiute *Oquirrh,* or "shining mountains." Mining has "brought low" the mountain near Midvale; it is now a colossal crater striated in red, gray, and brown, crawling with huge, snarling machines, producing gold, silver, copper, lead, and zinc. *The WPA Guide to Utah,* written in 1940, predicted that there would be "enough ore bodies to last until 1990."

Almost. People packing up in the little towns along what was once Bingham Canyon, amid exhausted earth and abandoned smelters, may quote to each other the words of Brigham Young in 1848, rebuking Sanford Bingham and his brother Thomas for prospecting: "Instead of

The Mormon landscape near Logan, Utah. *Utah State Historical Society*

hunting gold, let every man go to work at raising wheat, oats, barley, corn and vegetables and fruit in abundance that there may be plenty in the land."

The same WPA Guide (the most idiosyncratic, poetic, and uninhibited of the series) remarks on the older, sweeter sounds that could be heard on the slopes of those hills until they were drowned out by the roar and snarl of the machines. The Shoshone and the Paiute were very musical peoples, and so were the Mormons. The Indians put a high premium on "the man with a sweet voice," and the Mormons have always been famous for their choruses. Singing was important to these people. Brigham Young was a musical man as well as a master carpenter. The Mormon Tabernacle Choir and the extraordinary acoustics of the tabernacle both manifest his devotion to sweet voices.

It happens that in 1923 the Mormons around Salt Lake produced their first operas at the Lucy Gates Grand Opera Company under the aegis of Madame Gates, a coloratura soprano and granddaughter of Young, and her brother, B. Cecil Gates, a composer. The new West was crystallized in the presence of the most complex of Euro-American art forms upon the stage in Salt Lake City.

The Old West, the less harmonious West, the West of hatred and violence, had one gunfight left in it during the summer of 1923. Toward the end of that summer, "Old Posey," chief of the dispossessed Paiute of the San Juan Valley, made his last raid on the colonists near the town of Bluff. He broke two of his tribesmen out of jail, fought a running two-day battle with a posse, and at the end was mortally wounded in Comb Wash. He took shelter in a cave, propped himself up in its mouth, managed to stuff medicinal weeds into his wounds, but died — facing his enemies.

His kind of death was one answer to a world that had no place for him, as it had no place for the mountain that became a pit by order of the U.S. Smelting and Refining Company. Radical alterations like these, however, are not the common means by which the people of the desert Southwest have adjusted to the industrial, urban, corporate world of large units and exploded communities. Life has proceeded in innumerable minute adaptations, discernible only when assessment is made at the end or beginning of things, at funerals and weddings, at plant closings and Grand Openings, at the boarding up of exhausted houses and Open Houses.

The desert Southwest has new ruins every day, and new starts as well. It presents its accumulated uglinesses, mercilessly preserved by the dryness of the desert, without the underbrush and vines that disguise the worst of mankind's wastes in other parts of the country. And not far away, in the desert West, there may be gardens and buildings of a beauty so direct and spare as to make the opulence of other places seem anxious and fussy.

It is not true that all human interventions in the landscape make it worse; the intentional creation of comeliness thrives in this dry climate amid the natural drama of the West. Painters have congregated around Taos, architects, visionary and otherwise, around Scottsdale, and, more recently, filmmakers and writers at Sundance. There is probably no other part of America where so much good music is made per capita. After the Lucy Gates opera company came another one, at Santa Fe, and smaller ones elsewhere. Choruses and quartets, country fiddlers and pickers, are abundant.

And on the horizon there remain those meticulously joined walls of the Anasazi, as finished as a page of Mozart's music, the highest reach of attainment in the use of the materials at hand. When the Mormon Tabernacle Choir is singing what it most fervently believes, it reaches the level of the work at Chaco Canyon.

3

....

The Polygenetic South

The Carolinas, Kentucky, Tennessee,
and West Virginia

THE SOUTH has many voices: blues of the Delta, migrating to Memphis, becoming electronic Rhythm and Blues in Nashville; Country and Gospel everywhere, sung by Blacks and Whites in the hills and on the plains; the hymns of the Shakers still heard sometimes at Pleasant Hill; sentimental melodies spun around pianos throughout the South to the whirring of ceiling fans; work songs chanted by stoop labor in the fields; Moravian hymns in Winston-Salem; Robert Shaw's great orchestra and chorus in Atlanta; Menotti and Monteverdi at the Spoleto Festival in Charleston.

The South has a special strength derived from the diversity of its musical and genetic origins. Compared to colonial Connecticut, for example, the Old South was as diverse as the Balkans. It is a false idea that it was ever a place of sonic or racial "purity." Austrian German was spoken among the Salzburgers at Ebenezer, Georgia, and Rhineland German among the Palatines nearby. Rhenish was also the patois of the German Coast of Louisiana, though by the 1980s it had merged with French-Canadian (Cajun) into a dialect that has more in common with the English spoken by a businessman from Strasbourg trying to negotiate in Chicago than with the slow African-English of the Louisiana parishes nearby. French-Swiss was spoken among the Huguenot traders of Georgia and South Carolina who had been sent to Geneva for schooling; names like Manigault ("Many-go") and Huger ("Oo-jay") are still pronounced in Charleston not as they are in Indianapolis, but as in Paris — or, rather, as they were in Geneva.

Spanish was spoken in six dialects, including that of the Canary

Islands (in Florida and Louisiana), and these six inflections still exist. There were Italians and Minorcans at New Smyrna, Dr. Andrew Turnbull's colony in Florida; thirty or more Indian dialects began their fusions (like Gullah) with African languages originating from Senegal to Angola.

We could not attend in any detail to all these complexities even if we limited the discussion to those among the Euro-Americans. So in this essay I will attempt only a summary of their earliest relations to the African-Americans they brought to these shores to do their work and to the Native Americans they displaced. Then, because the distinction between Appalachian and flatland customs is the most obvious cleavage in a region divided by a mountain range, I will give particular attention to those who bestowed on the upland much of its special character.

Though some "seasoned" slaves came to the South from the West Indies, most of the ancestors of American Blacks were brought directly from Africa. The Deep South remains, after many migrations to the North, the most African portion of the United States. Any visitor to the Tidewater plain from 1740 onward might have thought it an African colony, with a few Europeans keeping guard. But of course these Europeans and their slaves did not come to an "empty" continent. Even before the Africans joined them, Whites had been a minority group in the Carolinas. As late as 1750 there were probably twenty-five thousand Europeans, forty thousand Blacks, and sixty thousand Creek, Cherokee, Choctaw, and members of smaller tribes. Thereafter, while the Native American population was diminished by death and forced emigration, the Black population increased more rapidly than the White.

The powerful but outnumbered Whites assiduously fomented divisions among the Indians and between the Indians and the Blacks to prevent these forces from combining. The English in Charleston had great success in recruiting Creek to join them in their slave hunts among the Guale and Apalachee. In the first decade of the eighteenth century, ten to twelve thousand Indians were brought to market with the assistance of other Indians.

Such alliances were replaced over time by reliance upon the militia, the function of which was to protect the plantations from Indians and, of course, from slave revolts. The English were so skillful in dividing their potential opponents that from 1708 to the middle of the century the militia was composed of equal numbers of Blacks and Whites. Though the fear of slave rebellion led to a diminution of the recruitment targets to one-third Blacks, half the force by which the governor of South Carolina barely succeeded in defeating the Yamasee in 1715 were Blacks. African-Americans also joined in the campaigns against the Cherokee in the 1760s.

The wars against the Yamasee and Cherokee were also Indian civil wars, as the remnants of other seaboard tribes were stirred up against these powerful nations. Blacks and Indians fought against each other and with each other against other Blacks and Indians in wars history has generally depicted as taking place between the European invaders of the continent. Blacks and Native Americans were actively deployed by the British in their wars against Spain in the early eighteenth century. The Spaniards, in turn, invaded Georgia in 1742 with an army that included a regiment of Blacks under Black officers superbly uniformed with lace at the collar and cuffs.

The American Revolution brought a new set of complexities and tensions to the region. In the presence of still-powerful confederacies of Cherokee and of a huge slave population, both the Whigs and Tories attempted to recruit those leaning toward them and to neutralize potential enemies. The British promised emancipation to the slaves in 1775. Thomas Jefferson estimated that in Virginia alone thirty thousand slaves responded and were "lost." Lost many of them were, for the British permitted thousands to die of starvation while awaiting shipment to freedom. It is possible some actually went free, but the records are very unclear as to how many — it did not seem important at the time. Nor do we know much about the twenty-five thousand slaves from South Carolina and the twelve thousand from Georgia who escaped to Florida or the West or were "stolen" by the British. There were many Free Blacks in the French army that aided the Americans at Savannah in 1779, and many more in the Spanish expedition that took the great fortress at Pensacola from the British in 1781.

Blacks also served in the American independence forces, more on sea than on land. In 1779 the Continental Congress offered freedom to three thousand slaves in South Carolina and Georgia in return for service in the Continental army, a proposal strongly supported by George Washington. It is a further demonstration of the selective blindness of American historians that we have apparently lost track of what happened to those who accepted the offer. Because we possess records of the conversations and deliberations of slave owners, but not of the behavior of slaves, we know only that John Laurens of South Carolina and Alexander Hamilton were unsuccessful in their effort to induce the Congress to make a fixed policy of enrolling Blacks. We can only wonder how the history of the Old South might have proceeded had it been otherwise.

(Laurens may not have known it, but during the Indian wars in 1710, South Carolina offered freedom to any slave who killed an enemy Indian. In 1865, Robert E. Lee favored recruiting Blacks for the Confederate army in return for a promise of freedom. This policy, essentially that of 1710 and of Laurens and Hamilton, was at the point of prevailing in the Confederacy when the Civil War came to an end.)

Slavery was not unique to the South; it was merely more successful there and inextricably associated with race. Europeans, like Africans,

John Laurens of South Carolina, one of the proponents of recruiting Blacks to serve in the Revolutionary War. *From the Collections of the South Carolina Historical Society*

had long imposed slavery as a penalty for losing in warfare. But in the English colonies slavery was the prize that provoked wars. In New England in the 1670s, Emmanuel Downing wrote his brother-in-law, John Winthrop, rejoicing in an outbreak of violence against the Narraganset to "deliver into . . . our hands . . . men, women and children enough to exchange for Moors [like Othello]."[1] Indian slaves were to be captured and exchanged in the South or West Indies for Blacks.

This habit of using conquered people to constitute a work force was applied by the English as soon as they stepped ashore in the Old South. Coffles* of conquered Indians dragged themselves eastward through the dust toward the Carolina coast and there met Blacks who, a few months earlier, had been marched westward toward holding pens on the coast of Africa.

Race and religion were correlated with caste and forced labor, though a few early Americans of English descent did not make such neat distinctions. Noting that the king of France encouraged racial intermarriage as part of his imperial policy, "in order that, having but one law and one master, they may form only one people and one blood," some reflective Virginians, like Robert Beverly and William Byrd, briefly urged a similar "Modern Policy" (their words) without "false delicacy" about race.[2]

But this was too much to expect from people whose experience with race was so different from that of Mediterranean peoples. The Spaniards had learned colonization in the lands they had "reconquered" — after seven hundred years — from the Moors. They had exterminated or exiled dissenters — Jews and Muslims — but also welcomed conversions. This was an important experience: if you try to save a man's soul by persuasion, you must learn something about him. If you give him up as a devil or a savage or a creature of another species, you learn less. Historians can be grateful for the results of Spanish inquiry — without being crass one might even call it market research. There is nothing in the English colonial literature to compare with the studies of Native American customs and mores provided us by the attentive though sometimes repressive Spaniards.

The conquistadors in Florida were instructed by their emperor, Charles V, to evangelize: "Our first intent in the discovery of new lands is that the inhabitants . . . may be brought to understand the truths of our Holy Catholic Faith." Accordingly, the first settlement in Florida was both a mission and a monastery of Saint Francis. Though Spanish conversion was sometimes coercive, it was an explicit statement that Indians were persons.

*Coffle, from the Arabic word for caravan, meaning "a column of men or beasts," is most often used to describe a column of Black slaves. But in the earliest days of the Carolinas, the columns of slaves were more often composed of Native Americans than Africans.

No similar directives were issued by Ivan the Terrible of Russia or Henry VIII of England, the contemporaries of Emperor Charles. Many Christian Indians came to live in Spanish St. Augustine and French Mobile, but there were very few in cities organized by the British. This is not to say that the Spaniards were wholly benign; they exploited and forcibly evangelized the Indians in Florida. In the Spanish colonies, both in the Southeast and the Southwest, racial comity proceeded further during the colonial period than it did where the British prevailed. Yet even among the Spaniards, coercive conversion led to bloodshed and bloodshed to slavery, though not initially based on racial lines.

It seems likely that if the Spaniards had elected to keep a few of the Frenchmen they captured on the South Carolina coast in 1565, they would have made them slaves — "as Protestants" and as losers. Instead, they were exterminated by the Spaniards "as Protestants," relieving the British of the task of doing so "as Frenchmen." Who in this sorry tale of enslavement and slaughter was the savage?

Black slavery united the seacoast, the highlands, and the plains beyond and distinguished the frontier experience of the South from that of the North. The historian Staughton Lynd has written: "Here the covered wagons had been followed by long lines of slaves; here, as Jefferson Davis observed in 1861, it was slaves not freemen who had made farms out of the wilderness; here the structure of power was aristocratic and not egalitarian; here the effect of frontier life was to coarsen and brutalize the peculiar institution, not to humanize it."

By 1780 the "peculiar institution" was producing more slaves than it could employ, so tidewater states made sure they sustained a market for their slaves. When North Carolina acquiesced to the organization of the territory of Tennessee in 1789, it did so in this language: "Provided always, that no regulations made or to be made by Congress shall tend to emancipate slaves, otherwise than shall be directed by the Assembly or legislature of such State or States."

The consequences of slavery still hover above the rich agricultural lands on both sides of the Appalachians. Visitors to the sunny islands along the Georgia coast can find vestiges of the world that preceded the onset of both European and African intruders and of the changes they wrought. On the seacoast, Europeans like the Irish-born Captain Pierce Butler learned much from the Africans about how to raise rice and use medicinal herbs. The best guidebook to those islands, issued in 1984 by the Georgia Conservancy, notes the presence of thousand-year-old bald cypresses near Butler Island in the Altamaha Delta. It speaks of Butler, on that island, as having been "responsible for the introduction of the rice culture into Georgia . . . with the help of several thousand slaves." We may reflect with some poignancy upon the special "help" of those slaves who brought to him the specialized knowledge of that culture as practiced in Africa. Fanny Kemble, the English actress who married Butler's grandson and wrote the eloquent *Journal of a Residence on a Georgia Plantation, 1838–39,* raised many questions about such matters, to the annoyance of some of her neighbors.

It was the founding Butler who made it clear to his peers at the Constitutional Convention in 1787 that the protection of slavery would be at the core of southern antebellum politics: "The security the Southern states want is that their Negroes not be taken from them." And not merely protection of slavery "in place," where it already existed. The planters of the Carolinas and Georgia sought room for expansion toward the West, as North Carolina's resolution for Tennessee demonstrated. At the same time they insisted that the slave trade be kept open, bringing fresh supplies from Africa. The Constitutional Convention heard Charles Pinckney manacle, for the first time but not the last, two principles, states' rights and white supremacy: "In every proposed extension of the powers of Congress, [South Carolina] has expressly and watchfully excepted the meddling with the importation of Negroes."

The legacy of Pierce Butler and the Negroes he imported can be observed on innumerable rice plantations along the coast, most of them abandoned but a few being restored to productivity by another kind of labor force. The original dikes of the rice fields on Butler Island and the ruins of its shucking plant are still there, in the custody of the state of Georgia. Little St. Simons Island, another Butler property, where Fanny Kemble's presence is palpable, remains in private hands but can be visited.

This lowland, slave-driven economy spread upland and westward with a new staple crop grown for world markets after the invention of the cotton gin. Butler's overseer, Roswell King, bought land north of Atlanta in the 1830s and laid out Roswell, one of the state's most beautiful small villages. It is now a suburb of the metropolis, with a cluster of those colonnaded Greek Revival houses that characterize the Georgia Piedmont, the cotton culture, and the plantation economy.

We are accustomed to thinking about African-Americans and European-Americans working out their destiny together in the cotton lands on both sides of the Appalachians. But there is a subtler amalgam to be found in the mountains between, where both these groups of newcomers merged with people who had been in place for thousands of years. Intermarriage among slaves who escaped from those plantations and Native Americans was common. This mixed heritage is manifest in the music of Appalachia, with African rhythms and African instruments such as the banjo, and in "mountain clothing," including moccasins, beading, and neck ornament. European elements are added in mountain storytelling, for the long, bardic, epic tradition is shared in the Cherokee, Celtic, and African traditions.

A vestige of a special European contribution to the hill country is the peculiar eighteenth-century Highland speech still to be heard — though less and less often in the age of electronic homogenization. These early African, Indian, and Celtic ballad patterns and inflections of both speech and song have made the southern mountains a laboratory for generations of ethnomusicologists and a revitalizing place for plain people who like old stories and music.

Beyond the neon and the moccasin kiosks, the motels and pottery flamingos of Gatlinburg and Pigeon Forge, is the real hill country, beautiful and unprofitable, into which European settlement seeped slowly and painfully. In some valleys it seems to have been completely resisted. There are places in the Nantahala and in the coves of the north slopes of the Smokies where the intruders left no evidence of their presence. I am told that there are reaches of the Congaree Swamp in central South Carolina that are exactly as they were in 1500 or 1800, as there are stretches of beach on the barrier islands where the wind and water have swept clear any evidence of humankind.

But it is important to stress once again that the Old South was an inhabited land when the Africans and the Europeans arrived and to emphasize that *two* sets of invaders, one driving the other, spread their occupation westward in quite different patterns from the frontiering of the North. One may think of the northerners as Europeans advancing — without Africans — in ever expanding waves, waves lapping upon a smoothly graduated, sandy coast. Too simple an image, but true enough. One cannot think this way at all about the pattern of advance across the South. There the frontier line was more like a marshy delta; Europeans, Africans, and Indians were mixed in paisley patterns of swirls and washes.

Perhaps that was because the land itself was not a marshy delta but the rough, complex, twisted jumble left as the Appalachian Mountains exhausted their energies and settled into the hot southern plains. Among the foothills, people on one side of a ridge had only distant knowledge of people on the other, and some preferred not to merge or fuse or modernize. By preference or necessity, there is an intractability among these upcountry southerners that is like the intractability of the upcountry itself.

The Indians of the region held their lands considerably longer than even the Iroquois in New York. The Mississippi Natchez were so tough that the French felt obliged to exterminate them (and, as has always been the custom of Europeans after genocide, to sentimentalize them in lovely poems and perfumed drama once they were out of the way). The Yamasee of South Carolina came to the brink of victory over the English in 1715. Later, in the southern Appalachians, there were Indian communities so obdurate that the Europeans were forced to ooze around them rather than try to crack their hard shells. The Creek (the name is English, not Indian), the Cherokee, the Chickasaw, and the Choctaw were all accomplished in diplomacy and war, shrewd in trade, and adept at architecture. They resisted conquest for three hundred years.

Now let us look more closely at the experience brought to the Appalachian highlands by people from the fringes of the British Isles. The polygenetic South has benefited from the presence of many ethnic strains, but it is well to observe how richly its life has been served by one set of immigrants often portrayed as if they themselves were homogeneous. There are great differences, however, in the ancestral memories brought to the southern highlands by the Highlanders of Scotland, by the Scotch-Irish who had been "seasoned" (to borrow a word often used for slaves who survived "breaking in" in the West Indies) by life in Ireland, and by the Irish-Americans.

Let us begin by going back to the Spanish-American force at Pensacola in 1781 with its African-American and Native American allies and the British and Native Americans ranged against them. Both those Spaniards and British had centuries of colonial experience in America behind them, and centuries more before they came to America. The Spanish experience of "reconquering" Granada was matched by that of the English as they "planted" agricultural colonies in Ireland.

Both the Spaniards and English described their acquisition of a subject people, and the tribute wrung from it, as a redemption. The English have always had considerable skill in rescuing people who do not wish to be rescued, sometimes from other European powers, sometimes from "savagery." Richard II set the tone in Ireland by describing the inhabitants as *"irrois savages, nos enemis."* Before England became Protestant, the Irish were said to be "pagan"; afterward they were "popish." But at all times they were expected to do the work of the fields.

The Scotch-Irish were largely Covenantors — Presbyterians — placed in Ireland by Anglican English landlords either to dispossess or intimidate the Roman Catholic natives. This Irish experience left its mark on the Scotch-Irish as well as the Irish themselves. The Scotch-Irish Jacksons (Andrew and "Stonewall" among them), Calhouns, and Hamptons came from a line experienced in the discomfort of being interposed between a people who disdained them and a people who hated them.

It was a grim life, and they remained rather grim in America where, if they went to town, they might be reminded of what they had left behind. The prototypes of the garrison villages built by the English from coastal Georgia to Fort Loudoun, Tennessee, were the fortified towns like Londonderry that the English built in Ireland and garrisoned with Scots.

Above, left: **The young and ferocious John C. Calhoun.** *National Portrait Gallery, Smithsonian Institution, Washington, D.C. Above, right:* **The young Thomas Jonathan Jackson, later known as Stonewall.** *National Portrait Gallery, Smithsonian Institution, Washington, D.C.*

Savannah, for example, resembled the geometric *bastides* that were designed to overawe the Irish and from which pressed outward plantations of Scottish Lowlanders who were to form agricultural garrisons throughout Ulster and the Pale.

The reappearance of such orderly town plans in Georgia, implying as they did repression together with religious, ethnic, or racial warfare, was discordant with the first, philanthropic phase of life in James Oglethorpe's colony. Like Florida, Georgia was founded with instructions from its proprietor to be respectful and kindly to the natives. It was to be entirely free of slavery and the use of alcohol as a means of trade and debauchment. Oglethorpe and his Quaker partners went even further: they restricted landholding to small tracts to keep out the hierarchic social system that was evolving in Carolina.

This was England's other face — earnest, intelligent, a little patronizing, willing to be generous, but always on the lookout for ingratitude. Though Oglethorpe was ahead of his time, other philanthropists followed him and had some success in settling European refugees. German Protestants came to what was the Saxe-Gotha township (now Lexington

Ebenezer, Georgia, in 1733: a tidy classical village based on the plan of a Roman encampment. *Georgia Department of Archives and History*

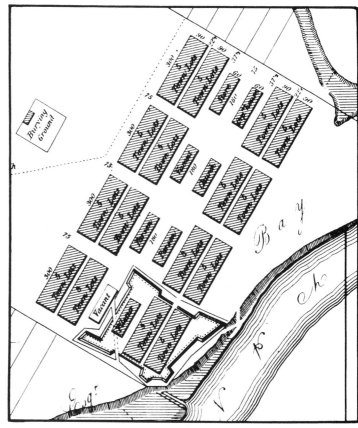

42

County) in South Carolina after 1735 — Dutch (Deutsch) Creek remains to remind us of their presence. More were brought to Georgia in the 1760s, after French ravages of the Rhineland. Compassion played a part in this transfer, and so did the hope that these tough people might help Georgia withstand the threat of Spanish invasions from Florida. As a result of the same mixed motives, Protestant refugees from persecutions in Salzburg and Moravia were helped to join the Rhinelanders.

We cannot tarry among these Germans, however, for our focus is on the Scots who came to the South at this time. One Scottish laird, Sir Alexander Cuming, dreamed of settling three hundred thousand Jews from Europe among the Cherokee, and though this venture did not prosper, he and other benign Scotsmen were successful in providing, in America, some release from the sufferings of their own Highlanders. Thus another Celtic strain entered the polygenetic South.

Cuming sought to rescue the Highlanders threatened in their religion (Roman Catholic) and deprived of their lands (and of other consolations, like bagpipes and kilts) after their Jacobite revolt was suppressed

General James Edward Oglethorpe of Georgia, philanthropist and professional soldier. *Georgia Department of Archives and History*

in 1746. The duke of Cumberland had brought to a bloody end at Culloden the Highlanders' assault upon modern firepower with claymores (broadswords) and pikes. Their leader, Prince Charles Stuart, escaped to exile and into sentimental tales as Bonnie Prince Charlie. (His widow was the sponsor of a far more beguiling adventurer, the discoverer of one of the possible sources of the Mississippi River; see Chapter 15.)

After Culloden an increasing amount of Gaelic could be heard around Darien, Georgia, and in the Carolinas. It expressed some sentiments uncomfortable to those who came after Oglethorpe and reversed his policies. Catholic Highlanders held out longer than others against the introduction of Black slavery and were very articulate, in public papers, against the imposition of forced labor upon any people, Black or White. One learns such things in the Highlands, where the lowland lairds could be as oppressive to their own people as the English, using Scottish agents, were in Ireland.

Unimpressed by the claims to deference of the Tidewater planters, the stiff-backed Highlanders living in the Carolinas and Georgia provided the backbone of the upcountry rebels against those planters. In the 1760s and 1770s, Highlanders (a term which, as time and uphill emigration went on, began to be used to mean settlers of the American highlands) became Regulators. Their revolt against the king's governor and the Tidewater was put down in 1771, after the Battle of Alamance, with a ferocity equal to that of William, duke of Cumberland, after Culloden.

Therefore it is not strange that some frontiersmen did not use the term "Cumberland Gap" to describe their route through the mountains and called a wildflower Stinking Willie rather than Sweet William, as it was renamed by the English after 1746.

The Regulator war anticipated the Revolution, though not in any direct or simple way. The rebels of 1770–1771 were rebels against the Tidewater *and* the Crown. In 1775–1783 many of the same men were rebels against the Tidewater and *for* the Crown, but more were merely rebels against any authority, Crown or Tidewater gentry, parliament, council, or Congress.

Many Jacobite Catholics of Scotland, including the most famous of Highland heroines, Flora Macdonald, immigrated to America. Flora had hidden Bonnie Prince Charlie from his enemies and allowed him to slip away to France. Now she had taken the oath of loyalty to the British king, and having a long tradition of oath taking to clan leaders, she, her husband, Allan, and their kin were serious about such things. Furthermore, Catholic Highlanders loathed Covenanting Lowlanders, so it was natural for them to choose any side but that upon which stood Ulstermen and Lowlanders, who were heavily committed to independence. Flora's husband fought for his British — actually, his Hanoverian — king. She fought too and was wounded in her last battle, on the decks of a ship attacked by an American privateer.

A veteran of Culloden, the eighty-year-old Donald McDonald, raised the king's standard in 1776 to gather the Highlander force that went into battle at Moore's Creek, North Carolina. McLeods and Stewarts, Campbells and McLeans rallied, with pipes skirling, tartans bright in the sunlight, pikes and claymores in their hands. Once again, as at Culloden in 1746, Scots charged into the face of modern military technology and died for it. Across the bridge over Moore's Creek they went at dawn, crying "King George and Broadswords!" though the cross planks had been removed and the unchivalric foe had greased the stringers. Two cannon and a thousand marksmen were waiting on the other side.

Four years later, in the fall of 1780, the Scotch-Irish and the Highlanders demonstrated how quickly they could learn Indian ways — in dress, in agriculture, and in warfare. They had learned to give a terrifying approximation of the Cherokee war scream, and give it they did as they assaulted the Tories ranged on the crest of Kings Mountain under

Flora Macdonald, Scottish heroine of song and story, savior of Bonnie Prince Charlie after the Battle of Culloden, here as a North Carolina dowager. *Ashmolean Museum, Oxford*

Major Patrick Ferguson of His Majesty's Seventy-first Highland Regiment. (This was the sound that became the "Rebel Yell" in 1861.) The scream of William Campbell's attack force came suddenly and frightfully over the battlefield; steadier was the wheeze and bleating of his pipers, answering those of Ferguson's Highlanders ranged against him.

Echoes of the pipes of both sides joined with the skirling that sounded as the Stewarts and McLeods went to their death at Moore's Creek in 1776 and resound in the tales told by Appalachian Scots to this day.

Prince Charles Edward Stuart, known as Bonnie Prince Charlie.
National Portrait Gallery, London

Apparently Major Ferguson was aware of the ethnic complexities of the north Europeans who had come to roost in what was even then an Old South. But so fixed were his prejudices that he drew out of that knowledge only a misconception, the same as that of Mr. Nakasone in our own time. Both used the term "mongrel" to derogate their American antagonists.

The Japanese gentleman is still a political force, though he has learned to be more discreet. Ferguson went to a gallant, ineffectual end. At Kings Mountain, his final battle, he was wrong in his tactics, wrong in his strategy, and wrong in his implication. It seems that he meant that the buckskinned men working their way from tree to tree uphill against his position were more racially mixed and therefore less formidable than the brightly uniformed Tories he commanded to defend it. Perhaps he felt that gentlemen do not hide behind trees and that a polyglot people using Cherokee tactics could not be composed of gentlemen. In any case, he ordered his men to respond with fixed volleys and feckless bayonet charges — and lost. In fact, nearly all the men on both sides were emigrants from Britain's Celtic fringe. All about him, rebels and Tories were killing each other in reciprocal slaughter of an ethnic purity remarkable for the South.

Ferguson's error has been compounded by subsequent historians who describe the battle as being fought between "the British" and "the Americans." The only person on the field who might have described himself as British was Ferguson. The others were all Americans, though before they became Americans most of them were Scots. Indeed, it might have seemed that Kings Mountain was merely another scrap between the clans, transferred to North Carolina, if one heard only the sound of battle and saw Colonel Campbell riding about wearing his claymore.

But there was considerably more at stake than another Celtic fracas in the hills. Moore's Creek and Kings Mountain were important to the outcome of the *first* American civil war, which was our independence. The *second* and even bloodier Civil War rectified the infirmities of the Constitution that independence made possible. As the Highlanders of Darien had intimated, ours was (and is) an imperfect society; the Constitution was an imperfect document, requiring amendments to provide a Bill of Rights and that second Civil War to remove from it provisions that maintained slave labor and unequal rights between Blacks and Whites.

On the golden isles and coastal plain, Blacks and Whites have continued to grow lowland cotton. Of late, rice has come back as a commercial crop. Far across the mountains, the deep soil of central Tennessee and Kentucky came to produce bluegrass, wheat, tobacco and upland cotton, fine cattle and fine horses (this was *not* the South reliant upon single staple crops for world markets).

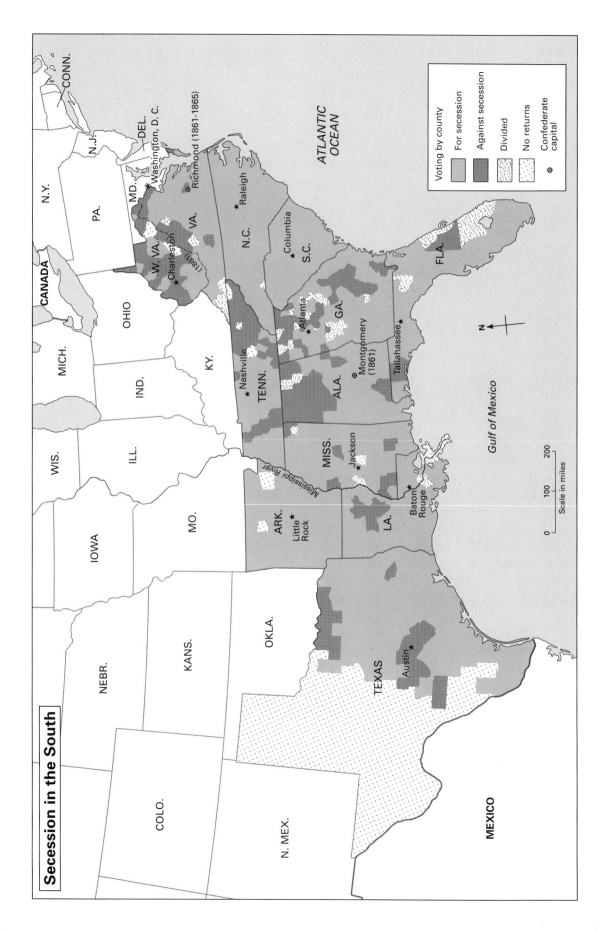

Secession in the South

Voting by county

- For secession
- Against secession
- Divided
- No returns
- ⊕ Confederate capital

ATLANTIC OCEAN

Gulf of Mexico

Scale in miles
0   100   200

N

CANADA

MEXICO

CONN.
N.J.
DEL.
MD.
Washington, D. C.
Richmond (1861-1865)
Raleigh
N.C.
Columbia
S.C.
Charleston
(1861)
VA.
W. VA.
PA.
N.Y.
OHIO
MICH.
IND.
KY.
Nashville
TENN.
ATLANTA
GA.
FLA.
Tallahassee
Montgomery
(1861)
ALA.
MISS.
Jackson
Baton Rouge
LA.
Little Rock
ARK.
Austin
TEXAS
OKLA.
KANS.
NEBR.
COLO.
N. MEX.
MO.
IOWA
ILL.
WIS.
Mississippi River

The Piedmont of North and South Carolina remained lightly settled until a boom in textiles and light industry following the Second World War. The mountains were more sparsely settled still. In the hills the descendants of fierce Celts became fiercer and watched their cousins growing rich in the Nashville basin with the same animosity that had turned their ancestors into Regulators and enemies of the Tidewater gentry. When the Confederacy was proclaimed under the leadership of the planter class, the mountaineers went into rebellion from rebellion. A convention in Winston County, Alabama, voted to take it out of the Confederacy; Rabun County, Georgia, never went *in*. The Ozarks of Arkansas sent eight thousand men to join the Union forces, and many more joined them from East Tennessee and the Cumberland region of Kentucky. West Virginia became a separate state. East Tennessee tried to do likewise, but failed because it did not have the endorsement of a resident Union army.

The Confederacy, like the Union, recruited forcibly. In the North there were draft riots. In the upcountry of the South, desertion was a remedy for conscription. Approximately one hundred thousand Confederates deserted, largely those from the hill country and the poor. To this day stories are told of the consequences to them of the Confederate response. Nice distinctions were not made between deserters and Union sympathizers. "They were driven from their homes . . . persecuted like wild beasts . . . hunted down in the mountains. . . . Perhaps no people on the face of the earth were ever more persecuted than were the loyal people of East Tennessee."[3] The echoes of Ireland and of the Highlands after Culloden could still be heard.

East Tennessee, western North Carolina, and the mountain corners of South Carolina, Alabama, and Georgia remained Unionist throughout the war, except when Confederate troops brought them to heel. General William Tecumseh Sherman was protected by a bodyguard of Alabama cavalry throughout his Georgia and Carolina campaigns. Reconstruction was less traumatic for these highland areas than for the Piedmont and Tidewater because there was less in the hills to reconstruct. The governors of North Carolina and Tennessee used militia units from the highlands to put down the Ku Klux Klan in the plantation country, and the poor remained poor. The few slaves who were there became free in legal theory and enjoyed a brief burst of hope that the poverty they shared with their White neighbors might somehow become less grinding. An economy of exploitation of natural resources replaced that of exploitation of human labor; coal and iron went to create prosperity elsewhere. There were a few pockets of affluence here and there: among the managers of mines and smelters and among those who organized the regiments of loggers who stripped the mountains of trees to provide timbers for mine tunnels and railroad ties for mining railroads and mining towns.

But the mountaineers of the East shared with the mountaineers of the West their role as economic dependents of absentee owners. Very little of the profits derived from mining and lumbering in Appalachia went to the replacement of its own economic resources. Those profits were sucked away to distant cities. Absentee ownership has been as much a characteristic of West Virginia as of Colorado.

Blacks and Whites together found work in the mines and on lumbering crews. But by the end of the nineteenth century discriminatory wage rates began once again to undo the work of Reconstruction. Reconstruction gave way to Jim Crow, and it was no longer so easy to distinguish the Republicans of the hills from the Dixiecrats of the flatland. Only during the period of southern biracial Populism in the 1880s and 1890s did there seem to be enough common aspiration among the poor country people of both races to bring them into alliance. After the Populist coalition came apart about 1895, Jim Crow prevailed everywhere, regardless of altitude.

Yet the politics of the Appalachians have roots more ancient than the Civil War of 1861–1865, older than sectional differences in the effects of Reconstruction or Jim Crow. Long before they invaded America, the highlanders differed from the great landowners and merchants of the shore. That difference had been heard in the pipes at Moore's Creek as it had been heard not long before at Culloden. Now it is no longer the pipes but the whining of mountain fiddles that expresses the contrariness, the separateness, the ancient, intractable, courageous cussedness of the highlander. And the descendants of Africans, Europeans, and Native Americans are still working things out.

4

....

The Conquest of Canaan
Massachusetts, Rhode Island, and Connecticut

THOUGH SOME Bostonians still like to speak of their city as the hub of the universe, it owes its prosperity to its place on a periphery. So does that eastern shoreline of New England of which Boston is the metropolis. This is the extremity of a continent and, reciprocally, the edge of a watery world. The people who live there have been, by necessity, amphibian.

This intersection of land and water is very ancient. For ten thousand years a great glacier weighted the earth with billions of tons of ice and in the process locked up enough water to fill the oceans to more than a thousand feet of additional depth. As it crept southward this great glacier also gathered rocks and sand and clay. When the thaw came this frozen booty was released, and Martha's Vineyard, Cape Cod, and the Shinnecock Hills were born. Even Rhode Island acquired a modest protuberance, now somewhat enthusiastically called Badger Mountain, the summit of which protruded seven hundred feet above sea level even after the glaciers melted and the waters rose. Long beaches and islands along the North Atlantic coast were inundated, becoming the shoals and banks upon which native fishermen found the means to respond profitably to protein deficiencies — their own and those of their agricultural neighbors. After these Indians were replaced by Europeans, catches were salted and sent to the West Indies and Europe.

Contrary to the empty continent myth still occasionally heard from public platforms (even in presidential debates), the peopling of this region did not come first from Europe. It is probable — though not certain, as Thomas Jefferson observed — that not long after the glaciers retreated, America was discovered from the west, from Asia, by those we now call Native Americans. As they worked their way from the Pacific to the Atlantic they grew very numerous, creating the urban complexes of Meso-America and Peru and the large but simpler cities of the Ohio Valley, Louisiana, and Georgia.

The penetration by Native Americans from the west and south took place over so protracted a period that we often forget the magnitude of their achievement. To be reminded of this, we may imagine them passing *eastward* through the "dark and bloody ground" of Kentucky, *eastward* through Cumberland Gap, then northeasterly *up* the Shenandoah Valley and the Ohio and Mississippi rivers, into the Great Lakes Basin. We may imagine some hardier souls bidding farewell to the lucky ones who would remain in the rich central hunting grounds and deep soils where they based their Adena and Hopewell ceremonial and residential centers and finding their way into the dark ravines of the Catskills and Adirondacks. Finally this advance guard came to the eastern edge of the continent where, about the year 1000, their hardiness was tested in their first encounters with the ferocious Scandinavians. But even as early as that, the density of Indian settlement amazed the newcomers — by 1500 much of the shore of Long Island Sound had been cleared and burnt to a depth of six or seven miles.

Who "discovered" whom? and when? Remains of Norse houses at L'Anse aux Meadows, Newfoundland. *Canadian Parks Service*

The Vikings, the terror of Europe, were themselves at first terrified by the Native Americans they called *skraelings,* but soon the few meadows and shelters along the northeast coast of the continent were being contested. Footholds were secured by the Europeans, perhaps as far south as Rhode Island or Martha's Vineyard.

It has been generally assumed that these early entrepôts did not survive, because we have no written assertions that they did. But most historians are now prepared to admit that the absence of a document does not prove the absence of an experience. Furthermore, it is entirely possible that there were renewed, though sporadic, European-American contacts over the next four hundred years; Basque, Portuguese, French, and English West Country fishermen may well have learned that the shallow waters off the American shores were crowded with fish. We *do* know that by 1525 these waters were becoming crowded with fishermen. Some ragged settlements on shore may have lasted a year or so on Newfoundland or even farther south, but fishermen have never liked telling others where the "big ones" are to be found, so history has only the barest hints of what Bristol and Galway knew before Columbus.

The Norse sagas suggest that Galway may have known something as early as the year 1100. They report that two "Scots" (probably, by contemporary usage, Irishmen) in the party of Thorfinn Karlsefni were congratulated for their discovery of a "productive land" after exploring the interior of Massachusetts — perhaps as far as Dedham or even Brookline — and bringing back grapes and wheat. (Perhaps they were religious fellows planning a service of bread and wine.)

Finally, fishermen's lore persuaded the skeptical British that some portion of the shore was worth colonizing. New England was not an impressive imperial prize. Its natural resources were scant; unlike Mexico it had no silver and gold; unlike the West Indies it could not grow sugar; even Newfoundland offered far more cod, mackerel, and haddock. The land between the lordly Hudson and the lazily looping Piscataqua was stark, bare, and harsh.

A curious traveler with a few hours to spare can get a sense of what the terrain looked like before the advent of the English. Along the shore there are still beaches and marshes and offshore islands with their colonies of gannets and gulls. Inland there are still swamps and barren, rocky hilltops. And here and there a pocket of old America can be found much as it was. Off Pine Street, a little way up Essex Road in Cornwall, Connecticut, the Nature Conservancy is tending the Cathedral Pines Preserve, and the Carlisle State Forest, near Carlisle, Massachusetts, contains some old-growth pines and hemlocks in a twenty-two-acre remnant spared by logging and hurricanes.

In 1620, very late in the European investigations of the region, seventeen years after the French planted their gardens in Maine, the Pilgrims

A reconstruction of the palisade built at Plimoth Plantation in 1627, with a costumed artisan at work. *Courtesy of Plimoth Plantation*

landed at or near Plymouth Rock. (If we were not bound so closely to the English historical tradition, we might use the term "Pilgrims" to refer to the *French* Protestants who settled in Florida in the 1560s. Theirs was actually the first Puritan attempt on the North American continent. But that settlement was, in any event, exterminated by the Spaniards.)

The English had already landed elsewhere — in the Carolinas and at Jamestown, Virginia, in 1607. They came so late because they had been distracted by their own civil and religious wars and paused in Ireland to rehearse for their American experience.

On that ravaged island they learned how to exterminate aborigines while forming "plantations" — the term has an Irish origin — and how to explain themselves to themselves. They wrote of the Irish and subsequently of the Indians in ways that later became braided into the older histories of New England: the natives were "savages" and their religion "idolatrous"; they were "nomads" because they moved herds from summer to winter quarters. (One reader of the Smithsonian guides wrote to us that this passage demeaned the Irish!)

Despite their conditioning, some of the Pilgrim Fathers and Mothers treated the Native Americans as respectfully as they themselves were treated at first, as their survival amply demonstrates. They had little

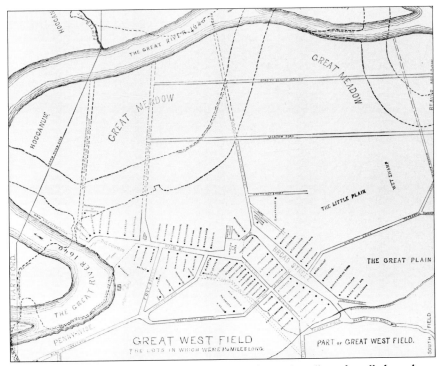

A map of Wethersfield, Connecticut, showing the ancient "meadows" cleared by the Indians and preempted by the Europeans. *Wethersfield Historical Society*

knowledge of the architectural and agricultural means by which to pass an American winter, learning barely in time about snowshoes and moccasins, about corn and beans and squash, about building with saplings and stockaded timbers.

In recent years we have been learning to rethink, as well, what can be discovered from the subsequent relationships between the Indians of southern New England and the pilgrims. This much is clear: the *Mayflower*'s passengers survived by sufferance of the Indians, by whom they were hopelessly outnumbered. It is difficult to estimate the numbers of Native Americans then living east of the Hudson, but the best guess seems to be about a hundred thousand.

In New England the invaders ultimately triumphed after a century of uncertain skirmishes, massacres, and alliances among changing clusters of colonies and tribes. Contributing to that victory, complete by 1760, were European diseases, which, by some estimates, eliminated nine out of ten Indians of New England. While the Indians could not adapt to imported viruses, the Europeans combined their technology of gunpowder with adaptations of snowshoes and moccasins and the dispersed forest tactics of the Indians and abandoned their European style of mass attacks.

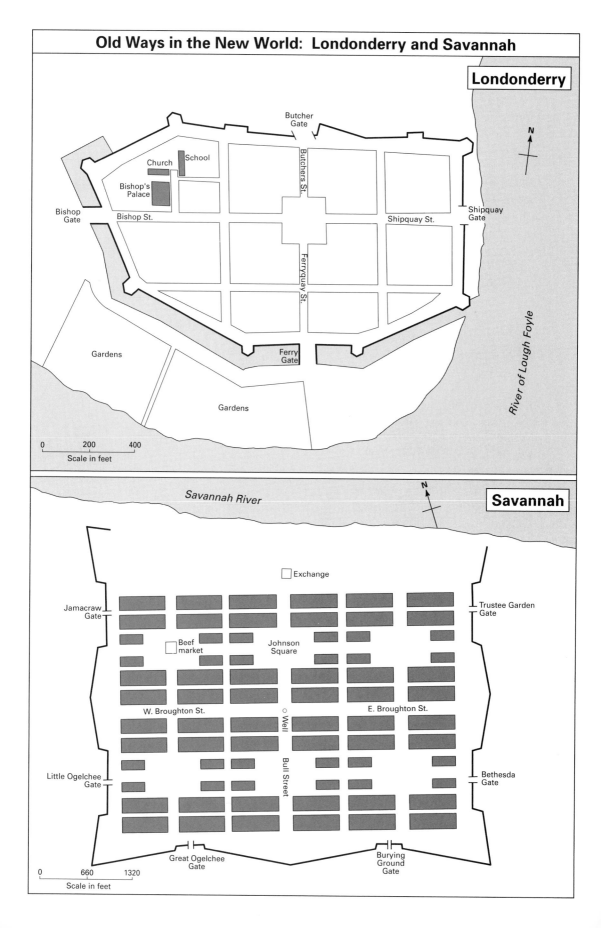

Old Ways in the New World: Londonderry and Savannah

Londonderry

Butcher Gate

Church
School
Bishop's Palace
Bishop Gate
Bishop St.
Butchers St.
Ferryquay St.
Shipquay St.
Shipquay Gate
Ferry Gate
Gardens
Gardens
River of Lough Foyle

N

0   200   400
Scale in feet

Savannah

Savannah River

N

Exchange
Jamacraw Gate
Beef market
Johnson Square
Trustee Garden Gate
W. Broughton St.
Well
E. Broughton St.
Bull Street
Little Ogelchee Gate
Bethesda Gate
Great Ogelchee Gate
Burying Ground Gate

0   660   1320
Scale in feet

Having learned their Irish lessons, the English were able to manipulate the rivalries of local chiefs and family groupings. Contrary to the Indian experience, the English knew all about a strategy of starving their opponents into desperate errors or submission. They burnt off food supplies and drove Indians from the small arable sections of the terrain, leaving them only the squalid life possible on barren headlands, rocky hills, sand dunes, and marshes. This strategy had worked well on one side of the Atlantic, and it worked again on the other. "Massacre," the killing of entire populations, including noncombatants, seems to have been an idea introduced by the English. All authorities agree that it had not been a convention of Indian warfare.

The Pilgrims were not the only English settlers to apply these lessons; New England is more diverse in its origins than that. To a stockade in Connecticut came a feudal settlement owing fealty to Lords Brooke and Saye and Sele (hence Saybrook). Maine and New Hampshire were Anglican and proprietary. Though the Saybrook proprietors were also

The traditional view of the terrain of the Puritan Wars of Conquest: Frederick E. Church's painting of the pilgrimage from Plymouth to Hartford as a tour through a peaceable kingdom. ©*Wadsworth Atheneum, Hartford, Connecticut. Photograph by Joseph Szaszfai*

Puritan, they were aristocratic, and their followers reflected the wide span of class origins and the low level of literacy to be found in Virginia, in contrast to the relative homogeneity of the middle-class, literate Pilgrims. Reforming Puritans, Baptists, and Quakers retreated to Rhode Island. These followers of Roger Williams fled from a system that coupled religious authority and political force. And the Connecticut River began to be lined by villages offering an anthology of sects, variations on Puritan, Dutch Reformed, and even Anglican themes.

There were also less desirable importations along the river — rough characters from the West Indies who abraded further the worsening relations between the invading Europeans and the Native Americans. A freebooter named Stone provided the pretext for the First Puritan War of Conquest. Having been banished from Massachusetts, this pirate courted martyrdom by kidnaping Pequot Indians. After the Pequot violently terminated Stone's predations and the Narraganset of Block Island murdered a trader named Oldham, the Puritans eradicated the male inhabitants of the island. Its twentieth-century summer colonists have reported that when the moon is right and the wind is low across the heath, you can still hear the keening of the women and children who saw their men die and then were sold into slavery.

The Narraganset struck up an alliance with the Puritans against the Pequot, their traditional enemies, putting more than six hundred warriors into the field. In May 1638 they joined Captain John Mason's troops in another expedition of extermination, this time against a Pequot fortified town on the Mystic River in Connecticut. The allies massacred eight hundred men, women, and children, after which Mason pronounced "the Lord was . . . pleased to say to us, the Land of Canaan will I give unto thee."

A generation later, in 1675, the Puritans turned on their late allies in the Second Puritan War of Conquest. A Harvard-educated Indian, John Sassamon, was found dead in a pond near Plymouth after he had gone to the English with charges that Metacom, a Wampanoag chief the English called King Philip, was planning to attack them. The evidence was ambiguous, but he may have been killed. The good people of Plymouth put some passing Wampanoag to death for the possible crime, two proclaiming innocence to the end. The third, hoping to save his skin, asserted that he was incited to murder Sassamon by Metacom.

In the war that ensued, Metacom became the first of several Native American leaders — Pontiac and Tecumseh come to mind as well — who approached victory over the Euro-Americans by creating an alliance among many tribes. He was also the first whose plans ultimately failed because he could not persuade one crucial tribe to draw a lesson from the European habit of betraying allies. In this instance — after a war costing three thousand Native American lives, six hundred English

An engraving, about 1850, depicting the Battle of Fairfield Swamp during the Puritan Wars of Conquest. *The Connecticut Historical Society, Hartford*

lives, eight thousand head of cattle, and many villages on both sides — the Mohawk attacked Philip from the rear, forcing him to fight it out on English terms. In August 1676 King Philip's War was over, and Philip was dead. (Some of the English regretted the loss of life on grounds that it raised the price of slaves.)

As these nations bloodily contended over the Land of Canaan, subtler political adjustments were wrought. The smaller English colonies, Plymouth and New Haven, were absorbed by larger Massachusetts Bay and Connecticut. The lordly enclave at Saybrook gave itself over to Connecticut as well. The age of feudal vestiges was over. This was the age of capitalist outposts led by middle-class intellectuals such as Connecticut's John Winthrop Jr. But one of the lords' agents, Lieutenant Luke Gardiner, slipped away to establish the longest persistence of medieval land tenure in any portion of the United States settled by the English. After sixteen generations the Gardiners of Gardiners Island still treat those bold enough to go ashore as poachers were treated in the sixteenth century.

And along the northern frontier it was becoming obvious that larger powers than Mohawk and Narraganset were coming into contention. One of the reasons the Mohawk turned on Philip was that an English alliance would help them stand off the French. It is well to recall that though the subjects of the Bourbon kings did not compete with the English in the number who chose to immigrate to North America, those who did come had been there considerably longer and knew far more about what might be found on the continent. Jacques Cartier had penetrated a thousand miles into the interior in the 1530s, nearly a century before the granite rock in Plymouth Bay felt Elder Brewster's footfall. The French were in Wisconsin and Missouri before the English had passed beyond the Berkshires.

Until the end of the seventeenth century the French were kept away from the Puritan colonies by the peculiarities of European religious, dynastic, and economic politics. In the middle of the century, while the two Puritan wars were being fought in New England, Oliver Cromwell, the leader of the Puritan commonwealth in England itself (having cut off the head of a king, Charles I, who was suspected of having Catholic sympathies), sent his Roundhead veterans into battle beside the Papists of France against the Dutch, who had given shelter to the Pilgrim Fathers and other dissident Protestants in Holland. Holland and England were competitors for the trade of the East and West Indies; commercial rivalry outweighed religious affinity. When Cromwell was gone, King Charles II turned loose his naval forces upon the Dutch, though they had been his hosts in exile from Cromwell's England. Thereafter New England continued to be sheltered behind European diplomacy as Charles, its Protestant king, accepted heavy bribes from the Catholic monarch of France to do nothing to upset the efforts of France against Holland. In return the powerful French forces in Canada, and their even more formidable Indian allies, abstained from snuffing out the embattled English colonies of New York and New England.

But Charles II had expensive tastes; his Parliament was reluctant to raise taxes; the subsidies he received from Louis XIV of France proved insufficient to his needs. So, to the incidental peril of his colonies in North America, he determined that his subjects' lust for war, commercial and religious, could no longer be resisted. There ensued one hundred fifty years of conflict between imperial Britain and imperial France. Until 1775 the Americans of the fifteen colonies were cobelligerents with the British; thereafter the thirteen that sought and gained independence became, through two world wars (1778–1783 and 1812–1815), cobelligerents with the French. (For some of the consequences of these arrangements for architecture, garden and fortress design, and town planning, see also Chapter 19.)

The Native Americans, ground between the great contenders and exposed to the deadly effects of measles and smallpox, were reduced more by disease than by military defeat. At the end Canaan became European. By the middle of the eighteenth century fields and pastures won from the Indians were producing increasing surpluses of food which, along with fish, could be sold at great profits to the slave-driven plantations of the West Indies. Maine and New Hampshire survived on the sale of maritime supplies and fish to the islands; South County in

Rhode Island, like the Carolinas and New York's Shelter Island, was a Barbadian subcolony organized along West Indian lines to send animals (for power and protein) to the Caribbean sugar plantations. Bristol and Newport grew rich on the Caribbean slave trade and later on the extension of that traffic to the descendants of the Barbadians in South Carolina.

By the beginning of the eighteenth century Boston was emerging as a center of commerce, including that with the West Indies and fishing towns and fleets all the way to Newfoundland. Salem and Marblehead, mackerel and cod ports in Essex County, Massachusetts, were growing despite their meager hinterlands. New Englanders made the best of their position between Canadian fish and West Indian sugar, trading and transshipping in both directions. The sugar ports of Rhode Island increased in size and wealth, and villages of Connecticut, far upstream on its ample rivers, built and managed ships for the oceans of the world.

Whalers set sail from these same river ports, as well as from those along the Hudson, from Sag Harbor on the north coast of Long Island, and from New Bedford and Nantucket. Whaling had been practiced by the Indians and Cape Codders in the seventeenth century, but not until after 1720 did a desire for lighting and lubricating oil turn Nantucket, New Bedford, New London, Stonington, Edgartown, and Provincetown on the New England coast and Newburgh, Poughkeepsie, and Hudson City on the Hudson into bases for expeditions ranging into the Arctic, Antarctic, and Pacific. Bath, Maine, supplied most of the steam whalers for the Arctic campaigns, developing the skills put to work more recently in constructing nuclear submarines.

Newburgh has gone through several booms and busts since the recession of the late 1830s brought a slow decline to the Hudson River whaling business. It gave the world one of its most convincing writers on architectural matters just when whaling fortunes were two or three generations old and ready to be sanctified by a simulated antiquity. Tasteful villas in the Gothic style began to appear in its suburbs, as they did subsequently in the environs of New Bedford and Nantucket. Newburgh's nurseryman-writer, Andrew Jackson Downing, knew how to combine a knowledge of horticulture with a vague Anglophilia that invoked the antique and the genteel sufficiently to endear him to his neighbors and to readers across a socially nervous nation. A dash of Downing could expunge the stench of spermaceti from the roughest of hands.

It was not only the Gothic Revival that characterized these fishing villages grown into port cities. The names of the proprietors of both Greek and Gothic mansions tended to be similar on the islands and up the rivers, wherever whaling clans established themselves. There were Coffins in Hudson and Poughkeepsie, Nantucket and Salem, thriving along with Jenkinses, Paddocks, Macys, Bunkers, and Folgers. The Rotches did not spread beyond New Bedford, nor the Starbucks from Nantucket; they remained in their great houses — Gothic for the Rotches, Greek for the Starbucks — looking to the past not the future, prosperous after the 1850s but turning to their brokers rather than their captains for profits.

Just in time to found a college in Poughkeepsie, Matthew Vassar, the local brewer, made one last fortune in the 1830s from "whale fisheries in the Atlantic and Pacific Oceans and elsewhere and in the manufacture of oil and spermaceti candles." (His partners were Paraclete Potter and Alexander J. Coffin; Potters and Coffins were partners in whaling companies from Maine to Staten Island.) Vassar, Coffin, and Potter had only twenty years or so to make a fortune. In 1857 oil from long dead plants and animals was discovered in Titusville, Pennsylvania. The petroleum-rich Rockefellers and Harknesses and Pratts replaced the whale-oil-rich Rotches, Coffins, and Starbucks in the pantheon of patrons of architecture. The scope of the new oil business, like the old, was worldwide, not in its sources at the outset, but in its destinations. Oil for the lamps of China, ran one slogan. Oil from Pennsylvania, then from Oklahoma and Texas, sold in immense quantities around the globe, providing fuel for the automotive age. The residences of its managers grew commensurately. No longer did the lighting business produce the "tasteful cottages" of Downing's Gothic Revival. Instead, huge neo-Renaissance palazzi appeared on Fifth Avenue and neo-Georgian country houses weighted the land at Glen Cove and Pocantico.

Some readers may find it of interest to turn from Downing's tepid taste-making for the Gothic Revival to revisit the architectural theories of the Abbé Suger of the abbey of Saint-Denis during the Middle Ages in France. He refashioned neoplatonic ideology into a comprehensive explanation for the light-seeking of the Gothic the first time around. We owe to Suger not so much the pointed arch, which he did not invent, but gothic theory, with its potent investiture in architecture of the concept, that "God is Light." And that is where the irony lies, for Saint-Denis differed from Peekskill and New Bedford, the Gothic from the Gothic Revival, Suger from Downing, not so much in the ephemera of solid form and ornament but in their difference in thinking about light. The Gothic Revival was engaged in shutting light out. It moped about in curtained and shuttered spaces, warming its hands upon overheated novels. Perhaps the whalers who gave prosperity to Downing's first clients were happy to see so much of their product used for lamplight even on the most sunlit of days. But after Titusville, it was no longer necessary to kill for light.

It is one of history's mercies that the automobile was not discovered before 1857, for the chief source of wealth to twentieth-century oilmen, the growth of automobile traffic, did not require the slaughter of more whales. The whaling towns experienced a brief resurgence in the 1870s, however, when whalebone stays for corsets and umbrellas brought some old whalers back into action. (The last steam whaler from Bath was crushed by the ice pack of the Arctic in 1919.)

Some New York and New England rivers were not important as harbors for whalers, but they had assets more important than sheltered space: rocks and rapids. The Merrimac, for example, illustrated a quality New England possessed which had been denied the region of the Chesapeake: its fall line was close to the coast. This meant that an obstruction became a blessing. The industrial development of New England began at this seacoast fall line. The rough and dangerous water that earlier had stopped the inland explorations of oceangoing shipping now produced power.

The Connecticut and the Merrimac, unlike the Hudson and the Susquehanna, were spared industrial development at their mouths, but not far upstream, where they broke into rapids, they nurtured mills. The "foothills" of "Badger Mountain" even gave Rhode Island a remarkable amount of water power; beside a waterfall at Pawtucket, American entrepreneurial genius and English technology gave rise to the first American textile plant. The Slaters of the Slater Mill organized a work force along military lines. Eight employees, none older than seven years, served interconnected machinery powered by what, by western standards, would seem a pitiable trickling of water. But it was enough. New England entered the industrial age.

Slater was financed by the adaptable Browns of Providence, one of those Yankee families who over eight generations have cannily decanted capital from fishing and smuggling to textiles, then into railroads and real estate, and eventually, we may assume, into electronics and financial services. In Boston there is a ruling elite phenomenally adaptable to economic change. Perhaps this is because during most of its history that elite has been content with a realistic self-definition. It is genteel but not aristocratic. It does not deny that it is a commercial class, but it has been proud to be led by intellectuals. Such diffidence is not characteristic of the English or the Dutch or the burghers of most American cities.

There may be another historic reason for this: Boston and Hartford, unlike Saybrook or Portsmouth, harbored no cast-off aristocrats to complicate the clarity of commercial vision. New England was spared the Cavalier pretensions that disabled the descendants of the merchant-planters of tidewater South Carolina and Virginia. Unlike the Huguenot merchants of Charleston, the Boston Brahmins did not have fertile agricultural lands nearby to seduce them from the countinghouse. They were therefore more likely to adjust themselves to the financial and industrial imperatives of the nineteenth century.

This is not to suggest that all those imperatives were noble. The consequences of heeding them were frequently ugly, though seldom within eyeshot of Beacon Hill. Out in the industrial landscape a new America of soot and slums was created.

That point requires little demonstration. It is there, all too visible in our cities today. But it is also there outside the cities, much camouflaged. Historians have been learning in the last thirty years or so how to cut below the picturesque surfaces of many New England villages to discover what "Colonial" or "Federal" New England was like. It is remarkable how skillfully and daintily that reality was altered after 1880. Much of what we see today is stagecraft. We might expect colonial towns to be re-created. Ample examples of that may be found, but what is more intriguing is the fresh creation of an imaginary industrial Arcadia.

The industrialization of New England began in the eighteenth century and with it the exploitation of women and children. This story does not require retelling here, but travelers may want to know what they are — and are not — seeing when they visit mill towns like Harrisville, New Hampshire, or Slatersville, where it all began.

The former is largely the creation of Austin Levy, who owned a woolen mill there. After 1918 Levy built twenty-two Colonial Revival worker's houses, a town hall, a library, and a courthouse. Under his philanthropic direction the Universalist Church was remodeled from the Victorian to the Colonial, and the Roman Catholic congregation was persuaded to build compatibly. The result is handsome, but no picture of what Harrisville would have been in 1800. It was considerably grubbier, dirtier, sootier, noisier, and crueler than this.

Slatersville was a real textile village with a fascinating past, but that past was insufficient for the revisers; while Levy was reconstructing Harrisville, Slatersville's multiple-family cottages were given side porches, porticoes, coats of white paint, and gentrified into single-family occupancy.

More important than coats of paint or colonializing trim for mill towns was the reordering of the entire shape of the colonial towns of pre-industrial — one might say anti-industrial — New England. Many were reconstructed in the Colonial Revival period (roughly 1880–1910), giving them the parklike greens the nineteenth and twentieth centuries thought appropriate to the seventeenth and eighteenth.

Few villages were sufficiently affluent to follow the lead of Litchfield, Connecticut. Its summer citizens engaged Frederick Law Olmsted to redesign the center of town and went on to remodel its Victorian buildings into the Federal, whitewashing their varicolored sprightliness, turning commercial structures into residences, reconstructing the town hall and the Tapping Reeves Law School.

As the result of all this, the pattern of settlement in colonial times has been obscured and colonial history made considerably duller.

Slatersville, Rhode Island, in the 1880s, on its way to gentrification.
Courtesy of The Rhode Island Historical Society

Place names, however, have been present all along to inform us of the true history of the region. A recent exhibition at Hartford's Wadsworth Atheneum reminded residents of that region of the meaning behind town names like Longmeadow, Springfield, Enfield, Topsfield, Hatfield, Bloomfield, and Greenfield. European settlers found waiting for them fields and meadows cleared and planted by previous occupants. Upon those sites they spread themselves very widely, for land was cheap. Only rarely, before the industrial phase of New England began, did they congregate around a central church.

In a few instances the nuclear village of England reappeared early in New England. Two of them are Hampton, New Hampshire, which *was* closely compacted, and Newtown, Connecticut, which was tight but linear. But Concord, Massachusetts, was the only inland town of any size that developed a commercial core before 1740 or 1750. Highway villages like Wethersfield and Northfield spread out along a single spine on the terraces the Indians had made habitable and arable. After they felt safe in leaving their initial stockades (faithfully reproduced at Plymouth) or the defensive gatherings of the first generation, as at Dedham or Andover, the colonials betook themselves to dispersed homesteads.

What of the white Colonial village church, with its Gibbsian spire and that well-mowed green before it? Spires were nineteenth-century

European-Americans at work in fields cleared by Native Americans. Frederick Church's "West Rock, New Haven." *From the collection of the New Britain Museum of American Art, Connecticut, John B. Talcott Fund. E. Irving Blomstrann, photographer*

additions, except for a few prototypical examples in major shipping cities like Boston and Newport. So too was the green as a park or common. It is a product of nostalgia in reaction to the industrializing phase of the nineteenth century. "Until then," we have learned from Thomas Lewis, "most commons were barren, unsightly places covered with stumps, stones, stagnant puddles and dead trees." That is how they appear in nineteenth-century photographs, often taken after a first meetinghouse, for which the common was created, had collapsed, or the common itself had been relinquished by a local clergyman for whom it may have been a glebe (a pastor's assigned field, where he might grub for his own vegetables).

We have our own interior images of the New England past, more powerful than any photographs and far more so than any monographs. We long to impose these ideal concepts of how our ancestors *must* have lived upon what we know of *how* they lived, though we may deprive them of the credit they deserve for surviving the harshness of their actual existence. There is more to this than architectural nicety; history has a moral dimension. There was more to living a moral life — back then —

The green or common at Branford, Connecticut, as it appeared after being cleaned up late in the nineteenth century. *The Connecticut Historical Society, Hartford*

than our reconstructions admit. If all was sweet and untroubled in colonial times, the triumph of democracy and tolerance would not be so remarkable. If serenity and openness and love predominated in the Peaceable Kingdoms of our imagination, and those which we have so carefully constructed, Anne Hutchinson and William Lloyd Garrison would have had tranquil lives and those calls to conscience for which New England has been famous would not have been necessary.

The history of New England did not stop when the nineteenth century began. Industrialism flourished. Emigrants from other nations were added to the Puritans from East Anglia. Determined men and women strove to live considered and responsible lives despite bafflements and complexities.

This essay must break off here, ruefully acknowledging that in an effort to give enough information to counteract some of the pernicious simplicities that have obstructed our vision of the accomplishments of southern New England, it has run out of space. That is how the writing of history always is: the story can never be fully told. All the historian can do is offer an invitation to inquire.

The physical evidence presented in southern New England itself offers many such invitations. Among the folded hills and in the Atlantic mists some villages remain as beautiful as the land itself that delighted the Native Americans, the Vikings with their Irish or Scottish associates, and the Pilgrim Fathers, when they first laid eyes upon this wonderful edge of the continent.

5

....

At One Extreme

Maine, New Hampshire, and Vermont

Hᴀ ɪsᴛᴏʀʏ is ineradicable in the North Country. It is an unforgiving land; the scars men make last a long time, as they do in the desert. Duff holds together grass and moss and pine needles in a poultice, but when it is ripped by a hiker's boot it opens a tear the wind will worry until all that is left is the gray-rock platform upon which northern New England is built. The miracle is that between the dark spruce forest of the far north and the hardwoods of Massachusetts so many tall pines managed to grow, finding nutriment in crevices, and anchorage as well. Some groves topped at one hundred sixty feet, rising on trunks six feet across at the base. When loggers wanted to climb a pine, they would drop a spruce diagonally against its trunk, to climb like a ladder to the lowermost pine branches, sixty feet up.

The first Europeans to search for the big pines wanted those branchless trunks entire for the making of masts; it was only much later, in the 1820s, that sliced pine for lumber became a great commercial crop. Whatever their ultimate destination, whether for fleets, floors, or furniture, the old-growth pines have largely gone. In Vermont there are thirteen acres of large, old-growth pines in the Fisher-Scott Memorial, two miles north of the village of Arlington on Route 7A, and sixteen acres of climax sugar maples and beech in the Gifford Woods State Park on U.S. 4, eleven miles east of Rutland. Not far away, in the Tinker Brook Natural Area on Route 100, 3.2 miles south of West Bridgewater, are forty-five acres of red spruce and hemlock. The diminutive size of these remnants makes the point: we have left very little of the terrain unaffected by our ambitions, even when we add in the Battell Stand in Middlebury, the more remote fragments of pine forest such as the Lord's Hill Tract in Marshfield, Vermont, and the Seven Ponds reserve north of Mount Katahdin, Maine. Seven Ponds is one of the two largest surviving tracts of unspoiled America north of the Smokies — the other is Ramsey's Draft, Virginia. (We will return to Seven Ponds in another connection.)

Paul Bunyan, the mythical logger, left large footprints. Some say they are the chains of elliptical lakelets of the North, but more likely the record of his passage is found in patches of desolate stumpage, slowly, slowly healing. This northland is irreconcilable, an Old Testament place of absolutes. Sky. Sea. Rock. Marsh. Ambiguities and meadows are luxuries for summer people.

This is not a terrain like that of southern New England, where the fields of deep alluvial soil along the rivers, sheltered by gentle ridges, have provided for agriculture for a thousand years and more. Nor are the evergreen woods of the North like the hardwood forests of Connecticut or Massachusetts, where a profusion of deer and small animals browsed on the berries, nuts, and acorns, on the peeling, edible bark and tender understory. Massachusetts was a hospitable wilderness, but, though bracing, Maine is only intermittently salubrious. The growing season is short, and in colonial times one might walk for days in the gloom beneath the giant pines without seeing a deer or turkey.

The casual assemblage of buildings in Dublin, New Hampshire, is characteristic of upcountry New England villages. Note the lack of a green.
New Hampshire Historical Society, photograph by Bill Finney

The North is spruceland, treacherous with unexpected bogs and disrupted by sudden granite mountains like Katahdin, so uncompromising that their slopes will have nothing to do with trees or even bushes. After the natives resisted the Europeans for two centuries, the land itself took up the defense. Nearly two hundred years passed before Senator William Bingham, General David Cobb, Lord Ashburton, and their successors in interest were able to get a hard surface applied to the road to those Penobscot speculations to which I will give some attention in this essay. In the centuries between the clearing and completion of their road, the outside world had so changed that what had been conceived as a carriageway became known as the airline highway.

North of the Saco River this terrain has always resisted agriculture. That river divided occupations for so long that the woodland Eastern Abenaki, who preceded General Cobb in their interest in the region beyond its eastern banks (and succeeded him, as well), spoke one set of dialects, and the agricultural Western Abenaki, who commanded much of New Hampshire and Vermont, spoke another. The eastern cousins knew as much about fishing as the western knew about corn and squash, beans and tobacco. Accents and occupations still are divided roughly along these ancient lines, though the coming of livestock and industry has confused things. The old ways of the forest, hunting, fishing, trapping, and lumbering, are still practiced east and north of the Saco as they have been for thousands of years. West and south of it, rural America truly begins.

The Abenaki were fierce fighters; they first held the English to a few starveling settlements along the coast and then drove them out of Maine entirely. Until European diseases and intertribal warfare weakened them, they also maintained their hold on villages and fields along the Connecticut River. When the Abenaki ultimately retreated northward to take shelter with their French allies, they left those terraces to be assumed by the English, who simply continued to plant as the Indians had done, though they did introduce sweeter strains of tobacco they had found in the West Indies.

In southern New England the first Native American settlers were replaced by thinly settled villages of dispersed Puritan yeomen who had no reason to defer to any hierarchy other than that of the intellectuals, whose authority was religious; there were no squires. The retreat of the Indians from northern New England came much later, after a century of uncertain warfare in which the English were often pushed back from the region by the French and Indians. When this set of wars was ended in 1763, and the king of England was acknowledged as somehow more important there than the king of France, the villages of northern New England were organized, but seldom into the patterns that had grown up in Massachusetts, Rhode Island, and Connecticut. (Originally the terms

This glass negative of Woodstock, Vermont, in the 1870s shows the jumbled residential, industrial, and commercial uses characteristic of New England before the great cleanup of the 1890s. *Courtesy of the Woodstock Historical Society, Inc., Woodstock, Vermont*

"town" and "village" meant an area organized within fixed boundaries for political purposes; they did not describe the tight clusters of houses and stores around meetinghouses that we call to mind as the ideal New England village. These were rare anywhere in New England until the commercial and industrial growth of the end of the eighteenth century, as noted earlier.)

Northern New England had a squirely hierarchy, civil not religious, and its people were not predominantly Puritan (in the far north next to Canada they were not, of course, Protestant). Massachusetts, Rhode Island, and Connecticut had been organized as Puritan commonwealths of one variety or another. But New Hampshire and Maine were Anglican; Portsmouth rivaled Boston, and in the absence of Puritan divines quickly developed a tight and seldom challenged mercantile oligarchy.

Maine, like Maryland or New York, was a proprietary colony owing fealty to grantees from the Crown. In the seventeenth century two courtiers of the Tudors and early Stuarts, Sir Ferdinando Gorges and Sir John Popham, thought of Maine as a fine place to colonize with English Catholics. Even earlier, in 1603, French entrepreneurs had established there the first European agricultural colony in North America. *They*

Governor Benning Wentworth of New Hampshire, the embodiment of the well-fed, well-satisfied North Country squire. *New Hampshire Historical Society, photograph by Bill Finney*

thought it ideally situated to receive French Protestants (this was after the Spaniards had exterminated the Huguenot colonies in South Carolina and Georgia).

Vermont, remote beyond the mountains, was at first more easily reached by the French from Montreal than by the English from the Atlantic shore. It became the creature of the Wentworths, innkeeping merchant-speculators risen to become royal governors in distant Portsmouth, New Hampshire, and of a succession of royal governors of even more distant New York, who distributed its best land to themselves and their supporters. These absentee grandees paid only grudging attention to the mixed lot of farmers and fur traders who percolated up the Connecticut Valley and who disputed their titles. As we shall see, it would have been wise for the New York and New Hampshire grandees to pay closer heed to the Green Mountain Boys.

Northern New England was like the Appalachian frontier, a new land little influenced in the colonial period by the special circumstances emanating from Plymouth and Boston. It was even more like central New York, a landscape dominated by the huge holdings of aristocratic proprietors. After independence those distant aristocrats and oligarchies were replaced by merchant-speculators — except in Vermont, which violently refused to follow the course of its neighbors.

Traces of these patterns of possession of the 1770s persist in the real estate map of the 1990s. Indeed, colonial legal arrangements have had a more tenacious hold upon the land than the natural conditions upon which they were overlaid. To observe this, we need only delay our inquiry into subsequent political history as we search for survivals of wildness to reveal the natural history of this early period.

That any wilderness has been left to us at all is undoubtedly due to Maine's reliance on lumber as a cash crop. Lumber is notoriously slow to become marketable, and as a result some of its proprietors have taken a very long view of their interests and responsibilities. Three quarters of the old-growth timber in all New England was recently transferred, in the block around Seven Ponds, north of Mount Katahdin, by the heirs of David Pingree, who acquired this tract as part of an enormous domain in 1820. Six and a half million acres of northern Maine are, to this day, served by five thousand miles of private roads traversing holdings as large as kingdoms. The Brown Company, a lumber conglomerate, is more important to the daily life of several townships than any agency of the state government.

Despite our democratic preference to think of this region as owing its charm to the reign of independent yeomen, there is no denying that some of its large landowners have bestowed upon it a benign tradition of conservation practices and public service. The recent benefaction of the Pingrees is one example; the remarkable legacy of the Gardiners along the warmer, pastoral coast is another. Robert Hallowell Gardiner still occupies one of the few continuous squirearchies in the United States, between the towns of Hallowell and Gardiner, on lands that have been in the family since the seventeenth century, when the Kennebec purchase was thirty miles square. (These Gardiners are not to be confused with those of Gardiners Island, New York, mentioned in Chapter 4, though the latter have held their isolated fief even longer.)

At the center of their holdings is Oaklands, a Regency Gothic manor house designed in 1835–1836 by Richard Upjohn to replace an earlier one destroyed by fire. Upjohn later became famous as the designer of more than a hundred churches, most of them Gothic and Episcopalian, and ninety houses, most of them round-arched and picturesque, from Maine to San Antonio.[1] He was not the originator of the Gothic Revival in America; that distinction, like so much else in our history, belongs to Benjamin Henry Latrobe and Latrobe's rival, Joseph-Jacques Ramée, both of an earlier generation. But Upjohn was its first proficient practitioner. Trinity Church in New York made his ecclesiastical reputation, and the Gardiner villa established him as fit to make country squires into aristocrats.

He was discovered in Boston, according to an early Robert Hallowell Gardiner (1782–1864), "an Englishman who was poor and supporting himself by carpenter work; the only job he had received as an architect was the fence around the common." Well, not quite — he had completed a handsome mansion for the lumber baron Isaac Farrar in Bangor (still there, though butchered) and was at work on another for Farrar's brother Stephen — but there is no doubt that the Gardiners put him in the public eye. They took him from the office of Alexander Parris, where he was one of a number of young associates, gave him some preliminary designs, and as they made his reputation, he made them barons: he "put in the turrets, battlements and buttresses, the hammered stone increasing the cost very much."[2]

The effect was splendid; it still is. When President James K. Polk visited Maine, all the expense and trouble was justified, as "the Executive procession . . . ascended the hill to the princely residence . . . built of granite, in the Norman and Lombard style, resembling a country seat of a British peer of the realm. . . . The escort of mounted citizens drew up in two lines, one on each side of the road, facing the carriages, and sitting uncovered as the train passed through. The company were at once ushered into the house, where a collation of cakes, fruits, wines, ices, lemonade, cordials &c. was spread out for them."[3]

The family was delighted; the house had nearly bankrupted them, and the ices might serve as a reminder of one of the reasons they were able to hold on to it — they had become successful ice merchants. From their piers on the river below, ships had carried blocks of it, insulated by sawdust, to the julep-drinking Carolinas, to the thirsty West Indies, and

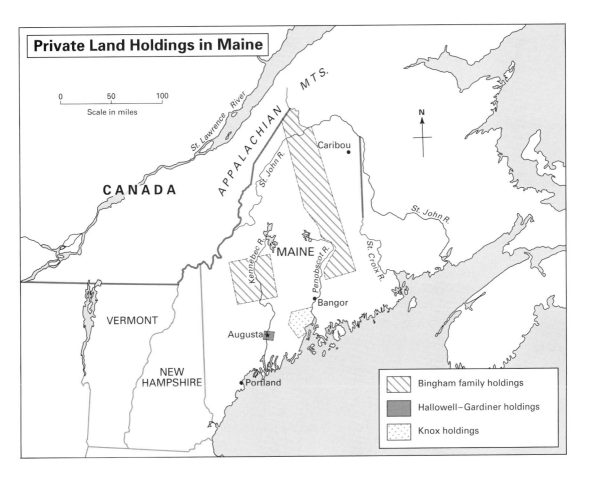

Private Land Holdings in Maine

0   50   100
Scale in miles

St. Lawrence River

APPALACHIAN MTS.

CANADA

Caribou

St. John R.

St. John R.

MAINE

Kennebec R.

Penobscot R.

St. Croix R.

N

VERMONT

Bangor

Augusta ★

NEW
HAMPSHIRE

Portland

▨ Bingham family holdings

■ Hallowell–Gardiner holdings

⋮ Knox holdings

around the Horn to Canton. The Gardiners have always been a practical lot, and their own account of the affair noted that "it was a dusty time, and so many horsemen raised a fearful amount of dust, so that it was impossible to distinguish one person from another. The President on his arrival was immediately conducted into father's room and furnished with the means of a thorough ablution, for which he expressed the warmest gratitude."[4]

Indeed, the accounts of the early Gardiners are good guides to Maine's other princely mansions of the early period, to which their attention was drawn for a number of reasons. The greatest of these was Montpelier, the seat of General Henry Knox, in Thomaston. Knox, according to Robert Gardiner, "had married a granddaughter of Brigadier Waldo, and partly by inheritance and partly by purchase of confiscated property had become possessed of the largest portion of the Waldo patent, embracing much fine land, many good harbors, excellent mill privileges, and valuable lime quarries." The asperity tincturing this passage may be explained by the fact that the Gardiners, who had remained loyal to the Crown, barely escaped being among those "confiscated."

Knox succeeded in selling a million or so of his acres to Senator William Bingham of Philadelphia, obtaining just enough cash to build what Gardiner described as "a splendid house, and lived in the style of an English gentleman. He had an open, generous disposition, was fond of society and extremely hospitable. He engaged in various schemes of business . . . all losing concerns. He died from attempting to swallow a chicken bone. . . . If he had survived a few months longer, his proud spirit would have been obliged to give up his splendid establishment and acknowledge himself a bankrupt."[5]

But until his death he was a splendid figure, this huge man, known to the local Jeffersonian press as "the Unmasked Nabob of Hancock County," proprietor of the first piano to be heard in Maine. So hospitable was he that friendlier reports had it that a hundred beds were made at Montpelier every morning, and he was a generous employer to the more than one hundred — one hundred seven, to be exact — people on his personal payroll. (Montpelier was burned in 1871, but it is very well represented by the replica erected upon another site in Thomaston, largely financed in the nostalgic 1920s by the publisher of the *Saturday Evening Post*.)

Visitors to Maine who may think its villas first appeared with the summer people in the 1880s might pause for a tour of Montpelier. The only surviving example of the French villa style of Charles Bulfinch, it has thirteen-foot ceilings, a double hanging staircase, and a vast oval drawing room bulging out in front.

Amid all this opulence it is easy to forget that Gardiner and Knox were poor by contrast to William Bingham, Maine's true nabob at the time. In the 1790s Bingham owned three million of its acres, along with one and a half million in Pennsylvania. He was a senator from Pennsylvania whose fortune had been made on his "golden voyage" to the West Indies during the Revolutionary War. In his lair at Martinique he and his French hosts had armed and shared in the profits of privateers. After the war he wisely invested in the depressed securities of the United States government, and together with his friend William Duer profited immensely as *their* friend and Duer's employer, Secretary of the Treasury Alexander Hamilton, redeemed those securities at par. As Gardiner noted, Knox and Duer had devoured confiscated Tory holdings; by the exertions of his friends, Knox escaped formal bankruptcy, but Duer went to debtors' prison after losing his head and his fortune in a frenzy of avarice. For a considerable period this handsome man had done very well indeed by coupling his old Etonian charm with a total absence of scruple. (To be fair to Duer, he was a gifted writer of political pamphlets as well as of land-touting brochures; he was the author of three of the *Federalist Papers.*)

Knox, a close political ally of Hamilton's, served as George Washington's secretary of war even though he was often absent on his extensive Maine business. (For example, Hamilton took over Knox's army during the Whiskey Rebellion in 1792 because Knox could not be spared from his land speculations.) The holdings of the Knoxes totaled at least two million acres. The two Knoxes, weighing in at five hundred fifty pounds of marketing persuasion, urged Bingham along, their arguments reinforced by Duer.

Bingham left no tangible evidence of his presence in Maine during the anxious decade in which he sought to liquidate what these charmers had sold him, but a fine brick house was built in Ellsworth by Colonel John Black, who carried on those efforts toward divestiture on behalf of Bingham's son-in-law, Alexander Baring. In the 1840s Baring, by then Lord Ashburton, uncomfortably retained a million acres of timberland in

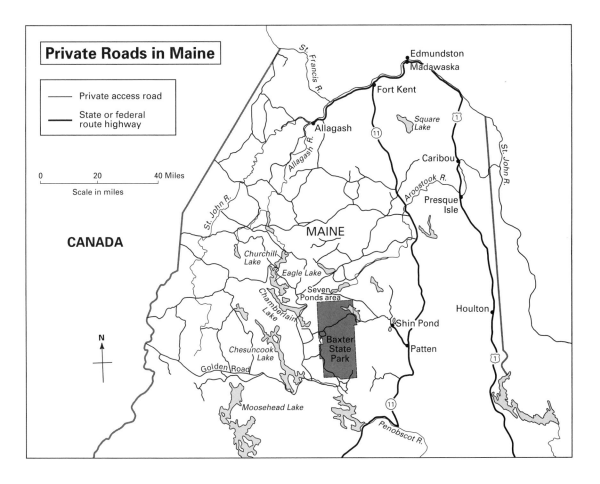

Maine and negotiated its borders with the government of the United States. One may bear this in mind when reading of our northern boundary being settled by the Webster-Ashburton Treaty of 1842.

The first Oaklands had been built in 1810 and, like the present version of Knox's Montpelier, was something of a reproduction, taking the shape of another Montpelier, the country residence of President James Madison in Orange County, Virginia. The two Montpeliers had been created at about the same time, possibly in sympathy with each other, for Madison and Knox could still be described as Federalists in the mid-1790s.

Tories might be sensitive to the subject, but not all losers in the colonial wars, Frenchmen or Tories, suffered confiscation. As noted, western Vermont and much of New Hampshire had first been organized between 1690 and 1750 into seigneuries, feudal estates, by the French and later into sections of the estates of George Clarke of New York and Benning Wentworth of New Hampshire. The seigneuries along Lake Champlain seem to have been sold cheaply, between 1763 and 1770, to British buyers who resold them to Americans after Vermont became independent of Britain in the late 1770s. The Clarkes, though Tories like the Gardiners, successfully managed a transition to American independence, and so did one set of Wentworth cousins.

This was not a satisfactory outcome in Vermont. Much of the eagerness for its independence (not quite the same thing as the independence of the United States) arose from a desire of the Green Mountain Boys to rid themselves of rentals arising from the seigneurs or to be paid to the Wentworths and Clarkes, who retained several hundred thousand acres. The grandees were as proud as ever; the extent of Benning Wentworth's reach had been disclosed by the very name of Bennington, Vermont, and the Clarkes owned 120,000 acres, some of them in the Green Mountain State. Ethan Allen had already given Vermont its patriotic text in an altercation with the Clarkes' lawyers: "The gods of the hills are not the gods of the valley."

The Green Mountain Boys were first organized in 1770, not to gain independence from Britain but to resist competition from landholders with title from New York. The Allens' claims arose from their having bought land from the Wentworths, who had always contended that the Clarke titles were defective.

Once rid of the "Yorkers," the Allens could deal with the Wentworths. From 1770 onward a small-scale civil war between the two sets of settlers was exacerbated by the founding by the Allens and other sons of Connecticut of the Onion River Land Company, dependent on Wentworth grants, in 1773. Ethan Allen moved to wrap himself in larger causes, and to unhorse the Wentworths, by leading the Green Mountain Boys against the source of all royal titles, the British Crown. They captured Fort Ticonderoga from the British in 1775.

Fort Matanzas, built to protect Spanish St. Augustine, Florida, from a British attack from the rear. *Photo by Jack Kotz*

The moon rises over Acoma, New Mexico, one of the two oldest continuously inhabited towns in the United States; the other, Oriabe, is nearby. *Photo by Jack Kotz*

Opposite: The concentric earthen ridges built around 1500 B.C. at Poverty Point, Louisiana, can be seen in this digitally remastered and colored aerial photograph. The structures were more extensive than those at Stonehenge. *Courtesy of NASA*

Complex masonry villages built by the Anasazi in Chaco Canyon, New Mexico, represent an immense achievement in a precarious ecological setting. *Photo by Jack Kotz*

Ethan Allen, it is asserted. The early statue of the Hero of Ticonderoga depicted here, said to be a good likeness, disappeared in 1852. The sculptor was B. F. Kinne. *Courtesy of the Vermont Historical Society*

Ethan Allen was captured in return later that same year. His followers, however, proclaimed Vermont to be a republic, independent of everybody. Some New Hampshire towns on the eastern side of the Connecticut enthusiastically applied to join, which enraged the American patriots of New Hampshire and encouraged Massachusetts to claim a portion of the new republic of Vermont for itself. The Vermonters were in a poor position to resist Massachusetts, New Hampshire, the British, or their Indian allies, because they were arrayed against a possible attack from New York.

Between 1779 and 1783 Ethan Allen, after release with suspicious ease from his Canadian jail, commenced negotiations as a representative of the republic of Vermont with the governor-general of Canada — the Green Mountain State might become reattached to the British Empire under the right conditions. But he was a little late: Lord Cornwallis soon surrendered at Yorktown. In 1783 the British conceded Vermont to the United States. Though its neighbors punished its ambiguities by denying it membership in the original thirteen states, Vermont was not quite

One of the great dramatic moments of the American Revolution: Ethan Allen at Fort Ticonderoga. *Courtesy of the Vermont Historical Society*

done with Balkan politics. As late as 1796 Ira Allen had twenty thousand muskets and twenty-four cannon on board a ship from France to provide for a new revolutionary army, this time to create "New Columbia." And northern Vermont supplied most of the provisions that fed the British armies of the North during the War of 1812.

Southern Vermont settled into the United States with greater equanimity as its seigneuries and the great Clarke and Wentworth landholdings came apart. There was a final reversion to medieval patterns in the 1830s. All America experienced the merino mania, a craze for the purchase of Pyrenean sheep with marvelous long wool. Historians at the time recalled that the wool export business had been the basis of Britain's prosperity three hundred years earlier. Now, following the British pattern of that distant time, small holdings, commons, and open pasture were enclosed by large landholders. This new enclosure movement was briefly profitable; the South had King Cotton and Vermont King Wool. In 1845 there were six sheep for every person.

But orthodox liberal economics prevailed: the Congress repealed the protective tariffs that insulated domestic wool from foreign competition and by the onset of the Civil War King Wool had abdicated. Only the wonderful mansions in Orwell and Castleton, built for his grand shepherds, are there to remind us of his reign.

Along the Connecticut are architectural vestiges of an earlier prosperity, which turned out to be equally precarious. These are the famous Connecticut River doorways, bold frames for door openings, curving into mannerist, overscaled celebrations at the top, supported, in their most magnificent versions, by piles of simulated blocks up the side. These doorways share many ornamental elements with headstones in valley cemeteries created at the same time. Deerfield, Massachusetts, has the most famous of these pompous artifacts, and other examples are to be found all the way to the headwaters of the river. They were more than doorways; they were signboards, proclamations of the haughtiness of the occupants of houses otherwise quite plain though capacious. The great merchants of the Connecticut Valley were called the river gods by their contemporaries. Some may have repeated the term in private among themselves if they were not yet mindful of Ethan Allen's appropriation of rhetoric about gods of the mountains, gods of the valleys — or of the rivers.

The Wilcox-Cutts House in Orwell, Vermont, an unorthodox essay in the Greek Revival by Thomas Dake.

A Connecticut River doorway: the Ebenezer Grant house in South Windsor, Hartford County. *Photography by and courtesy of William Hosley*

These merchants, many of them Tories, shared their lordship with such absentees as the Wentworths, a point made in the qualities shared by those doorways, by the headstones of the same merchants, and by the extraordinary ornament of the Council Chamber of the Wentworths at Little Harbor, two miles south of Portsmouth. In its presence we can recall that moment of pre-Revolutionary obsequiousness in New Hampshire when, in the final hours of its ancien régime, some citizens petitioned that the Wentworths be made officially what they had become de facto: hereditary governors of the colony. The Crown's chief officer, John Wentworth (1671–1730), had started the house. The great room to which he summoned his council was probably built around 1695 rather than in the time of his son Governor Benning Wentworth (1696–1770) or his grandson Governor John Wentworth (1737–1820).

There is no other space in America in which one can better sense the imperial ambitions of the European powers before the Treaty of Paris in 1763 and the panoply of power created by their representatives. Men like the marquis de Beauharnois in Quebec, Sir Edmund Andros in New York, and John Wentworth in Portsmouth deployed every artifice available to them to overawe the colonists who were straggling ashore and setting themselves up in such unprepossessing places as the rocky estuary of the Piscataway.

John Wentworth's caryatid mantelpiece, based on a design by Inigo Jones, was truly imperial, whereas his brother Mark's midcentury door piece, taken from William Salmon's *Palladio Londinensis,* is merely colonial. (Mark Wentworth's house is grandly situated on the Portsmouth waterfront. Known as the Wentworth-Gardiner House, it was once owned by the Metropolitan Museum of Art, which considered moving it to Central Park.) By the time the house was completed in the 1760s, the taste of the Portsmouth Wentworths and that of the small group of related families with whom they ruled New Hampshire was becoming tame, cautious, deferential — and genteel. Though Mark Wentworth's doorway is taken from the same page in Salmon's book as the entrance to William Byrd's Westover on the James River in Virginia, Byrd's was rougher hewn, carrying greater conviction. Unlike the urban coterie of Portsmouth, with their borrowed graces and hesitant fashions, Byrd was a merchant turned squire whose taste in literature, invective, and architecture sustained the spirit of the freebooting early imperial age.

In France, Spain, and Latin America that age expressed itself in the baroque, and it is sometimes said that the Connecticut River doorways and headstones and the Wentworth Council Chamber are "baroque." But using that word is misleading and pernicious, because the term blankets out the origins of their vigorous style in *northern* Europe and, worse, may distract us from the glorious American work done in its spirit in the nineteenth century.

The baroque mantelpiece of the Benning Wentworth House, in Portsmouth, New Hampshire, carved by a local craftsman about 1752 from a design plagiarized and published in 1737 from an earlier design said to be by Inigo Jones, as published by William Kent. *Photograph by Douglas Armsden, courtesy of the State of New Hampshire*

Long before Britain imported the baroque from France and Italy at the end of the seventeenth century, the nouveaux riches aristocrats and courtiers of Queen Elizabeth's court (such as Maine's founders, Messrs. Popham and Gorges) were building chimney pieces and doorways like the Wentworth chimney piece and woodwork. This strutting stuff is known in England as artisan mannerism. Despite this somewhat patronizing title, given it by lovers of Palladian restraint, it was exceedingly sophisticated and never dull. When it appeared in the décor of the true Elizabethan grandees, the Cecils and Howards, it was, of course, considerably more sophisticated and of richer materials than anything Popham or Gorges could afford, but the same bellicosity is found in most Elizabethan and Jacobean work. This is the passionate, Shakespearean side of the English character.

It has nothing whatever to do with Puritanism, nor did Portsmouth in its ancien régime, even in its relatively genteel phase. Expanding our focus, we can truly say that the Shakespearean frame of mind was present in northern, as distinct from southern, New England, from the 1690s to the 1850s. In the 1830s, for example, there appeared in Maine a jubilant variety of American popular classicism constrained only with difficulty within the Greek Revival. Something very like artisan mannerism reappeared in social and economic circumstances that had much in common with the reign of Good Queen Bess — rapid growth amid turmoil and social instability.

The river gods had a brief reign; toward the end, in the 1780s, their doorways shut out an increasingly disrespectful outside world and their headstones seemed to become entryways from that increasingly revolutionary world into the silent order of the grave.

In the 1830s and 1840s a sedate Greek Revival appeared in upstate New York, Ohio, and Michigan, on the western slope of New Hampshire along the Connecticut River, and on the western slope of Vermont below Lake Champlain. There are beautiful small Grecian towns in all these places. But it is in the wild profusion of Belfast and Bangor and a dozen shoreline towns of the 1830s that Maine shows its neighbors how artisan mannerism might flower again with only the faintest Hellenic sanction. There is nothing in America to compare in virtuosity with the carved doorways of Wiscasset, that is, nothing created between the doorways of the river gods in the 1780s and the banks designed by Louis Sullivan and George Elmslie between 1907 and 1913.

It is not easy to think of Belfast and Bangor as boom towns, no easier than it is for some Bostonians to reconcile themselves to the fact that Sullivan's genius makes Owatonna, Minnesota, the hub of the American universe, from an architectural point of view. But one final quotation from the promotional literature of the early nineteenth century may assist us in visualizing the circumstances within which American Free Classicism flourished a century before Sullivan revived it. Things quieted a little only after the deaths of Bingham, Knox, and Duer.

> The wildest speculation that ever prevailed in any part of the United States was in the timber lands of Maine. In 1832, or about that time, it became known to the people of Massachusetts that a good deal of money was being made by a few investors in Maine timber lands . . . at very low prices. . . . Those who bought early . . . did make . . . large fortunes.

Summering in Maine: the veranda of the Poland Spring House, Poland Spring, Maine, in 1939. *Maine State Archives, photograph by George French*

. . . The desire became so strong, and the excitement so great, that a courier line was established between Boston and Bangor, by which offers to buy, and subsequently to sell, were rapidly transmitted, and for months nothing was talked about but Maine lands. Brokers' offices were opened in Bangor, which were crowded from morning till night. . . . Not one in fifty knew anything about the lands he was buying. . . . The same lands were sold over and over again. . . . Dishonesty was in the ascendant.[6]

The *Baltimore Advocate*, in May 1835, took the occasion to get in a little "nativist" (meaning anti-Catholic and anti-Irish) gossip: "The timber lands are all the go in this, and even the worthy Catholic Bishop, it is understood, is dipping in, having purchased a whole township which he is selling to the Irish to make a Catholic State somewhere in the woods of Maine."

The land boom came crashing down in 1837, and Bangor acquired its present look of having been heavily bombed and its rubble carried away. It is, in fact, the Boston that almost was, the difference being that Bangor had no canny Puritans to carry it through crises and decant capital from one speculation to another just in time.

In the interior, northern New England has become a land of less frenetic ensembles, villages not uniform or disciplined but restrained, respectful, and coherent. Here the parade of nineteenth-century "styles" passed through without altering the landscape very much, and great emigrations deprived the region of those disposed to change anything.

On the shore, summer people came to be waitered upon the verandas of great hotels and then to compete in the shingled expanses of their cottages and the verdure of their putting-green lawns. But in the rest of the year life went on, and goes on, much as it did in the past. Fishermen and subsistence farmers remain as suspicious of strangers as the Abenaki had been.

It is to such old continuities that I wish to draw attention, to the extent of northern New England's landholdings, to its perpetual clearing of land for planting and grazing, and, despite the felling of white pines so tall that their first branches were higher than the rooftops of a Manchester textile mill, to the intractability of the fundamental North Country to any human intervention.

The moose go on searching for succulent stems of arrowroot, the mosquitoes for the nourishment of blood, the eagles ride the currents sent upward by the sun's earnest effort to thaw Katahdin. And the wolves, it is said, are coming back.

6

....

The Middle Atlantic States

New Jersey, New York, and Pennsylvania

THE EUROPEAN colonies that became the Middle Atlantic states were, from their earliest days, tied to the West Indies by a cat's cradle of trade and trade warfare. New Netherland, which became New York, was a colony not of Holland but of the Dutch West Indies Company, which had absorbed New Sweden which, in turn, had been intended to serve as a base for Swedish assaults on the Spanish West Indies. Even Canada was ruled for a time by the French West Indies Company. George Washington's Mount Vernon was named for Edward Vernon, the British admiral whose assault on Cartagena, on the southern shore of the Caribbean, provided the Washington family with its first opportunity for military glory, in 1740. And despite a general impression that Pennsylvania was named for William Penn, its mild Quaker founder, it was so denominated to honor his father, like Vernon an admiral of the Spanish Main, whose fame arose from his capture of Jamaica in 1654.

In 1699 William Byrd of Virginia, himself a shipper of foodstuffs to the islands, noted that "Pennsylvania has little trade with England but pretty much with the West Indies, and . . . not precise in consulting what trade is lawful and what is not." New Netherland kept looking southward even after it became New York, and looked very southern itself. As late as 1800 there were more slaves per capita in Dutchess County than there were in North Carolina. Many of the sweet Dutch Colonial houses along the Hudson (like the Van Cortlandt house in Croton) were built by the twelve thousand slaves resident there — though not, of course, for themselves. It is worth noting that Black slavery was still legal in New

York in 1827 and that a prime reason for the laggardliness of the legislature in abolishing it was the resistance of the Dutch farmers along the Hudson. After nearly two centuries they were still carrying on the type of plantation life, with small gangs of slaves doing the heavy work, that had been the pattern in the West Indies before the onset of the sugar culture and the deployment of Africans in regiments.

These West Indian connections were more apparent before urban growth replaced the villages that once lined the shores of upper Manhattan Island, Queens, Brooklyn, and the Bronx. The "typical New York cottage" had long Caribbean verandas; some, like Alexander Hamilton's

A pastel sketch of
Alexander Hamilton at the
age of forty. *National
Portrait Gallery, Smithsonian
Institution, Washington, D.C.*

The Grange, country seat of Alexander Hamilton, Esq., the consummate
creole in residence in a city that first waxed wealthy in the West Indies trade.
Courtesy of the New-York Historic Society, New York City

The Grange, had fragile tropical plants under glass and hardier species out of doors. This most prominent of New Yorkers was from the island of Nevis. In the early years of the republic, Hamilton's close ally was William Bingham of Philadelphia, whose fortune was made privateering on Martinique. Philadelphia's second and third richest men, Stephen Girard and Robert Morris, were also West Indies traders.

Much of the prosperity of the English mainland colonies depended upon commerce with the Caribbean. Sugar and slaves made the Livingstons rich; one branch of the family, headed by Philip Philip (*sic*) Livingston, devoted itself entirely to its plantations on Jamaica. The lordly Clarkes, rivals to the Livingstons, presided over more than one hundred thousand acres scattered about Hyde Hall, their mansion near Cooperstown. The Clarkes and their Hyde relatives derived most of their income from the 1760s until the 1820s from Jamaica, and spent it in London and New York.

It is startling to come upon such survivals of this period as the Van Cortlandt House at Croton, the Dyckman House on upper Broadway, or the creole cottage that acts as the southern wing of Hyde Hall. They seem out of place until we recall that New York, like Newport, Rhode

The Van Cortlandt House in Croton, New York: the West Indies format applied to a slave-built Hudson River plantation house.

A West Indian survival: the Dyckman House on upper Broadway in Manhattan.

Island, once paid to pave its streets with a tax laid on the importation of slaves.

The slave-and-sugar economy came first, followed by the trade in furs. That lively, though subsidiary, interest on the part of the European trading companies explains another set of geographic relations that are strange at first glance. Fort Orange (Albany) was established before New Amsterdam (the city of New York — the colony was New Netherland) for the same reason — the fur trade — that a Dutch stockade near Hartford, known as the House of Hope, preceded settlements at the mouth of the Connecticut River, and the French built a post far up the Mississippi at Natchez before they founded New Orleans. The ports where rivers issued into the sea were then needed only to provide harbors for refitting vessels bound for the lucrative West Indies. Upriver stations could turn a profit in trade goods with the Indians.

The West Indies trade was important to the Puritans of New England and the Quakers of Pennsylvania as well as to the merchants of New Amsterdam. But there was a fundamental difference in the founding intentions of the entrepôts along the Hudson and those of the other two colonies. Plymouth and Pennsylvania were conceived as Christian utopias thriving from farming, not commerce. They were to be places of refuge, drawing settlers inward, so to speak. By contrast, New York was formed as a salient thrusting after trade, into the continent. *They* were not quite Arcadias, but *it* was a clearly an emporium.

This distinction was apparent in the Hudson Valley, which remained sparsely inhabited throughout the colonial period. The Dutch in their fortified trading stations were long indifferent to settlement, which accounts for their generally compatible relations with the neighboring Indians. This was true, though some of their entrepôts appeared on the map as the center points of large landholdings called patroonships. It is an important key to understanding the disposition of villages, houses, and boundary lines in the Hudson and Mohawk valleys and southwestern Vermont to recall that these commercial, thinly settled Dutch holdings evolved, in British hands after 1674, into a manorial system of land tenure forbidding to settlers.

This evolution is unique to that region and accounts for much in its appearance. Though there persists to this day in England itself an aristocratic sentiment for land, according to which a man's acres assert at least the basis for his status, in colonial Virginia, New Hampshire, and Pennsylvania this tradition was never strong. Merchants who acquired many acres (the Carters and Byrds come to mind) held on to only a few thousand around their home plantations and disposed of the rest as soon as they could take speculators' profits. This was most un-English of them.

But not so in New York and Vermont. One might think the patroons and manor lords would inherit the practical Dutch view of things, viewing sod as a commodity. Holland was a mercantile country with little land and less of a landholders' mystique than anywhere in Europe except perhaps Venice. But along the Hudson the Dutch, Anglo-Dutch merchants, and English merchants (by this time they included Scots) who became patroons and later manor lords were as tenacious as Warwickshire squires. Though presented with immediate cash offers, they declined to sell. Well into the nineteenth century, the Livingstons and Van Rensselaers and Clarkes sought to live on tenantry.

In the process they denied the best soil to small independent farmers. Along the Hudson a poor man, even after he got a little money together, could be only a tenant. Few land-hungry Europeans would come all the distance to America to settle for that. America was profuse with land to take from the Indians or to purchase from those who already had.

Even today the counties of the central Hudson Valley show the consequences of this peculiar experience. From Hyde Park north nearly to Albany, the great sweep of countryside on the east side of the river north of the Highlands remained closely held by the oligopoly that chose the winning side in the Revolutionary War — largely the Van Rensselaers and Livingstons. To this day it is a land of great estates. But because most of Putnam County was held by Tory manor lords whose property was confiscated after that war, it was divided into many small holdings.

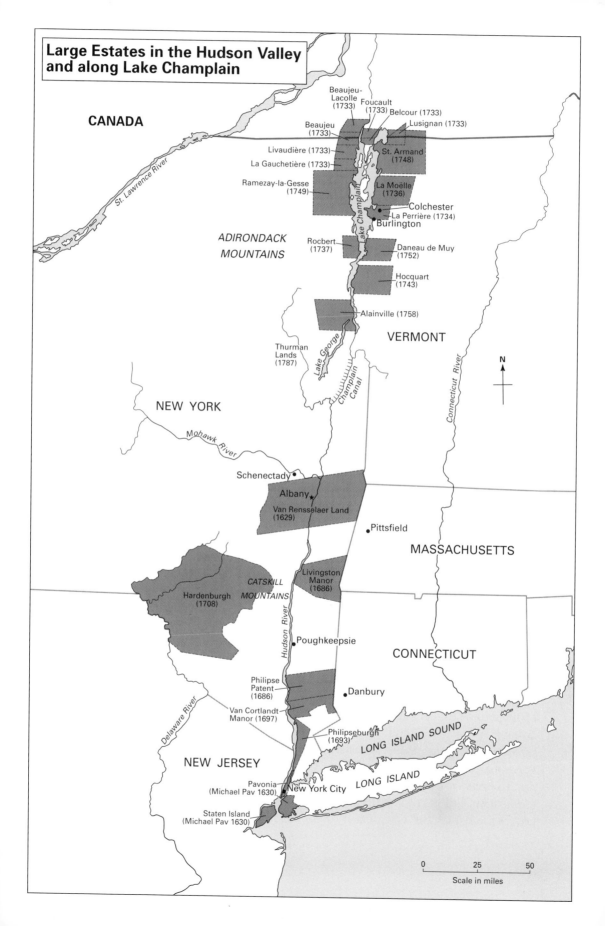

Large Estates in the Hudson Valley and along Lake Champlain

CANADA

St. Lawrence River

ADIRONDACK MOUNTAINS

Beaujeu-Lacolle (1733)

Foucault (1733)

Belcour (1733)

Lusignan (1733)

Beaujeu (1733)

Livaudière (1733)

La Gauchetière (1733)

St. Armand (1748)

Ramezay-la-Gesse (1749)

La Moëlle (1736)

Colchester

La Perrière (1734)

Burlington

Lake Champlain

Rocbert (1737)

Daneau de Muy (1752)

Hocquart (1743)

Alainville (1758)

VERMONT

Thurman Lands (1787)

Lake George

Champlain Canal

Connecticut River

N

NEW YORK

Mohawk River

Schenectady

Albany

Van Rensselaer Land (1629)

Pittsfield

MASSACHUSETTS

Livingston Manor (1686)

CATSKILL MOUNTAINS

Hardenburgh (1708)

Hudson River

Poughkeepsie

CONNECTICUT

Philipse Patent (1686)

Danbury

Van Cortlandt Manor (1697)

Delaware River

Philipseburgh (1693)

LONG ISLAND SOUND

NEW JERSEY

Pavonia (Michael Pav 1630)

New York City

LONG ISLAND

Staten Island (Michael Pav 1630)

0   25   50

Scale in miles

Though the patroonships were established as rewards to merchants, British rule in the 1670s altered them into something anachronistic for that period — they became feudal.[1] It was a curious coincidence that the same remedievalizing was taking place in New France. The French were the first of the three European nations to contest for this region against the Native American powers already there and to make use of feudalism for that purpose. They placed in fortresses in the wilderness "men of war, of approved trust . . . to hold the inhabitants to their duty within, and repel the enemy from without." This language, which might have been taken from a document of the Carolinian period, was used in 1667 by the intendant Canadian Jean-Baptiste Talon. He led the reintroduction in the seventeenth century of the system the French had invented in the ninth — or was it the seventh? No one is really sure.

At the extremities of empire, the wars between Britain and France after 1670 recreated circumstances much like those of Europe after the collapse of the empire of Charlemagne. Large estates were granted by the Crown: seventy-two percent of this land was held by four closely related families. Across the St. Lawrence from Montreal stood the turreted stone château of the greatest seigneur of them all, Charles le Moyne, afterward baron de Longueuil, proprietor of three fiefs. In the ancient fashion, some simple fiefs became the basis for more pretentious titles: Talon's seigneury of Des Islets was elevated into a barony, on the island of Orleans the fief of François Berthelot became an earldom, and not far away René Robineau became a baron.

The structure was in place, the seigneurs eager for tenants and retainers. But the climate was not propitious, and the age of happy retainers was over. In agriculture, capitalism was well under way. One of the seigneurs in what is now Vermont wrote the king to complain that he could not "find any farmers . . . to place on his seigneury . . . [though] if he should find any, he is willing to furnish them with axes and picks for clearing and one year's provisions." The sieurs de Contrecoeur and de la Perrière asserted that they had "done everything to settle their grants" but failed.

That failure ordained the return of many, but not all, of these grants to the king's personal holdings in 1741. Some of these fiefs and feuds in the Champlain Valley survived very late, as did the Dutch patroonships, in their new incarnations as British manors, along the Hudson and Mohawk. For a hundred and thirty years the domains of the Bourbon kings of France had been said to include both Canada and the Mississippi Valley. The word "domains" may seem a little archaic, but the Bourbons and their British rivals treated their North American possessions as fiefs — personal possessions. In Quebec the persistence of the Middle Ages can be felt to this day, for much of that city remains as it was in colonial times. Quebec was a *bastide,* a fortified village containing within its walls a cathedral, a governor's palace, stone warehouses, and hives for bureaucrats. New France, of which it was the administrative center, was the most intensely urbanized of the European colonies in the eighteenth century (a fifth of its population already lived in cities). But those cities were perched on the edge of a wilderness.

As the neat arrangements with Charles II that had kept the peace between England and France came to an end, and imperial warfare between the two became increasingly likely, the king of France, in 1676, promulgated a decree establishing subfiefs in the Champlain and St. Lawrence valleys.

At the time, absolute monarchy, guided by such princes of the Church as Cardinals Mazarin and Richelieu, was turning the independent nobles of France into gorgeous but impotent courtiers at Versailles. Some "irreconcilables," turbulent young men of old noble families, resisted being converted into gilded and gelded butterflies, and a few among them accepted Richelieu's invitation to remove their energies to Canada. In 1627 the Company of the Hundred Associates gave expiring feudalism a renewed span of life on a new continent.

Threadbare gentry left drafty castles behind to reenact the heroics which, centuries earlier during the old barons' wars, had established their families upon those domains. Their energies were turned toward the fringes of the king's domain in what are now New York and Vermont. As a result there came to be a true feudal revival, though it must be admitted there was more knightly commerce in furs than slaying of dragons or rescuing of fair damsels.

As the seigneuries struggled to serve their functions as buffer states, after 1730 the marquis de Beauharnois, governor of New France, was increasingly affronted by the evidence of British aggression close upon the outworks of Quebec. Too often there was smoke on the horizon — another farmstead aflame, another cornfield burning. Even within sight of his walls, scalps were being taken by the British and their Mohawk allies.

To aid in understanding how Beauharnois felt under these provocations, we can turn to the eloquent pages of Francis Parkman and reverse the polarities. Parkman, greatest of New England historians, established for many generations of Americans the dramaturgy of the French and Indian Wars. His depiction of the behavior of the French seigneurs as they carried those wars into New England will do nicely as a description of the way British leaders of Native American auxiliaries, such as Sir William Johnson, Lord of the Mohawks, may have seemed to Beauharnois:

> He was at home among his tenants, at home among the Indians, and never more at home than when, a gun in his hand and a crucifix on his breast, he took to the war-path with a crew of painted savages and

Baroque Quebec in the 1770s. *Courtesy of the Library of Congress*

Frenchmen almost as wild, and pounced like a lynx from the forest on some lonely farm or outlying hamlet of New England. How New England hated him, let her records tell. The reddest blood-streaks on her old annals mark the track of the Canadian gentilhomme.[2]

Though he had a few such gentlemen at his disposal, the governor of New France was painfully reminded again and again that his defenses were weak; there were too few Frenchmen living in Canada. More were needed to replace the disease-ravaged Indians in league with France and to stiffen his frail and febrile garrisons. Though New France, like New Amsterdam, was initiated to accommodate neither those who wished to trade nor those who wished to farm, colonization was becoming necessary. It was then that Beauharnois reinvigorated the feudalization of New France.

The British in their outpost at Albany thought themselves in a similar pass. They had succeeded to the lands and policies of the Dutch who, at the last minute, had taken a sudden interest in colonizing. Some of the investors in the Dutch West India Company had been rewarded with ample landholdings, carrying titles more capacious than responsibilities. When the British took over, some of these patroons were still holding on in a kind of rural capitalism.

Patroonships, despite their name and much sentimental nonsense written about them, were not so feudal as the British manors that, for military reasons, replaced them. The core of feudalism had been reciprocal obligations of defense and deference. But the merchants who became patroons, taking title not from the Crown but from a slave-trading commercial company and the States General, had no intention of leading anybody into battle on the frontier, nor could they expect more deference than that imparted by ready cash. The patroonships lapsed into mutual rancor, enriching their owners but discouraging settlement. The Dutch had no illusions about this; the early patroons like Kiliaen van Rensselaer, safe in Amsterdam, were no more interested in the administration of justice than in military adventure. They did not expect to raise, sustain, or rally their tenants or levies. How could they? The first generation of Van Rensselaers and Van Cortlandts was not expected to live on its grants and did not do so.

To this situation the British governor, Thomas Dongan, brought something new — new, that is, to it, but old to him and the British: the experience of forcing military colonies, fiefs, on a resentful and turbulent populace in Ireland.[3] So Dongan reversed the modernizing, capitalist Dutch pattern and attempted to "settle" experienced soldiers in little domains along the border. Both he and Beauharnois attempted to set the clock back in the same way, expecting their border lords to keep order from their own garrisoned houses, where grain might be stored and to which villagers could go for shelter in time of trouble.

Both governors understood the importance of marshaling law and religion for the defense. The local seigneur, knight, or, later, squire served as justice of the peace and judge of courts *baron* for civil cases and courts *leet* for criminal and administrative matters. Furthermore, he need brook no "seditious curates"; all clergymen must have his approval, by what was called right of *avowdson*. After 1688 the New York patroons were turned nostalgically into manor lords as they were presented with the full panoply of powers — courts *leet* and *baron* and even the power of *avowdson*.

Captain Thomas Chambers was given a "manor" near Kingston, on which he was expected to maintain a mansion house defensible against the French and Indians. At the same time, the authorities in Quebec made grants in "*fief* and *seigneury,* with high, middle, and low justice," parceling out most of what is now western Vermont and that portion of New York lying along Lakes Champlain and George. (Some New Yorkers and Vermonters still hold chains of title reaching back to Dongan and Beauharnois.)

It was too late, however, for the English grants in the Hudson Valley to become replicas of medieval institutions. Few of them were actually assumed by soldiers. Most went to merchants, such as the Livingstons and Van Cortlandts. These canny folk had no intention of acting as squires holding fiefs. They deliberately avoided the chief device by which European estates were held together in the hands of the first-born son, the rule of primogeniture. Some first-born sons had a tendency to run up debts encumbered by mortgages. These obligations were avoided by placing family lands in many hands, as far from the reach of creditors as from the follies of the first-born. Practical, but not feudal.

Furthermore, Charles II had abolished the reciprocal obligations of land tenure and military leadership in 1660, so the few captains who did become manor lords in the New World were reduced to mere landlords and speculators. Yet they had this much in common with the truly feudal landlords of the Middle Ages: they did very little farming themselves. They squeezed tenants for high rents and hoped for windfalls such as improvements made by the tenants that reverted with the land after a term of years, a system leading to revolts in Ireland in the seventeenth and eighteenth centuries and in New York until the 1840s.

At the very end, however, another ironic switch took place. The early manor lords of New York, New Jersey, Vermont, Maine, New Hampshire, and Pennsylvania were absentees, as noted, taking little active part in agriculture. But as their system was expiring in the nineteenth century, Stephen Van Rensselaer and George Clarke read the novels of Sir Walter Scott, assumed the bearing and habits of squires of old, and, a little too late, became as active in agriculture as some Virginians had been all along.

In the foregoing discussion there was some mention of Irish precedents. Let us follow them up in order to dispose of a few pernicious stereotypes. New York and Pennsylvania benefited from three quite distinct Irish immigrations well before the potato famine led to the great removal of the Irish peasantry to America and even before New York benefited from cheap Irish labor on the Erie Canal. The first of these earlier settlements, begun in the seventeenth century, was led by tough Scotch-Irish frontiersmen. The second brought to the fore equally hard but considerably more affluent and courtly Irish squires. The third produced, in Pennsylvania, a number of Irish artisans.

Let us take them in order. The Pilgrims were not the only Puritans to come early to America, though the Scotch-Irish, Presbyterian, plantation-trained military clans did not arrive in force until the 1730s. Some indication of their presence can be found in place names like Londonderry, New Hampshire, and Orange and Ulster counties, New York, and in western Pennsylvania, where they began their occupation of the Appalachian valleys. From there they spread south into western Virginia, where one of their number, George Croghan, and his partners acquired two and a half million acres, and on into the Carolinas, Tennessee, and Kentucky. Though they carried with them the bitter memory of being ground between Anglican landlords and Roman Catholic peasants, and though their early photographs make them all seem as grim as

Stonewall Jackson and John C. Calhoun, they knew how to laugh as well as to scalp.

Some of them, and some Catholic squireens as well, rose to become the dominant landowners in the inland empire of New York and Pennsylvania, managing huge estates on the edge of Iroquois holdings from the Adirondacks to the Genesee and the Ohio. The Johnstons, Warrens, Constables, Lynches, Croghans, Duanes, and Delanceys vied with the Van Rensselaers and Livingstons until 1783. But many of them chose the losing side in the Revolutionary War, leaving behind only their names on streets and villages. Nevertheless, it is arresting to recall how different was the implication of a brogue in the streets of Lynchville (Rome), Constableville, Warrensburg, Johnstown, Duanesville, or along Delancey Street in 1800 than after the famine and the canal.

We know very little about the social life of the Irish glass-making elite who dominated the cultural life of Pittsburgh in its early days, but we do know of the generosity of George Croghan's heiress, Mary Elizabeth Schenley. She clung to two hundred acres in the heart of that city but did not cling to all the revenues derived therefrom. A great philanthropist, she almost matched the benefactions of Stephen Girard at the other end of the state. Two rooms from her "picnic house," Pittsburgh's finest Greek Revival interiors, were rescued recently and flown, in a kind of seraphic adaptive reuse, to repose on the upper floors of the University of Pittsburgh's Cathedral of Learning. Her gift of land for a great cemetery still provides green relief for the citizens of the city. It also offered employment to John Chislett, a practitioner of the English Regency style, who was the city's most distinguished architect until the advent of Henry Hobson Richardson fifty years later, in the 1880s.

The mention of Chislett permits a final note on the architecture of the Greek Revival, of which he was a skillful practitioner. We can leave to others description of the urban accomplishments of the twentieth century. They are easy to find, from Buffalo, with its anthology of works of genius by Richardson, Louis Sullivan, and Frank Lloyd Wright, to the parade of vanities along lower Park Avenue and "Arragansett." Here we focus on the wonders of the interior of the Middle Atlantic states and limit ourselves to the Greek Revival.

Any American who wishes to show European friends why the rural areas of our country differ positively from theirs should take them into the countryside, anywhere from Lakes Erie and Ontario to Altoona, Schenectady, and Cooperstown. This inland empire centers on the incomparable beauties of the Finger Lakes, America's supreme pastoral landscape, and the Hellenic subtleties of its villages. Niagara Falls will do; so will the World Trade Center. But Geneva or Cooperstown, Skaneateles, Baldwinsville, Aurora, Ovid, or Poolville do not need to raise their voices to make their point.

There was a time when Elias Baker in Altoona, William Gurley Strong in Geneva, and ten thousand less affluent people built clean, clear, classical houses deferring to one another but full of justifiable pride in each individual achievement. Isaac Meeson had shown them the way as the century opened, in a somewhat earlier style (his Mount Braddock languishes untended and decaying south of Pittsburgh, though it is the finest Georgian house west of the Appalachians). But the inland empire did not organize its aesthetics fully until the resumption of American self-confidence in the 1820s. Then, and for thirty years thereafter, a new psychological and economic exuberance expressed itself in a hundred thousand sudden columns.

This classicizing of the inland empire coincided with the settling of the uplands. Then were established the vineyards and orchards that continue to provide us with wine and fruit and a well-tended, deliberate landscape. The uplands were also, of course, given their first planting of the grain for export that made the Irish squires whose fortunes had their origins in the trade in furs even richer.

To find places where this land can be seen as it was in the age of the fur trade, we can seek out mountaintops, beaches, or bogs. They are difficult to ruin. An Adirondack crag or scree is unlikely to be much altered over centuries unless it bears metal or draws lightning. It would not be true to state that scrub is always the result of human intervention, for fires made barrens and acted as nature's cleaners of woodland before the advent of humans. The pine barrens are little affected by three centuries of human intervention; wildness is to be found in thousands of acres of bog contained in the granite uplands of central Pennsylvania.

There is something more consoling, however, in large trees. In New York, old-growth timber is not so common as one might think, nor is it to be found where one might expect. The largest tracts are near Claryville, on the west side of the Catskills. After a century of depletion for tannin, for fuel for iron and potash furnaces, and for both fuel and lumber for cities downstream, there is much that has been abandoned in the Adirondacks, but not much virgin timber. One patch lies at the end of a good half-day hike in the Five Ponds Wilderness, off Route 3 near Wanakena.

Stretches of moorland, like Tug Hill southwest of Watertown, and the duneland along Lake Ontario have miles of remarkably unspoiled open land. The cliffs and beaches at the extremity of Long Island are much as they were when first sighted by Verrazano and Henry Hudson, though no one would mistake Montauk for a wilderness. For that one has to go to northern New Jersey, which has some fifty-acre stands of climax hardwoods, one tended by Rutgers University near New Brunswick, and to the pine barrens.

Pennsylvania has several times been stripped of most of its forest cover, but in the following places remnants of the old world can still be found: around State College are patches of old-growth trees, but one needs a good map and a guide to find them. Fortunately, that is a city with a good bookstore, and the State Forest office at Mifflinburg can help.

The Alan Seger Natural Area in Huntingdon County is eighteen miles southeast of State College on U.S. 322. Drive to the Laurel Creek Reservoir and west a few hundred yards on Stone Creek Road to a right turn, which one follows for seven and three-tenths miles to a half-mile trail through old hemlocks along Stone Creek.

Ricketts Glen Natural Area in Luzerne County, larger and more remote, has huge white pines as well as hemlocks. Look on a good road map for the intersection of Routes 118 and 487, about forty-five miles west of Scranton as the crow flies.

While we are looking, some of our animal cousins will be looking back at us, as they have all along. Humans were not the only seafarers to reconnoiter the interior of North America. Whales penetrated far into the continent; two disported themselves far up the Hudson within sight of the Dutch garrison at Fort Orange in 1647. Another was observed making a slow, ruminative "circle tour" of Manhattan Island in 1773.

Perhaps even now, if we humans can sustain a respectful stance toward our neighbors and cousins at sea, this mutual inspection may once again lead to visits by whales to us and by us to them without further civil war among mammals.

7

....

Tobacco and Paper

Delaware, Maryland, Virginia,
and Washington, D.C.

I N THE 1780s, before there was any city at Washington, the Chesapeake region already demanded the constant attention of people
interested in American politics. The tobacco gentry were the most
powerful political elite in the new nation.

As the United States commenced their independent career, still refer-
ring to themselves in the plural but reaching toward unity, Virginia and
Maryland had more leverage upon the policies of the republic than any
combination of two of the other eleven, except perhaps Pennsylvania
and Massachusetts. This was true because agriculture was still the chief
source of wealth. Among the crops raised for export, tobacco was the
most important, so the power of the people of the area arose from the
amount of tobacco they produced (whereas it now arises from the
amount of paper consumed).

Green tobacco fields stretched toward the Blue Ridge, interspersed
with red-splotched expanses of exhausted soil returning to broom sedge
and briars, and rectangles of yellow wheat (the planter's resource when
tobacco prices were low). Now in their place sprout the girders and
cranes of the feeder exurbs. Corporate offices, like the cells of mud
wasps, are every day being laid in steel combs about Tyson's Corner,
around Manassas, and along the Dulles corridor.

Tobacco was the most important factor in the life of the Chesapeake
region in the first two centuries of European occupation. As we now
know, it is a dangerous drug. It was dangerous to those who smoked or
chewed it, and it was dangerous to those who cultivated it, for very soon

after they began to produce it in commercial quantities, they incorporated their plantations within the slave-driven system based in the West Indies. That system was lucrative but violent, and in 1865 it came to a violent end.

The history of tobacco in the Chesapeake began two centuries earlier, soon after the British learned from the Dutch, French, and Spaniards the general shape of the coastline of Chesapeake Bay. They explored the land and found on it a "sot weed" similar to the tobacco already found valuable in the West Indies. An exploring party sent out by Columbus to Cuba had reported in 1492 that its natives perfumed themselves by burning a dried leaf with a pleasant smell. Before a decade was past, other Spaniards noted the use of the same leaf for snuff and chewing. A hollow wooden tube in a Y shape, called a *tabaco*, was held to capture the burning fumes and transmit them into the nostrils.

The Spaniards cultivated tobacco in the West Indies, but sugar, a sweetener used to induce consumption of powerful caffeine stimulants, proved to be more cost-effective even than tobacco for planting in the subtropics. So the West Indian islands were turned into sugar plantations, while the low-lying, readily accessible alluvial plains of the Chesapeake were put under tobacco, plus a few patches of food crops to sustain life.

Thus the Spaniards lost their tobacco monopoly. Until then, they had sold the weed at high prices to the English; the French ambassador to Spain, Jean Nicot, immortalized himself by sending its seeds to his queen. Ralph Lane, the first governor of Virginia, Sir Francis Drake, and Sir Walter Raleigh made its use fashionable in Britain, despite solemn warnings of its medical dangers (there were apprehensions concerning it as early as 1600).

Tobacco culture in Maryland and Virginia was easily commenced, since the soil was fertile and the plant throve amid stumps on barely cultivated ground. The market was avid; there was a rapid increase in cultivation, which brought prices down so rapidly in the early seventeenth century that many of the first generation of planters were bankrupted, while much of the land they first planted became exhausted, no longer able to produce "sweet" leaf. But soon there was land aplenty as the once numerous Indians were reduced by disease and driven from the shores.

The seventeenth century was a violent time; not only were there constant Indian wars, but life was destabilized by vehement surges and collapses in prices. Rushes of affluence encouraged planting of new areas and overproduction; heavy debt at the planting season led to sudden liquidity at harvest. There ensued that gluttonous demand for fancy goods which is characteristic of unsteady and speculative agricultural economies. Nor was colonial life tranquil politically; Bacon's Rebellion broke out in Virginia and Jacob Leisler led an insurrection to seize power in New York. This was also a century of religious wars in Europe, and psychoreligious antipathies spread into the British colonies. Maryland was seized by anti-Catholic frenzies in the last decades of the seventeenth century at the time when Salem was finding its scapegoats among people who were either unattractive or unorthodox or both and were called witches.

Maryland had been a sort of Holy Experiment in proprietorship; its Roman Catholic owners were tolerant of Anglicans, Quakers, and Dissenters. At the outset, Maryland extended all the way from the Anglican, and corporate, colony of Virginia to the Puritan outposts of New England, which were chartered by the Crown. But turns of fortune in London brought about obligations on the part of an Anglican king to his brother, the duke of York, and to William Penn, the Quaker son of a powerful admiral. New York and Pennsylvania were lopped away from Maryland's Calverts, Lords Baltimore, and their deputies the Carrolls. The Calverts are gone, but the Carrolls still celebrate Mass in their private chapel at Doughoregan Manor near Baltimore.

As the Protestant succession in England was secured by the Glorious Revolution of 1688, a Protestant junto brought the end of the rule of the Catholic proprietors in Maryland, and its capital was removed from St. Mary's City, seething with Papists, to Protestant Annapolis. By the 1690s this Holy Experiment was over, having lasted about as long as another experiment, the slave-free border province established by James Oglethorpe in Georgia.

Annapolis, tobacco capital of the Chesapeake and citadel of the old order.
Maryland Historical Society, Baltimore

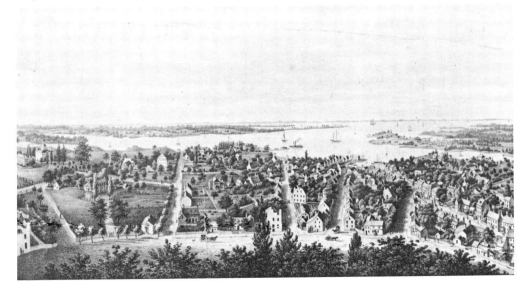

Slavery at this stage was only beginning to be an important component in the life of the Chesapeake planters. Though slaves had been sold there as early as 1619, mainly white indentured servants (founders of some of the first families of Virginia) worked the land beside the small planters (founders of others). Newcomers such as the Carters, Burwells, Byrds, and Beverleys rose to eminence only after 1720 or so and remained eminent, in economic terms, for only sixty years thereafter.

Little remains aboveground to tell us what life was like for the Native Americans of this region or for Europeans during the first century of their settlement. Archaeologists have been busily reconstructing the "impermanent" structures of the latter from postholes and debris: St. Mary's City has been quite completely explored. But the most tantalizing finds are those catalogued at the Thunderbird site in the Shenandoah Valley. Eleven-thousand-year-old faint markings of an oval structure, perhaps with a veranda (my interpretation), have been found. The striking thing about this evidence is the degree of permanency this sort of building implies. Its creators apparently expected longer occupancy than did the first two generations of Europeans who came to the area.

As the plantation system settled down, Europeans built for a longer haul and surrounded themselves with Africans they regimented into slave quarters. Searching the tranquil terrain of the interior of the Delmarva Peninsula and "South-side" Virginia, we can find a few remaining medieval buildings that record the humble beginnings of plantation permanency.

Amid ephemeral triumphs and frequent disasters, Indian wars, and slave risings, some Englishmen built little peaked houses that in their apparent antique serenity now belie their scrambling, harried, bloody-handed origins. They did not arise from a stately and hierarchic world. Slavery, a system of institutionalized violence, did create somewhat later the balanced red-brick-and-white-trim buildings of the Georgian period. But we should be careful to "read" them skeptically. Life was not as quiet as all that.

There are successive messages to be read, first of medieval insistence, then of classical assurance. In rural areas there are still buildings that are in essence proclamations of both. Upon the flat, sandy, ageless, endless land they present to travelers' eyes scenes similar to what was seen there in 1700. The architecture was medieval — Gothic, if we use that term capaciously.

Among the most accessible examples of the medieval are Bacon's Castle in Surry County, built by Arthur Allen about 1665. Saint Luke's Church, east of Smithfield, was built around the same time and is nearby. Near Virginia Beach is the Thoroughgood family house, built around 1680 and several times restored; Lynnhaven house, not far away, is fifty years younger. Both show how the Gothic tradition persisted into

"Bacon's Castle" in Surry County, Virginia, built about 1665.

the eighteenth century and beyond, into the revival period of the nineteenth century. Bremo Recess (a private house in Fluvanna County *not* open to the public) was composed in 1834 by people who still had memories of the medieval Williamsburg (specifically of a Gothic Custis house) that preceded the classical town that has been restored for us.

Classical Williamsburg and plantation houses like Westover and Carter's Grove replaced all that. They were a new order of things. We sometimes call them Georgian, though their prototypes were first introduced into England by the courtiers of Charles II who returned with him from Holland, and then by the Dutchmen who went to England in the train of William III. The Dutch, Francophobic in politics, by 1660 were Francophilic in architecture. So our early Georgian might be called (proximately) Franco-Dutch, though its roots stretch back — by way of England, Holland, and France — to sixteenth-century Italy.

The first architects to publish their work using the Renaissance invention of print were Andrea di Pietro della Gondola ("Palladio") of Padua and Sebastiano Serlio of Bologna. Palladio's most important clients were found in Venice and Serlio's in France, but it was their books, not their buildings, that had their effects along the James River.

Westover, the seat of the Byrds of Virginia, built 1730–1735 in the Franco-Dutch Wrenaissance style. *Virginia State Library and Archives*

Serlio, more than Palladio, was conscious of the possibility of a posterity not of princes but of gentry; he created the prototypes for the high-roofed, symmetrical, five-bayed, brick manor houses often found along the tobacco rivers of the Chesapeake. From Italy he went to France, and his books went from France to Holland, Scotland, and England, and from there to Virginia and Maryland.

Multinational in its origins, this style became in the Chesapeake region the symbol of the success of a local tobacco culture that had its brief moment of opulence in the eighteenth century. Tobacco accounted for as much as half the total exports of the thirteen original colonies but declined in importance after independence. Cities and industry burgeoned in the North, and cotton began its reign over the expanding South; by 1850 the sot weed accounted for less than thirteen percent of American exports.

Prescient people like Thomas Jefferson had always lamented the pernicious effects of reliance on tobacco cultivation through the deployment of slave labor. He called the combination of the two "a culture productive of infinite wretchedness. . . . Men and animals on those farms are barely fed, and the earth is rapidly impoverished." His own Albemarle County was "worn out, washed and gullied," and a British traveler reported that the washing was so severe that the rivers carrying the earth in the spring run-off "appeared like a torrent of blood."

Another torrent washed out of Virginia and Maryland after 1780, a torrent of its most vigorous talent. The denuded and increasingly sterile soil of the Tidewater could not support even the levels of population of the 1770s, and the consequences of natural increase had to be decanted elsewhere. Great planters were able to find funds to pay for fertilizers, but most others could not; large estates engrossed more and more unprofitable land. Yet they did not thereby become richer — merely more extended. Yeomen departed in tens of thousands. More than a third of the white children born in Virginia and Maryland around 1800 immigrated to the West. Three hundred thousand slaves were sold to planters in the new South; some Virginians fell into the detested practice of breeding human beings for sale.

One of the early WPA Guides to Virginia described those dispirited times: "Fairfax County by 1833 had become a ruin; Norfolk . . . had lost half its commerce. In much of the Piedmont and the Tidewater, plantations were so run down that they could support only their masters. . . . Land values fell from $206,000,000 to $90,000,000 from 1817 to 1830."

As early as 1816 a committee of the Virginia legislature lamented that while "many other states have been advancing in wealth and numbers . . . the ancient Dominion . . . has remained stationary. A very large proportion of her western territory is yet unimproved, while a considerable part of her eastern has receded from its former opulence. How many sad spectacles do her low-lands present of wasted and deserted fields, of dwellings abandoned . . . of churches in ruins!"

This was not the work of the War Between the States; the destruction of the tobacco economy of the Tidewater was well under way before Robert E. Lee was born. During his lifetime the decline of his native region was rapid. It was lamented and irreversible.

These were hardly years Virginia and Maryland and Delaware would have cause to celebrate. Instead, they reached the apogee of their relative importance before the new nation was launched and held on awhile thereafter. But it is a somewhat mysterious characteristic of our own time that we have chosen to lavish our most diligent care upon the preservation of our dependent rather than our first, independent past. We have Williamsburg and Winterthur, Annapolis and New Castle, James River plantations and societies of Early American Life. The tobacco-raising gentry are easy to summon to the stage, but they had less than a century to create the remarkable heritage of cultivated living we have so diligently preserved.

Though the colonial period is reasonably clear to us (we have been busy "restoring" it), it is more difficult to bring into focus what this region was like after British rule had been thrown off but before there was a federal city.

In 1790 the national capital had just moved from New York to Philadelphia, driven by yellow fever, rioting veterans, and regional jealousies. Only such urgencies could have induced the Congress to sentence itself to bucolic retirement on the Potomac, at some distance from the center of the new nation's intellectual and mercantile life.

The Potomac awaited them, to be probed upward in its lazy loops from Chesapeake Bay until the Piedmont appeared at the rapids just above Georgetown and Alexandria. These were two of the seaports competing for the tobacco-exporting business, though much of that trade was still carried on by the great planters at their own wharves.

Baltimore was barely a village; its merchants were only beginning their boisterous intrusions into the wheat country behind Philadelphia to draw off the business of prosperous German farmers from the senior and somewhat smug Quaker community. Annapolis, the capital city of the tobacco culture, was soon to be eclipsed. The wheat and corn economy nourished bakeries, distilleries, and retailing; wheat, unlike tobacco, gave rise to a multitude of mercantile subcultures and to the rapid industrial growth that was appearing along the tributaries of Delaware Bay, the Brandywine, and the Schuylkill. Though these power-producing streams were barely twenty miles from the head of the Chesapeake, culturally they were a million miles from its lower reaches, dominated by the planters of the James, the York, and the Rappahannock.

The Chesapeake was even more important than our reverence for the intellectual power of its leaders might lead us to suppose. Pause for a moment and jot down your impression of the relative populations of Virginia, New York, Massachusetts, and Pennsylvania in 1790. Then jot down their size in acres, not including their claims beyond the Appalachian chain. I did so before checking the census figures and was startled by how far off the mark I was.

The population of New York was 340,000, somewhat smaller than that of Massachusetts, with 380,000. Pennsylvania was in the same general range, with 430,000. Virginia had 750,000 people, forty percent of whom were slaves. Their number almost equaled the entire population of New York, White and Black. Maryland, the other great tobacco producer, still anticipating the growth of Baltimore, had nearly the same population as New York, and it is noteworthy that its proportion of slaves was not much smaller than that of neighboring Virginia. (This is not to be taken for granted; the Old South was extremely diverse. Only fifteen percent of the population of North Carolina were African-Americans, not a much different proportion to the total population than in Dutchess or Westchester County in New York.)

The Great Smoky Mountains. This fastness for the Cherokee has been "settled" since the earliest days of the Republic, yet it contains the largest parcel of unspoiled land in the eastern United States. *Photo by Jack Kotz*

The Hermitage in its final version: headquarters and residence of the great border chieftain Andrew Jackson. *Photo by Jack Kotz*

Opposite: Rattle and Snap (1845), pride of the Polk clan of Bluegrass Tennessee. Recently refurbished and painted, it is still a private home. *Photo by Jack Kotz*

Next page: Port Clyde, Maine. It could be Eagle Harbor, Michigan, or a fishing village on Washington's Olympic Peninsula. *Photo by Robert Lautman*

As to sheer physical extent, Massachusetts, urbanizing and commercial, was the smallest of these states; Maryland was twenty percent larger, New York and Pennsylvania about four times its size, but Virginia outstripped them all. And the Old Dominion, with more than six times the area of the Bay State, had already relinquished its claims not only to Kentucky and Tennessee, its two primary colonies, but also to the Northwest Territories north of the Ohio.

Virginia's population grew only to a million by 1850, having remained fairly static since 1820; Maryland, with very little increase for forty years, reached only a half million. Massachusetts equaled Virginia, Pennsylvania was 2.3 times larger, and New York had a population of 3 million.

The relative decline of the tobacco-growing Chesapeake area was very rapid. Long before the Civil War, Virginia and Maryland lost ground to their quickly growing neighbors. Nonetheless, they themselves were changing in character, though not in ways celebrated in legends of an imaginary antebellum world. Richmond was becoming the Ruhr of the South, a steel and iron town presaging Pittsburgh, and brash Baltimore was slugging it out with Philadelphia. Land values in the Chesapeake began to rise again just before the War Between the States. Crop diversification and fertilizing were undertaken. So was the investment in heavy industry that produced the growth of Richmond.

The South's strategy for the war would be incomprehensible without recognition of the central economic importance of that slave-driven industrial city. It was not only to protect its capital city that the South fought so hard. It was also desperate to keep its Bellona and Tredegar Iron Works, its armory, navy yard, ordnance laboratory, its munitions industry, and its uniform-making plants.

Two additional points about that struggle should be made because they are often forgotten. Those plants were largely state enterprises, created by taxing the rural economy to produce by forced draft an industrial base to compete with that of the North. Aside from the Tredegar works, these enterprises were managed by Confederate government employees working in a kind of wartime state socialism.

Second, in 1864 President Jefferson Davis, urged by a dozen generals in the field, proposed to relieve the acute shortage of fighting men in the Confederate armies by emancipating those slaves who would volunteer for military duty. Furthermore, Confederate emancipation in Davis's plan included a kind of citizenship and a homestead. Obviously this desperate, final measure was taken only when things could scarcely have become worse, but it is interesting to record that the Confederate Congress went so far as to approve recruiting an army of Blacks.

When the war was over, human property was removed from the asset side of the balance sheets of wealthy southerners. The less wealthy returned to a countryside that had been torn by war in tidewater Virginia.

The antebellum South revisited: Richmond as an industrial center.
Virginia State Library and Archives

But the war left the Delmarva Peninsula untouched and scarcely affected western Virginia. (This area, largely mountainous, had been broken off into the new state of West Virginia; its White population, like most of that in the upland regions still remaining in the Old Dominion, had held few slaves in any case.) After 1865 it went about its life of bare, subsistence agriculture, lumbering, shallow or surface mining, and growing people for a new economy based on steel and coal.

Industrial growth, initiated by the genius of the du Ponts and their affluent, well-connected, and charming partner, Pierre Bauduy, spread outward from Wilmington, while Baltimore expanded its grain-producing hinterland by means of railroad entrepreneurship. Yet as one contemplates the economic map of the region today, it is striking how much power and population is concentrated in those regions of Virginia which seemed most depressed in the immediate antebellum years. These were poor, bedraggled Fairfax County, now a huge suburb of the federal city, and the ravaged, now resurgent, maritime complex around Norfolk and Newport News.

The urban industrial corridor that commences at Portsmouth, New Hampshire, and advances with scarcely a green break through New York, Philadelphia, Wilmington, and Baltimore, terminates at Richmond. Its color changes from sooty to glassy to papery to sooty again, and its culture is not uniform. The cities and technoburbs have been imposed upon localities of radically different history. Beneath the asphalt carpet are to be found the middens of squires and slaves; sachems and West Indiamen; China traders and clipper captains; immigrants from Asia, Africa, and Europe; femurs of mastodons and axles of Mack trucks; floppy disks and tobacco.

It has been the ironic fate of Virginians, who developed the most eloquent and consistent theoretical basis for opposition to the expansion of federal power and supplied the crucial economic and intellectual leadership of the Civil War fought against that expansion, to find themselves the chief beneficiaries of the growth of the federal bureaucracy. Regiments of civil servants are bivouacked in suburbs where once a ring of forts protected the federal city from the armies of the South. However they may lament the passing of the rural delights of Montgomery and Fairfax counties and the rapid replacement of pastures by parking lots and paddocks by industrial parks, Maryland and Virginia landowners and developers are enjoying what used to be called unearned increment as the federal lava ineluctably inundates the landscape.

There remain in 1990 few unsullied sylvan scenes from Fredericksburg to Frederick and from Port Tobacco to Annapolis. Baltimore remains a real city, but it is now continuous with Washington; Richmond, only barely beyond the commuting distance of GS-15s, is once again under siege at its northern extremities.

Yet farther afield there remain vestiges of aboriginal America. The largest stretch of virgin timber between the Catskills and the Smokies is to be found in Ramsey's Draft, west of Staunton, near Headwaters, Virginia. There are patches of old-growth hemlocks along the headwaters of the Hazel and the Thornton rivers in Shenandoah National Park, and high up near Skyline in Limberlost. Ravaged West Virginia can still show surprises in the alpine tundra of Dolly Sods and the cranberry glades. A surveyor's error has left a wedge of virgin spruce near Gaudineer Tower, and there is a good "climax" stand in fifty acres along Route 50.

At the extremes of the region one can still feel the proximity of the primitive past. The fifty-five-hundred-foot crest of Mount Rogers is well above the encroachments of the twentieth or even of the nineteenth century, and in the swamps south of Norfolk nothing much has changed for a thousand years. The water snakes glide, the great trees add another ring, the insects rise at sundown, and the most exciting activity of the day is photosynthesis.

Now let us take a closer look at the nation's capital itself, keeping the WPA Guides of the 1930s and 1940s in hand as means to discern what has happened to that city in the last half century.

It is easier to find one's bearings in Washington than in most other American cities. The capital pivots around a huge obelisk, the Washington Monument. In New York, Houston, Chicago, or even in Boston, we may find ourselves in gridlocked bafflement before any one of many nearly identical steel-and-glass office warrens, wondering where to find that one which is our destination. But in Washington we need only look to the horizon for the Monument, set, appropriately for the nation's leafiest city, in the midst of an expanse of green.

We think of it now as our ultimate statement of republican simplicity, eight thousand tons making a single point. It does so quite contrary to the original intentions of the Congress and of Robert Mills, often described as its architect. What we see is a tribute instead to the researches of a foreign service officer, George P. Marsh. Marsh instructed a much later Congress about the architecture of obelisks, after it finally got around to completing Mills's teetering, off-plumb tower.

What Mills originally had in mind would in truth have been a better symbol than Marsh's obelisk for the real nature of Washington the city, though not for Washington the man. It was to be international and shamelessly eclectic. The Egyptian shaft would emerge from a Babylonian base surrounded by a Greek temple housing a statue of Washington in a Roman toga, "sitting in a Greek chariot drawn by Arabian steeds driven by an Etruscan *Winged Victory,*" in the immortal words of the 1937 edition of the WPA Guide.

Even in its present, much simplified form, the Monument is a more complex sign than it appears. It is, of course, a reminder of a person, our chief Father Figure. It is also a political statement: it creates an uncommonly political skyline. The older European capitals were not, like Washington, created for political purposes. They were the outgrowth of commerce, and most were also cathedral towns. Rome and Istanbul are rounded; they give us domes. London and Paris are spiky; they give us spires (despite Saint Paul's, one thinks of London's skyline more for Wren's pinnacles than his domes). Except for the Monument, our city is squared off, because in the nineteenth century the city fathers set a height limit to match the capacity of fire companies to reach upward from the street. They found such a limit so important aesthetically that they retained it. Despite a popular belief to the contrary, it was not the Monument that set that limit, but it has been the beneficiary —and so have all of us who without it would lose our way.

Let us start at the Monument; many visitors do. Standing at its huge base, we feel the impositions of order — lapidary, constitutional order — upon nature, including human nature. Washington is beautiful not so much because of its site, which is unremarkable, but because it is the result of the operation of will upon circumstance, as is our political system. Washington appears to be serene and remarkably clean, and its

**The Washington Monument, centering point for visitors and symbol of
assertive republican simplicity.** *National Museum of American History, Archives
Center, Donald Sultner-Welles Collection*

architecture is predominantly rational, not romantic (unless one thinks
of any aspiration to rational order as romantic). So one can begin at the
base of the Monument and take a breath and be proud, even in this
querulous time.

Then we can walk down the little hill toward Constitution Avenue,
where shine, white and superb at a distance, the imperial government
offices that show another kind of pride, which long ago replaced republican simplicity. It is a bold person indeed who does not cower before
that front; there is no place on (relatively) dry land where one can sym-
pathize more easily with the feelings of an Eskimo paddling a kayak
under the overhang of a glacier.

The difference between such a glacier and the columnar massif along
Constitution Avenue is that the latter is intended to impress. Like the
other artificial cities created to be capitals, ours was meant to be awe-

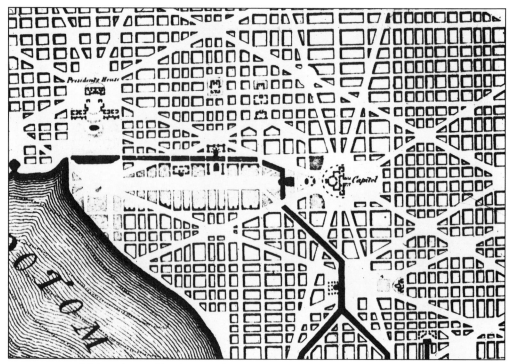
Major Pierre-Charles L'Enfant's plan for Washington following the same scheme as Versailles.

some. This was true for the first government building in the neighborhood, the White House. Very early on, George Washington rejected Thomas Jefferson's suggestion that it be of a domestic scale, preferring instead that it denote the power of a rising nation. Jefferson complained that it was "big enough for two emperors, one pope, and the grand lama in the bargain." Others did not find it offensive, because it did not, after all, house emperors or kings but merely an elected chief magistrate who could be unelected every four years. Anyway, the White House was the nation's, not the person's.

The whole official city is like that — even more grand and, when one realizes it is set in a swamp, grand as much for what it tries to be as for what it actually is. It tries to be a fit place to serve as capital of a free country. That is no small ambition. Achieving grandeur in a swamp requires a lot of money and a lot of determination. On only one other occasion has a capital been deliberately placed on a site more than half of which was a bog. There are such claims for Mexico City, but they are mythical. The other example is St. Petersburg, staked out in the delta of the Neva by Peter the Great. Eighty years later our Founding Fathers settled upon the area between the slow, tobacco-colored Anacostia

An early view (c. 1826) of Washington, showing the wide open spaces separating the White House, the Capitol, and the scattering of residences and boardinghouses.

River and Rock Creek. Through the site meandered the mosquito miasma called Goose Creek, which they solemnly renamed Tiber Creek.

To this day, if we cleanse our eyes of the rotogravure familiarity of Washington and look only at its topography, we can see how tidal basins and reflecting pools have been scooped out to collect the run-off and how the level of the water in those artifices rises and falls with the tide in the Potomac. With a little Spielbergian imagination we can conjure up a vision of the Jefferson Memorial, set only recently upon filled land, or the Lincoln Memorial, so weighty and so white, disappearing into the ooze with barely a plop. The Jefferson rotunda might leave only a dome exposed, like a white bowler hat floating in the Potomac.

This outcome would not be very desirable. These two most effective pieces of architecture in Washington express what can be done in difficult terrain. They are, in this way, parables of our political experiment, which aspires to order — equal justice — despite all our confusions. They are, like us perhaps, a little solemn, but also like us, they are respectful of solid engineering like that which, simultaneously, put museums in the bed of the Tiber. Goose Creek, after its brief Roman apotheosis, is now reduced to an underground river. On rare occasions it has its vengeance, rising in its subterranean bed to send directors and curators scurrying about the basements of museums along the Mall to rescue artifacts from their dampening depositories below sea level. (An alluvial sandbank protects the site of the Smithsonian's truly underground museums, the Sackler and the Museum of African Art.)

Outside the retaining walls, encrusted in the streambeds, are the remains of predecessors who scarcely ever scurried. Too bulky to move very rapidly, dinosaurs and later mammoths crossed the Potomac. Where Washington now reposes, some remained, as we can determine from the boneyards found recently.

Other, later migrants, also gone now, are revealed by mansions rather than middens. Washington is no longer what it was before the Depression of 1931–1941, a wintering colony for the international rich who built palaces along New Hampshire and Massachusetts avenues, near Dupont Circle, and out Sixteenth Street, most of which now house legations. Beaux Arts mansions were built in the same period — 1890–1920 — by silver and copper kings who once came to Washington to keep an eye on how Congress, through its currency policy, was pricing their assets. Because there are more "sovereign nations" in the world today than at any time since the Holy Roman Empire, Washington has made good use of its palatial legacy. It is the temporary home of an unusual number of ambassadors and ministers, with or without portfolio, plenipotentiary or powerless, from people's republics and imperial potentates around the world.

Since 1700 or so, capital cities seem to have been born international. The first of them in modern times, now called Leningrad, was after all christened first with a Dutch name, Puitersburg, and its most famous buildings are the products of a Scottish architect (Cameron) and a French one (de Thomon). One of the latest to be built, Chandigarh in the Punjab, is a museum to the genius of the Swiss-French Le Corbusier. New Delhi was primarily designed by the great British architect Sir Edwin Lutyens, which is not so strange given the date of its composition, 1910–1920. But it is worth remembering how offended were the members of both the British and American institutes of architects when the Australians decided that only Australians would serve on the jury which selected the architect for their capital city, built at the same time. That jury had difficulty deciding between an American, Walter Burleigh Griffin, and a Finn, the elder Saarinen. It settled on the former; the international community need not have worried.

In Washington, too, the first architects spoke in many accents. Washington and Jefferson, both gifted designers, spoke the Virginia variety of eighteenth-century English, which apparently sounded a little like present-day Australian. Major Pierre-Charles L'Enfant, a military engineer who was laying out avenues four hundred feet wide through the swamp, talked in French with Étienne Hallet, architect for the Capitol, and so did Jefferson. The Capitol's first design came from the West Indian physician William Thornton, and its construction was supervised by George Hadfield, who was born and received much of his education in Italy.

The White House was the product initially of the Irishman James Hoban, who made it look like the duke of Leinster's house in Dublin, with details suggested by several country houses in Ireland. Other improvements, including the porticoes and colonnades, were added by Jefferson and by Benjamin Henry Latrobe, whose father was a Huguenot-Irishman and whose mother was Pennsylvania Dutch.

Though all this international talent was assembled at the outset, nobody, as Hadfield lamented, was in charge of any single project, Capitol, White House, or office building, very long. In the 1820s the Capitol was given greater coherence and a huge cast iron dome by Thomas U. Walter. Though we have summoned here a succession of celebrated designers, it remains true that it is not to Washington that one should look for the highest reaches of America's achievements in architecture. It does have two or three world-class monuments, of which one, the East Building, or East Wing, of the National Gallery, bears the indelible signature of genius. By comparison to, say, Chicago or Columbus, Indiana, the best one can say for the general tone of Washington architecture is that it is competent. Somehow the ensemble is not bland, however; its controlled scale and green releases from the insistent works of man make it remarkably hospitable, taken all in all.

The internationally trained architects who could rise to a high standard in America in the eighteenth and early nineteenth centuries are not well represented in Washington. Latrobe never had a large commission here. His Decatur House on Lafayette Square is polite, as is his country villa for Henry Steier, now called Riversdale (or the Calvert Mansion) near the University of Maryland campus at College Park. His three churches — one on Capitol Hill, one in Alexandria, and one beside Lafayette Park — have all been remodeled or were not built as designed; none of these survivors is on the same level as two other Washington houses of his, which, disgracefully, were destroyed. His masterpiece is the Cathedral in Baltimore, not so far away.

Nearby Annapolis contains splendid examples of the best work of the preceding generation of builders still at work in a genuinely Colonial style. Hadfield's Arlington House, above the national cemetery, is the most conspicuous private house in America and a very effective residential reliquary for the Washington artifacts collected by Hadfield's client, George Washington Parke Custis. Most Americans probably associate the house more with his son-in-law, Robert E. Lee, than with Custis, but it took its shape as a second Washington monument. Hadfield's

George Hadfield's Washington City Hall (1817–1821), the most important neoclassical building then completed in the capital city (the Capitol was unfinished), now the District Court building. *Courtesy of Douglas Evelyn*

Washington City Hall, now District Court, is probably the most fastidious classical exercise in town, though it was not completed; his design called for a great shallow dome, which would have made it the grandest, regardless of size.

Washington once had the Hay and Adams houses designed by Henry Hobson Richardson, America's midcentury genius, but they are gone. The titans of the Beaux Arts style, Daniel Burnham, John Russell Pope, and the firm of Carrère and Hastings, all have left us their recollections of older styles, highly competent and *very* big.

Washington was not the beneficiary of the work of American originals like Frank Furness, Louis Sullivan, or Frank Lloyd Wright. Canberra got Griffin, who studied under Wright, but Washington had nothing of the Prairie geniuses until the Pope-Leighey house was trucked onto the grounds of Woodlawn, which was one of George Washington's secondary plantations.

In 1911 the *Encyclopaedia Britannica* said, rather severely perhaps, that St. Petersburg (soon to be renamed Leningrad) had "no tradition, no history beyond that of palace conspiracies, and there is nothing in its past to attract the writer or the thinker." *The City in American Life* tells us that "only Bonn, being the seat of government, yet generating few of the country's heartbeats of finance, commerce, education, or cultural ferment, has some of the same characteristics" as Washington.[1] People who want all capitals to consolidate all power, in the manner of Paris or London or Rome, are hard on places like Washington, Canberra, Brasília, Bonn, or New Delhi, which concentrate on one kind of power only. Such critics are wrong to ask them to be something they were not intended to be. Congress gave up on Philadelphia as a national capital because it was generating too many heartbeats; it was a turbulent commercial city, an exciting intellectual center. The legislators thought it might be quieter where there might be fewer mobs and, perhaps, fewer distractions by scientific and technological experiments.

Washington was intended to be a seat of government. Some of the Founding Fathers, like George Washington, rightly thought of it as a great commercial city, which it is. But nobody thought of it as full of engines, like Manchester, Pittsburgh, or Stalingrad, which became interesting primarily for what they made. This is also true for intangibles — even after the creation of Wolf Trap, the Kennedy Center, and the Arena Stage, Washington does not originate a deluge of drama or dance. It consumes culture as New York consumes industrial products.

But it has always attracted writers and thinkers; it is a pleasant place, despite the testimony of politicians. John F. Kennedy once said that Washington was a city of southern efficiency and northern charm. Like many things said about the capital, this was a handy way of separating the speaker from the subject. Every presidential candidate since John Quincy Adams has pretended to an aversion to Washington. People who are running hard toward the capital find it expedient to pretend that they are running away from or, in fact, against it.

We are a people with a strong antiurban bias, and Washington is not only a big city but an international city. Politicians tend to speak about it as if it were a sink of international iniquity, like Shanghai in the 1930s. They further suggest that it is depraved because it is where the work of government is done, work they very much enjoy but must pretend to loathe. So it is part of the liturgy of American public life to say nasty things about Washington; John F. Kennedy had the distinction of being witty on the subject.

It is in this context that we can come to the strange story of the two editions of *The WPA Guide to Washington, D.C.* Franklin Delano Roosevelt expressed horror at the 1,041 pages of the Guide as it was originally published in 1937. He ordered it cut in half — of course, he was a president who read books and may have had a number of good reasons to see that it was cut. Perhaps it offered too easy an example for the charge that the WPA Writers' Project shared his government's propensity for surplus. More likely its chief liability was that all those pages were about Washington.

The 1937 edition was impractical; no tourist could have used it as a guide. As the pruners of 1942 said of it, "Not even Samson" would have carried it "from depot to hotel." And it was rough. As its Preface said, it had been "a training ground for the editorial staff. In compiling the volume they learned how the job should be carried on." But sometimes roughness is a virtue. Though the portable 1942 version is by far the best guide to Washington, it is a little bland.

We have already observed that the 1937 version could be irreverent, even about the Washington Monument; the 1942 Guide lost that irreverence. Other cuts showed that something more deadly than the deletion of fun was occurring. There was also a systematic elimination of references to discrimination against African-Americans. Some such references remain, but the roughest and most eloquent were cut.

Why was this done? Perhaps the New Deal reforming zeal had diminished. Perhaps it had declined into bureaucratic shrewdness. By 1942 the Writers' Project was, to some extent, a patronage system; the editorial staff might have had in mind a domestic political objective. The Roosevelt administration and its patronage were facing a severe test, the third-term campaign of 1940: victory required sustaining the coalition of the segregationist South and the liberals of the northern cities.

In any case, when the 1942 Guide emerged, its differences from the 1937 version began on the very first page of text. This sentence went out: "And always there are the myriad dark-skinned children of the South upon whom the city is largely dependent for the performance of its manual work." We are led to skip to the chapter on the Negro in Washington, only to find it a shred of what it had been.

Gone is the discussion of "the shabby contrast between the profession of democracy and the practice of slavery," as are sections on Washington as "the very seat and center of the domestic slave traffic"; on attempts by Negroes to flee slavery and laws intended to prevent their escape; on Washington's alleys ("disease infected sties"); on its Negro fraternal clubs; on Negro heroism in the First World War; on the details of the race riot of 1919; on discrimination in housing and employment; and on the fraud of "separate but equal" schooling.

Unlike the 1937 version, the 1942 edition can really function as a guide for a tourist. The anonymous and rather rambling essay on architecture of 1937 was replaced by a feisty but good-humored discussion by Elbert Peets, now so long departed from newspaper memories that his Dickensian name might persuade us that he was a mild man. Peets was a model of restrained passion, a critic and urban designer who loved the town and knew it well.

One of the virtues shared by both editions is that they afford us an opportunity to compare the city they describe with the city we inhabit, then to pursue the paths they suggest on a tour of our own, filling in the new places and noting what has been added and what subtracted.

While the 1937 Guide was being revised into the 1942 version, the Pentagon was being built. That edifice had originally been intended for a site right across the Memorial Bridge, but President Roosevelt heeded the advice of his architect uncle, Frederick Delano, and ordered it moved to a less conspicuous site. It contrives to be remarkably demure, considering the fact that each of its five sides is the length of Britain's largest house. (This is Wentworth Woodhouse, still owned by the family of the marquess of Rockingham, who persuaded King George III to accede to the military skill of the predecessors of the Pentagon's tenants and agree to our independence.)

Not yet had the highway engineers made the Pentagon inaccessible by land at rush hour; the Shirley Highway had not become Washington's closest invocation of Los Angeles. (It is a good thing that generals have helicopters as alternatives to the Fourteenth Street Bridge.) The Guide reported that only fifty to seventy-five thousand people commuted to Washington in 1942; a million or more do today. In 1942, one in three adults in Washington owned a car, a statistic thought remarkable because the national average was one in 5.5. Today the average family in the region owns more than one car (1.2, to be exact); this probably reads through to about one for every two adults.

The city itself had about the same population in 1942 as it does in 1990, around 650,000, but the automobile has created suburbs that have grown from 300,000 people in 1937 to over 2 million. We should not see in that number a vast ooze of government workers across the countryside. Only half the people in Washington and its suburbs worked for the government in 1942, and only about a third do today. In truth, more Washingtonians work *on* the government than *for* it. As everybody knows, the great growth of government in the past two decades has been at the state and local levels; the growth of the Washington area from the eleventh to the eighth largest in the nation occurred during the war years just after the 1942 Guide was written. It is a fair guess that since that time, despite its status as a sunny city (it ranks not far behind Los Angeles in days of sunshine and ahead of Chicago), Washington has not blossomed as much as the Sunbelt cities.

The absence of a great university in Washington has meant that it has not benefited, like Boston or various California towns, from high-technology urbanism. Springfield, on the Richmond Highway, has some computer companies and a streambed, but it is not yet Silicon Valley, nor is the Beltway Boston's Route 128. The District has no MIT or Harvard, Stanford or Berkeley.

On the other hand, it has a remarkably high level of education, spread very widely. A glance through *Who's Who* suggests that Washington's intellectual qualities, like its architectural qualities, are not spectacular but amiable and distinguished. The "rules statistics have laid down for our guidance" (in Lady Bracknell's words) instruct its citizens to be commendable, comfortable, and competent, not extraordinary. The Board of Trade tells us that thirty-eight out of one hundred Washingtonians have college degrees. If travel educates, they are pursuing a lot of continuing education. They take more air trips and hold more passports than the citizens of any other city.

They average out impressively; Washington is an averaging, civil-servicy kind of place, enlivened by a few redeeming eccentrics. Its inhabitants have the nation's highest after-tax household income (twice the national average), though they fall well below the national average number of millionaires per thousand. Nearly three times as many of them as the national average pay rents of over $500 a month; twice as many have mortgage payments over $750. The average value of their homes is twice what it is for the nation, yet they have only half the national average of deposits over $100,000.

Your image of lots of handsome young people bustling about on Capitol Hill and sipping exotic drinks in Georgetown has some legitimacy. Six percent more Washington men and women are eligible to marry than the national average, though the number of divorced people is right on the national mean, as is the average age. Washington's per capita consumption of alcohol is twice the national average, second only to Nevada's. Despite all this toping, Washingtonians seem to remain in good enough shape to win twice as many Presidential Health Awards as the national average, though curiously, the number of those who walk to work is not much larger.

Architecture in the capital city has acquired two major monuments since 1942: the Jefferson Memorial and the East Wing of the National Gallery. As an admirer of classicism of the Jeffersonian, Latrobian, and Hadfieldian sort, I am grateful for the deferential reference offered by the Memorial to these, its greatest local predecessors, and by the architect of the East Wing, I. M. Pei, to the Memorial and to the preceding building of the National Gallery.

The Jefferson Memorial harkens back to Jefferson's love of Palladian rotundas with porticoes, and so does the "old" West Wing of the National Gallery. This is not strange, since both were designed by John Russell Pope and completed after his death by his partners, Otto Eggers and Daniel Paul Higgins. The 1942 Guide says rightly that one of the supreme pleasures of Washington is to stand before the Gallery in the late afternoon after a rain, watching the delicate gradations of its marble from white to light strawberry under the caresses of the sunset.

Then you can turn and watch the sun break right through the stone prisms of Pei's East Wing. Pope offered a reverberation of the rounded romantic classicism of Latrobe and Hadfield and Thornton, echoing the expression of the moment when the city was founded. Pei did something considerably more subtle: he gave us a careful linear contrast, a cleansing of the eye, yet a twentieth-century variation on the same theme.

The East Building of the National Gallery, I. M. Pei's hard-edged hieroglyph of a rotunda form. *Photographer, Robert Lautman*

That subtlety speaks most readily to joggers on the Mall, who see both buildings at a pace that forces one to comment on the other. Subtlety speaks again when one enters the East Wing to find a huge open space with galleries all about, and a great deal of escalating here and there for pedestrians. It is, of course, an abstraction of a rotunda without roundness, severely linear but composed of the same elements. Like the entrance hall at Monticello, like the rotunda of the National Gallery, like any of the great central, airy spaces around which one can hang balconies or extend wings, the East Wing evokes feeling — awe, amazement — by the use of disciplined geometry. It is, therefore, like the central rotunda of the National Gallery, an example of romantic classicism — revisited.

In the East Wing you will probably get an exhibit worth your attention, but the space is exhibit enough. Save the main portion of the Gallery for leisurely moments, the basement for cooling off later, if you can find a table in the grotto by the underground waterfall. On the way you can imagine what the Mall, upstairs and outside, was like when there was no National Gallery and the Smithsonian's Castle stood romantically Romanesque amid verdure planned by Andrew Jackson Downing before the Civil War.

The Mall has been rectilineated since Downing's time; it has lost his ponds and bosky dells, his glades and copses, but the Park Service elsewhere in the city has kept his fructifying spirit alive. The cherry trees need no celebration in these pages. They are what they were in 1941, a springtime glory. Daffodils and forsythia and cultivated grasses of wondrous simplicity make Washington in the spring the sort of place a horticulturist like Downing could visit with pride. Let there be heard a cheer for the Park Service and for the committee of the House of Representatives that appropriates for daffodils!

There are other gardens, some of the best open to the public but not dependent on the Congress or the Park Service.

At the other side of Georgetown is Dumbarton Oaks. Its garden is described by Henry Mitchell, who knows about such things (and writes about most things better than anyone else in town), as "one of the best places in Washington to be quiet and happy in," surrounded by acres of forsythia and old boxwood, formal parterres, and even a small Oriental garden. The main house, an enlarged version of the bricky, sedate Georgetown style, is a warren of Byzantine scholars from Harvard, but the public is invited into a polished little crystal of a museum by Philip Johnson.

Do not expect to get there quickly. Georgetown is no longer the "quaint, romantic suburb" it was called in the 1937 *WPA Guide*; in fact it had ceased to be so by the time the line was cut for the 1942 version. It still had "old warehouses — relics of a once extensive commerce" crumbling along the waterfront, but an even more extensive commerce has replaced many of them with boutiques and condominiums. Georgetown has some backyards to be romantic in, but M Street is about as quaint as Lexington Avenue in midtown Manhattan, and as difficult to traverse in a hurry.

Other changes are less easy to describe but perhaps more important to the life of the city. During the last forty years Washington has been radically altered by a combination of the top-down impact of what was called urban renewal and by the bottom-up movement of hundreds of thousands of relatively poor people, most of them Black, out of the dispersed poverty of the rural South into the compressed poverty of the city. About a third of the city's population was Black in 1937, two-thirds at the end of the 1980s.

The arrival of so many people from farms and villages into a great city was not made easy by the policies of the authorities who managed that city. Stable Black communities were bulldozed aside to accommodate huge residential buildings, parking lots, and freeways. Urban renewal was one of a series of large-scale social experiments for which the nation's capital served as a testing ground in the years before home rule.

In Southwest Washington alone, eight hundred acres were redeveloped. Population movements racked the life of the city, which at the same time was catching up more rapidly than most of the nation with the delays of justice and the imperatives of the Constitution: the District of Columbia schools were integrated in 1953, before the Supreme Court made such integration a national imperative in the *Brown* decision.

Social tensions that accumulated during the late 1960s burst into flame in the riots of 1968. The riots marked the nadir in the life of the community; Whites and affluent Blacks immigrated to the suburbs, whole reaches of the central city were burned out, the schools were described as jungles: things seemed bleak. But the tide turned, and by the early 1980s there was discernable movement back into the city on the part of those who had the resources for choice. The subway system, finest in the nation, was tying the city together and creating villages like Capitol Hill, from which people actually commuted to the suburbs.

Architecturally the subway entrances provided some of the most exciting processional spaces in town, and at its edge twentieth-century transportation called forth a masterpiece: Eero Saarinen's Dulles Airport Building. One of the virtues of the Dulles terminal was that it prompted a respectful reappraisal of Daniel Burnham's older entrance to the city, Union Station, an instance of the architecture of "great expectations." When it was built, early in this century, all seemed possible to those who thought big and were unafraid.

Uphill from the station, symbols appeared in the 1960s and 1970s of other, even larger expectations: the imperial role of the United States was expressed in huge white adjuncts to the Capitol, which itself was given an even larger façade. There appeared two new Senate Office buildings and one for the House. A new palace for books, the Madison Building, was added to the Library of Congress, and the Roman spirit was made even more explicit in facilities for circuses: Robert F. Kennedy Stadium and the Convention Center.

Yet all was not imperial in scale. Washington's virtues had been intimate virtues all along behind its colossal façades. As the subway made it possible to live without an automobile, people rediscovered residential neighborhoods in the city itself. The powerful black middle class continued to live as it had for three generations, quietly and confidently "up Sixteenth Street" and "Northeast." Adams-Morgan grew into a subculture like New York's Upper West Side. Georgetown had always been there, of course, though at times even Georgetown was creaky. The combination of a new transportation system and the accumulating sense of loss, nurtured by the historic preservation movement, sent back into the center of the city a flow of people and money. In the nick of time people noted the loss of acres of fine nineteenth-century housing between the White House and Dupont Circle and lamented their replacement by a clutter of developers' boxes glowing putrescently with blue-white fluorescents. Regret is not always debilitating, and nostalgia does not always sap the will; in Washington, historic preservation has been a powerful affirmative force that has led to a recrudescence of neighborhoods.

These are some of the same neighborhoods to which the WPA Guide refers, though the use of individual buildings has changed. The condominium has replaced the boardinghouse. Many office workers in the thirties and forties lived in boardinghouses, like the Founding Fathers. It is said that when Thomas Jefferson was elected to the vice presidency his fellow boarders did not even offer him a place closer to the fire. When the Guide was written, "the big-but-homelike boarding house" was still a happy accommodation for those who "must live economically but are used to living moderately well." The author of those words, the redoubtable Elbert Peets, obviously preferred boardinghouses to "ducky little FHA love-nests" or the apartment buildings that "began to grow like popcorn when the New Deal came to town . . . machines for that way of living."

The boardinghouses so beloved of Peets have gone. I am told by one senior citizen that the last, Hartnett Hall, was closed in 1972 and that the building is now occupied by one of Washington's larger gay bars. The suburbs have sprawled and the condominia have divided the airspace of Washington into as many compartments as the boardinghouses did, but at higher altitudes. Rosslyn, across the Potomac from Georgetown, has bristled with a demonstration of what might have happened to Washington itself if the fire companies had had longer ladders or high-pressure hoses when the height limits were set.

The skyline is a bit the worse for Rosslyn, and there are, as one might expect, some changes in four decades, but not enough to make the Guide of mere antiquarian interest. What it says is by and large still true, and well said. Elbert Peets was right: "Washington . . . is a beautiful place, as American cities go, made beautiful by its trees, skies, fogs, rivers, and low green hills, even by the rich chaos of its buildings, a chaos subdued by its magnificently ordered plan." The chaos has been subdued somewhat in the center of town, squeezed out to the edges, where it presents an effulgence of the unplanned. The suburbs act as a transition from Washington's artificial order and the rich chaos of the rest of America. The classical impulse, represented in much of Washington's architecture and in the very artificiality of its plan, is the same impulse toward order that leads us to make constitutions, to demand justice, to struggle for self-control, and to rejoice in a seemly order of sentences. *The WPA Guide to Washington, D.C.*, gives us many a good sentence to describe a city whose physical appearance at least attempts some conformity with its political — and therefore moral — reason to exist.

8

....

Western Adventures

Arkansas, Oklahoma, and Texas

ENERAL SAM HOUSTON's victory at San Jacinto gave Texas
its independence in 1836. It also made him the military hero
of a new power in a region beyond the effective control of
any of the European empires or of their successors, the
United States and Mexico. Between the Mississippi and the Rio Grande
there lay an open stage offering adventurers an invitation to become
sovereigns.

Colonel Aaron Burr died in 1839, having noted Houston's achievement and observing that he himself had been "thirty years too early." In
1805 and 1806 Burr had attempted to set himself up in his own domain in
Arkansas. No one knows how independent he intended to be, but it was
conventional at the time to assume that the United States government
could not hold on to its western provinces. The seat of that government
was weeks away, across a formidable mountain range still largely in the
hands of independent Indian nations and beyond an immense, unbroken, hostile, and forested mystery — Kentucky and Tennessee. And
between Texas, Louisiana, and Arkansas and the rest of the United
States lay the Mississippi, a moat so broad and unpredictable in its
moods as to seem beyond bridging to the easterners who first beheld it.

James Madison said that "no colony beyond the river could exist
under the same government, but would infallibly give birth to a separate
State having in its bosom germs of collision with the East." And as early
as 1795, Burr discussed an expedition to found a colony beyond the river
with anyone who would listen, while Alexander Hamilton consulted his
friends about a competing colony for himself. John Jay, later Chief Justice of the United States, was no fonder of Hamilton than of Burr. Jay

129

Sam Houston pointing the way to Texas. *San Jacinto Museum of History Association*

was not at all affronted by Burr's disclosure of his plan in 1796; it apparently seemed inevitable to him that energetic military heroes disappointed in politics in tranquil terrain would seek more exciting careers. He supported Burr for governor of New York as late as 1804. After all, Thomas Jefferson was writing about the states of the East, much more tightly bound together than those of the West, that they were "as independent, in fact, as different nations."

In the end, what Burr and Hamilton intended, Houston achieved. Until their final duel, fatal to Hamilton in the literal sense and fatal to

Aaron Burr as military hero: C. H. Stephens's depiction of Burr carrying General Montgomery's body at the Battle of Quebec. *From* Blenner-hassett *by Charles F. Pidgin*

Burr politically, *both* colonels were military heroes, and Burr the more heroic of the two. During his four years of service in the Revolutionary armies, he may well have saved Hamilton's life in the second Battle of Bunker Hill (on Manhattan, not near Boston). Before that, Burr carried the corpse of his commander, General James Montgomery, through a snowstorm from the field of battle before Quebec; engravings of this scene once offered inspiration to schoolboys. And it was Burr's cool courage that salvaged some scrap of pride for the American army from George Washington's defeat at Monmouth Courthouse.

Burr has not had a good press — like Adlai Stevenson, he bore the burden of wit. He could not resist cynical one-liners. He was not admired by Thomas Jefferson; indeed, one can say with certainty that he was feared by Thomas Jefferson. And he killed a former secretary of the Treasury. Those are not good ways to assure a chorus of praise from American historians. Furthermore, until recently, many of those historians have seen him not only as an enemy to Jefferson, whose ambiguities they felt a need to simplify, but as an enemy to the institution of slavery, upon which Jefferson's political base was, unhappily, built.

This does not mean that Jefferson favored slavery. He was stuck with it — "a wolf by the ears," as he said. But Burr actively opposed it, proposing its abolition in New York in the 1790s, where it had powerful defenders, especially among Dutch farmers who had as many slaves per capita as the people of North Carolina. Burr provoked Jefferson on the subject; in his final act as Jefferson's vice president, he broke a tie in the United States Senate to assure that trade with the Black republic of Toussaint-Louverture on Haiti would continue, despite the president's strenuous efforts to cut it off.

One of the chief reasons given by members of Jefferson's cabinet for preventing the success of Burr's proposed colony in the West was that Burr would liberate its slaves and provide an asylum for runaways. Of course, this was precisely what the Mexicans did in 1824, thereby provoking the series of attacks that led to the establishment of the slave-holding colonies later consolidated into Texas. Many early Texans opposed slavery, but because the plantation system had become established there, Texas was seen by the government of the United States — from the administration of one slave holder, Thomas Jefferson, to that of another, James K. Polk — no longer as an asylum, but as a barrier against the contagion of emancipation sweeping up from Latin America.

In the light of these facts, we must reevaluate both the reputation of Aaron Burr and the early history of Texas and Arkansas. The idea of creating one or more proto-Texases — satellite states situated between the United States and Spanish possessions — was probably first proposed by General Francisco de Miranda. He was a Venezuelan patriot who hatched such a scheme while commanding one wing of the French revolutionary armies in Flanders in 1792–1793. By so doing, he brought into this story that theme of French swashbuckling in the region which is as important as the grand adventures of American military colonizers.

Miranda and the French commander, Charles-François Dumouriez, shared the proto-Texas scheme with American soldiers of fortune in their army, while other French leaders took it up with George Rogers Clark and John Paul Jones. The highest-ranking hero of the American Revolutionary War to pursue the thought was not a Frenchman, how-

Francisco de Miranda, the Venezuelan patriot and cosmopolitan foe of absolutism in Europe and the Spanish dominions. *Bild-Archiv der Österreichischen Nationalbibliothek, Vienna*

133

ever, but a German, Baron Friedrich Wilhelm Ludolf Gerhard Augustin von Steuben, godchild of King Friedrich Wilhelm of Prussia and drillmaster of George Washington's army. After the Revolutionary War, Steuben came to believe himself rudely treated by a Congress that should have been more grateful and by fellow officers who should have been more respectful. He was conspiring with the Spaniards for independent status in the West at the time of his death. (For another side of Steuben's character, see Chapter 19.)

Soon thereafter William Blount, governor and senator from Tennessee, entered into a new conspiracy to set up an independent fiefdom with European support, in this case that of Great Britain. Blount was caught so red-handed in the attempt to make himself satrap of a secessionist western state that he was drummed out of the United States Senate in 1798.

These were the plots of the 1790s, when it was doubtful that the United States could extend itself to take control of the other side of the Appalachians, much less the other side of the Mississippi River. The exhausted Spanish Empire was relinquishing its feeble control over the immense expanse of desert, rock, swamp, prairie, and savanna lying beyond the line of missions and forts guarding its truly valuable possessions, the silver mines about San Luis Potosí.

"Treaty title" to portions of this region was on various occasions assigned to Spain, Britain, France, Mexico, the United States, and Texas, but claims manufactured in distant chancelleries and salons did not have much effect on people in the bayous, the dry mountains, or the high plains. It was never very important whether a king in Madrid or in Paris or in London, or a president in Washington or Mexico City, was currently the asserted suzerain of the sagebrush kingdom, the marsh-lands of Barataria, or the fastnesses of the Davis Mountains, the Ozarks, and Ouachitas. The absence of a real ruler was an immense invitation to adventure, especially after two events that occurred during Burr's life-time.

The first was the invention of the cotton gin on the Georgia planta-tion of another of his old comrades in arms, General Nathanael Greene. Eli Whitney's contraption arrived just in time. The world's population was surging for reasons we still do not fully understand, and surging with it was the demand for cloth to cover these new human bodies. Southern uplands quite suddenly became good for something beyond subsistence agriculture. Their only cash crop had been a little corn whiskey — now they were to clothe the world. Aaron Burr was one of the first to recognize that the world's rapt and rapacious attention would

The spike-toothed, or wire-toothed, cotton gin, as described in Eli Whitney's original patent in 1794. *National Museum of American History, Smithsonian Institution*

fall on the upland South on both sides of the Mississippi River, with profitable consequences.

Even if it took a while for a cotton boom to develop, a second great event drew the attentive Burr to the trans-Mississippi West. This was a coup of finance, not of invention. Ingenuity of a fiscal rather than a technological sort threw the spotlight of the world of finance back once more upon Mexico's silver mines around the city of San Luis Potosí and renewed the centrality of those mines to imperial politics.

Between 1804 and 1809, seventy million pesos of silver shipped from Vera Cruz to Europe kept the Emperor Napoleon solvent. The collapse of Napoleonic finance was averted. American seafarers had carried much of the metal with the compliance of the British Admiralty (for reasons too complex to review here but presented at some length in *Orders from France*). The American government complied as well, despite Jeffersonian protests about neutrality and nonintercourse in European broils. The motivation of President Jefferson and Secretary of the Treasury Albert Gallatin was simple: the commodity-producing South was always short on specie, the metal to back up a currency, and the American government was reluctant to tax away what there was. As a result it was delightful for this enormous and coordinated shipment of contraband to be compensated in the metal it carried. Americans took their commissions in the shavings from the silver scheme and restored the fragile monetary system of the United States.

A number of Burr's friends were conspicuously enriched, and several of them regaled him with tales of ingots tarnishing in warehouses in Vera Cruz or stored in the vaults of churches at San Luis Potosí.

So it became established in the minds of every ambitious scalawag in the Western world that he who controlled a source of silver might control much else. A vacuum on the edge of a bonanza will not go long unoccupied. In 1804 Burr had disqualified himself from further service in high office of the United States by killing Hamilton on Weehawken Heights, New Jersey, and soon Burr was in New York competing for expeditionary talent with Miranda.

Too shrewd to head vaguely westward into Arkansas or Texas, he put all his remaining capital into a tract of land lying along the Ouachita River. Upon his domain of 350,000 acres Burr could be far enough into Arkansas to be safe from any casual rake of claws by President Jefferson and sufficiently distant from the Mexican garrisons to provide a sheltered workshop for the training of a disciplined army of invasion. When he was ready, that army might make a cross-country expedition to San Luis Potosí or progress downriver to New Orleans, and in alliance with the pirates of Barataria he could set sail for Vera Cruz.

Burr began assembling a general staff of experienced French officers headed by Colonel Julien de Pestre to aid in recruiting French trappers on the plains. Apparently he also opened negotiations with the brothers Jean and Louis Laffite, French pirates who knew the shores of the Gulf. The wisdom in his method belied the apparent madness of his plan, a madness, like Hamlet's, that was quite sane south by southwest. His compass was drawn not by iron but by silver. This Franco-American group found in Arkansas a well-watered and fertile plain unoccupied by permanent settlers on which he might grow cotton and plot about silver.

Burr made his move in 1805–1806, but he was both too early and too late. Jefferson was ready for him and pounced. The Sage of Monticello had weakened Burr by acquiring as his own agent Burr's duplicitous second in command, James Wilkinson. Jefferson and Wilkinson had led Burr along over more than a year of open discussion. At first it was possible that Burr could be a useful weapon against the Spaniards, but Burr was unmanageable. In a war with Spain he might prove heroic once more, restoring his political reputation. Alternatively, he might not bother with such mundane matters; he might set himself up as an independent power and become the true beneficiary of Jefferson's labors to acquire Louisiana. Furthermore, in such a role he would serve the British, French, and Spanish objective of preventing the further expansion of the United States into the Southwest.

So Burr's manifest, fully disclosed, and brazenly public activity was suddenly described as a conspiracy and disavowed (like Miranda's at the same time by the same people). In each of five trials and hearings, the allegation that Burr's intentions were treasonous failed of proof before judge or jury. But his career as a public figure was over. He was driven into exile.

In 1818–1820, a new group of Frenchmen, generals and colonels of Napoleon's staff, attempted a renewal of Burr's plan, with the base and the contemplated invasion route shifted a little to the south. Soon after Waterloo they had come to Philadelphia, gesturing westward with their muscles bulging, limping somewhat, scarred somewhat, but still very energetic. They terrified the Quaker merchants and demanded ships, recruits, and money to depart in the general direction of Texas.

They received the ships, recruits, and money, some of it from Stephen Girard, the French-American banker who had by that time become the owner of Burr's property in Arkansas. Probably more important to Girard, however, was a political objective in common with other Bonapartists — the establishment in Texas of a base to acquire financial resources (silver would do) to liberate Napoleon from his island prison on St. Helena. Burr had left maps and proposals with Napoleon that could be used for the Texas portion of such a Bonapartist expedition.

The heroes of the South's first lost cause, veterans of Waterloo, estab-

An imaginative depiction of life among the Bonapartist colonials of Alabama. Their colony in Texas was just as unlikely to look like this. Both colonies were gone before this engraving was published in Paris in the 1830s. *Courtesy of the Archives Division, Texas State Library*

lished themselves at a place they called le Champ d'Asile in the valley of the Trinity River above Galveston. After Texas would come an assault upon the silver mines. But the brothers Laffite, who might have aided Burr to reach those mines, were, as usual, playing two games. Still in the pay of Spain, they were hiking their rates to match those paid to the Napoleonic heroes. Worse, from the point of view of Bonapartist historians, was that they failed to instruct those heroes in desert nutrition. Dysentery is always a threat to armies, but the consumption of a plant they called desert lettuce can bring it on fearsomely.

Though a passing Indian offered another plant as palliative, the heroes were so weakened that they had difficulty in building the three small forts comprising their threat to the Spanish Empire. Though that empire could summon only a puny expedition to deal with them, rumor magnified that force. After an orderly but inglorious French retreat to Galveston, the final humiliation was provided by a hurricane, which flooded the island and destroyed their remaining stores and morale.

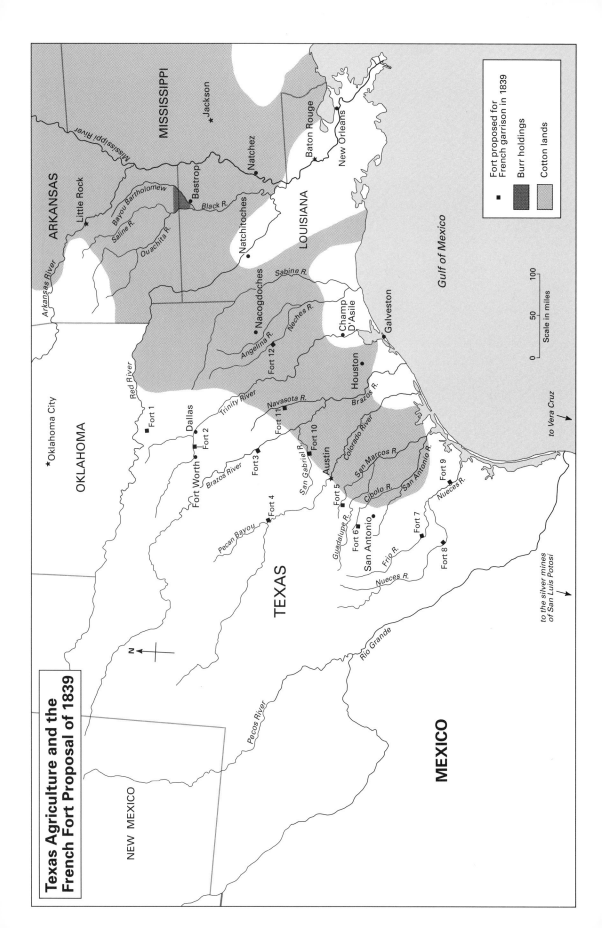

Texas Agriculture and the French Fort Proposal of 1839

Legend:
- Fort proposed for French garrison in 1839
- Burr holdings
- Cotton lands

Scale in miles: 0 — 50 — 100

N

States/Regions: ARKANSAS, MISSISSIPPI, LOUISIANA, OKLAHOMA, TEXAS, NEW MEXICO, MEXICO, Gulf of Mexico

Cities/Places: Jackson, Little Rock, Natchez, Baton Rouge, New Orleans, Bastrop, Natchitoches, Nacogdoches, Champ D'Asile, Galveston, Houston, Oklahoma City, Dallas, Fort Worth, Austin, San Antonio

Rivers: Mississippi River, Arkansas River, Bayou Bartholomew, Saline R., Ouachita R., Black R., Sabine R., Red River, Trinity River, Angelina R., Neches R., Navasota R., Brazos River, San Gabriel R., Colorado River, San Marcos R., Cibolo R., San Antonio R., Nueces R., Guadalupe R., Frio R., Pecan Bayou, Rio Grande, Pecos River

Forts: Fort 1, Fort 2, Fort 3, Fort 4, Fort 5, Fort 6, Fort 7, Fort 8, Fort 9, Fort 10, Fort 11, Fort 12

to Vera Cruz →

to the silver mines of San Luis Potosí →

They crept away into civilian life. Their leader, General Jean-Joseph-Amable Humbert, who once captained the famous invasion of Ireland in 1798, died a drunken tavern crawler in New Orleans.

A vacuum of power remained in the region even after Mexico achieved independence from Spain. Sea pirates like the Laffites and land pirates like James Wilkinson demonstrated that the grasp of Mexico did not extend as far as the Brazos. In the 1820s and 1830s this land, now Oklahoma, Arkansas, and Texas, was still beyond the imperial reach of either the United States or Spain. Furthermore, the independence of Texas remained a fixed objective of British and French diplomacy. But the Comanche and Kiowa and the resurgent Mexicans remained dangerous forces on the western frontier. In the 1830s President Andrew Jackson of the United States told his old companion at arms, President Sam Houston of Texas, that his new nation could expect no direct aid from Jackson's government. Houston thereupon knitted together many of the strands of this story. In 1839 he and General Albert Sidney Johnston, his secretary of war, proposed that Texas reimport French soldiers of fortune — a new set; the Bonapartists were getting old — to man a series of nine forts along the ninety-eighth meridian.

139

The plan came to nothing, for Texas pride balked at the proposed pay for these mercenaries — three million acres of land — and the implica-

Galveston in the 1850s still retained the aspect of the pirate settlement of Jean Laffite thirty years earlier. *Courtesy of the Archives Division, Texas State Library*

tion that the country would become "the puny fraction of a French colony." (Visitors to the French consulate in Austin, one of the pleasant pillared mansions of the republican period, might wish to bear this in mind.)

Many common friends united Jackson, Burr, and Houston, some of them too colorful to consign to footnotes. One was Sam Swartwout, a Dutch gentleman swindler from New York who occupies a central role in Gore Vidal's novel about Burr. Jackson and Swartwout were devout Burrites; Jackson pledged support to Burr and, true to his word, supplied it. Swartwout went to jail for that offense, while Jackson escaped prosecution: he was already too dangerous to be dealt with peremptorily. Even after prudent western Burrites like Henry Clay dropped Burr when it was apparent he could not lead them to a proto-Texas, Jackson would not abandon the cause. He went to Richmond for Burr's trial, challenging supporters of Thomas Jefferson to tavern fights and murmuring imprudencies that would have been enough to terminate the career of a less ebullient politician.

Jackson sustained a lifelong friendship with Swartwout. So did Houston. Swartwout introduced Houston to the Galveston Bay and Texas Land Company, and in 1835 Houston introduced Swartwout to a "piece of land on the Red River." The very thought of getting back into that terrain, to which Burr had led him long before, made Swartwout "too *appy* as poor old Genl La fayette used to say. Why man," he wrote Houston, "my 50,000 acres, if I ever get them, will be a fortune . . . 11 leagues . . . *due to me,* for my sufferings and trouble in that old Burr scrape of mine." Swartwout's fifty thousand acres were, it seems, a part of Burr's four hundred thousand. (Another connection: Charles Edwards Lester, Houston's amanuensis for his autobiography, was Burr's cousin.)

Even after Texas was folded into the American Union in 1845, the hopes of adventurers for independent sovereignties were not extinguished. Governor John A. Quitman of Mississippi, a hero of the Mexican War, asserted publicly that his leader, General Winfield Scott, should make himself emperor of Mexico, distributing to his fellow officers titles, lands, and mines. Scott disappointed him, so Quitman thought next of setting himself up as president of an independent Mississippi, and after that as the monarch of a slave-driven empire in Cuba. Neither his secessionist plot of 1850 nor his filibustering in the Caribbean worked out, so Quitman repaired to a stately old age in Monmouth, a handsome mansion in Natchez. It is said locally that he was poisoned by abolitionists while attending a banquet for President James Buchanan, whose politics were closer to Quitman's than to Houston's.

But it is not to mansions in Natchez that we should look for grounding of these general observations in the specific places travelers may visit. In this region the most magnificent of possibilities for lovers of architec-

John Quitman of Mississippi, filibuster, governor, and fierce southern separatist. *Courtesy of the Mississippi Department of Archives and History*

141

Monmouth, John Quitman's mansion in Natchez. *Courtesy of Monmouth, Natchez, Mississippi. Ron and Lani Riches, Owners.*

ture is a dream, not a historic site. This was an imperial capital that might have been designed in 1805–1806 by the great Benjamin Henry Latrobe. Latrobe, English born and German educated, was then working for Thomas Jefferson as superintendent of the construction of the United States Capitol. Though Jefferson treated Latrobe as a friend, the Capitol project was subject to dispiriting delays and endless bickering with contending architects and politicians, and Latrobe was an adventurer at heart.

He nearly forsook all that to work for Aaron Burr in Arkansas. Burr could be most persuasive. Among his admirable qualities was a love of good architecture, and he dreamt of building something splendid upon a site provided him by yet one more military adventurer, a man as tall as Houston and as crafty as Burr, "Baron" Filipe de Bastrop.

Burr's Arkansas holdings had been acquired from the Spanish Crown by way of Bastrop and two Kentucky speculators. The soi-disant baron, who was *very* tall, had once been handsome enough to catch the eye of Frederick the Great of Prussia. According to Bastrop, Frederick bestowed the title of baron upon him when Bastrop was very young, but not even then naive. After a scrape with Napoleon in France, the beautiful Bastrop found favor with a Spanish official from whom came the grant of land.

There is little in either the Texas or Louisiana towns named after this man of indisputable charm to remind us of Bastrop's artistic taste, but we do have evidence of Burr's architectural sophistication. At the end of the 1790s Burr obtained a baroque design from a great engineer, Marc Isambard Brunel, for a house which, after his duel with Hamilton, he could never build in New York. (Brunel produced this design for Burr in the last stages of a rather ignominious American career before he went to England, sponsored by the Livingston family, and became Sir Marc, builder of the Thames Tunnel and great bridges.)

In 1805–1806 Burr attempted to prevail upon Latrobe to become his court architect in Arkansas. The inducement was to be a grant of ten thousand acres in that portion of his holdings lying about the present city of El Dorado. Thomas Jefferson told Latrobe that Burr's empire was an impregnable valley surrounded by ramparts of mountain — Jefferson's view of the Ozarks was a trifle emphatic — and Latrobe's imagination was so much engaged in assisting Burr's army to get there that he designed riverboats to serve as Burr's troopships. Then, despite encouragement from mutual friends, he lost his nerve just in time. Burr was soon thereafter betrayed by Wilkinson, who had been persuaded to expect greater preferment from Jefferson.

There was no Emperor Aaron the First, and Burr probably had no intention that there should be. But we can imagine the white Latrobian domes of Burr's El Dorado — like those built in our own time for the

Fort Ward, Virginia: a Union outpost in the Civil War, now engulfed by a suburb of the Federal City. *Photo by Jack Kotz*

The persistence of Gothic: Saint Luke's Church in Smithfield, Virginia (1632).
Photo by Jack Kotz

The interior of Saint Luke's. *Photo by Jack Kotz*

The governor's mansion in Austin, Texas (1855), designed by Abner Cook. It is one of a number of Greek Revival governor's "palaces" created during the antebellum years. *Photo by Jack Kotz*

National Gallery and the Jefferson Memorial in Washington — glimmering above the great trees of Arkansas, reflected in basins drawn from the meandering Ouachita River.

If the notion of a Latrobian, neoclassical capital city for Aaron Burr seems too fanciful, one can get a more concrete sense of what Burr might have had in mind by visiting the Old State Capitol in Little Rock. It is a classical complex designed by Gideon Shryock, a mystical Kentuckian who learned the style from Latrobe's own student William Strickland. Burr's capitol might have looked like that. And with Latrobe about for encouragement, Arkansas might have had many neoclassical villages over the ensuing decades. It does have one, Old Washington, where Sam Houston plotted the fulfillment in Texas of Burr's design for Arkansas.

Old Washington is one of the nation's most perfect expressions of the spirit of the 1830s and 1840s, a miracle of survival into our time of the architecture of Burr and Houston. There are individual survivors of the period in another Washington, on the Brazos, in San Augustine (one of Houston's many capital cities), in Seguin, and especially in Huntsville, his favorite town.

Like "Baron" Bastrop, Houston has a city in Texas named after him, and so does Stephen Austin, the dour alternative to Houston as first president of the Texas republic. Austin did not live to see the creation of the range of Tennessee-style mansions that are still the pride of his city — he may have disapproved of their opulence if he had. They were the work of Abner Cook, who learned his architecture where Houston learned his politics, in Andrew Jackson's Tennessee.

These Roman-proportioned, central-porticoed, rectilinear houses spread widely across the domain we can call Greater Tennessee. The old Jacksonian, Tennessee-trained ruling elites of Texas and Arkansas, like that of Florida, housed themselves this way when they could. They grew corn and cotton, bred horses and cows, and built Roman.

Richard Keith Call, the Sam Houston of Florida, lived in a Tennessee-style mansion while he was governor, as did Houston in Austin at the end of the 1850s. Houston did not build the governor's mansion; during his terms as president and then as governor he lived in a boardinghouse, preferring either his house in Houston City, a white frame dog-trot cottage, or the Steamboat House, his later creole cottage in Huntsville, or Raven Hill, the country place he designed. Raven Hill — the home of "Co-lon-neh the Raven," as Houston had been called by the Cherokee — reminds us of Park Hill in the Cherokee country of Oklahoma. Here the leader of the Cherokee nation, John Ross, built his Rose Cottage, a mansion which, it is said, looked much like Raven Hill.

In the 1830s the Creek, Choctaw, Cherokee, and Seminole had been "removed" to the region that is now Oklahoma, their independent nationhood guaranteed by treaties. Some of the Cherokee leaders, like

Ross, were rich before they were removed; they remained rich enough to build grand houses containing grand pianos and to be served by many slaves. The leaders of the other independent Native American nations in the region lived in almost equal elegance. Robert M. Jones of the Choctaw was said to have owned five hundred Black slaves, several steamboats and stores, and five Red River plantations, the largest of which covered five thousand acres. The Chickasaw and Creek also included a number of rich, slave-owning plantation owners, as did the recently arrived Seminole. Even after the great boom in slave and land purchases in Arkansas in the 1850s, the proportion of slaves to nonslaves in that state was no higher than that in the Indian nations.

Slavery was the central fact shaping the history of this region in the nineteenth century. (It could be argued that the shadow of slavery has remained so throughout the twentieth.) Texas was incorporated in the Union; in the presence of slavery it brought with it disunion. The acquisition of so great a slave-owning state rearoused the expansionism of the slave owners. How else could their regular crops of slave children be marketed except for equipping new plantations? Yet northern opinion was reaching the point at which no new slave state was acceptable, and even in the slave states there was a growing revulsion against the traffic in humans. Conflict was irrepressible. The House was divided.

It was especially so among the independent Native American nations of the proximate West. The reason we do not know much about how Rose Cottage looked is that the mansion of John Ross was burned by the troops of another Cherokee, General Stand Watie, during the civil war fought among the Cherokee at the same time the Civil War was being fought among the people of the United States, and with equal ferocity. Though the Confederacy skillfully drew into alliance most of the slave-owning elites of the Chickasaw and Choctaw and some of the Cherokee, Creek, and even the Seminole (who included more people of mixed Black and Indian blood), there were many Unionists among the people of this region. Arkansas had come within two votes of admission as a free state in the United States Congress in 1819, and fewer than one in ten in its White population qualified as plantation owners. Some of these stood with the Union, as did John Ross and Sam Houston of Texas.

Houston went forth from his governor's mansion to address a crowd in Galveston and told them what was coming: "Your fathers and husbands, your sons and brothers, will be herded at the point of the bayonet. . . . After the sacrifice of countless millions of treasure and hundreds of thousands of lives . . . the North . . . will overwhelm the South."

The old Jacksonians and Whigs of Arkansas, together with its mountain yeomen, voted down secession in the first Arkansas convention of March 1861. In April, however, Governor Henry Rector, representing the radicals, replied to Abraham Lincoln's call for troops. "The people of

A portrait of the Confederate and Cherokee general Stand Watie.
Archives & Manuscripts Division of the Oklahoma Historical Society

this commonwealth are freemen, not slaves," said Rector without the least implication of irony. Sixty thousand Arkansans out of a total White population of 324,000 served the Confederacy, but 9,000 Whites served the Union, together with four regiments of Arkansas Volunteers of African Descent.

Among the Indian nations, each tribe was riven against itself. John Ross went off to live in Philadelphia. (Several Unionist refugee planters of Natchez repaired to New York; today the home of one of them is the scene of a Confederate ball.) Meanwhile, Stand Watie rose to become a Confederate general and, two months after Appomattox, was the last to surrender to the Union forces.

Early in the war Union forces withdrew their protection from antisecessionist areas of northwestern Arkansas and the Cherokee, Creek, and Seminole nations, and Confederate depredations were severe. Albert Pike, the New England–born representative of Jefferson Davis in the region, sought to turn the Wichita, Comanche, Shawnee, Delaware, and

Osage against Unionist Kansas. Later, however, the victims of the war's destruction were the Indians who sided with the Confederacy, as Union troops and their savage allies, White and Indian, moved southward to the Red River and Texas.

The most conspicuous casualties of the war, however, were the treaties guaranteeing to the major "civilized tribes" the status of independent nations upon lands solemnly said to be theirs in perpetuity. That status and those lands had come to them in return for their submission to removal from their eastern possessions in the 1830s. But in 1866 Kansas wanted to dispossess its Indians, to have them "removed" to the lands of the independent nations in what was subsequently called Oklahoma. Half the lands previously guaranteed to the consenting nations went to appease the Kansas free-soilers, whose irony in the use of that term was only surpassed by Henry Rector's willingness to speak of slaves and freemen.

The Civil War was over. The last spate of Indian wars upon the plains were yet to be fought. Aaron Burr was finally dead, and Sam Houston too. Not long before Houston, and on the brink of the Civil War, the widow of Burr's competitor Alexander Hamilton went at last to her grave.

A small war remained to be fought in Oklahoma, to deal with the Cheyenne. At the Battle of the Washita, near the present town of Cheyenne, the Hamiltons' grandson Captain Louis Hamilton was killed. His pallbearers were Philip Sheridan and George Armstrong Custer.

9

....

The Great Lakes States

Minnesota, Ohio, Michigan, Illinois,
Wisconsin, and Indiana

Here is Frederick Jackson Turner country. Here is Middletown, U.S.A., and Sangamon County; here are the birthplaces of Warren Harding and of Frank Lloyd Wright, of Ronald Reagan, Orson Squire Fowler (the phrenologist and prophet of octagon houses), and Studs Terkel.

The Old Northwest is a region in which diverse dreams have swirled and settled and formed crystals — villages like New Harmony and Zoar, Union Village, Nauvoo and Kirtland, Amana, Bishop Hill, and Saint Nazianz — and then, of course, Grosse Pointe, Shaker Heights, and Lake Forest. There are few Shakers in Shaker Heights, and little milling is done in Gates Mills, but the history is there, and as one travels the Great Lakes states, one comes upon startling reminders of Mormons and Icarians, Rappites and Amish, along with Old Believers and the Eastern Orthodox.

The Roman Catholics, Spanish and French, were the first Europeans to arrive. Then came Protestants of innumerable persuasions and Jews of several, all tinctured by their residence in older American areas before settling or pausing in the Midwest.

Because this is a region of considerable expanse — from Moorhead, Minnesota, to the eastern edge of Ohio is as far as from London to the frontier between Poland and Russia — one has to be cautious about making general statements about geography and climate. The terrain is not uniform. In the state of Michigan, Mount Arvon and the rest of the ridge that includes the Huron and Porcupine mountains rise nearly two

"Twilight in the Wilderness" by Frederick E. Church. The landscape resembles that of the Porcupine Mountains and Lake of the Clouds along the Lake Superior escarpment in Michigan. *The Cleveland Museum of Art, Mr. and Mrs. William H. Marlatt Fund, 65.233*

thousand feet from the south shore of Lake Superior — enough, if taken too fast, to make a mountain man pant. And any simple notion that latitude or even altitude alone determines climate can be dispelled by contrasting the chill of Milwaukee one day in late fall with the Michigan fruit belt directly across Lake Michigan, where an overcoat may not be needed. The prevailing winds from the west pass across the lake and sop up heat stored in that great basin during the summer, producing a mini-climate more like that of Virginia than of Saskatchewan. Cairo, Illinois, shares the latitude of Williamsburg, Virginia, and, for that matter, of Tunis; northern Minnesota is closer to the Arctic Circle than the Gaspé Peninsula at the frigid mouth of the St. Lawrence. So the land may be relatively smooth, but it is not flat. Its people may seem on first acquaintance to share certain "midwestern" characteristics, but they are far from uniform. And its many subclimates have altered the behavior and appearance of the area's multitude of subcultures, rendering them even more varied.

All this may seem somewhat removed from "history," if what we generally mean by that word is written records of human activity. But we would miss much of the Midwest's magic if we restricted ourselves to literary records. Ever since Gutenberg, European-Americans have printed so much about their history that they have lost the capacity to learn about it from other than written sources. As a consequence, historians have much to learn from archaeologists.

To give an example that arrived on my breakfast table as this essay was going back to its editor for the last time: Bruce Smith of the National Museum of Natural History, whose office is only a few hundred feet from mine — though across a throughway tunnel and the gulf fixed by the parochialism of the information systems of historians and archaeologists — reported in the journal *Science* that the Native Americans of the Ohio Basin became agriculturalists independently of the more celebrated cultivators of Central and South America and long before the Europeans did.

Nearly four thousand years ago, Smith reports, the residents of Illinois, Kentucky, and Tennessee were cultivating sunflowers and their cousins, marsh elder, lamb's quarters, and *Cucurbita pepo,* an ancestor of today's acorn squash. These plants invaded ground cleared or burnt by expanding human settlement; "from there, it's a relatively small step . . . for people to save some of the seeds they harvested over the winter and to try to expand the stands of plants they were already growing." And expand them they did. By about 250 B.C. they were also cultivating grain — barley, at first, for the growing of maize (corn) did not become common until another millennium had passed.

There were artifacts upon the ground to suggest inventions not only in agriculture but also in gastronomy — pots, for example. Reading those artifacts was made immeasurably easier by an invention of our own time, accelerator mass spectrometry, which makes it possible to obtain radiocarbon dates for seeds. Smith associates the presence of large caches of edible seed at some sites with ceramic vessels permitting the combination of vegetable food with meat to produce stew.

Archaeology, recovering seeds or pots, is one means of learning from the past. The recovery of our own symbolic sense is another. Ours has been blunted and confused by advertising and the promiscuity with which we debauch and desecrate our most sacred symbols. Our preliterate predecessors were more careful, and as a result had a livelier sense of symbolic life. In Europe they learned from stained glass images, from statuary, from stories told by elders and minstrels, from liturgical drama, and from small objects in daily use. They were thereby reminded of certain continuous truths.

The early history of the Middle West can be learned this way, too. The absence of written records is an inducement to relearn the language of objects, to reawaken our symbolic sense. When we visit the wonderful Ohio Historical Society in Columbus or the Field Museum in Chicago and examine the artifacts gathered from the thousands of years of human habitation in the Midwest that preceded the arrival of a written language, we are staggered by the power and skill of the artistry revealed in them.

Our desire to flex again our ability to learn symbolically, to begin to share the feelings of the people who made those objects, is increased when we encounter the profusion of architecture left by them. The great mound at Cahokia across the Mississippi from St. Louis is the largest of those remaining to us. Larger in extent than the Great Pyramid, it was a stepped platform for a ceremonial structure now lost. The base alone was more than one thousand feet by nearly eight hundred, and one hundred feet high. Many smaller earthworks remain in the area despite the work of plows, bulldozers, and parking lot proprietors.

Ohio contains a rich diversity of ancient architecture, much of it — like the Serpent Mound in Adams County — in animal forms and abstract patterns like, and roughly contemporary with, the famous geometric pottery of the Aegean: octagons, ellipses, trapezoids, and circles. Wisconsin alone has more than twelve thousand prehistoric buildings, Illinois more than ten thousand. The eerie fact is that almost none of these were inhabited when European explorers first arrived and began to record their detailed impressions in the seventeenth century. Sometime during the preceding centuries there seems to have been a series of devastating disruptions of the life of the peoples of this region, leaving them vulnerable to outside conquest.

We know that the Iroquois engaged in a war to eliminate the competition of other tribes from the hunting grounds south of the Great Lakes and were so successful that large areas were depopulated. We know that the climate changed somewhat and that European microbes, carried by Native Americans who had encountered those diseases on the coast, preceded the Europeans themselves into this region. But we do not know all that happened to leave this area exposed like the abandoned places of the Old World — Petra, Persepolis, or Leptis Magna. Across a terrain of a thousand miles, Europeans found ruins only occasionally visited by the remnants of the people who had built them. Those native survivors had tales to tell of these ruins, yet lacked the written records either of their grand days or of the subsequent disasters.

The land was not empty, but it was no longer occupied by the descendants of a thriving and vigorous agricultural society. In the thirteenth century the midwestern Native Americans lived in towns larger than any the European-Americans would build until the eighteenth century. But by the seventeenth century the region had reverted to scattered bands of hunters and a very few agricultural settlements without ambitious or even permanent architecture. The Cahokia mound was built between A.D. 1025 and 1250; nothing like it was attempted again for four centuries. Never again did Native Americans build anything as grand.

The Great Serpent Mound, Adams County, Ohio: an immense statement of mankind's relationship to other creatures of the earth. *Photograph courtesy of the Museum of the American Indian, Heye Foundation*

But they did create villages such as Angel Mounds in southern Indiana with its mile-long stockade with fifty-three bastions and rectilinear houses painted black, red, and gray. Finally the French began their occupation of tiny strips of arable ground in the central Mississippi Valley, bringing to it after 1740 the stockade-under-a-hat form of creole cottage characteristic of their villages from Quebec to Guadeloupe.

That the Native Americans were weakened does not mean that they were weak. Pontiac made this point to the British and Americans after he was deserted by his French allies in 1763. Rousing the tribes of the region, he waged war on a front a thousand miles long, taking every British fort except Detroit and Pittsburgh, inflicting casualties at least ten times his own losses, and forcing a radical change in British imperial policy. It is too easily forgotten that his successes actually convinced the government in London to constrain its citizens from further invasions of the territories Pontiac was defending. The working alliances he wrought, from Virginia to New York, were dissolved only after the British had him assassinated in 1769.

In the Northwest Ordinance, twenty years later, the Congress of the United States set out to build a new society. In the Northwest Territory Americans might start fresh to form a better reality than that possible within the refractory original thirteen states, cluttered and clogged by inexpungible bad habits such as human slavery and an unsuitable appetite for the luxuries of Europe. Emboldened by such a prospect, they laid upon the land a grid — a geographic and psychological matrix — into which their fellow citizens might place schools and colleges and churches, villages for those who liked villages, and plantations for those who wished to avoid coming together too much.

There was nobility in these plans, but in retrospect it appears as a flawed nobility. The founders shared in the human condition; they may have had angels' dreams, but as with the rest of us, their understanding was earthbound. Even as they were laying their exalted aspirations before the world, they betrayed how indistinctly they discerned their own surroundings. They envisioned the Northwest Territory populated by free men and women, but some of them did not like to think of that population including free people who were black. (The Northwest Ordinance forbade slavery in the territory, but it contained a clause permitting the return of fugitive slaves to their "owners" — the new land would not be allowed to become a haven for slavery's refugees.) And they marked out, neatly, towns and houses, gardens, farms, and burial places, overlooking the presence of the numerous Native Americans already there who had houses and villages, fields, and burial places. From the 1820s onward, the region lying between the Ohio River and the Great Lakes received a rush of settlement from the East, some of it by water along the lakes and rivers, some along the National Road (now Route 40), a straight path from Pittsburgh to the Mississippi River.

The northern tier of the region took upon itself a Yankee quality, building in the materials used traditionally by Yankees — pine horizontals painted white, and when these were not at hand the settlers used exotic materials like cobblestones. The region of Yankee settlement is still marked by a distinctive glottal speech pattern and by a density of Greek Revival architecture; indeed, a region we could call Greater New England extends from New York's Finger Lakes into the Western Reserve of Ohio. This is, or actually was, the Western Reserve of *Connecticut,* a remnant of its colonial-era holdings west of Pennsylvania. West of the Western Reserve lie the Firelands of Ohio, compensatory acreage for property burnt by British raiders scorching out resistance on the Connecticut shore.

The Yankee province continues into northern Indiana, around the corner of Lake Erie where Commodore Oliver Hazard Perry scored one of the few victories achieved by the Americans over the British in the War of 1812, and on across the band of counties in southern Michigan and northern Illinois. "Greater New England" includes the Saint Croix River Valley, dividing Minnesota from Wisconsin, which in 1860 was the extreme reach of gentility in the contiguously settled United States. Minnesota's Taylors Falls, Afton, and Franconia and Wisconsin's Saint Croix Falls and Hudson were the last outposts of Yankeedom before it leaped a thousand miles of prairie and desert, eerie badlands, mountains, and western rivers. It came to earth again and founded its penultimate colonies in Oregon and Washington (the ultimate Yankee colony was on Oahu).

Amish carts beside a meetinghouse. Even in motion, though at a pace established before the motorized age, they remind us that many Americans of many races have resisted cultural homogenization and have refused to be budged. *George A. Tice, photographer*

Brick had been the preferred building material of the Tidewater, the Upper South, and the central colonies, and it was generally found in the band of settlement descending the Ohio River and penetrating its small tributary streams. In the belt of counties along the Ohio River one feels as if one is in Virginia; many of the region's people came from there or from Virginia's western dependencies, Kentucky and Tennessee. The brick band has extensions northward into Illinois and Indiana, swinging around the tip of Illinois and up the Mississippi into the mining region of southwestern Wisconsin and northwestern Illinois. There was a good deal of brick where the planters of the Deep South had heavily invested in Abe Lincoln's central Illinois. The brick-building tradition in the Midwest was occasioned by the declines of Virginia and South Carolina and the inhospitality to agriculture of Appalachia.

Southern migration was not as likely as Yankee migration to produce religious communities such as those of the Mennonites or Shakers or experiments in sectarian utopianism such as New Albany, Indiana. It was neither so lofty or so hearty; instead, it sustained certain habits of courtesy. This polite regard to neighbors expressed itself in an architecture somewhat more deferential to its surroundings than the more obtrusive forms and colors and siting to be found in the North. It can be discerned in beautiful villages like Vevay and Madison, Indiana, and what is left of Lexington, Kentucky, and Shawneetown, Illinois.

It is arresting to note how differently these two bands of settlement evolved. The Butternut areas, so called because their people dyed their clothes with walnut or butternut oil, were dominated by the culture of the South and Pennsylvania. They tended to produce corn, sweet potatoes, and corn-based whiskey. James McPherson, the historian of the Civil War, has pointed out that they were also known for their antibank and anti-Black sentiments and illiteracy. They voted overwhelmingly for Democrats, and more of them were Baptist than anything else. The Yankee counties voted Whig and later Republican. They produced wheat, cheese, and wool. Statistics show that they had higher farm values, more improved land, farm machinery, banks, and probank sentiment. They had more schools and greater literacy, tended toward Congregational and Presbyterian churches, and opposed slavery.

The Butternut migration had its northern outpost at Galena, Illinois, a red brick, templed little town removed far to the northwest of the main current. Even those Butternuts who settled Wisconsin did not build like Yankees and did not talk like Yankees; the Scotch-Irish had been trained for centuries to resist the English and the bland, deaspirated speech of the English that had been inherited by the New Englanders. The other edge of Wisconsin was for a time pure Yankee; it still has fishing villages with nets drying in the sun, wooden boats pulled up on shore for painting, gray houses under gray skies, fireweed, and people who know the moods of the waves. They might be in Maine.

There are not many places in the Great Lakes region where one can find evidence of the countryside before the coming of humankind. The land has been scarred, plowed, skinned, stripped, and paved. But there are gorges in the southern Ohio hill country where virgin timber can be found. South of Paoli, Indiana, there remain those "few black walnuts 130 feet high with trunks 5 feet in diameter, 70 feet high to the first limbs; oaks poplars etc. in proportion" that amazed the naturalist Andrew Hepburn nearly fifty years ago. There are islands and patches of old-growth pines in the north woods of Minnesota, Wisconsin, and Michigan, though not nearly so many as were there when I guided canoe trips in the Boundary Waters in the 1940s.

155

The Joseph Hoge House, one of the brick buildings created by emigrants from the South in Galena, Illinois, near the Wisconsin border. It could be in piedmont Virginia or in east Tennessee. *From* Architecture of the Old Northwest Territory, *photo by Hedrich-Blessing*

Frank Lloyd Wright's country house–studio compound at Spring Green, Wisconsin, in 1915. *Photograph courtesy of the Frank Lloyd Wright Foundation*

Since the first person singular has entered this essay, it may not be amiss for me to suggest to you that from my point of view the clearest justification for the conviction that human intervention in the landscape may ennoble as well as desecrate it is to be found in this region of America. To my eye, Louis Sullivan's bank in Owatonna, Minnesota, is America's Parthenon. William Gray Purcell's little house on Lake Place in Minneapolis, restored by the Minneapolis Institute of Arts, is far more important as a record of human achievement than most of the "period rooms" in the great museums of the nation. And a single visit to Frank Lloyd Wright's Taliesin East in Spring Green, Wisconsin, should be enough to make Americans proud of their country and induce them to wonder what were the qualities of the culture that could produce these three masterpieces all within a decade of one another.

10

....

Some Reflections on Winchesters and Corn Fields

The Dakotas, Iowa, Kansas, Missouri, and Nebraska

O N JULY 19, 1881, Sitting Bull rode into Fort Buford, Dakota Territory. He did not surrender his .44-caliber model 1866 Winchester to the post commander directly. Instead, he handed it to his eight-year-old son, Crowfoot, saying, "I wish it to be remembered that I was the last man of my people to surrender my rifle." He did not say, "I wish it to be remembered that I was the last man of my people to surrender my bow and arrows."

Twenty years earlier another Sioux army, under Little Crow, had attacked Fort Ridgeley in Minnesota. The Sioux were defeated largely because its defenders had a twenty-four-pound howitzer, and Little Crow did not. One of Little Crow's officers observed Fort Ridgeley's twenty-four-pounder scattering canister amid his troops and commented, "With a few guns like that, the Dakota could rule the earth."

It is doubtful that he was wistful; more likely he was making plans. They were very adaptable, these warriors of the plains. Evidence from fired cartridge cases at the Little Big Horn shows that the Sioux made good tactical use of their repeating rifles.[1] It is foolish to describe as "primitive" cavalrymen who use Winchesters and know the capability of howitzers. It is time we rid ourselves of this and other misconceptions about these shrewd and adaptable resisters to agriculturization.

Sitting Bull, with his horse, his stirrups, and his Winchester, demonstrated that the Native American resistance was not technologically primitive. Armed with his weapons, he could have disposed of Julius Caesar or Charlemagne, armed with theirs.

The great Sioux coalition builder and strategist, Sitting Bull. *Nebraska State Historical Society*

158

The story of Native American adaptation up to that point can be told by twice focusing, fading, and refocusing on columns of horsemen bearing guns as we move into the past. The blue coats of the Seventh Cavalry are first to come to mind, lithographed into our memories. Then they lose focus and in their place come other horsemen, other rifles. By the time the Seventh arrived on the scene, the Sioux were already making full use of the rifle and the horse; the Stone Age was long gone. Then behind the Sioux, fading through into our picture, are the Spaniards, the providers of horses, the first users of gunpowder on the plains.

In the 1540s the Native Americans, pedestrian peoples of the region, had not been so amused by the absurdity of Europeans riding through summer in Kansas encased in armor as to fail to observe that they were, in fact, *riding*. In the ensuing three centuries the Cheyenne, Kiowa, Comanche, and the loosely related nations of the northern plains we call the Sioux made themselves masters of cavalry tactics. They learned to use muskets soon after they first observed Europeans killing one another with them. After muskets came rifles.

Artillery might have come next, but the plans conceived by Little Crow's captains never quite matured. None of the detachments of militia or of the U.S. Cavalry wiped out in the succeeding years were towing howitzers or even Hotchkiss guns. The Indians were only able to add rifles and carbines to their arsenal. They never gained cannon.

At Wounded Knee in 1890, Hotchkiss guns fired repeated rounds at men, women, and children, showing who did, indeed, "rule the earth": those who possessed the surplus capital to acquire advanced technology or the industrial skills to create it. The way had been shown by the generals meeting aboard the steamboat *Far West* on the Missouri River to plan the strategy that ultimately brought Sitting Bull to surrender. The generals were the motorized advance agents of agriculture, the farmers' skirmishers. They won, those masters of steamboats and railroads, of artillery and repeating weapons, communicating by electricity.

The Native Americans were successful in standing off the immense numbers of their opponents for a whole generation until nature itself, the nature of their own region, defeated them. As a result, historians do not have available a "decision battle" to mark the final victory of any one of the succession of generals sent against them — Sherman, Sheridan, Miles, Crook, Custer. The European tradition has a fondness for decisive battles — Zama, Chalons, Agincourt, Waterloo, Sedan, Stalingrad. But we cannot even name a decisive battle in which Little Crow or Red Cloud or Sitting Bull was defeated. Most of us can name one or two, such as Little Big Horn, which they won. Why can this be? Why, instead of scenes like that at Yorktown — stacked arms and exchanges of swords, of military bands playing "The World Turned Upside Down" — do we recall a few hundred starving women and children following their warriors into acquiescence?

This is because the bloody history of the plains records no large military encounters that settled very much. Armies decided nothing. Microbes and malnutrition settled something. Demographics, driving agriculture onward, decided more. Finally the climate and soil decided things. Red Cloud and Sitting Bull mastered the political skills necessary to build coalitions of tribal groups and were able to put several thousand men on a battlefield under coordinated leadership just a little too late. The dry, thin soil of the western prairie could not sustain the forage, game, water, and fuel sufficient to keep an army together unless it was supplied by steam-powered boats and trains.

What if? one asks. What if the Sioux had captured some artillery? What if Native American coalition building had occurred on a large scale a little earlier? The Indians put up an extraordinary fight using all the latest weapons they could capture, but they were starved into submission.

The Sioux and Cheyenne victory over the troops led by George Armstrong Custer. *Courtesy of the Library of Congress*

Another way of putting the matter is to remove the military from the scene and visualize the Native Americans as being forced, ultimately, to give way to an ecological transformation brought about by farmers. In only two or three decades agriculture replaced hunting as the chief occupation of the human race on the plains. In 1879, the year in which the Ute defeated a force of Colorado prospectors and stockmen at Milk Creek and three years after Little Big Horn, sixteen thousand homesteads were entered in Kansas and Nebraska, covering 2.3 million acres. It is, perhaps, symbolic that an Indian agent named Nathan Meeker precipitated the events at Milk Creek by telling the Ute to plow up the land where their hunting ponies grazed and shoot the ponies.

The western third of Kansas held only 38,000 people in 1885; two years later there were nearly 140,000 farmers there, increasing crop acreage by 265 percent. Such transitions are seldom peaceful. It had not been an easy thing to place 2 million people in Iowa in fifty years, where a hundred thousand had been before. Nor could 1.5 million quietly crowd into Kansas around the 50,000 whose hunting required plenteous

Life on the prairie frontier: the photographer, Robert Guy Barber, standing at the entrance of his "soddy," around 1890. *Archives & Manuscripts Division of the Oklahoma Historical Society*

space. Seen this way, the European-Americans who won the Indian wars of the plains never wore a uniform.

Neither the details nor the pacing of their victory was inevitable. Other outcomes were possible all along. If there is inevitability in the story, it arises from the massing of individual lives into population trends so great in the aggregate that they could not be forever resisted.

Some leaders fared better than Sitting Bull in forcing adjustments in those outcomes. Even before he relinquished his Winchester, another rear-guard action commenced against the apparent inevitabilities of the kind of industrial and urban life that was altering Americans' lives. This time it was the farmers who found themselves facing a new foe coming over the horizon from the East. This time there was some success. The farmers organized themselves as Grangers and Greenbackers in the 1870s, in Alliances in the 1880s, and as Populists in the 1890s.

A reevaluation of the plains people of the past, including the twentieth-century past, is necessary not merely because we know new facts. As the passive 1980s become history, and as the peoples of Eastern Europe demonstrate that it is possible for large numbers of individuals to act together to alter their history, we may be enabled to jettison some of the prejudices by which we have justified political indolence on our own part. Most Americans are politically inert in 1990. Half of them may vote, but only a tiny percentage exert themselves to alter their circumstances through the political process. Consonant with this passivity there has grown up a scholarship of torpor, endorsing inaction by a sophisticated disdain for the active. The indolent have been consoled by derogating those who refused to be victims.

I do not mean to suggest that we go on the warpath, nor to insist that there is a close identity among those who did and those who soon afterward organized the largest peaceful political movement in American history. I simply wish to point out that we have not been sufficiently respectful of either. (And to note that the American tradition of self-determination survives even in its nostalgia as a subtext of exhortation in so apparently escapist a film as *Field of Dreams*.)

Native American resistance was violent, as the forces imposing unwelcome change upon them used violence to achieve it. The Greenbacker-Alliance-Populist resistance was within the conventions of constitutional politics: it was an agrarian revolt that first coincided with and then survived the Indian wars of the West. What the two had in common was a denial of the inevitability of any economic or political change and a willingness to pay the price of resistance. The farmers began by helping each other, not by turning to the state. The Alliances forged cooperatives, means by which an earlier America might have regulated prices and production. But by the end of the 1870s the power of the transcontinental corporations was too great to admit such exceptions. The railroads, engrossing millions of acres of farmland, engrossed state legislatures as well and worked their will in the Congress of the United States.

Government was turned against the farmers (and borrowers in general) in the interest of corporations (and lenders). The public's chief asset, the land in the "public domain," went to corporations in enormous grants. The public taxing power was dedicated to transferring wealth from farmer-debtors to banker-creditors. Taxes were levied on the former to "buy back" — "redeem" — Civil War paper money, which was in effect a promise to pay on the part of the government. Most of it had been purchased by the creditors in sixty- or seventy-cent dollars. The debtor-taxpayers paid for it in one-hundred-cent dollars. The Supreme Court of the United States began to interpret the interstate commerce and contract clauses of the United States Constitution in entirely new ways, all resulting in the transfer of economic power to corporations.

So the farmers responded by counterattacking through the same political process. Loosely related Granges and Alliances were linked into

Indian Nations, Major Battle Sites, Forts, Major Cities, and Railroads

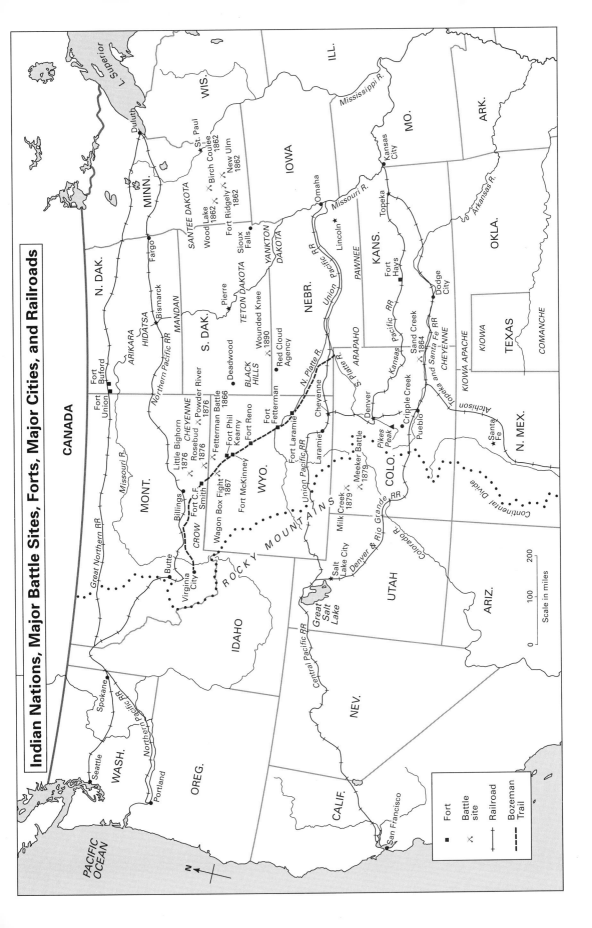

CANADA

PACIFIC OCEAN

L. Superior

WIS.

ILL.

MO.

ARK.

OKLA.

TEXAS

N. MEX.

ARIZ.

NEV.

CALIF.

UTAH

COLO.

KANS.

NEBR.

WYO.

MONT.

IDAHO

OREG.

WASH.

N. DAK.

S. DAK.

MINN.

IOWA

Duluth

St. Paul
Birch Coulee 1862
New Ulm 1862
Fort Ridgely 1862
Wood Lake 1862

SANTEE DAKOTA

Fargo

Bismarck

MANDAN

ARIKARA

HIDATSA

Pierre

Deadwood

BLACK HILLS

Little Bighorn 1876
Powder River 1876
Rosebud 1876
Fetterman Battle 1866
Fort Phil Kearny
Fort C.F. Smith
Fort Reno
Fort McKinney
Wagon Box Fight 1867
Billings
CROW
Butte
Virginia City

Fort Buford
Fort Union

Fort Laramie
Laramie
Cheyenne
CHEYENNE

Wounded Knee 1890
Red Cloud Agency

Sioux Falls
YANKTON DAKOTA
TETON DAKOTA

Denver
Cripple Creek
Pueblo
Pikes Peak
Meeker Battle 1879
Milk Creek 1879

ROCKY MOUNTAINS

Continental Divide

Salt Lake City
Great Salt Lake

Spokane
Seattle
Portland

San Francisco

Santa Fe

Omaha
Lincoln
PAWNEE
Topeka
Fort Hays
Dodge City
Sand Creek 1864
CHEYENNE
ARAPAHO
KIOWA APACHE
KIOWA
COMANCHE

Kansas City

Missouri R.
Mississippi R.
Arkansas R.
N. Platte R.
S. Platte R.
Missouri R.
Colorado R.

Northern Pacific RR
Great Northern RR
Union Pacific RR
Kansas Pacific RR
Topeka and Santa Fe RR
Denver & Rio Grande RR
Central Pacific RR
Northern Pacific RR

Fort Fetterman

Legend

■	Fort
✕	Battle site
┼	Railroad
- - -	Bozeman Trail

Scale in miles
0   100   200

N

William Jennings Bryan, Democrat and economist.
Courtesy of the Library of Congress

164

the People's Party. Contrary to all the expectations of cynics then, and discomfiting to cynics now, most of the programs espoused by the People's Party became law. The party has disappeared, but the farmers, of course, were not so much interested in the *means,* the party, as in the *ends,* the programs. By and large, they won.

Only by and large, for they were traduced by the silverites, led by William Jennings Bryan (a Democrat, not a Populist), and maligned and betrayed by some of their leaders. And they failed in two important regards. They were unable to forge an alliance with the remnants of the Reconstruction Black leadership in the South in time to stave off Jim Crow, though some tried. And they were unable to effect the proto–New Deal coalition with organized labor, though some tried. It was many years before urban laborers became ready for that sort of coalition. Samuel Gompers was not ready for Ignatius Donnelly.

The chief contribution of the academic research of the decades of the 1970s and 1980s to the history of the Populists is to permit us to treat them with proper respect. For too long, historians (such as Richard Hofstadter), economists (such as Daniel Bell), and even playwrights unjustly derided the Populists' understanding of their economic context, despite the fact that they understood it quite correctly. They were fighting back against a deliberate governmental policy of deflation. As borrowers they were quite correct in doing so. They observed the deployment of the power of government in the hands of their antagonists, and they resisted that attack with remarkable success.

Populist economics are not easy to read at a glance, but after a little reflection it would be foolish for us to dismiss them as intellectually primitive. They had much to teach their contemporaries, and much to teach us as well. These much-derided people believed in governance of economic life through plebiscite, especially in what one might call a democratic agriculture. They also believed in the governance of industry by choice. Their cooperatives were at both the producer and consumer ends of the Great American Transaction. They required uniform weighing and measuring of products for both producer and consumer protection. They turned to government to establish rules for the use of children in factories and to set industrial hours and working conditions.

We have not sufficiently honored their accomplishments or their point of view. This is not to say that the devices of Populist politics of 1890 would be precisely applicable to the requirements of 1990. The circumstances are different. But admitting that, we may ask once more, why are we so reluctant to take them seriously? And the answer is, once more: we find that their activism, their intense expectations of each other, imply uncomfortable expectations of us.

Because their modes of discourse were not genteel, it has been customary to make light of the remedies they recommended; even among historians it was fashionable to deny the intellectual sophistication of the Populists. Yet there was as much learning on the platform at their convention in 1896 as there was at the time in the faculty of Harvard College. (Ignatius Donnelly, the vice-presidential candidate, might count as a faculty by himself.) The difference was that this was a period in which the faculty of Harvard did not include many people devoted to changing their world. The Populist intellectuals — Harry Demerest Lloyd, Clarence Darrow, Ignatius Donnelly, James Altgeld, and the unclassifiable Thorstein Veblen — did.

To give them their due, it is not necessary to prove that Donnelly in his library at Nininger was a better economist than Thomas Jefferson had been in his at Monticello. Reading their works side by side, one can only be awed by the breadth of understanding of each as against the prevailing wisdom of their times. Neither was successful in bending the outcome of economic history very much in the direction he desired. But Jefferson won great office while Donnelly did not; Donnelly is often called the wild jackass of the prairie, while Jefferson is called the Sage.

It may seem strange to juxtapose these two. But speed of change in the history of the United States makes for strange propinquities. Take the group of babies born in the middle years of the 1830s. Sitting Bull was born in 1834, Andrew Carnegie in 1835, Jay Gould in 1836, and John D. Rockefeller in 1839. If Sitting Bull had lived as long as Rockefeller, had chosen to vote, and had developed a fine ironic sense of history, he could have cast a ballot for William Jennings Bryan, for Theodore Roosevelt, or for Robert La Follette.

The fact that Sitting Bull and Carnegie were contemporaries encourages us to look more closely at the easy progression from primitive to developed stages in conventional history. Despite its apparent serenity today, the Missouri Valley was the scene of intense struggles throughout its history. For a thousand years it has provided a violent demonstration of the clash of cultures, perhaps most dramatically shown in the wars between the Native Americans and the European invaders, but just as dramatically in the political struggle of the proprietors of individual family farms against trusts and conglomerated corporations.

Nor in the succeeding period was the determination of what kind of agriculture should dominate the region without conflict. There were arguments, and sometimes skirmishes, about how its products should be priced, transported, weighed, evaluated, and brought to market. As late as the 1930s there was armed struggle in midwestern streets as to how government should be conducted.

This story is unintelligible if we limit it to events on the ground and within the last part of the nineteenth century. Those events were set in motion a little earlier in Europe. They were among the results of what European demographers call the vital revolution.

For reasons we often pretend to understand but truly do not, the pattern of population growth in Europe and its colonies was broken in the last half of the eighteenth century, when there began an immense, unprecedented increase. Until that time there had been several occasions on which one might have looked to a previous century and remarked how many more people there had been then. This could have been said in A.D. 400, 500, or 600, or in 1400, when the population of Europe was about 25 percent lower than at its previous peak. In 1650 it could have been said poignantly of a period only two decades earlier. A graph of the population until that time would have shown a wavy motion, not a hilly one rising upward.

The population in the Western Hemisphere had been growing slowly as well, but after the Europeans arrived it fell sharply. In 1600 there were probably 25 percent fewer people in the Americas than there had been in 1500. And strangely, as America was being invaded by Europeans, while we might expect a great rush of reproductive energy in the homelands from which that invasion came, there was instead a remarkable decline in the European rate of growth — from 28 percent in the sixteenth century to 12 percent in the seventeenth.

This decline is one puzzle. An even greater enigma is its subsequent reversal. It has been suggested that industrialism provided the basis for accelerated population growth, but the Irish, who had few factories, multiplied more rapidly than the English, who built many. The other two European nations to achieve similar bursts of increase were the industrially mismatched Swedes and Dutch. There is no completely convincing explanation. Like so much in history, it just happened.

The demographic revolution in Europe had a successor in North America, with cataclysmic consequences to the central valley. The total population of what is now the continental United States, including the invading European-Americans and the Native Americans, was about a million in 1700, as it had been in 1500. By 1750 it doubled; by 1800 it was 6 million; by the Civil War it stood at around 30 million; and it would double again by 1900. During this entire period the number of Native Americans was declining. Furthermore, the invaders were moving into the plains in enormous numbers, shifting their nationhood west of the mountains. Even though 97 percent of the European-Americans lived east of the Appalachians in 1790, and Europe was sending its surplus population largely into eastern America, the shift of Americans to the West was so great that fewer than 41 percent of them lived east of those mountains in 1907. In that year more immigrants from Europe appeared on these shores than the number that made up the entire population in George Washington's youth. In each of the last five years of the 1850s, Ireland alone had provided enough new arrivals to replace all the European settlers living in 1700.

The plains filled with newcomers. They radically altered its ecology, killing its animals, burning its timber, overgrazing its grass or replacing it with cultivated annuals like wheat and corn. These farmers did what the ragtag army of the United States was never able to accomplish in pitched battle. The Plains Indians were reduced to starvation by growers of food.

Upon this larger scene we may observe the resistance of the Plains Indians. The Teton Sioux defended against an attack by John L. Gratton upon the camp of Sitting Bear in the North Platte Valley in August 1854; Gratton led soldiers to capture a warrior who had shot an arrow into a farmer's ox. In 1862 Little Crow, having been told by a corrupt Indian agent that his starving people might eat grass, drove back the farming frontier in Minnesota by two hundred miles. Red Cloud's greatest successes were inducing the government of the United States to deny to immigrants passage over what had been the Bozeman Trail through Sioux territory, thereby abandoning four forts along the trail, and to deny to agriculture, by treaty, all of South Dakota west of the Missouri River.

These victories were insufficient to hold back an army of "settlers" who included not only miners, trappers, bison hunters, and speculators

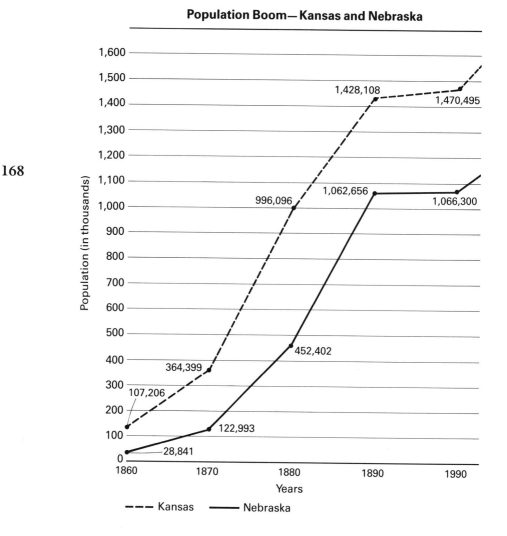

Population Boom—Kansas and Nebraska

who never intended to settle, but also millions of farmers who did so intend and had the pertinacity to do it in the face of an implacable, intelligent, and adaptable foe.

In *Field of Dreams*, a classic motion picture fresh-fledged for us in 1989, an exchange occurs twice. The central character, an Iowa corn farmer, is asked the same question by two ghosts. He answers it the same way each time, in case we missed it the first time and in case it takes two tries to reinstate a national myth.

> "Is this heaven?"
> "No, it's Iowa."

It was once thought that "Iowa" covered a lot of territory. In two years of the 1870s, four million acres of eastern Colorado were sold to corn-growing homesteaders. They were told by the railroads, the news-papers, and the state government that "Iowa," or at least the climate of Iowa, extended across the high plains to within eighty miles of Denver. Corn had been the crop of the pioneers; it did well amid the stumps of the forest and it did well on well-watered prairie like Iowa. Where you found thriving corn fields, you found successful pioneering. More to the point, where corn grew happily year after year, one could believe in a benign, changeless, independent family farming. The proper size of a family farm had been implied in the Northwest Ordinance in 1787: "forty acres and a mule" ought to be a good start, eighty better. Three hundred twenty acres is a big corn field.

169

What this implied, of course, was sufficient fertility and rainfall to sustain a family prosperously on such a farm. Those were not the con-ditions of eastern Colorado, western Nebraska and Kansas, and the Dakotas, as the unfortunate homesteaders found to their sorrow. They learned that lesson at about the same time Sitting Bull and Red Cloud

"Young Corn," Grant Wood's Iowa: the fields of dreams, feminine, fertile, generous. *Cedar Rapids Community Schools*

were learning that similar country farther north could not sustain an Indian army.

We do not think of Indian warfare when we think of Iowa. As the immense success of *Field of Dreams* instructs us, we impute to Iowa qualities of rural tranquillity and duration, which we find sadly lacking in, say, California, or Cambridge, Massachusetts. We long for such a corn-growing agricultural Arcadia. This movie is likely to become an important reliquary for American nostalgia. Its message is that the American past is to be found in a corn field.

170

Some part of that past *is* surely there, that part which abruptly replaced the past of Sitting Bull and Little Crow. Quirkily, in defiance of population patterns in most of the rest of the country, that part has remained into our own time. It is likely that Californians are moved to make a cinematic heaven out of Iowa or Kansas, and millions of urbanites are moved to think of going there — "They'll come!" — because the demographic and industrial history of Kansas and Iowa has been so unlike that of, say, California. Kansas and California had the same population in 1900. Since then Kansans have added few to their numbers, while Californians multiplied by ten by 1950 and twenty by 1975. Iowa, changeless, heavenly, nostalgic Iowa, had about the same number of people, mostly farmers, in 1900, in 1950, and in 1980.

This apparent changelessness is of course rooted in the nature of the terrain itself, its climate and the natural resources, which do not include either waterfalls or sufficient petroleum to provide cheap, on-site energy for industry. But there is a larger lesson here, one for which there are no ecological or economic imperatives. Over two centuries the people of this region have refused to acquiesce in changes they did not like. The most important constant in the political life of the Missouri Valley — a quality shared by the Native Americans, the Grangers, Greenbackers, Populists, Alliancemen, and the Cooperative movement — is that its people do not take well to being imposed upon.

As suggested earlier, this quality is discomfiting to others. It is abrasive to those who encounter it when they hope to get rich by imposing. Perhaps it is even less endearing to the beneficiaries of that imposition who come later. Least of all does it commend itself to people who know that they themselves might well summon the energy to improve their circumstances but prefer to console themselves with a passive version of the doctrine of "progress."

Progress is self-justifying change, the inevitable replacement of something worse by something new. It has become as deeply ingrained in the American myth structure as the notion of Indians as primitive and corn fields as durable as heaven. Believers in progress derogate the past. They sometimes fail to resist the imposition of the worse upon the better. Indeed, they tend to be passive in the face of changes they do not entirely understand and assume to be inevitable. Sitting Bull, Red Cloud, and Little Crow did not make this mistake. Neither did the Populists. The best thing to be said for *Field of Dreams* is that it is a tract using nostalgia as a pretext for political exhortation. It is an illustrated sermon about responsible citizenship; its heroic corn farmer stands in the tradition of Sitting Bull, Jerry Simpson — orator and senator from Kansas — and Ignatius Donnelly.

The Missouri Valley has a tradition of resistance to unwelcome change. Its history is a chronicle of people refusing to be victims. That does not mean that they refused to accept reality; Sitting Bull guided his Spanish horse with Spanish stirrups to the place where he would hand in his Winchester. And after him other Native Americans have had to make an even more wrenching set of adaptations to a new world.

Here is the point at which we must be careful of the dude-ranch or even the corn-field version of the West. The scene at the end of *Field of Dreams* in which thousands of automobiles are bringing tourists to visit the Arcadian past could as easily be a time exposure with the headlights facing the other way, bearing corn to market. Heaven has a hole in it. The corn growers of Iowa and the wheat farmers of Kansas and Nebraska were not, nor had they ever been, making lives apart from the rest of the world. Their populism arose from a determination to have something to say about how that connection operated. We did not learn much about the corn market in *Field of Dreams;* if we had, we would have had a movie about the Chicago Board of Trade and world markets.

As early as 1790 Thomas Jefferson recognized that the Mississippi Valley was not intended by nature for small farms devoted to subsistence, or to any other self-contained agriculture. The free and independent yeoman out there did not farm for himself or even for his neighbors: he farmed for the urban populations of the world. Jefferson wrote to George Washington that the Mississippi must be kept open for trade in order to convey the "surplus" of the valley to the rising population of Europe and the West Indies.

Soon the population explosion, the "vital revolution," was felt as pressure on the plains and as suction at the mouths of the great interior rivers. The Native Americans gave way to the farmers, though the region did not and could not become one great corn or wheat field.

Between limitless land and infinite sky lay the world's greatest pasture, a grassland extending two thousand miles. Even today a hundred million bees attend the pollination of springtime, buzzing through a forest of billions of grass stems across the plain so straightforward that we feel that by climbing a stepladder we could see a hundred miles. (This image is not intended to suggest that the region as a whole is lacking in variety of terrain. It lies between two mountainous regions: the state of Missouri includes a large portion of the Ozarks, a crinkled protuberance at the junction of the prairie province and the southern hardwood forests. South Dakota possesses the Black Hills, which rise above seven thousand feet in another kind of forested upland oasis, still remarkably wild in places. From the highlands of the Dakotas can be seen the thirteen-thousand-foot peaks of the Bighorns.)

In the beginning of historical time these grasses were so luxuriant that sixty million huge, horned, ungainly, hungry, and thirsty bison could survive there in herds so vast as to carpet the land from one horizon to another. Many of the highways and railways we follow today were first leveled by the tramp of these herds. Bare, compacted earth would have paved the prairie where so many bison passed but for the prompt aeration that ensued from the tunneling and burrowing of millions of smaller animals, especially gophers and prairie dogs.

"Profusion" is a word conjuring up domestic opulence or perhaps a surplus of agriculture ripe for harvest, implying a manageable magnitude acquiescent to human control. But the profusion of the Missouri Valley was not domesticated when Europeans first came upon it with Coronado in 1540. It was frequently very dangerous; sometimes it was a horrid abundance.

First came a murmuring and a new cloud on the horizon, then a swelling of sound until the earth shook with the pounding of hooves of ten thousand bison, twenty, thirty thousand furry locomotives, wild and red of eye and foaming at the mouth, terrified and contagious with terror, and they would keep coming for hours at a time, the noise and dust and madness accumulating until the human skull could scarcely keep it all out and the brain was penetrated. Then they would be gone, leaving the earth still trembling, and the people trembling, too.

Abundance in this region was not always overwhelming. Sometimes it was merely wonderful and amusing. How startling it must have been to the Sioux as they emerged not many centuries earlier on the open plains. They came forth from the cover of trees and observed squirrels behaving insanely. Instead of dashing upward into leaves and limbs, these succulent companions of the forest were darting downward into holes in the earth. Prairie dogs are squirrels brought to earth. Like the bison, they throve on the open prairie, where their presence was not so obvious, but their numbers were even greater. Under the prairie sod the earth was aswarm with living creatures. Peter Farb tells us that one prairie-dog community extended over twenty-five thousand square miles and may have housed four hundred million animals.

Men had much to learn from squirrels. Adaptation to this region took many forms, as the "woods Indians" and after them the "woods Europeans" became accustomed to a rich but treeless terrain. Beyond the forest a new culture developed, first for the Indians, then for the

"Buffalo Chase" by George Catlin. *National Museum of American Art, Smithsonian Institution, gift of Mrs. Joseph Harrison, Jr.*

European-Americans. One kind of pioneering came to an end: no clearings now, no fences or turkeys, and rarely any fish.

This adaptation was quickly succeeded by the other earlier noted; the image of the Plains Indian as a hunter on horseback is a modern invention. It has no prehistory. The hunter on horseback came into existence *with* history, specifically with Spanish-American history. But the Spaniards made no effort to plant agricultural colonies in this vast portion of their extended dominions. All Europeans at first doubted that the prairie could be attractive to settlement. It was not thought to be a destination for farmers but an intervening inconvenience. And so it was, at the western edges of the Missouri Basin. Yet even here, as the bison and squirrels had demonstrated, there was nutriment for ambulatory grass eaters.

While it was still assumed that land without trees could not be productively farmed, even the eastern portion of the great valley was used for pasturage. Earlier still it was merely a roadbed for bovine delivery.

Because railroads were largely built to carry agricultural produce, there was little purpose in placing them in the Great American Desert. So at first cows were not driven to picturesque towns like Dodge City, Ogallala, Abilene, Ellsworth, or Cheyenne — there was no railroad there to collect them. The earliest cattle trails, such as the Sedalia and Baxter Springs Trail, took Texas cattle into central, forested Missouri, where the herds often got lost in the woods and quite a few strays became pot roast for Missouri farmers.[2]

Part of the story of the cattle kingdom, which lasted only a little more than a decade, will be told in Chapter 11. After the collapse of that brief kingdom in the 1880s, the national pasture became the national experiment station for cultivated grasses like wheat, corn, oats, and rye. The destruction of natural species came on at a greater pace. In the eastern reaches of the prairie province, natural grasses had grown as high as the stirrups of the Sioux. Now that deep sod was broken by the plow. Farther west, short grasses were torn from their deep roots, and even the bunch grass of the high and arid plains was ripped away to feed the ris-

174

The fecund plains of Kansas in the 1880s, from a glass negative.
The Kansas State Historical Society, Topeka, Kansas

The National Farmer's Bank in Owatonna, Minnesota: America's Parthenon and Louis Sullivan's masterpiece. *Photo by Robert Lautman*

Previous page: **Angel Mounds, Indiana, is one of the thousands of important works of Native American architecture in the Midwest.** *Photo by the Indiana State Museum System, Angel Mounds State Historic Site*

Interior of the National Farmer's Bank. *Photo by Robert Lautman*

Next page: **Wheat "in the rough" and one of its potential containers.**
Photo by Robert Lautman

ing cities. Farmers interposed their cultivated grasses on the land at extremities of farming. Some of it survived, though most of these plantations disappeared long ago in the true high plains.

Remnants of the old natural prairie grasses can be seen even today, along with ample evidence of the hardiness of the cultivated grasses that replaced them. Near Manhattan, Kansas, lie nearly five thousand acres of tall grass prairie (the Konza Preserve), and there are even two hundred twenty acres near Lincoln, Nebraska (Nine-Mile Prairie). Not too far away, the Willa Cather Prairie near Red Cloud has six hundred acres of midgrass, but the glory of natural Nebraska is the Sandhills Region, mostly midgrass and nearly ten thousand square miles in extent. Here are lakes and grassy plains as they were when the first humans came upon the scene, when horses first cropped that small portion of the vegetable systems appearing on the surface. Here the high plains can be seen as they were when the Oregon Trail was crawling with westering Americans.

Travelers today who come in search of peace may cross this vestige of primitive America along Highway 83, amid the lakes of the Valentine Migratory Waterfowl Refuge, or in the environs of Nebraska's Hyannis — yes, Cape Codders and Camelotians, Hyannis — where the prairie lakes in spring and fall are crowded and noisy with a profusion of bird life that recalls the effulgence of America before we plowed and paved it. Only the lake country around Aberdeen and Brookings, South Dakota, and Tule Lake in California can rival the midgrass aviary in this profusion.

Central California again comes to mind when one works one's way westward and upward into the short-grass prairie, perhaps best seen in the Coronado National Grasslands near Hugoton, Kansas, in the Ogallala National Grasslands near Chadron, Nebraska, and over vast stretches of the Dakotas. This was the heart of that region dismissed by forest-biased Americans as the Great American Desert. John Muir came into a similar bunch-grass region and said of it that it seemed "all one sheet of plant gold, hazy and vanishing in the distance . . . one smooth continuous bed of honey-bloom."

These are the nation's bee gardens, their sources of nectar differing, of course, from one garden to another. In North Dakota after the snow recedes, one would look first for the bold, blue-gray pasqueflower, then yellow violets, wild parsley, purple avens, meadow rue, silverberry, harebells, and squawweeds. Then come prairie roses, oxeyes, mallows, flame lilies, coneflowers, and in the lakes — and there are many little lakes — lazy white and yellow water lilies.

Except in a few places, however, the bee gardens have gone under the plow. The farmers have conquered, and the industrial world has been fed. But the farmers could not make Iowa out of Colorado. They could not make a dry climate wet, though for a time in the 1870s it was believed that they could. They were told that when the prairie turf was broken, rainfall would come, and "the forest would follow." But at the end of that fierce decade droughts demolished that hope. Irrigation was tried along the rivers, but on the dry prairie in most seasons, the rivers are nasty and intractable. Matted with driftwood and treacherous with ice in the winter, they are sluices of sand in the early spring, quicksand traps for cattle in the summer, shallow and shifting all the year except when they run dry.

176

These are not domesticable bodies of water, facilitating travel and unifying communities like eastern rivers. Nor had they offered means of access to the interior of continents, though for a while the great Missouri itself had seemed such an avenue as it passed from St. Louis to St. Joseph. It still seemed a good eastern river, an east-west convenience for those seeking new lands to plow. But from the moment one crosses the Missouri-Kansas line, one knows the great river is changing its disposition.

As a Mrs. Frissell wrote in 1852, "From this river is time reconed & it matters not how far you have come, this is the point to which they all refer, for the question is never, when did you leave home? but when did you leave the Mississouri river?"

Beyond the Missouri-Kansas and Missouri-Nebraska lines, going north and west, the Missouri indulged in a six-hundred-mile northward deviation from its duty to convey Americans toward their targets, Santa Fe and Oregon. And beyond Fort Union, at the North Dakota–Montana line, water ceases to float travelers predictably. The transition to the perversity of western rivers was marked by Meriwether Lewis in 1804, .when he saw for the last time the little flotilla that had brought him and William Clark only so far.

Clark's elder brother, George Rogers Clark, had been one of the great explorers of the well-watered, riverine woodland of Ohio and Illinois, a citizen of the Atlantic world who had offered his military services to the French Revolutionary government. On the Missouri, William Clark was in quite another setting, where nautical images had to be abandoned like their bateaux themselves and attention given to feet instead. Said Lewis:

> The little fleet altho' not quite so respectable as those of Columbus or Capt. Cook, were still viewed by us with as much pleasure as those deservedly famed adventurers ever beheld theirs. . . . We are now about to penetrate a country at least two thousand miles in width, on which the foot of civilized man has never trodden.

Yet even in that country, the western streams were still willing to supply water for animals and for irrigation. Then humans altered that disposition, too. They drilled deep wells for irrigation, mining for

Bonanza farming in Kansas with panzer columns of wheat combines.
The Kansas State Historical Society, Topeka, Kansas

aquifers, thereby reducing the water table. They eroded the water-holding poultices of turf that had seeped downward to resupply those aquifers, replacing the magnificent diversity of the primitive grassland with monoculture. All across the prairie empire, from Manitoba to Oklahoma, a few selected strains of grain seed have been planted where once a thousand interrelated plants had been. The annual re-creation of the prairie from its own seeds has been replaced by the planting of a single set of seeds requiring purchase, mechanical distribution, and chemical encouragement every year. Native grasses with fifteen feet of self-renewing root systems have been replaced by in-and-out, shallow-rooted annuals, the familiar corn of *Field of Dreams* and the "amber waves of grain."

The scale of some of those fields was, and is, very large. In the late 1870s the Northern Pacific railway, in one of its periodic cash and probity shortages, sold hundreds of thousands of the acres it had received from the government to its shareholders for as little as forty cents an acre. Three of these purchasers combined their holdings into the first of the "bonanza farms." The largest of these, with nearly sixty-five thousand acres under wheat, was the Grandin Farm, where battalions of farm workers soon operated panzer columns of farm machines from one horizon to another across the flat Red River Valley of North Dakota and Minnesota. Not long after the Northern Pacific relinquished its acreage to its managers' friends, technology came to their aid with a new purifier for spring wheat, to make white flour, and a new roller mill, which could cope with hard wheat. For a time several of these "legumacies" produced crops greater than those of many a German principality. By 1906, despite the breakup of the syndicates that controlled the largest bonanza farms, they were selling land for $40 or $50 per acre. Technological change has been at the heart of American agriculture since the tinkerings of William Byrd II, George Washington, and Thomas Jefferson. Oliver Dalrymple supervised one hundred thousand acres by telephone as early as 1876; on the Houston farm nearby the first roll-film camera was developed during the long, inert wheat farmer's winter. The name Kodak may or may not have a Dakota origin — George Eastman was not clear one way or another.

German, English, Dutch, and Bostonian shareholders not only owned shares in tens of thousands of cattle in the western Dakotas and Montana but became absentee farmers of tens of thousands of acres in the wheat belt. It was not until the droughts and bitter winters of the mid-eighties raised the anxieties of the syndicators that they fell out among themselves. The bonanza farms are gone; the most magnificent of the bonanza farmers, the Dalrymples and Grandins, live in Minneapolis; but the ghost of the agglomerated past lives on in North Dakota, where the average farm includes four hundred sixty acres, three times the national average.

In the 1880s and 1890s another long, difficult transition began in this territory, a move away from the dominance of the prairie province by great corporations. The American Fur and Hudson's Bay companies had been there first. Then came the Union Pacific, Great Northern, and Northern Pacific, the cattle kingdoms and the bonanza farms, the elevator companies and the Armours, Swifts, and Cudahys. Now there appeared a mixed economy of cooperatives and the prairie-socialist enterprises in the Dakotas and the variegated legacies of the Farmers' Alliance and the Greenbackers, Populists, and Progressives.

And all the while, on farms large and small, hardy annuals were being planted and reaped, producing an enormous abundance, an abundance as astonishing as the herds of bison had been. Anthony Trollope strayed far enough from the Pallisers and the characters of his other novels to fulfill "the ambition of my literary life to write a book about the United States." In 1862 he observed what Americans did with cultivated grasses.

> I went down to the granaries, and climbed up onto the elevators. I saw the wheat running in rivers from one vessel into another, and from the railroad vans up into the huge bins on the top stories of the warehouses; — for these rivers of food run uphill as easily as they do down. I

saw the corn measured by the forty bushel measure with as much ease as we measure an ounce of cheese, and with greater rapidity. I ascertained that the work went on, week day and Sunday, night and day incessantly; rivers of wheat and rivers of maize ever running. I saw men bathed in corn as they distributed it in its flow. I saw bins by the score laden with wheat, in each of which bins there was space for a comfortable residence. I breathed the flour, and drank the flour, and felt myself enveloped in a world of breadstuff. . . . God [had] prepared the food for the increasing millions of the Eastern world, as also for the coming millions of the Western.

179

What God had prepared, humankind distributed. That is the history of the nineteenth and twentieth centuries in the Missouri Valley.

11

....

The Mountain States

Colorado, Idaho, Montana, and Wyoming

THE LONE GUNFIGHTER. He appears from nowhere, provides the plot with a spasm of heroic violence, refuses the tug of domesticity, and rides off into the sunset. "Shane!" the child in us cries after him, but he is gone.

It is just as well. He never was very important in the real West. A single horseman has little chance of inducing many cattle to go anywhere; cowboys worked in groups, often staying in their "outfits" longer than Japanese industrial workers stay in theirs. But the rest of us want to dream other dreams, so we have brought forth the myth of the lone cowboy. It is an eastern creation arising not from the needs of the cattle business but from the psychological requirements of urban cowboys seeking fantasies of relief from the abrasions of city living.

Chief among those urban needs was a desperate desire to be dumb — dumb in the literal sense: to be able to get by without articulate speech. The boy who called out "Shane!" grew up to become Dustin Hoffman's buddy in *Midnight Cowboy*. He was just as fragile, but instead of being solemnly silent in the shadow of the mountains, he talked all the time. Like all city people he had to. City folk, crowded and beset by the innumerable indignities of urban life, go to the movies to be caught up in the myth of the loneness of the lone cowboy. Forced to explain ourselves at every turn as we shove, prod, and push our way through the day, we yearn for a world in which we might survive without making use of any of the nuances between "yup" and "nope."

The Hollywood cowpoke needs but two facial expressions: a squint of disapproval implying an immediate intention to perforate and a

A rare instance of a single cowboy managing a string of cattle.
Wyoming State Archives, Museums and Historical Department

jaunty, asymmetrical grin of beguiling narcissism. No more is needed to communicate with the critters, though occasionally he does vouchsafe a meaningful lurch.

Inarticulate he is, but enormously persuasive. He has convinced us that the high-plains-and-mountain frontier was a place for the lone male'— without parents, wife, or progeny. That may have been true for lone American males during the mountain-man generation in the early 1800s, but even then, as we shall see from an economic point of view, that lone American male was far from independent.

It was not only the cinema that distracted us from the true history of the West; before there were mythmaking motion pictures there were mythmaking historians, apparently moved by the same desire to depict this vast region as if it were largely barren of life except for an occasional lone horseman or farmer. The Harvard historian Frederick Jackson Turner was magnificent in describing the agricultural Midwest — the realm of the family farm — but he faltered in the Southwest and failed as a guide to the high plains, because the frontier in each of these regions was different from the others.

Turner did distinguish between two agricultural experiences in the East. The first was that of the southwestern pioneers, exemplified by

Andrew Jackson and Sam Houston, who seized the land only after dispossessing a native population that had lived over many generations in densely settled agricultural villages. These southern pioneers drove their slaves before them into the West and required a world market for the crops they sweated out of them. This was not the experience of Turner's own Wisconsin parents. The northern pioneer cleared the forest to make and work his own place and planted for a local market.

Tennessee and Texas, Colorado and Wyoming, were not all Wisconsin. The Midwest had been fertile, well watered, well timbered, and divisible into one-hundred-eighty- or three-hundred-sixty-acre family farms. This, if anywhere, was the natural habitat of a nation of independent yeomen. One might call them lone husbandmen, as each of them constituted an economic unit. But matters were not so simple on the plains and around the Rockies. This was not the agricultural frontier of Turner nor the West according to John Wayne. There were, and are, few family farms in the midwestern sense, just as there were few lone cowboys.

Another Harvard historian, the magisterial Charles A. Beard, proposed a view that was at the opposite extreme from Turner's, suggesting

Fort Laramie, Wyoming, the intersection of two cultures. *Wyoming State Archives, Museums and Historical Department*

that the real West was so disgusting a place that it justified exploiting. His scruffy sodbusters and savage Indians confirmed the expectations of the western wilderness that had been held by New England intellectuals since the days of Cotton Mather and Timothy Dwight. The Puritan founders had seen the sunset horizon as red with the fires of Satan. The Harvard faculty, reeling from the presence of Turner in their midst (perhaps that should be "mist"), formed ranks behind Beard and rejected the frontier as a source of anything culturally useful. If the West on its own could contribute nothing important to America's development, one could exploit it without remorse and return quickly to the cultivated side of the hedge. The exploitation goes on, though in our time Turner's sunny view of the agricultural frontier has once again supplanted Beard's crabbed one, and the vitality of cultural life west of Cambridge has recovered from the defoliation of Beard's scorn with sufficient vigor to require no help in these pages.

"The prairie is uncongenial to the Indian . . . only tolerable to him by possession of the horse and rifle." So wrote another influential mythmaker, Lewis Henry Morgan, in 1859. The horse first became available to the Indian in the seventeenth century, the rifle in the nineteenth. If Mor-

The Medicine Wheel in northern Wyoming, one of a number of sites where ritual practice was apparently related to astronomical observations.
Wyoming State Archives, Museums and Historical Department

gan was right, the intolerable high plains would have been unoccupied before those times except for herds of bison and the lone eagle. But archaeology tells us otherwise: for ten thousand years families, tribes, gangs, and more recently corporations have left their remains upon the plains and in clefts of the foothills of the Rockies.

Bighorn Medicine Wheel in Wyoming, seventy-five feet in diameter, presents spokes that form alignments with celestial bodies more accurately than do the spaces between the monoliths at Stonehenge. This was, it seems certain, a ceremonial center for many people in an area where agriculture was and still is difficult. Not far away at Sheep Mountain in the Absaroka Range, a hunting net was recently discovered that is six feet high, two hundred feet long, and composed of more than a mile of cord. It is thousands of years old. Just over the Canadian border is the Head Smashed-In kill site, where for at least five thousand years, and perhaps as long as nine thousand years, large numbers of people kept rock walls and cairns in good repair to funnel lines of bison toward a cliff over which they could be driven by crowds of hunters.

Over thousands of years in this region a substantial population was supported by agriculture and a widely diversified supply of game. Clusters of small circles of stones that once held down the edges of tepees are frequently found throughout even the high, arid fringes of the plains. At the opposite border of the region, near Kansas City, there was a mound complex marking the extremity of the densely settled, agricultural woodland culture. In between, along the rivers, there were many smaller agricultural settlements where the Mandan and other village tribes lived in earthen houses roofed with sod and built upon massive wooden frames. These were the prototypes for the "soddies" of European settlers, who for a long time lived less densely upon the ground than did the Native Americans before them.

One aspect of the old image of the high plains as a mere bison pasture has real value in helping us to visualize it as it was and as it is no more. That is the aspect of multitudinousness. Bison beyond counting, in herds so vast as to defy comprehension, moved in masses often a hundred miles across. As a report to the Smithsonian Institution observed in 1880:

> Of all the quadrupeds that have lived upon the earth, probably no other species has ever marshalled such innumerable hosts as those of the American bison. It would have been as easy to count or to estimate the number of leaves in a forest as to calculate the number of buffaloes living at any given time during the history of the species prior to 1870.

Twelve million animals might move in a herd; one herd followed by Grenville Dodge covered fifty square miles. Bison were not limited to the Great Plains — the Spaniards reported them in Mexico in 1527, as did the English on the Potomac in 1612 — but they were to be seen in

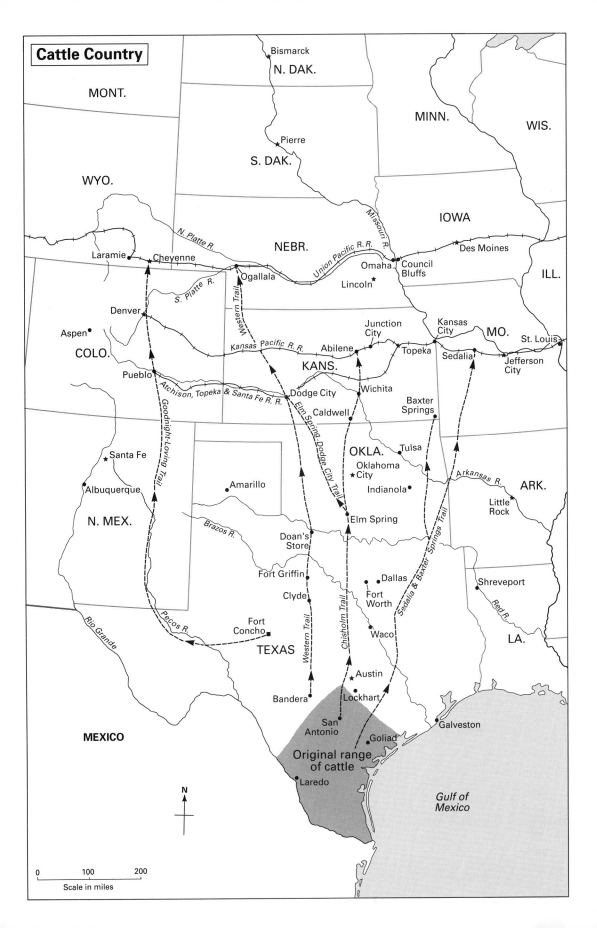

Cattle Country

MONT.

N. DAK.
• Bismarck

MINN.

WIS.

S. DAK.
★ Pierre

WYO.

IOWA

N. Platte R.

NEBR.

★ Cheyenne

Laramie •

Ogallala

S. Platte R.

Union Pacific R. R.

Missouri R.

• Des Moines

Omaha
Council
Bluffs

ILL.

Western Trail

Lincoln ★

Denver •

Aspen •

COLO.

Kansas Pacific R. R.

Abilene

Junction
City

Kansas
City

MO.

St. Louis •

Topeka

Sedalia •

Jefferson
City

Pueblo •

Atchison, Topeka & Santa Fe R. R.

KANS.

Dodge City •

Wichita

Caldwell

Baxter
Springs

Goodnight-Loving Trail

Santa Fe ★

Elm Spring-Dodge City Trail

OKLA.

Tulsa •

Albuquerque •

Oklahoma
★ City

Indianola
•

Arkansas R.

ARK.

N. MEX.

Amarillo •

Little
Rock
•

Brazos R.

Elm Spring

Doan's
Store

Sedalia & Baxter Springs Trail

Dallas
•

Shreveport
•

Fort Griffin

Fort
Worth
•

Clyde •

Western Trail

Chisholm Trail

Waco
•

Red R.

LA.

Pecos R.

Fort
Concho ◻

TEXAS

Rio Grande

Austin
★

Bandera •

Lockhart
•

San
Antonio •

Goliad •

Galveston •

MEXICO

Original range
of cattle

Laredo •

Gulf of
Mexico

N

0   100   200

Scale in miles

immense numbers only in the grassy region where the plains approached the Rocky Mountains. The great roundups and drives of the cattle kingdom were the successors to these immense animal assemblies. The West was the unbounded arena for the spectacle of multitudes, not of isolated, singular movement.

The myth of the lone cowboy has distracted us from the real drama enacted on the high plains and the first rearing ranges of the Rockies, a drama of groups, of cowboys whose only real work was concerted, of the crews building railroads to bring the riches of the West to market. In return, the same rails brought food and manufactured goods from the East to make it possible for settlers to survive in a region that could not feed, clothe, or shelter them.

And there is the other drama, subtle and invisible, of huge enterprises whose power spanned thousands of miles and controlled the lives of Westerners from the very beginning of European-American settlement. The West's semiarid terrain lent itself to a kind of dry-country plantation system, a pattern with which the Spaniards were thoroughly familiar from their experiences on their own peninsula. Their ancient predecessors on the Iberian Peninsula, the Romans, had organized the land into latifundia, very large plantation units that were owned and ruled from a distance.

In a similar fashion, the West has been exploited by outsiders from a distance and organized into huge spreads. Colorado's own Robert Athearn, a very good historian indeed, made this point thirty years ago. (The Populists had made it fifty years before that.) As Athearn told us, "The most persistent theme [in western history] is that of exploitation and experimentation carried on by remote control from the more settled parts of America. From the day of the mountain men, down through that of the miner, the cattleman, the land speculator, the timber baron, and the oil wildcatter, the region has been regarded as a place to capitalize upon natural resources with precious little concern about what was left when the stripping was finished."

What was left? Raw, sterile tailings on a thousand hills, bleached and yellow and unforgiving, the creaking of doors dangling on rusted hinges as the high-country wind blows through exhausted gray rows of abandoned houses. From the tailings and ghost towns, from the saloons of Butte and the shanties at the edge of Denver, there are trails leading eastward to marble fountains, walnut paneling and rich carpets, *boiseries* and silver wine coolers and opera boxes. At the eastern end of those trails one can also find Western buildings — Western not in architectural style but Western because the West's ore and oil and cattle paid for them. The Guggenheim Museum in New York is as Western in this sense as Fort Laramie, and a dozen "cottages" at Newport are as Western as Main Street in Leadville. In a country retreat just outside New York City there

Butte, Montana, "the richest hill on earth," about 1910.
The Montana Historical Society, Helena

is an exquisite Japanese garden that is, in its financial origin, not from the Far East but from Montana.

Athearn's "persistent theme" links the mountain man Jim Bridger to Ward McAllister, the New York social arbiter of the Gilded Age — an odd couple to any observer but an economist. The mountain man, gathering his furs in some desolate canyon, served Mr. Astor, sitting in his countinghouse in Manhattan, and was compensated sufficiently to buy himself rum and rough fare in squalid trading posts. McAllister served a somewhat later Mrs. Astor, providing for her needs and being compensated in rich food and champagne, a magnum or two of which were, in effect, provided by Bridger.

The persistent theme stretches invisible lines of economic force across the western landscape, tripping up the horse of the lone cowboy, throwing him to the ground, snarling him in foreign entanglements, and trussing him up so that he can be forever prevented from riding forth again as a symbol of independence. Those lines start, as the cowboy often did, with the cows in Texas. An estimate in 1830 counted only 100,000 head of cattle in Texas, but another in 1860 found an astonishing 3,535,000. Such a rate of increase caught the attention of the shrewd investors of the City of London. The American Civil War, ending in 1865, produced a group of men accustomed to riding long distances, sleeping out, making lethal use of firearms, and unwilling to return to sedentary hardship on the rocky farms of New England or the burned-out cotton fields of the South. Applied to a potential beef crop with such a rapid rate of increase, their talents could have substantial money value. The American cowboy was becoming interesting, and so was his native habitat.

The high plains, it was becoming clearer, were not a Great American Desert but an enormous rectangular pasture, two thousand miles from north to south. Into that pasture cowboys drove 260,000 Texas cattle in 1866. C. W. Dilke told his readers in London three years later that Colorado and Wyoming were destined to be "the feeding ground for mighty flocks." The British landscape was full and Ireland overgrazed, but already there were half a million cattle and a million sheep between Denver and the Wyoming boundary. This was true despite the Sioux and Cheyenne, whose livestock interests were confined to bison and horses and who had not relinquished their claims to most of the pasture.

By 1871 Wyoming cattle were feeding both sides in the Franco-Prussian War; millions were on the plains, driven by tens of thousands of cowboys working in battalions. A hundred thousand ponies went north from Texas in a single year to provide them mounts. One operation in the Beaverhead Valley of Montana in the early 1870s contained three thousand sheep and three thousand cattle, and enough cowboy help to require five hundred horses. The valley was bounded by escarpments on either side, so steep as to serve as ha-has, as the British might say; that is, no fences need obtrude upon the view. Across the midriff of the valley a six-mile-long fence belt was in place, and upstream another, a little shorter, ran in parallel. The greensward within covered 19,200 acres.

By the end of the 1870s this was a small spread compared to those being financed in the London money market. Huge sums were being aggregated to purchase land, livestock, fencing, and food. Scottish, English, Dutch, and German investors scrutinized cash-flow projections to cover the outgo while the four-legged subjects of all this attention ate themselves closer and closer to the slaughterhouse and toward the income side of the financial statement. At the outset there was consider-

Cowboys on a wintry day in Wyoming about 1890, encouraging their animals toward provender after an early snow. In blizzard years many cattle did not make it. *Wyoming State Archives, Museums and Historical Department*

able skepticism on the part of British cattlemen as to the quality of American cows, but it was a pleasure to observe how they survived on bunch grass, drinking from puddles. A British sportsman observed that "a herd of 5,000 head will feed the year round and grow fat on a stretch of arid-looking table-land, where an English farmer, if he saw it in the autumn, would vow there was not sufficient grazing for his children's donkey."

In 1872 the Scottish-American Investment Company began borrowing money at low Scottish rates to lend to cattlemen. The British-American and Anglo-American companies followed, then dashed ahead to invest directly in operating ranches. Fifty thousand British-owned cattle grazed along the Tongue and Powder rivers in Wyoming. Two and a half million acres of Carbon County were controlled by the British, about the same expanse of land (mostly gorse) held in Scotland and England by the duke of Sutherland, the greatest landowner in Great Britain. To the south lay the holdings of the Swan Land and Cattle Company and the British-capitalized Prairie Cattle Company, which owned two and a half million acres in Colorado alone and nearly as much elsewhere. In the Dakotas were the Matador Land and Cattle Company and the vast oper-

View of the William Tweed Ranch in Red Canyon, near Lander, Wyoming, about 1885. *Wyoming State Archives, Museums and Historical Department*

ations of the marquis de Mores. The EK Ranch of Sir Horace Plunkett and the principalities of beef owned by Otto Franc and another German, Charles Hetch, stretched from horizon to horizon in Wyoming.

During the late 1870s and 1880s the power of these foreign investors was so feared that it was possible for American investors to induce state and territorial legislatures to pass the kind of laws restricting foreign investment that we associate with Japan in our own time. Meanwhile, huge pools of capital from Boston, New York, and Philadelphia were poured into the cow country. As a result, a cowboy's life was characterized by a military-style organization and a lack of independence. The cattle economy was like the sugar economy of Barbados in the seventeenth century, as enormous remittances flowed back to overseas investors and to the city folk who owned the West.

Cotton had once been king, though its prices were set in Manchester and London; now people said that grass was king and spoke of the cattle kingdom. It was a kingdom and remains so in our memories, not because of its wealth but because it was organized like a kingdom with baronies and dukedoms, vast domains operating on a spectacular scale, its owners using violent means to discipline their realms.

Though the cattle kingdom was a potent presence in our national mythology, it was not as potent a presence in our national economy, nor even in the cattle economy, as it seemed at the time. Walter Prescott Webb, the historian laureate of the Great Plains, pointed out long ago that "after all, the West (even including Texas) did not produce many cattle." He cited statistics showing that the plains area, including Texas, produced only about twenty-eight percent of the total cattle in the United States in 1880. The plains states themselves, without Texas, rounded up only about fifteen percent of the total.

And the reign of the cattle kingdom was very brief, lasting only a decade between the internationalization of its economic base and the terrible vengeance wreaked upon its excesses by the weather in 1886 and 1887. Coming out of the world depression of the late 1870s, international investors had expanded the scale of the American cattle business and taken powerful roles in the already oligopolistic organization of the production and marketing of cattle. Their additional power and traditions of predatory behavior altered the cattlemen's associations of the Great Plains. These associations became organized into cartels as effectively as the railroad and industrial trusts that came after them, but drought and savage winters in the middle 1880s could not be organized away. The grass was seared by unremitting sun; the rains refused to fall; cattle died of thirst. Then came the blizzards. There are stories of ranchers driven mad by the sound of their cattle lowing for food. When the winds stopped, cattlemen emerged to find thousands of carcasses filling ravines and bunched along fence lines.

The collapse of the bonanza decade was more rapid than its boom, and the cattle kingdom did not recover. As a depression diminished the market for beef, many of the great companies, such as Swan, went to their creditors, who sold the herds into already flagging markets. Some smaller operators hung on, but many gave up. A pair of apparently colorless statistics tells much: in 1887 one quarter of the cattle sold for slaughter in Chicago were cows and nearly one in twenty were calves.

There are still large ranches and herds in the West, but nothing like those of the bonanza years, just as there are no wheat farms along the Red River of the North to compare with the huge aggregations of those same years that deployed combines like panzer armies from horizon to horizon. The 1880s were the decade of agricultural and pastoral pageants that were never seen again.

Spectacle — it was there overwhelmingly from the outset. Nothing mankind could offer could compete with the marvels provided by nature. Perhaps that is why Cecil B. De Mille never attempted a true western — cinematic stunts like Ben Hur's race would have seemed ludicrously diminutive in Jackson Hole. (The Hudson River School painters, especially Albert Bierstadt and Thomas Cole, went west to do their best work; it was not done on the Hudson.) The great roundups and drives of the cattle kingdom are forever fixed in our minds —hundreds of thousands of animals moving beneath clouds of dust rising a mile into the sky past a backdrop of mountains a mile and a half higher yet.

BIRDSEYE, WYO.

Birdseye, Wyoming, halfway to somewhere. *Wyoming State Archives, Museums and Historical Department*

Lost in those clouds of dust is the truth that these spectacles came about at the behest of distant corporate managers who manipulated the cowboys and the mountain men and the miners as pawns on an intercontinental chessboard.

I wonder what John Wayne would say to that.

12

....

The Imperial Basin

Oregon, California, Washington, Hawaii, and Alaska

THE PACIFIC STATES are so called not because their inhabitants are more noticeably benign than others but because they are unified by a region of water in a way that has more to do with their history than a land-bound view of things would suggest. They are deployed about the northeastern quadrant of the Pacific Ocean — a modest description that might lead one to think they are closer together than they are. The Pacific, taken as a whole, is the largest single element in the geography of the globe; one of its quadrants is an immense expanse by comparison with the relatively modest ranges of wave and trough shared by the five Gulf states, the two Long Island Sound states, or the four Lake Michigan states. The members of each of these minor maritime congeries could float messages to each other in bottles, but only the Pacific states came into the present century with a history in which water was more important than land.

Americans do not customarily center a story on a featureless watery terrain whose edges are shorelines; Americans, like the Russians (about whom more in a moment), are a continental people. To most of us emigration does not imply traveling over water, though to a Polynesian, a Nantucketer, or an Aleut it might. Instead we think of the Oregon Trail, of Conestoga wagons, of Mormon handcarts, of pack trains, railways, and highways — it requires some effort of imagination even to conceive of dog teams and the Yukon. Furthermore, most of our land travel, like that of the Russians, has been across fairly level grasslands, where a straight line on a map is the shortest distance between points.

193

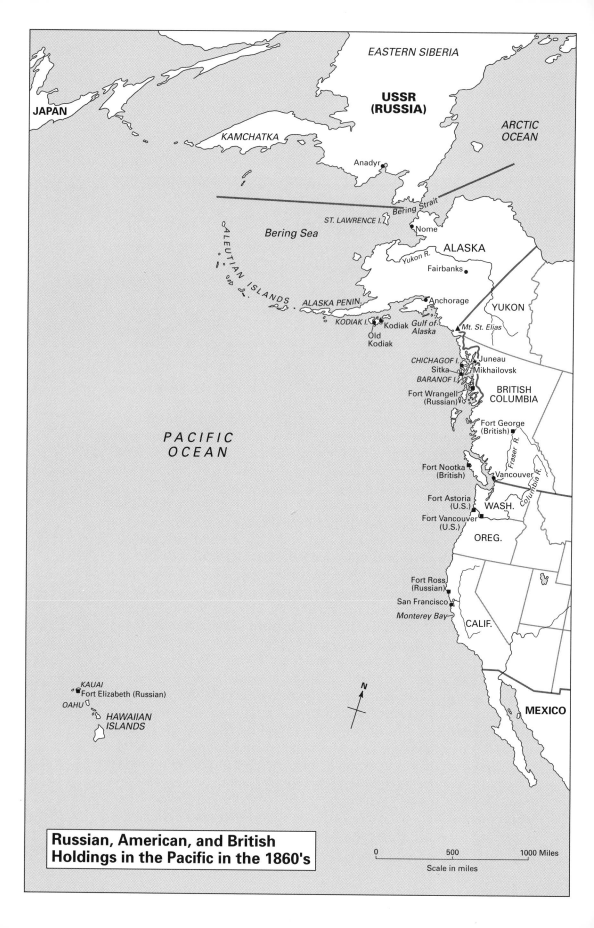

EASTERN SIBERIA

**USSR
(RUSSIA)**

*ARCTIC
OCEAN*

JAPAN

KAMCHATKA

Anadyr

Bering Strait

ST. LAWRENCE I.

Bering Sea

Nome

ALEUTIAN ISLANDS

ALASKA

Yukon R.

Fairbanks

ALASKA PENIN.

Anchorage

YUKON

KODIAK I. Kodiak

*Gulf of
Alaska*

Mt. St. Elias

Old
Kodiak

CHICHAGOF I. Juneau

Sitka Mikhailovsk

BARANOF I.

**BRITISH
COLUMBIA**

Fort Wrangell
(Russian)

*PACIFIC
OCEAN*

Fort George
(British)

Fraser R.

Fort Nootka
(British)

Vancouver

Columbia R.

Fort Astoria
(U.S.)

WASH.

Fort Vancouver
(U.S.)

OREG.

Fort Ross
(Russian)

San Francisco

Monterey Bay

CALIF.

N

KAUAI
Fort Elizabeth (Russian)

OAHU

*HAWAIIAN
ISLANDS*

MEXICO

**Russian, American, and British
Holdings in the Pacific in the 1860's**

0   500   1000 Miles

Scale in miles

But Polynesian navigators knew a thousand years ago that they could not set sail directly for any ultimate goal; the invisible tugs and pressures of wind and current required that, in order to get there, they warp the theoretical geometry of the earth's maritime surface with elaborate calculations.

In the age of paddle and sail, Hawaii was at the extreme northeastern reach of an indirect triangular pattern of canoe-borne emigration that had been important in human affairs for a thousand years before Russians or Americans arrived on the scene. Along this ancient pathway moved thousands of migrants, sometimes as a few people in a single craft, sometimes in fleets under the command of chiefs. They went island by island, eastward first from the southeastern edges of Asia, to create a new culture on the islands of the central Pacific. Then, after a long pause, they moved again, northward to Hawaii.

The medieval Polynesian achievement staggers the imagination: by A.D. 300 the Samoans had already colonized Tahiti and the Marquesas, and during the next five hundred years the islanders spread not only across the open ocean to Hawaii but also in the opposite direction, to New Zealand. By the fifteenth century two hundred thousand of them were living in the Hawaiian archipelago; that number remained fairly stable until the onset of Europeans and European diseases in 1778. The population was reduced to fewer than thirty-five thousand by 1900.

In the Far North, human settlement was much older. The earliest linking of Siberian and Alaskan cultures — presaging our links with the Russians — may have been as early as fifty thousand or as late as twelve thousand years ago and is seen in the similarity of ancient artifacts found in Siberia and America. There is substantial archaeological evidence in the region to support the hypothesis that the ancestors of the American Indians passed through it on their way to populate North America. Once in place on this side of what became the Bering Strait, some of these people showed a remarkable predilection for staying put: the settlement of Anangula in the Aleutian Islands lasted longer than the Roman Empire.

There is evidence of Japanese or Chinese voyages to the western coast, and of Russian castaways there in the seventeenth century, but the original inhabitants of our five-state region discovered Europeans digging in upon their shores with clear intention to remain only in the eighteenth century. Juan Rodríguez Cabrillo had touched the California coast in 1542, and Sir Francis Drake made a landfall there fifty years later. These first probes were events chiefly interesting to map- and mythmakers, not serious intrusions. Though the Manila galleons made landfalls at Cape Mendocino as early as 1600, and Sebastián Vizcaíno established a base at Monterey to protect their passage southward, California was only pricked along its western skin until Father Junípero Serra commenced the laying down of missions after 1769.

A Spanish fortress-village in California: the Presidio at Santa Barbara.
Santa Barbara Historical Society

Shortly thereafter, the Russians put down their first permanent settlement in North America at Unalaska in the eastern Aleutians; after a precarious winter or two, it was firmly established by the outbreak of the American Revolution. American domestic history — common people living their daily lives without the presence of court chroniclers and commissioned biographers — bears remarkable similarities to the history of these Russian pioneers. While we tend to regard the log cabin as a western European contribution to this continent, the Russians had perfected the form by the fifteenth century, and as one of them proudly said in the 1840s, "A Russian is everywhere the same. No matter where he chooses to live, whether it be in the Arctic Circle or in the glorious valleys of California, he everywhere puts up his national log cabin." And we have a common history of fur hunting and fur trading. The famous Captain James Cook did not arrive in the North Pacific until 1768, almost two hundred years after Sir Francis Drake, but the fur traders had probably preceded him. Russians had reconnoitered the North American coast as far south as what is now British Columbia.

Cook was not commissioned to make a survey of natural resources, however. His assignment was to test the possibilities of taking a Northwest Passage from the Pacific to the Atlantic, and he performed that task. Pressing through the Bering Strait into the fogs and ice floes of the Arctic Ocean, Cook put a final quietus on the dream of an alternative route to the long voyage around Spanish South America. He returned to the Hawaiian Islands, where he was the first European to intervene in the civil wars among the residents — who needed no discovering by him — and paid for that intervention with his life.

Visitors appeared in Hawaii from another direction as well. The continental inconvenience around which Cook had sought a Northwest Passage had a Southwest Passage, but a distant one around the Horn. Mariners who followed that passage on their way to San Francisco or the northwest coast found that the imperatives of Pacific winds and currents created a navigational triangle, with its western and most pleasant vertex at Honolulu. Before the narrow waist of America was cut by order of Theodore Roosevelt to allow for a canal across Panama, Boston traders had to sail a jump-rope course around and under the feet of that landmass. Then they were impelled to move not northward along the South American coast but northwestward to Hawaii before pressing back eastward to California, Oregon, or Washington. This would have been true even if the South American coast had been friendly, which in the hands of the Spanish Empire it was not.

Yankee traders went around the Horn and then to the mouth of the Columbia River well before Lewis and Clark reached it overland. By 1807 New Englanders knew more about Oahu and Nootka than they did about St. Louis. They saw Mauna Loa before they saw Pikes Peak. Every important early English or American explorer went to Alaska, Washington, and Oregon by way of Hawaii. This was true of Cook in the 1770s, of Robert Gray at the end of the 1780s, and of George Vancouver in the early 1790s. They established the route to the fur ports and, fifty years later, for the suppliers to the mining frontier of California.

This was the sequence: furs first, then gold, and much later the harvesting of the forests. Some people farmed where and when they could, but not until the twentieth century did agricultural products from this region become important in world markets. Instead, Americans and Russians were engaged in a converging campaign of destruction of fur-bearing animals. Insatiable, brutal, relentless, heedless, and improvident, the pursuit of fur on the part of European hunters had led to the near extermination of such animals, first in Europe itself and then in many parts of eastern America and western Siberia. One historian of modern Russia has depicted its eastward expansion as being essentially a sequence of conquests "of successive river basins . . . the speed of expansion being determined by the exhaustion of fur-bearing animals in each successive basin."

At about the time Puritan merchants in England first introduced the conical beaver hat, the Stroganov family of merchants was turning a displaced army of Cossacks away from their own salt-mining domain near the Urals toward the neighboring khanate of Sibir. Within a single lifetime these Cossacks and their sons exhausted several river basins. They reached the Pacific shore in 1638. In the North Pacific the fur hunt and fur trade also induced the indiscriminate degradation and in some instances slaughter of the native peoples who had since ancient times lived in a balanced, self-renewing relationship with the animals of the North.

198

From the outset of the English invasion of North America, the native peoples were perceived chiefly in utilitarian terms — as agents to hunt for fur or later, after the animals bearing commercial fur had been exterminated, as no longer useful and therefore as impediments to other uses of the land. It has been wisely observed that the indelible image of Indians as *hunters* was fixed in the European mind not because that was their essential character or occupation when Europeans first came

Neoclassical Russian-American architecture in Sitka in 1867.

among them, but because that was how the Europeans used them: as units of production, as hide seekers.

It may seem strange to stress the fur trade so heavily in an essay dealing with California and Hawaii as well as with the north-coast Pacific states, but even if we revert to overland history, American fur traders came that way first to California, and other fur traders intervened at the pivots of modern Hawaiian history. Their cannon enabled the king of Hawaii to complete his conquest of the islands, and they later brought Hawaii into the imperial contests of Great Britain, Russia, and the United States.

199

The convergence of European fur hunters from east and west on the North Pacific came after the long scouring of two continents for fur. Russians from the lower Volga and Dnieper valleys pressed eastward toward the Pacific as American pioneers out of the Appalachian highlands pressed westward toward the same destination. By the end of the eighteenth century, Russians and Americans were selling beaver hair to

R. N. De Armond Collection, Alaska State Library

the same customers. During the 1780s and 1790s the commanders of Russian forts sumptuously entertained British and American sea captains; a Spanish administrator in California was even willing to consider a Russian administrator as a son-in-law. There was a bloodless Nootka Sound crisis among the imperial powers in 1790, after which Spain courteously relinquished its exclusive claim to Vancouver Island, marking the first stage in its withdrawal from the North Pacific.

These were the decades in which the native populations were being decimated by war and disease, especially in the North. The Russians there did not trade furs in exchange for commodities as did the English, Dutch, and French, relying instead upon extracting tribute from native populations. The rigor of their means of extraction, together with the diseases the newcomers carried, produced even worse losses than those resulting from European disease and warfare in North America. The Russians' systematic program of elimination reduced the native population in the region under Russian control by ninety percent, but only after the most effective resistance to European imperialism offered anywhere in North America. Russian efforts to apply the same methods in Hawaii were successfully resisted by a relatively densely settled, centrally governed, and technologically sophisticated people.

European diseases wrought their usual consequences from Kauai and Vancouver to Santa Barbara. War and radical changes in social structure ravaged the densely settled region we now call the Pacific Northwest. Villages of great architectural sophistication were depopulated and some left uninhabited. Buildings of heavy planks laid upon frameworks of post and beam (more European in appearance than any others on the continent) were left eerily empty, presided over by immense wooden sculptures. These "totem poles," removed to serve purely ornamental purposes in New York and Washington, continue to justify gasps of wonder — urban Americans seldom expect such grandeur from people they have been taught to think of as savages or nomads or hunter-gatherers.

The decline of Spanish power in the Northwest after Spain abandoned Nootka in 1790 was followed by the revolt of California from Mexico and its ultimate acquisition by — some would say merger with — the United States. California settled into statehood in 1850 without passing through territorial status.

The Russians had simplified matters eight years earlier by selling their California base, Fort Ross, to John Sutter, a private citizen. (Fort Ross was named not for some Anglo-American Ross but by the Russians for "Rossia.") Alaska was sold later, but only after a Hawaiian adventure. Since Alaska was not hospitable to the traditional food crops grown by Russians, Hawaii, fertile and fecund, assumed a fresh importance. Russian ships arrived off Hawaiian ports in 1804, and there is evi-

Fort Ross, California, about 1877. *Inset,* the Russian Orthodox church as it appeared in 1988. *Vancouver Public Library*

dence that they intended to establish a base on the islands in 1808. To the end of the 1850s many of the needs of Alaska's fur gatherers were answered on the shores of Kauai and Oahu, where beachheads were established.

The Russian presence in Hawaii was most welcome to American skippers during the War of 1812. There was a powerful British fleet in the Pacific, so American ships were "sold" to the Russians and operated by the Russian American Company. The company proposed to reciprocate this stratagem in the 1850s, offering to "sell" Alaska to a San Francisco ice company (with a right of repurchase three years later). This was, again, to keep an asset out of the hands of the British, with whom tensions were gathering that would lead to the Crimean War.

One of the American vessels conveniently transferred to the Russians, the *Atahualpa,* renamed the *Bering,* was cast ashore on Kauai during a gale, and the local prince availed himself of the conventions of the law of salvage to make off with its cargo. Under the pretext of liberating that cargo, the Russian American Company sent a German surgeon, George Anton Schaeffer, to Kauai on an American ship to secure a base and then see what might be done on Oahu.

Schaeffer complied; from 1815 to 1818 he filibustered about the islands, building Fort Elizabeth of lava blocks on the south shore of Kauai, Forts Alexander and Barclay on the north coast, and the beginnings of another fort at Waikiki on Oahu. The Russian flag flew briefly over the Kauai forts until Schaeffer was sent packing by the Hawaiians. The Russian

Ruins of a Russian fort on the island of Kauai, photographed from the shore about 1890. *W. E. H. Deverill, Bishop Museum*

emperor declined to support Schaeffer's endeavors. Though two years later the czar created a flurry of diplomatic activity by claiming the North American coast nearly as far south as Nootka, he made no mention of Hawaii.

The Crimean War of 1853–1856 led to the abandonment of Alaska by the Russians in 1867. The weakness of the Russian armed forces in the Pacific was demonstrated by the pummeling of Siberia's ports by a British squadron. Fearing that the British would take this opportunity to add Alaska to Canada, the Russians made their offer to sell Alaska to the ice company, thereby alerting the expansionary Americans. Though its economic value had declined steeply as the fur seals were exterminated, Alaska was a possession worth keeping out of the hands of the British. The required price — two cents an acre — was reasonable, so Alaska was purchased in 1867, though it was not effectively governed by the United States for decades thereafter.

The Hawaiian Islands remained independent, though their central government was "advised" by Americans and their arable land engrossed by American corporations. In the 1890s a series of nationalistic revolts threatened those arrangements. After members of the Hawaiian royal family joined in these last efforts to resist the Americanization of the islands, the kingdom was replaced by a republic in 1894, and four years later Hawaii became a territory of the United States.

It is noteworthy that a new power in the North Pacific, Japan, vigorously protested that step. As the Russians backed away the Japanese took their place, commencing a contention with the United States from the Philippines to the Aleutians. The first climax to that contest occurred at Pearl Harbor in 1941, the second in Tokyo Bay four years later.

However, the ruins of Fort Elizabeth, now moldering in the underbrush on the bank of the Waimea River, remind us that the United States might have had to purchase, not only the forty-ninth, but also the fiftieth state from the Russian emperor.

13

....

How the University of Virginia Became Ohio, and Other Thoughts About Original Sin

THE TEMPLES and colonnades around the Lawn at the University of Virginia compose the most satisfying assemblage of beautiful structures in the Western Hemisphere and, to my eye, the highest expression of American humanism. Late at night, when things quiet down and the place itself can be heard to speak symbolically, the visitor who walks slowly through those colonnades may enter into the minds of Thomas Jefferson and of Benjamin Henry Latrobe, who was Jefferson's most important assistant in this masterpiece.

This is a holy place, to be approached as one would the cloister at Moissac, in southern France, or at Gloucester, two other masterpieces of architecture. Moissac offers in one enclosed space a distillation of the courageous spirit of Romanesque beauty in defiance of a brutal world. At Gloucester the Gothic spirit burst forth in a paean of hope, sustaining those who might flag, reinspiriting the defeated.

The University of Virginia is cooler, as befits the sanctuary of humane reason. It is at first somewhat confusing, more midwestern than we expect *and* more southern. Somehow it feels familiar — *and* very strange. I believe these mingled feelings arise from the presence at Virginia of symbols we midwesterners have become accustomed to considering secular — and our own. Furthermore, those symbols, while particular to neoclassicism, partake in an archetypal potency that arises from common human experience but is especially poignant in Albemarle County, Virginia. And they are holy in an unexpected way.

Thomas Jefferson's symbol of an ordered universe: the Rotunda at the University of Virginia. *Photo by Robert Lautman*

The founders of the University of Virginia meant it to be a paradigm of an ordered society. They were moved to do so both out of the cosmopolitan confidence of the Enlightenment and out of the specific anxieties of the American South. These sophisticated founders made deliberate use of a set of classical symbols that still retained their incandescence — their symbolic potency — to assure their contemporaries and us, their beneficiaries, that architecture is a weapon in the contest against chaos. Any human institution, be it a university, a government, or a marriage, is fragile. The founders had every reason to know that. But they built a university to show the way to a civilization as they might build a patent model to show the way to a machine. This was to be a disciplined, instructive mechanism to help form an ideal commonwealth.

The University of Virginia was intended to be a template for a Jeffersonian America. Templates and models — the use of miniatures to suggest great machines — is a Roman idea. The University is permeated by Roman ideas. It is classical — meaning "hierarchic," each part distinguished from each of the others. "Every professor," said Jefferson, could be the "police officer of the students adjacent to his own lodge," to enforce the discipline of his temple precinct.[1] If that sounds like a drill sergeant — well, it should. For a Roman lawn is not for croquet or volleyball; it is a campus where the militia is mustered.

The classical ideal: the Parthenon, a temple set within a sanctified rectilinear space. *Courtesy of the Library of Congress*

Here is where the classical note is sounded; in Rome the mustering occurred at the sound of a trumpet called *classicus,* a trumpet long and shining in the sun, like an alp-horn. This ungainly klaxon would sound, and the citizens would take their assigned places in the campus by degrees, by station, and by role, achievement, and expectation.

In deference to this Roman tradition the University might consider a classical festival, perhaps once a year. Virginia's students and their bachelor sergeant-professors could turn out to muster before each of the pavilions or lodges, each little battalion in its own uniform, or at least its own neckties. Imagine that from the portico of the Rotunda they were summoned by the sound of a Roman trumpet.

As the *classicus* finished its last braying, the student battalions would rank themselves in accordance with their performance. The best and the brightest first, then the not so good and not so bright, descending down the Lawn to the last, where, in their disheveled ranks, one would find on one side the bright and bad, and on the other the good and stupid.

The classical spirit seeks order through hierarchy, deferring *to* hierarchy because it may bring tranquillity if it does its job. That is why it makes use of classification, the rank ordering of people. (Incidentally, it rank-ordered literature, of which the best became classified as classics.)

This University has become a classic. It has been called the comeliest creation of man upon this continent, and is so, I think, because it is orga-

Trimountain, Michigan, one of the varieties of midwestern landscape.
Photo by Robert Lautman

The shell of Barboursville, the grandest of Thomas Jefferson's designs for rotunda-centered mansions in the Virginia Piedmont. *Photo by Jack Kotz*

Opposite: The paradigm of an ordered society: the rhythmic pattern of the colonnade at the University of Virginia. *Photo by Robert Lautman*

Next page: The West of the imagination: Beartooth Mountains, Wyoming. *Photo by Robert Lautman*

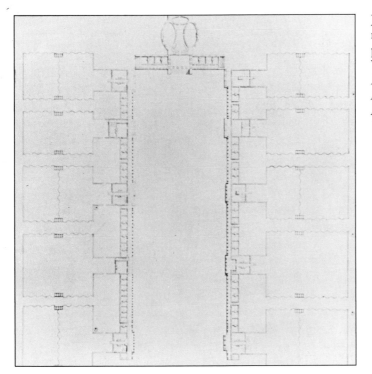

Jefferson's "squares," the rectilinear modules of the plan for the University of Virginia. *Thomas Jefferson Papers (N–100), Manuscript Division, Special Collections Department, University of Virginia Library*

207

nized by the use of four classifying devices: the square, the circle, the rectangular *temenos* or sacred precinct, and rhythmic repetition.

The first of these is as Roman as the *classicus* — it is the grid of "squares." Here they are not quite square, though Mr. Jefferson called them so. They were 200 by 235 feet as he laid them out on July 18, 1817. They formed the blueprint of his empire of reason. These squares were, he said, to form "in fact a regular town, capable of being enlarged to any extent." They might replicate themselves until they stretched beyond the Lawn westward, ever westward, their rhythms recurring over and over; and as their steady beat was felt, another would be felt as well, reinforcing theirs: the pattern of the floor of the Pantheon in Rome.

That building lies behind the Rotunda at Virginia as the spirit of Hadrian, the philosopher-emperor who created it, presides over its entire campus. What was said of Hadrian by William Macdonald, the great scholar of the Pantheon, could be said of Thomas Jefferson, though he was also the prototypical American: "He was a Roman, and must try to conquer and order the unknown."[2]

And those squares tell us one of his means. Here is what Macdonald has to say about those upon the Pantheon's floor: "The grid underfoot, in appearance like the Roman surveyor's plan for a town, appeared overhead in the coffering, up in the zone of the mysteries of the heavens. To unify unities is to produce the universal, and this is perhaps the Pantheon's ultimate meaning."

To unify by imposing a discipline of squares — there's a Roman idea! And to unify, or at least organize a wilderness according to a Roman surveyor's plan — there's a Jeffersonian one. We recall that George Washington and Thomas Jefferson were both trained in surveying and that Jefferson came of a long line of order makers, surveyors. The first American Jefferson, another Thomas, was surveying neat rectangles in 1616; the latest was Peter, the surveyor father of the famous Thomas.

Surveyors seem to us as drab and workaday as accountants. But they were not so in the eighteenth century; they were magicians, outsiders who might suddenly appear unbidden on the fringe of a clearing to decide what you owned and what you did not. They stood upon hilltops in strange costumes, carrying occult instruments, making use of the strange signs of mathematics, and they were derisive of commonsense meets and bounds. The surveyor was known as a measurer, and as John Stilgoe has said, was thought to have "an evil magic that trapped . . . [the] land in a web of invisible lines drawn by a mysterious figure knowing things beyond common knowledge." Thomas Jefferson was one of these; many frontiersmen distrusted him, too, and his "deep philosophical mind." He had a predilection for squares, arbitrary impositions upon the rounded hills and the coilings of streams, upon the undisciplined swellings and recedings of the landscape.

As early as 1777 he was suggesting that all Virginia's ancient counties be divided into school-support townships five or six miles square. In 1785 he proposed that all America between the Great Lakes and the Ohio River be divided into 640-acre-square townships. His serene indifference to the roundness of the earth induced Timothy Pickering to note that a square grid calculated for a flat surface would certainly produce disorder upon one that was curved. "A difference of six hundred yards in ten miles must surely produce material errors." Pickering was correct — but the 640-acre square marched westward with Euro-American settlement until frustrated by the Rocky Mountains.

Jefferson spoke for the ordering, classifying impulse of his century. There was much talk of nature's laws, but in practice the late Renaissance he represented was insistent upon *man's* laws — *for* nature. In New England appeared a tract called "The Ordering of Towns," which asked Yankees to regulate themselves within six-mile-square towns, and Virginia required an arbitrary platting of the Piedmont into square plantations of two hundred acres each. Less philosophical folk did resist: the people of Groton, Connecticut, asked not to be "strictly tied to a square form."

As this University *was* being so strictly tied in 1820, John Quincy Adams expressed the fervency of the ordering impulse in his *Report on Weights and Measures*. His father, John Adams, had said to Jefferson that John Quincy was as much the son of the Orderer of Monticello as his

The Pantheon as painted by Giovanni Pannini around 1740. The pattern of
the floor anticipates the pattern of land allocation under the Northwest
Ordinance. *National Gallery of Art, Washington, D.C., Samuel H. Kress Collection*

own, and with regard to the imposition of rectilinear rationality upon the recalcitrant earth, he was. Here is the voice of John Quincy Adams singing his hymn to the metric system: "If the Spirit of Evil is, before the final consummation of things, to be cast down from his dominion over men, and bound in chains for a thousand years, the foretaste here of man's eternal felicity, then . . . the metre will surround the globe in use as well as in multiplied extension." Heaven awaits the Northwest Ordinance, and the angels are surveyors.

There is something militant here that invites us to look back to previous encampments laid out in squares. It was not only to Roman surveyors that Jefferson calls our attention, but to centurions and generals, the makers of neat, gridded Roman garrison towns. The University of Virginia is called a campus, I gather, though the term "campus" was first applied to an academic establishment, not a military installation, at Princeton, Aaron Burr's school. Virginia (but not Princeton) looks Roman — a group of buildings arranged around a drill ground. And in case we forget the military meaning of the term, we need only look at the first large building to be constructed within Mr. Jefferson's philosophical grid for the Northwest Territory, the Campus Martius at Marietta, Ohio.

I am underlining the impositional character of an Enlightenment relationship to the landscape, presaged here and carried forward in the federal land policy of the United States. It was first expressed in the laying out of a series of gridded garrison towns in Georgia by the military engineers brought there by General James Oglethorpe in the 1730s

Campus Martius, Israel Putnam's *bastide*, or fortified village, in Marietta, Ohio. *American Pioneer, March 1842*

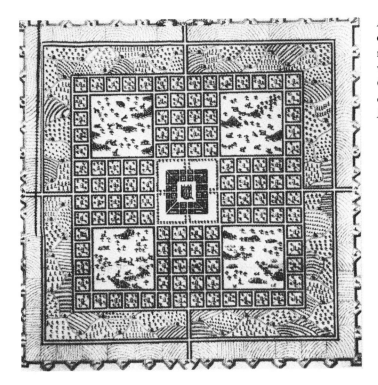

211

through the 1750s. He had fought with the Austrians against the Turks in central Europe and observed the "planting" of neo-Roman *campi martia* along Europe's eastern frontier. At the same time French military engineers were laying them out for the Russians along the upper Volga. Savannah was not the only Roman garrison town contemplated for Georgia; there were a half dozen others.

When the surroundings are fearsome, when violence may come at any time, when disorder lurks in every shadow and murder behind every tree, a geometric grid is very consoling. It is the product of twenty centuries of military consolation and consolidation.

A hundred years before the Northwest Ordinance, and a hundred thirty before Mr. Jefferson surveyed the squares of this campus, Oglethorpe's pattern was anticipated by an earlier Georgia proprietor, Sir Robert Montgomery of Skelmorley, who gave this formation to his chimerical margravate of Azilia. (Montgomery's project was part utopia, part pretext for a campaign against the Spaniards, and part land speculation. In that last role it ran afoul of the collapse of various other manias and collapsed in 1720.)

A margravate is a border province — a "march." Marquises and *marquis* and *marchesi* were marcher lords. From Scotland to Spain and Hungary they used square encampments for military purposes — garrisoning and squaring away — anticipating their use by the Enlightenment for

Jefferson's capitol in Richmond: Franco-Romanism and time-tested taste.

psychological purposes. The eighteenth century delighted in bounding, ordering, gridding; it doted upon system.

So far all our examples have been two dimensional. Now let us observe the square as it raises itself from the ground, swells, and straightens itself into the implacable form of the cube. The mystery of three dimensions, of solid geometry, is before us.

With it appears Mr. Jefferson's image of the Virginia capitol, which he described as a building in the "cubical style." What a square was, a cube might be with infinitely greater force: obdurate, insistent, militantly pedagogical. The capitol was to be "an example of architecture in the classic style of antiquity . . . for . . . study and instruction."

The Sage of Monticello had been explicit in designing the capitol at Richmond; around it he intended to provide a group of buildings for his fellow citizens, a *civic* village "for their study and instruction." *That* village, like the campus of the University, was to be "academical." Not only would the wise legislators lay down laws within it; while they orated, instructively, its very shapes would be, instructively, teaching how to build.

That village was never completed. The capitol was the only structure in the planned group to be finished. No other temple-form buildings were created until a full generation had passed. Then, at the end of his life and at the end of the Renaissance tradition he exemplified, Jefferson saw to it that there should appear around the Lawn at the University an anthology of Roman and Palladian models taken from British and French books, "models of taste and good architecture . . . no two alike, so as to serve as specimens for the architectural lecturer." Symmetrical, orderly, antichaotic.

Architecture is always a device for public instruction, and no man has ever known its pedagogical potency so well as the Sage of Monticello. Monticello itself was his academical *house,* and the University of Virginia, down the valley where he could see its dome and instructive porticoes, was his academical *village.* He was from first to last a professor of architecture. Jefferson provided this academical village, with the emphasis upon "academical," for the delectation of the sons of the new South come for instruction in the ways of the Old.

What lesson was it teaching? What was the primary symbolic curriculum of all this "academical" architecture: "academical" houses, "academical" villages, and "academical" rectangular buildings called cubical lest we miss their point?

To get an answer we must proceed from squares and cubes to circles and spheres, to the second of Jefferson's ordering methods, the deploy-

The final plan for the mountaintop at Monticello, with a rotunda form in the center, akin to the plan for the university. *Special Collections Department, University of Virginia Library*

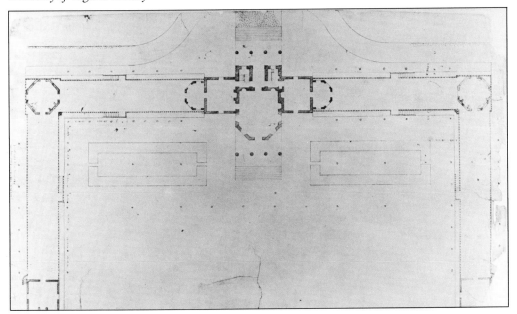

ment of the rotunda. We must square the circle, or with even greater difficulty, cube the sphere.

It is remarkable how similar the ground plan of Jefferson's private paradigm of ordered living, Monticello, is to his public paradigm of civic instruction, the University of Virginia. At the center of both is an evocation of another grand Roman idea, the Pantheon of the Emperor Hadrian, known suggestively throughout the Renaissance, and especially to Palladio, as Santa Maria Rotunda.

Jefferson built two little pantheons and tried to induce his architects to build several more. In the private one, at Monticello, the Sage was at the center of things, as Hadrian had been when he dispensed justice in his Pantheon. Hadrian was making a symbolic point: rationality would prevail because justice would be done in that immense space, with all its implications of system, consistency, and openness, in contrast to his predecessors, who had too often operated in secret.

In the previous American rotunda-centered campus, that of Union College, Schenectady — the plans for which were exhibited in Philadelphia with plenty of time for Benjamin Henry Latrobe to study them and offer the rotunda form to Jefferson — the central rotunda was to be occupied by a chapel in which the college president, Eliphelet Nott, one of the great liberal preachers of his time, would hold forth. In Virginia the mysterious, sacred vault was a shrine to something more abstract, less idiosyncratic, and deriving from an ordered universe — human reason.

Theology was not to order things at the University of Virginia. Indeed, Jefferson's correspondence leaves no doubt about it: this was to be an antitheological, man-centered campus. Which reminds us again of Hadrian. That philosopher-ruler preempted for his Pantheon the spherical space previously reserved for mystery cults in Asia Minor. He thereby brought the gods down to earth, trivializing them by making them all equal, in a pantheon, and putting in their midst the lawgiver, himself, the greatest of Romans, the emperor.

This sounds as if the Romans were men of the Enlightenment, sharing the anticlerical views of Jefferson and Latrobe, who sixteen centuries later merely reiterated a point. But this time they erected a complex of buildings putting human reason in the place of the emperor who had put *himself* in place of the gods. The Rotunda of the University is the pantheon of the empire of reason. Instead of mystery cults, instead of the deified emperor, it is the temple of a process by which mankind participates in the creating and ordering of the world.

Powerful symbolic messages are communicated when one uses a pantheonic form, a rotunda, for that sort of business. What Frank Brown once said of the Pantheon is even more true of Jefferson's Rotunda: "The form . . . [is] the form of the cosmos with man at the center."[3]

But man is not cosmos. Actually, the man or woman who *is* at the center of the University is the *reader,* the student, the seeker after whatever general truths may be left in the universe among the ruins of the Enlightenment. Man or woman is at the center of the vast, numinous, mysterious power of the interior of a sphere. The pantheonic, containing form is, in the words of Shelley, "the visible symbol of the universe; in the perfection of its proportions, as when you regard the unmeasured dome of Heaven, the idea of magnitude is swallowed up and lost."⁴

The scholar of the Pantheon, William Macdonald, to whom I referred and to whom we are indebted for those sentences of Brown and Shelley, put the matter even more powerfully in his own terms: "Order and the system were synonymous, and the most orderly of geometric, and therefore of architectural, shapes is the circle. It is without corners and without seams, and has no beginning and no end. It stands for continuity, and, when raised in form to a great height and vaulted over, it intimates an inclusive security."⁵

Shelley spoke of the perfection of the Pantheon. So had Sebastiano Serlio, Palladio's contemporary and competitor, three centuries earlier. The rotunda was "the purest form, that is the round form. . . . The Pantheon seems to me to be the most perfect piece of work I ever saw."⁶

"Perfect" is a capacious word. It is used with care in the Bible, in which it is said that "in heaven there shall be no marrying or giving away into marriage," for in heaven there *is* perfection. There the opposites are joined in a seamless circle of utter smoothness. The roughness, the edginess, the anxiety, are all gone. That is why so often in medieval art the Holy Spirit is depicted as a sphere or circle of fire, a cool conflagration in the heart, burning sweetly in wholeness, completion, in circularity.

I suggested, whimsically, a little earlier that John Quincy Adams thought surveyors were angels. He didn't, of course, but sometimes *architects* are touched with angelic qualities, and one set of them, so inspired, provided us those intimations of perfection we feel at the University of Virginia.

Now for some thoughts about the two other ordering methods evident in that campus, the *temenos* and repetition.

The *temenos* is the rectilinear sacred precinct. It demarcates the domain of the sacred, the area before which you take off your shoes and purify yourself. Some of us have the habit of pausing at the door of a church and ritually washing, even if we have forgotten how our predecessors once washed their bare feet at the door of the synagogue. Holy water is a symbol of ritual cleansing before the *temenos* is invaded. In Roman times rectilinear temples were raised on platforms, so the sacred space was obvious. For the Greeks things were more subtle. Everybody knew the domain of the gods.

The area of the Lawn is a sacred space; each of the temples placed about it — each lodge, each pavilion — shadows its own smaller sacred space. Mr. Jefferson and Mr. Madison meant for attending the Univer-

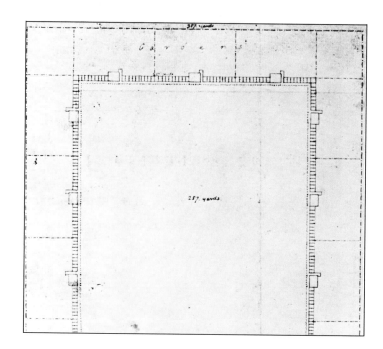

216

sity of Virginia to be felt as a serious undertaking. That is one of the reasons Jefferson wept when discussing the antics of riotous students who did not seem to understand that what had been created for them here was sacred space.

We who are constantly exposed to a roar of commerce, contrived crises, and twenty-second noise bites are in peril of becoming symbolically deaf. Blind, as well. Our symbol-sight is blurring. But in the 1820s Jefferson and Madison saw quite specific symbolic associations in classical forms. They were not finicky as to which were Greek and which were Roman derived from the Greek. Such distinctions were not so important to them as they are to architectural historians. These were philosopher-statesmen. They put their attention on the impact, not the derivation of symbolic forms. So though neither of them made use of specifically Greek massing in their architecture, it was no coincidence that Greece itself was coming alive again while Jefferson deployed classical forms for the enlightenment of Virginia students.

By the 1820s Jefferson's affinity to Greek ideas (not its architecture, specifically) added symbolic poignancy to his feeling for the temple form within a sacred precinct. As soon as the United States was free of Britain, his thoughts had turned to Greece. In 1785 he wrote from Paris to Ezra Stiles that independent Greeks "would easily get back to . . . classical models. . . . We might then expect, once more, to see the language of

An engraving of the University of Virginia published in 1827, showing the grandeur of its temples in the eyes of contemporaries. *University Prints, Manuscript Division, Special Collections Department, University of Virginia Library*

Homer and Demosthenes a living language." Two years later he said to George Wythe: "I cannot help looking forward to the re-establishment of the Greeks as a people, and the language of Homer becoming again a living language." In his old age, as he was planning this University, Jefferson expressed regret that he had become too infirm to join George Ticknor of Harvard in a voyage to the Aegean.[7]

The Greeks did not achieve freedom quickly or easily. And Jefferson's successors did not share Jefferson and Madison's feeling for Greece — reference to Greek independence was stricken from what we call the Monroe Doctrine. But there remained among ordinary Americans intense feeling for Greece. It may be gauged by the names they gave their towns, created in the 1830s and 1840s on those Jeffersonian grid patterns of the West. And they erected thousands of temple-form buildings in towns with names such as Corinth, Sparta, Athens, and Homer.

When Americans like Ticknor did travel abroad, they went to Greece itself and saw it as a *temenos,* a place ravaged, pillaged, and burned, but retaining a sacredness, a numinosity. The suffering of its population was like the ritual scourging of the acolytes of a temple. Though its sacred sites might appear to be abandoned, to a person responsive to such things they were — and are — alive with unseen presences.

Even the cold, appraising, commercial eye of the early nineteenth century saw Greece as "a land set apart." Not only were its temples "approached by a portico and surrounded by a consecrated enclosure," but to one American traveler of Jefferson's time, it seemed as though "the whole land of ATTICA itself was a sacred TEMENOS."[8]

Americans in the 1820s and 1830s displayed in their architecture a resurgent pride in their own nation. After the first disappointing decades of independence and the disasters of the War of 1812, thousands of them, not just a handful of intellectuals, felt themselves to be the heirs to the glories that were Greece.

The Lawn was set aside as a *temenos* to learning, and each of the pavilions or lodges — temples, as they really are — is set aside within its own sacred precinct.

Pavilion III at the University of Virginia, the prototype for many mansions.
Photo by Robert Lautman

These individual columned spaces are linked in colonnades, which means that they partake in the fourth of the means by which the University was to order nature, ritual repetition. These arcades are at once encompassing and consoling barriers; column by column they are composed — musically — to reinforce one another. Thomas Jefferson brought to this place the principle of repetition, as ancient as Egypt, as modern as Mies van der Rohe, out of a lifetime of experience and a lifetime's desperation for order.

To repeat is to affirm the previous instance, a conservative act. I submit that the key to understanding Jefferson's intentions and capturing fully what he accomplished is to know how conservative he was. He was not interested in the *unnecessarily* new.

This view — my view — rejects two popular myths about Jefferson: the myth of the bloodthirsty revolutionary and the myth of the revolutionary architect. He *was* guilty of youthful, revolutionary rhetoric. He *did* spend an embarrassing term as a wartime governor. But almost alone among the leaders of the Revolution, he had no experience whatever of violence. Though his lifetime included two world wars and two revolutions, each of which cost many lives and maimed tens of thousands of people, Jefferson never experienced bloodshed. His famous letter from the apparent serenity of pre-Revolutionary Paris, about nourishing the tree of liberty with patriotic gore, was the sort of effulgence possible only for someone who has never experienced the suffering of war. And nothing in his actual behavior or his recommendations for political action after events in France turned sanguinary justifies the conclusion that he was bloodthirsty. He was merely vehement.

Jefferson was for ordered change carried on by the gentry in the interest of what he and his contemporaries called a system of ordered liberty. Liberty, yes, but "regulated liberty" or, as Edward Everett said, "liberty enshrined in constitutions, and organized by laws."[9]

Though the *Richmond Enquirer* called the Federalists the Friends of Order, so were the Jeffersonians, as President Jefferson made clear in his Second Inaugural. What he himself had called the Revolution of 1800 was not to be taken as disruptive. Its purposes were "that *peace* be cultivated, civil and religious liberty unassailed, *law and order preserved* . . . and that state of property, equal or unequal, which results to every man from his own industry or that of his father."

And as he was designing the University of Virginia, he spoke of the chief virtues of the American system as being "the combined blessings of liberty and *order*," while his friend Madison underlined "the necessity of . . . [blending] *stability* with liberty."

When we talk of Jefferson's revolutionary generation, we are apt to forget how unrevolutionary they were. We could be reminded by reciting again the poems or singing the songs they invented. Some of us may remember Philip Freneau's lines of 1787:

> Here reason shall new laws devise
> And *order* from confusion rise.

And many can sing:

> America, America, God mend thine ev'ry flaw
> Confirm thy soul in *self-control*
> *Thy liberty in law.*

Jefferson could have as easily expressed as John Quincy Adams did the epiphanous tidiness of the *Report on Weights and Measures.* Even if he had not been disposed to order, Jefferson's post-Revolutionary experience as a member of George Washington's cabinet in the 1790s would have brought home its virtues. Shays's Rebellion burst forth in Massachusetts, the Liberty Boy riots in Charleston, the artisan riots in New York, and the Whiskey Rebellion in Pennsylvania. It was altogether consonant with his own views that Washington should establish Thanksgiving Day by somewhat anxiously asking prayers of thanks for a government that had established "liberty with *order.*"

Now there is a second false impression about Jefferson which must be vanquished if we are to engage with the mind that built this masterpiece. Somehow it has gotten abroad in the land that he was sympathetic to the so-called revolutionary architecture of Ledoux and Boullée, which he observed in Paris in the 1780s. This is not likely; their ideas were disruptive of the eighteenth-century tradition, of which Jefferson was the chief American apostle. In fact, he did not approve of them at all. More important, his response to their work contained the clearest possible statement of his aversion to innovation in architectural form and, implicitly, his respect for repetition and continuity.

"Experience," he said, "shows that [when something radically new is attempted] about once in a thousand times a pleasing form is hit upon." He wanted no part of novelty in architecture, no "brat of a whimsical conception never before brought to light." No architect, he insisted, should be able to "draw an external according to his fancy."

His taste was very conservative. We recall his advice to Madison to use a portico at Montpelier derived from a seventeenth-century French text, Perrault's version of Vitruvius, to which he returned twenty years later for Pavilion I on the University campus. He recommended the 1675 façade of the Louvre for reuse by Major Pierre-Charles L'Enfant in the public buildings of Washington. America should benefit from "some model already devised and approved . . . [or] copied from the most precious, most perfect model of ancient architecture" something that had gained "approbation . . . [for] nearly 2000 years."

This is being conservative *about* a conservative reverence for a very conservative culture for, as Sir Moses Finley observed not long ago, "the artistry which has been so much admired" by men of Jefferson's bent and has had their "approbation" for two thousand years "was at all times firmly rooted in the conventions of an extremely cautious and conservative [ancient Greek] building industry." This is important. We are talking here not about dried-out archaeological restorations of Greek architecture but about that architecture itself. The Greeks, and the Romans after them, knew the value of repetition.

Along the colonnades that bound the sacred Lawn of the University of Virginia recur the rhythms of repetitious architecture beating slowly, column by column, as each is reexperienced in the next. This is reassurance, steadying, a metronome telling us that we are experiencing what others have experienced for two thousand years. We partake in an order of things that has continuity. There is nothing here of modernity — no desperate desire for innovation, for personal, emphatic "statement," which by the act of estrangement from tradition sets itself outside the common experience.

Repetition need not be boring. Indeed, repetition is the consequence of intense experience and feeling. In architecture as in sexuality, Carl Jung was right in insisting, "any kind of excitement, no matter in what phase of life, displays a tendency to rhythmic expression, perseveration and repetition." Breathing hard, we repeat sounds and phrases of intense excitement. In architecture that sort of sustained excitement gives seemliness to the vernacular.

The assertion of order through a regular beat, expressed in the architecture in colonnades, is one of the fundamental principles upon which the University of Virginia, that masterpiece of spatial organization, was built.

In a chaotic world populated by erratic and violent people like us, it is reassuring to come into the presence of a hopeful spirit like Mr. Jefferson's. The University is a credo, a statement of the belief that order is possible in the world, a statement expressed in symbolic terms at least two thousand years old.

Dr. Jung and I would argue that those symbols are as old as our species and that drawing upon them is not docile but at once courageous in the face of current news and at the same time diffident before the long continuities of the universe.

If there were no world out there, no history, nothing but art, that would be my ending. We could let it go at this, a celebration of the wonders of mankind's participation with nature as the eternal laws of geometry are articulated in brick, stone, and ordered form. But the University of Virginia is not a campus placed *anywhere*. It is the central artifact of the antebellum South.

As its guardians, we have an obligation to those who struggled so long to create it and to build a civilization in America, who grappled with America's original sin — human slavery — and whose dream of order was overcome by slavery's bloody, chaotic consequences. We must acknowledge their travail and their courage.

The campus of the University of Virginia is not merely a consummate work of architecture. It is a statement of feeling arising from the circumstances of its creation. "Statement" is too cool a word; the campus is at once a gesture of defiance and a cry of pain.

Thomas Jefferson did not live out his old age in a sweet, seemly, untroubled imposition of Enlightenment principles on an ordered terrain. The South was not tranquil. The plantation system lived in terror; its work force was created, organized, and held in subjection by violence, and there was always, in the back of the southern mind, the apprehension that it would meet its end in violence. The "firebell" that Jefferson said he heard in the night in 1820 was the firebell of slave insurrection. His neighbor John Randolph feared revolution led by African-Americans, but he feared emancipation just as much. It would be, he said, an invitation to the freed slaves "to cut their masters' throats." Jefferson in his youth had spoken of emancipation, but only when coupled with shipping the emancipated back to Africa. Later he gave up any hope of relief from the horror that haunted his imagination and tried, without that hope, to impose architectural tranquillity in Virginia. He implied a permanence he did not anticipate, contemplating the possibility that "all the whites south of the Potomac and Ohio must evacuate their States and most fortunate those who can do it first."

Jefferson lived out his life upon his hilltop looking to the horizon for the smoke of burning houses and crops, recalling the slave revolt in Haiti and what he called its cannibal republic. He wrote of "horrors . . . beyond the reach of human thought," while John Marshall predicted "calamity" for his beloved state inevitably arising from its denial to the slave of "the natural right to the fruits of his own labor."

Recalling Jefferson's despair of the consequences of slavery, especially in association with the growing of tobacco — "a culture productive of infinite wretchedness" — we can observe that by the time the first buildings on the campus were completed, Albemarle County beyond its *temenos* was "worn out." Though the decline of Jefferson's native region was most rapid during his lifetime, it had begun long before then. A romanticized view of life among the James River planters, encouraged by the non-Virginians who have descended from Chicago to remodel their houses, has given them the serenity of antiques. But we should not be so dazzled by the shine of twentieth-century remodeling as to forget how few of the houses that have been given so much attention remained in the hands of the families who built them as late as 1800 — Westover and Stratford are just two that did not.

Nor should the apparent composure of the University, its clean, untroubled classical evocations, permit us to forget how narrowly it escaped destruction. In 1865 the trajectory of vengeance stopped just short of it. The implacable Ulysses S. Grant was at Appomattox. William Tecumseh Sherman was coming up from the south, and Philip Sheridan, the scourge of the Shenandoah, from the north. The worst fears of Thomas Jefferson came true.

The South is that region in the United States which has a tragic history unlike any other. Only here does half the population find constant, visible reminders of its enslavement and the other half monuments to its defeat and occupation. "Tragic" does not, however, mean "pathetic." There clings to the word "pathetic" an aroma of passivity that does not describe Jefferson's life, or the life of the South. "Tragic" implies a *refusal* to be acquiescent even to one's own limitations, an unwillingness to accept defeat even at the hands of one's own error, a determination to keep on striving to make the world better, to give it some order, to rise to a higher aspiration, though one knows one's own imperfections.

It is conventional to say that Jefferson had only something conventional in mind when he took a few moments from his work upon the University to write to a French friend that "error is the stuff of which the web of life is woven." So to say would once more simplify the complexity of Jefferson, of his living in full consciousness of his tragedy and that of his beloved region. He was not wasting his ink on convention. He had thought deeply and carried in his psyche what is known by any person who has lived very long in public life, or perhaps life in general. All our endeavors are ambiguous. All that we achieve is imperfect. Terror awaits on the fringes, and all our structures are brittle. But we do keep on trying. We do make use of the classical tradition to piece out our imperfections, to create some small domain of continuous and ordered civility, even though we ourselves may not be worthy of or benefit wholly from it.

A noble and tragic life is a brave try. We feel the University of Virginia as such a brave try. We feel it to be noble *and* its circumstances to be tragic. That is why its dream of order is so inspiriting. It has been provided to us not in childish ignorance, not in bland naiveté, not in cynicism. No, it arose in full consciousness of sin, of the imperfection of all human endeavor, of uncompleted obligations, of past defeats and defeats likely to come, of chaos beyond the doors. The University of Virginia and the Jeffersonian dream of a decent and orderly America *are* heroic. It is a miracle that both still survive.

14

....

A Field Guide to the
Southern Greek Revival

AGLIMPSE of white columns in the moonlight.
     A scent of magnolias.
     A rustle of crinoline and the sound of laughter in the
shadows.
Buttered grits for breakfast and, after a reasonable interval, mint and
bourbon whiskey.

Antebellum South and Greek Revival.

Memories from life, or from fiction as real as life, twine together
as tenaciously as wisteria, as insatiably as kudzu. They are shared memories, so familiar to us all that we understand instantly what architectural historians mean when they write, as one did not too long ago,
that "Greek Revival plantation houses . . . *symbolized* the Antebellum
South."[1] (In the South "Antebellum" is one word, capitalized, like
Damnyankee. This is our first example of the American Free Classicism
to which this essay is devoted.) This is not to say that the columnar big
house *characterized* that South; its "*characteristic* architecture . . . was not
the fabled mansion but . . . the dogtrot."[2] (A dogtrot is a structure probably composed originally of two one-room log cabins roofed together
with an open hallway between. Later, in frame versions, it sometimes
added one or even two rooms to each side.)

In the difference between the symbolic and the typical lies a world of
imagination and yearning. Columned mansions were rare. Few people
rose from dogtrot to Greek Revival mansion, though many yearned to
do so. More than a century after the Greek Revival period (1825–1860)
the popular imagination strives to satisfy that yearning retrospectively.

224

We make it happen; the Greek Revival mansion occupies the foreground of our dream of the South that *was,* as the window air-conditioning unit occupies much of the foreground of the South that is.

The Greek Revival. Yes indeed. What comes to mind? Probably Tara in David Selznick's movie version of *Gone With the Wind,* though it was much too big and too white and had too many columns for the Georgia house the author of the book, Margaret Mitchell, described. Greek Revival is a very broad term. Within it there are, as the Bible says, "many mansions," meaning "many meanings," of which few are the same.

Everybody knows what southern Greek Revival houses look like, though "frankly, my dear," they do not look alike. Perhaps that is because they come from two entirely different traditions, one from the North and East, the other from the South, each given a little Hellenizing after reaching the South. The Hellenizing commenced around 1820 in the Mississippi Delta and in northern Alabama. In the 1830s it flourished among the new occupants of the region, the European-Americans, who applied motifs derived from Anglo-American builder's guides, together with similar but not identical elements drawn from French Renaissance practice, to forms made available from the West Indies.

This creole-Yankee Greek Revival swept back into the older South, the Carolinas and Georgia, bypassing quite another composite of Renaissance details, largely Virginian and Palladian in origin, which took firm root in bluegrass Tennessee and Kentucky and their dependencies. All together, these diversifying variations in American Free Classicism reached their fullest expression in the 1840s and 1850s.

It is important to note, however, that the Greek Revival did not thrive everywhere; the columnar mansion became the symbolic architecture of the culture of the uplands, but not of the Tidewater or of the mountains. The Greek Revival plantation house scarcely exists in the truly old South, tidewater Virginia and South Carolina, and it is even rarer in the mountain South.[3]

It is the chief expression of a planter class raising sugar and cotton with slave labor and selling those staples into world markets at violently unstable prices, going deeply into debt to buy land and labor, enjoying huge profits in some years and suffering disaster in others. The classic sobriety of their architecture gainsaid the rampant alcoholism of the planters' lifestyle; its implications of duration and stability belied the terrifying fluctuations of the planters' fortunes.

The key to understanding the history of the columnar mansion is that it represents a fresh synthesis of new ordering ideas and traditional forms, a synthesis forged in the heat of the expansion of the plantation South into the Mississippi Delta and northern Alabama. After the old forms acquired their new components along that western frontier,

226

The Greek Revival style of the North: the Fitch-Gorham-Brooks House, built around 1840 in Marshall, Michigan. *Photo ©1990 by Jack Kotz*

the columnar mansion, so created, was carried backward into central Georgia, Tennessee, and even to the Carolinas. It spread into central Florida and even, by a quirk, into the region between Boston and Worcester, Massachusetts, carried there by Yankee architects who had encountered it while working for their Georgia clients.

After laying out something of the story of how the two traditions, the Jeffersonian-Palladian and the creole, came to be available in the

Delta, we will observe how three gifted architects, one English, one German, and one emphatically a Yankee, effected the synthesis to which we have referred and created the Old South's predominant symbol. They were Levi Weeks, William Nichols, and Charles Reichardt.

Why Greek?

Let us jettison at the outset any embarrassment about accepting the term used by the Americans who built the Greek Revival. They called it that and we may too — though we may note in passing how unscholarly they were, if so doing makes us proud — to cover any orderly buildings with columns, rectilinear or square, constructed in the first half of the nineteenth century.

These might just as well have been called Roman Revival, but at the time they were built Americans were intensely sympathetic with the Greek struggle for independence from the Turkish Empire. And the Founding Fathers had made it clear that it was Greece, not Rome, that had the sort of history with which a gentleman would wish to associate his columns.

Besides, both George III and Napoleon had been celebrated as Roman by their court painters, tailors, and architects. Americans felt little affinity either for the king, against whose imperialism they had remonstrated in the Declaration of Independence, or for the emperor, whose regime they perceived as a betrayal of the ideals of the French Revolution. Bonaparte had quite explicitly preempted grand-scale Roman architecture to glorify himself — the Arc de Triomphe celebrated the triumph of despotism.

So the antebellum South received its symbol. This essay is about the diversity of Greek Revival houses in the antebellum South, suggesting something of what that diversity means. Architecture is a useful tool in understanding the culture that creates it; that is why many travelers buy architectural guides. We can learn a great deal about the South if we are not troubled by a wild variety of buildings all claiming to be Greek, something none of them are.[+] They are American. What about "revival"? They do not actually claim to revive anything the ancient Greeks would readily recognize as akin either to their temples or to their houses. Greek temples upon the Acropolis, including the Parthenon, and those at Paestum, Segesta, and Agrigentum, are rectilinear stone buildings with tiled gable roofs. They have thick, heavy columns on their gable ends, with more columns or pilasters along both sides. No southern house looks like that.

Neither, of course, did the houses of classical Greece. They were more like those of Santa Fe, New Mexico, than any of the open, extroverted, porticoed, and pillared buildings of the Old South. Greek residences did not wear their columns on the outside, but inside, sparingly, and around an atrium. Greece, like New Mexico, is hot and dry, not hot and wet like most of the Old South. The ancient Greeks conducted much of their business and social life in open public places, as New Mexicans do today. Accordingly, they did not build very large houses, and they do not seem ever to have built houses with porticoes. Porticoes were for temples, showy colonnades for markets and voting places and public squares.

There is only one Greek temple building in the South and that is in Nashville, where in the early 1890s a reproduction of the Parthenon was erected for a World's Fair and has been left standing to baffle future archaeologists.

A handful of southern houses are Grecian in some of their elements or proportions, having a little better claim to the description than the others, and as we come upon them it may be useful to have at hand a small glossary of descriptive terms to identify those elements.

Some pillars are stubby, some attenuated. Roughly speaking, in Greek history they began short and grew long, from archaic Doric to Hellenistic, so when displayed in chronological order for us on the pages of textbooks, they seem to benefit from nutritional improvement, like children of the same age but in succeeding generations in family portraits.

The function of a column is to hold something up, and the shape of that something is important: a triangular burden is called a pediment, while a flat beam held up by a series of columns becomes an unpedimented colonnade. Pediments are associated with gable roofs that produce two triangles, one at each end.

Most Greek temples and Roman temples that were patterned after them were rectilinear with gable roofs. The Parthenon is the most familiar model: pediments at each end, colonnades along the sides. However, other temples also contributed ideas to the American Greek Revival. Many Roman temples were *not* rectilinear in plan but roughly round, with a pedimented portico jointed with great difficulty in front; the Pantheon is one example. The Greeks had used round forms also, but as burial places, not as temples in which they might expect much foot traffic.

A portico is a short stretch of gable roof borne by columns, like the end of a temple, sliced off. It is called monumental when it looks so. More often than not, that means that it is at least two stories tall. In this essay the word "porch" is used to mean a little portico, and "veranda" or "piazza" to mean a space outside a building under a roof, but not a gable roof.

We will not need to parse out all the American uses of ancient styles, but it is useful to bear in mind that the Greeks developed a number of distinct orders, or classes, of columns. Roman and Renaissance com-

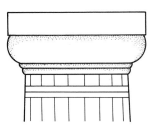

The ancient Greeks developed three orders, or classes, of columns. The Doric was the simplest, the Ionic had whorls like ram's horns, and the Corinthian was the most complex. *Illustration by Laurel Cook*

mentators insisted that each of these required quite distinct sets of associated forms.

The Doric is the simplest and stockiest of their column forms and the least animate. It is a thing straightforwardly doing its job of keeping up a roof. Its intentions and its capitals are plain.

The capital of an Ionic column has whorls, like the horns of a mountain ram. It is the most animal of the orders, recalling the use of Greek temples as places of animal sacrifice. Ionic columns are thinner than Doric columns.

The capital of a Corinthian column is the most elaborate and botanical of the three. It does its work effortlessly, almost casually, saving its energy for the aesthetic.

A column capital composed of American tobacco leaves, by Benjamin Henry Latrobe. *Monticello, Thomas Jefferson Memorial Foundation, Inc.*

The Romans made all this more complicated, the architects of the Renaissance more complicated still, and Americans patriotically added tobacco-leaf, wheat-sheaf, and corn-cob orders.

Let us look at what does exist in the South and how it came to be there, beginning with the giant portico and the biloggial portico. Architectural historians are especially irritated when the biloggial format — with one loggia above, under a triangular pedimented gable, and one below — is ascribed to a Greek revival, because there is no evidence that the Greeks ever made use of such a form. But from the onset of its reappearance west of the Appalachians, about 1825, it was called Greek and is no less so than the Roman-proportioned giant portico.

The giant portico and the biloggial portico were firmly established in America in colonial times, but neither became widely popular until the Greek Revival period. Both were deployed in hundreds of variations from the Virginia Piedmont to central Texas. I will tell their stories separately.

The Giant Portico

So far as I have been able to learn, the first Virginia portico on a "heroic" classical model was that added to James Madison's Montpelier in the 1790s, with the assistance of Thomas Jefferson. As noted in Chapter 13, neither Jefferson nor Madison made use of Greek architecture. They were Franco-Palladians, and therefore their classicism came from Rome through France by way of Venice; the name of Madison's house, its garden design, and the plans for its portico and little temple-icehouse were all French. The chief design elements were selected from the drawings in Claude Perrault's revision of the works of Vitruvius and from impressions of Palladio by Charles-Antoine Jombert and Fréart de Chambray. Later, in the 1820s and 1830s, more of these Perraultian porticoes appeared, one of them on Pavilion I at the University of Virginia.

Scions of Virginia and graduates of its University went west to the central plains of Kentucky and Tennessee. They built more Perraultian porticoes amid fields into which they introduced a crop many believe has been there for a very long time: bluegrass. Yet the architecture was "introduced" at about the time the grass was "introduced." In both the botanical and artifactual realms, the exotic has become the typical. As a result, it is pardonable to call this sort of Cumberland classicism country and western or, perhaps, Bluegrass Greek Revival.[5]

This regional expression of the Jeffersonian and Palladian — and before that the Roman — tradition became available on the Cumberland Plateau and throughout the Piedmont after three immense transitions were negotiated to get from Pericles to Andrew Jackson. The first resulted from the conquest of Greece by Rome and the absorption of

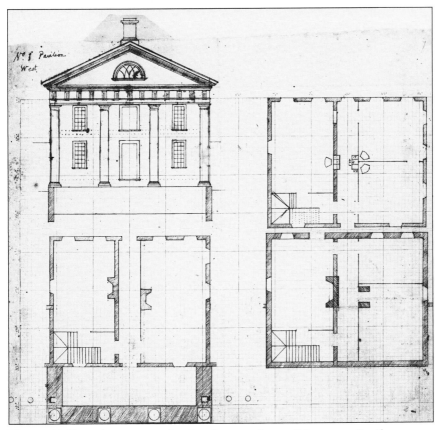

Thomas Jefferson's prototype for the giant porticoes of the upper South: Pavilion I of the University of Virginia. *Thomas Jefferson Papers, Special Collections Department, Manuscript Division, University of Virginia Library*

many Greek ideas by the Romans. Beginning with Augustus Caesar, Roman emperors expressed in architecture the vainglorious notion that if the army makes a man chief of state for life, it makes him ex officio sufficiently godlike to give his house a portico. Porticoes, even in Rome, had hitherto been reserved for temples, the habitations of gods. Commencing about the time of Christ, the religious significance of the portico was trivialized as it was domesticated by a succession of Roman juntas.

The additions by the Romans to the post-and-beam repertory of Greek domestic architecture — their use of rounded forms: domes and arches — were carried over into the American Greek Revival without regard to archaeological niceties. Our public buildings and most of our larger Greek Revival residences are Romanized by roundness at their apertures — doors and windows — and along their hallways. Our courthouses, churches, and banks designed in this style are generally built about central spaces topped by domes or entered by interior vaulted arcades.

There is another Roman element in our Greek Revival: its delight in contrived and artificial effects — sham, Louis Sullivan might have called it. Form followed fancy, not function; American Free Classicism is full of dropped ceilings, false domes, and tricks with light for which the classical sanction is Roman, not Greek.

The second transition was from a real Rome to an imaginary one reconstituted from ruins by the Italians of the sixteenth century. The architectural consequences of bringing the gods down to the imperial level and emperors up to meet them reappeared in Renaissance Italy after 1500 and in the United States after 1830. The American Greek Revival is indebted to this second transition, carried out not by a junta but by a syndicate. The residential portico was deployed by Venetian architects to flatter the members of that syndicate, a closely related set of merchants who were recoiling from the Levant trade and reinvesting their profits in estates on the Italian mainland, thereby creating splendid commissions for new plantation headquarters. Palladio, Sansovino, and before them the painter Mantegna used porticoes to assure these trader-planters that if not godlike or even imperial, they were, in the terms of Palladio, "munificent" and "glorious."[6]

Scholarly eighteenth-century Virginians and Carolinians knew their Palladio, who made available to them this process of glorification of traders-become-planters. In Virginia the descendants of English townsmen like the Byrds, Washingtons, and Carters became squires, and by the 1770s Thomas Jefferson, the most widely read in architecture of these cosmopolitan countrymen, completed the first, bookish phase in the transfer of Renaissance ideas to America — completed it; he did not initiate it. The process had been powerfully at work for half a century.

As a result, the groundwork was laid for the Greek Revival during the colonial period, though its full flowering did not occur until the 1830s and 1840s. This was true for the giant portico, and as we will observe, it was true as well for the biloggial portico and the creole cottage ripe for classicizing. Though in the first two, Palladian elements were little changed by the Greek Revival, in the 1830s and 1840s they entered a field of psychological and political force that exploded their use from the occasional deployment by an elite into immense popularity. Only in the United States was the classical revival popular enough to enter the vernacular; it became an expression of resurgent nationalism and pride. Tens of thousands of humble citizens became classical builders.

The monumental portico of Roman proportions, later so conspicuous at the University of Virginia and in Tennessee and its colonies in Florida, Arkansas, and Texas, first appeared in a forgotten protoportico

233

for Saint Philip's Church in Charleston in 1723. Saint Philip's was destroyed in 1835, but Saint Michael's (1751–1760) is still there to remind us of Charleston's prodigious Palladian 1740s and 1750s and of another of its lost monuments, the pediment and monumental pilasters of the Charles Pinckney House, built in 1745.

While Saint Michael's was under construction, the parishioners of Prince William's Chapel in Sheldon, South Carolina, created a perfect, small, brick Roman temple. Burned twice, it is now a ruin. Prince William's was drawn from a Scottish–neo-Palladian design by Colin Campbell, just as Saint Michael's comes from a Scottish–neo-Palladian concept of James Gibbs. Campbell or Gibbs or William Kent could claim paternity for the basic design of the porticoed Redwood Library in Newport, Rhode Island, adapted by Peter Harrison, a local architect, in 1748. As far as we know, America's first house with a giant portico

Colin Campbell's design for a church "in the Vitruvian style" was a prototype for Prince William's Chapel in Sheldon, South Carolina, and many other buildings.

234

appeared outside Annapolis when Governor Horatio Sharpe of Maryland built Whitehall in 1764–1765.[7]

The Biloggial Format

A second element to find its way into the Greek Revival reached the American lexicon in these same decades. It also owes something to the propulsion of Thomas Jefferson's influence, though it too was an Italian idea already "in play" in the British colonies in North America before Jefferson discovered it. This was the biloggial portico, using two tiers of columns under a pediment as the centerpiece of a main façade, a Venetian idea *not* picked up by the English Palladians. Instead, it became commonplace in France from the time of Hardouin-Mansart (1646–1708) onward. Somehow this un-English, Franco-Venetian idea reached

The ruins of Prince William's Chapel, the first temple-form building in North America.

South Carolina at the end of the 1730s and coastal Virginia twenty years later.

Drayton Hall, on the Ashley River near Charleston, was built between 1738 and 1742, and Miles Brewton redeployed the format for his mansion, in the city itself, at the end of the 1750s. Brewton had made a town house out of a Palladian villa, as Major Pierre-Charles L'Enfant made a nation's capitol of it when he designed Federal Hall, the first capitol of the United States, in the 1790s. By that time the Brewton town house scheme had spread southward from Charleston along the coast to become the dominant motif in Beaufort in the 1780s and thereafter crept westward into the Piedmont of South and North Carolina.

It had appeared in Virginia between 1750 and 1753. The second capitol at Williamsburg acquired biloggial porticoes. One was added to a strange Franco-Dutch plantation house on the James, Shirley, which already had a mansard roof, an *allée* of poplars, and a tight, anti-Palladian, un-English forecourt.[8]

Thomas Jefferson's sketch for the first Monticello, of the 1770s and 1780s.
Massachusetts Historical Society

These were the circumstances when Thomas Jefferson reached architectural consciousness. He wrote of the second Williamsburg capitol (not its predecessor, reconstructed in the 1930s) that it was "the most pleasing piece of architecture we have." His approval was made tangible in the 1770s in his first version of Monticello, a biloggial house like Shirley and the second capitol.

Jefferson tore down this unfinished version of Monticello after he returned from France in 1789; he had encountered such enormous French and Dutch demonstrations of the grandeur of the format, in marble, that it may have lost its lure (see *Orders from France*). But he continued to recommend it to such friends as Matthew Page of Annfield.

It is touching and perhaps ironic that this form, rejected by Jefferson for his own use, was taken up by Andrew Jackson for the third Hermitage in Tennessee in 1831. Like Monticello I, Hermitage III has disappeared. It burned and was replaced by Hermitage IV, the final version one visits today.

Meanwhile, however, the biloggial example had been pursued by planters in Tennessee and Kentucky. From there it spread through northern Alabama, eastern Arkansas, and into the upland red-clay cotton-growing sections of Louisiana and Texas. It was a shy flower of Jeffersonian classicism compared to the trumpeting Romanism of the descendants of the University of Virginia. But it sustained its charm as late as 1851, when some wanderer made use of it to complete the central building of Fort Union, on the Missouri River on the Dakota-Montana line. Far from the Veneto, fur traders marked the extremity of the Renaissance. Smoking cigars at sundown, they were unlikely to have given much more thought to Mantegna, Palladio, Hardouin-Mansart, or Jefferson than they did to Greece.

The Classicizing Professionals Arrive

In the 1780s and 1790s the American Greek Revival was brought closer by three Europeans who knew Greek and Roman work at first hand and aided the infant republic in making use of the lessons of these classics to develop its first national style. While Jefferson was in Paris in 1784–1789, he was assisted by Jacques-Louis Clérisseau, antiquary and archaeologist, in designing a Roman temple form for the Virginia state capitol. Nothing like it had been built in Europe for human occupation (as distinguished from garden ornament or stage scenery), nor would another appear there until twenty more years had passed.

A decade after the Virginia capitol was in place, the first two professionally trained architects, Benjamin Henry Latrobe and George Hadfield, appeared in the United States. Like Clérisseau, they had actually seen Greek work in Italy, though Latrobe, while proclaiming the purity of his Greek intentions, brought more of Rome than Greece (and more of Palladio than Rome) to America. In all the buildings in which Latrobe made use of porticoes with Greek proportions, he placed a domed space behind — the Pantheon, and its spherical form, was often in his mind; he never made anything so much like the rectilinear, pedimented, domeless Parthenon as Jefferson's capitol.

From Jefferson, Hadfield, and Latrobe sprang, after a lapse of nearly two decades, the flowering of American Free Classicism. (It was never scrupulous about the exactitude of its references, Greek or Roman; though we Americans ought to leave quotation marks around "Greek" in our Greek Revival, we don't.) At its core was a small number of residential buildings and a few more public buildings that can almost properly be said to be Greek. They are largely the progeny of Hadfield's two great buildings in the nation's capital: Arlington House, Doric and residential, and City Hall, Ionic and monumental.

The Politics of Style: The Greek Revival, Federalist and Whig

The first building in America to be created with massive Greek proportions — though with un-Greek wings — was Arlington House, built by

Arlington House, also known as the Custis-Lee Mansion, in Arlington, Virginia, was designed for George Washington Parke Custis by George Hadfield and built between 1802 and 1819. *Photo ©1990 by Jack Kotz*

238

George Hadfield for George Washington Parke Custis between 1802 and 1819. It was a patriarchic and political statement, and so were all the other Greek temple-form houses built in the South thereafter.

Arlington House was a shrine to General George Washington, Custis's stepgrandfather by adoption. He was also the Father of His Country and of the Federalist party. It is probable that the granddaughter of the arch-Federalist chief justice, John Marshall, looked back to Arlington in 1840, when she added a Greek portico to Ashleigh, near The Plains, Virginia. She had no special reason to defer to the other amalgamator of Grecian and conservative sentiment, Nicholas Biddle, to whom the other Greek temple-form house in the South, Berry Hill (1842–1844), was implicitly dedicated. It was built by James Coles Bruce as a tribute to Biddle, his mentor and patriarch of the Second National Bank. Biddle was assiduous in propagating the Greek Revival. He helped establish it in Philadelphia, remodeling his own house, Andalusia, into a temple and influencing the creation of Philadelphia's two most important civic buildings of the era, Girard College and the Second

Tennessee Romanism: Clifton Place in Mount Pleasant. *Photo by Jack Kotz*

Neoclassicism comes to Mississippi: the rotunda of the old state capitol in Jackson, designed by William Nichols in 1839 and subsequently remodeled and extended. *Photo by Jack Kotz*

The Senate Chamber of the old state capitol. *Photo by Jack Kotz*

America's finest Regency interior: Gainswood (1842–1860) in Demopolis, Alabama. *Photo by Jack Kotz*

Berry Hill, the James Coles Bruce house near Halifax, Virginia, was built between 1842 and 1844. It is the central structure in a Greek Revival complex that drew upon the lessons taught by Bruce's mentor, Nicholas Biddle, in Philadelphia. © *Wayne Andrews, ESTO*

Bank of the United States. Even before the construction of Ashleigh, Levin Marshall, a cousin of its mistress, though drawn by political and commercial ties to Philadelphia and the Whigs rather than to Washington and the Federalists, provided a Greek front section to Richmond, his house in Natchez, around 1832. Levin Marshall was one of Biddle's financial and political agents.

A similar addition was made to Donelson Hall (sometimes called Cleveland Hall) near Nashville by Andrew Jackson's nephew, Andrew Jackson Donelson, after he had gone over to the Whigs from Jackson's party in 1839. His was a gesture of disaffection rather than full-tilt, whole-house revolt — just an addition, not an entire new Biddlean creation.[9]

Though the temple-form Greek Revival house with prominent Palladian wings is a northern, not a southern, phenomenon, the exception to

Richmond, the Levin Marshall house in Natchez.

that rule is one of its finest American expressions, Madewood (1846–1848), on the Bayou Lafourche near Napoleonville, Louisiana. It was designed by the Irish-trained Henry Howard for Thomas Pugh, an arch-Whig and sugar magnate. Its similarity to many other Whiggish mansions in the Finger Lakes region of New York, in Ohio, and in Michigan is very suggestive, but to follow the suggestion and inquire as to how it came to be would lead us on a scenic detour by way of New York, Brooklyn, Northampton, Massachusetts, and the Erie Canal, a detour lying beyond the Mason-Dixon Line and the bounds of this essay.[10]

The Creole Cottage in a Village Tradition

The other most important and widespread variety of the southern Greek Revival was the classicized creole cottage of the Mississippi Delta and of piedmont Georgia.

Opposite: **The Louisiana creole cottage has a long history and a wide range. The earliest known example appears in the background of this painting of 1641 from Brazil. Later instances can be found from Hawaii to Manitoba and Arizona, well into the twentieth century.** *From Thomas Thomsen's* Albert Eckhout

Its history is not like that of the Palladian plantations of Greater Tennessee or of the temple-form houses in the South or North. It is a new creation, without precedent in the Old World. It revives nothing; its bone structure is continuous with that of the American raised cottage, and though it became clothed with classical columns and caparisoned with classical details, it remains the least Greek of all Greek Revival forms."

But it owes its existence to the presence on the southern land of professional, classically trained architects to a greater degree than is the case in the Palladian progression, which was largely conveyed through books.

In Louisiana the term "creole cottage" is customarily confined to a vernacular form, often asymmetrical and one room deep, under a high-pitched roof with galleries all or nearly all around. Louisianians have come to describe this simple West Indian format as having abandoned its "vernacular" status and having gone "high style" when it straightens itself into symmetry and acquires another range of rooms to become "double pile." They regard it as deprived of vernacular purity when the unbroken French sequence of rooms is interrupted by a central hall of Anglo-American Georgian origin. But there is a good reason to use the term "classicized creole cottage" to describe all hip-roofed, two-story, roughly cubical houses with columns all or nearly all around and classical — Greek or Roman — details. By doing so, we are more likely to give proper credit to the West Indian influence that supplied the basic cottage form to be classicized and extended far beyond the Caribbean.

We have observed that most of the essential elements which later developed into the American Greek Revival were in place by the end of the colonial era. Among them was the raised cottage with an extended high-pitched roof supported by spindly posts, common since the 1750s along the seaboard from Maine to Florida and west to Texas. Americans had completed the adaptation of this Caribbean idea to their own materials and behavior. Then, after 1816 and in large numbers after 1830, Americans were emboldened to classicize this cottage by thickening its columns, formalizing the rectilinearity of its doorways and window openings, and adding their own free versions of Greek ornament.

As a result, the classicized creole cottages that cluster in the villages of Georgia, along the lower Mississippi, the Louisiana bayous, and in low-country Texas differ from the Jeffersonian plantations to be found in the interior of the South. Whatever else they may have in common, the "pure" cottages do not have pedimented porticoes, whereas the houses descended from Palladio and Jefferson, best seen in western Virginia, Kentucky, and Tennessee, do.

Europeans did not invent the creole cottage. Native Americans were building their own versions when the Europeans arrived, and Africans

The Waoli Mission on the island of Kauai, apparently a creole cottage in the mid-Pacific, but in reality a natural adaptation to a climate similar to that of the Windward Islands of the West Indies. *Photo by Robert Jay*

had been building somewhat different but related cottages, with tall roofs and extended eaves supported by posts, for centuries. Its evolution to the format of Tara required several stops along the way; it is strange but true that this evolution has until recently received almost no serious study. Lately, however, we have been able to piece together a plausible timetable of the stages by which Mr. Selznick's fundamental symbol first became available in the Old South.[12]

When I wrote *Architecture, Men, Women, and Money* in the early 1980s, a survey of received wisdom indicated that no galleried houses had been described or depicted in the New World prior to 1730, and a few previously *thought* to have been earlier had been demonstrated to be additions of the mid-eighteenth century. But since then, Louisiana's Jay Edwards has found examples in Brazil from 1637 to 1644, in Jamaica from 1655, one in Louisiana from 1704, another on the Gulf Coast from 1726, and documentary hints that there were some built in the late 1720s in New Orleans. As the result of his delving we know that travelers coming to anchor in ports from Albany to Bahía, Port Royal, or Galveston might, indeed, have seen on the shore houses with galleries well before 1730. The general outburst of gallerinizing occurred after that date, true, and

The La Cour House, a creole cottage of about 1750 and the oldest extant house in Louisiana.

that gallerinizing seldom took on classical proportions until yet another century had passed.

After 1730 there *was* a craze for galleries and piazzas by people building along the shores of the navigable rivers of both North and South America and on innumerable islands between. Piazzas and "sitting porches" appeared everywhere: on the St. Lawrence, the Hudson, the Tombigbee, the bayous of the Mississippi Delta, on Shelter Island, Staten Island, Jamaica, and Barbados. There were few professional architects available, even among the extravagantly rich planters of the West Indies (probably the richest private citizens in the world). There were not even enough copies of the printed texts carrying pictures or descriptions of classical buildings to permit the creation of colonnades of columns of classical heft — so far as we know.

Massive classicism seems to have awaited the appearance on the scene of people who were sufficiently serious about themselves as architects to give that as their profession and, as if so emboldened, to lead their clients to classicize their raised cottages. That happened first in Mississippi, then in Alabama, and thereafter throughout upland North America, though seldom on the seaboard.

The first raised cottage to be surrounded by a range of classical columns instead of two tiers of spindly posts was a house called The Forest, built by the widow Dunbar in Natchez in 1816 or 1817. The likeliest runner-up is Forks of Cypress, erected in northern Alabama a decade later. Only after these prototypes were built came that rush of classicizing which did, indeed, make the form the most familiar symbol of the antebellum South.[13]

The Forest replaced a "big square white plantation house deep in the oak woods . . . [with a] verandah . . . one floor above the ground" built about 1790 by the scientist, physiocrat, physician, and planter William Dunbar soon after he determined that he would make his career in American Natchez rather than in Spanish Louisiana. Dunbar died in 1810; his widow, the equally remarkable Dinah Clark, tore down the old house and built in its place "a large square brick mansion surrounded by a double gallery" of Tuscan columns, two stories high.[14]

The Forest, probably the first house in America to have classical columns all the way around. *Courtesy of the Mississippi Department of Archives and History*

Stubby one-story Tuscan pillars had earlier appeared in Louisiana, supporting a *gallerie,* above which a second, thinner set of posts would rise to the extended eaves of the roof. But the great pillars at The Forest are probably the deliberate classicizing legacy of a friend of the Dunbars, a feisty, relentlessly creative architect bent upon bringing the "orders" to the raw villages of the West. He was Levi Weeks (1776–1819), formerly of Deerfield, Massachusetts. In 1800 he had rallied the carpenter-builders and contractors of New York City into a professional society called the Brethren of the Order of Vitruvius, a subset of the Masons. Alone of its members, Weeks refused to describe himself merely as a builder or artisan. Like Latrobe or Hadfield, he thought of himself as a gentleman, insisting that though he was self-taught, he be called an architect.

Weeks had a way of intriguing the gentry into taking him seriously. His charm and energy served him well in New York, where his career might have come to an end on the gallows. Powerful friends rallied to his support when he was charged with murdering his mistress and dumping her body into a public well. His successful defense was managed by Alexander Hamilton, Aaron Burr, and Brockholst Livingston.

Weeks followed his friend Burr to Natchez, where he found other powerful clients among the Yankee Burrites who dominated the town. Weeks built a bank, a church, and finally, in 1812, a complete residence, Auburn, for Lyman Harding, formerly of Massachusetts. Weeks gave Harding, who had been attorney for Burr, "Ionic columns with the Corinthian entablature . . . the first house in the territory on which was ever attempted any of the orders of architecture."[15]

Like The Forest, Auburn is an immensely important prototype in American architecture. Yet in another sense it is a retrotype, for it looks backward to the middle of the eighteenth century. Only one of the builder's guides in Weeks's library was written after 1760, so it is not surprising that he produced another retrospection in his Jefferson College design of 1817. This was a year for looking backward; Thomas Jefferson began, at the same time, offering Virginians an anthology of Palladian paradigms for the University of Virginia. This Natchez-Charlottesville axis set the tone for the conservative Palladian tone in the residential architecture of Greater Tennessee, which prevailed over the more venturesome, more Greek forms appearing elsewhere over the next three decades.[16]

That was not the audience to which The Forest was addressed by the widow Dunbar and by Weeks in his other, bolder mood. Though the conservatives thought Auburn "the handsomest house about Natchez," those who wanted to apply classical ideas freshly to American conditions turned to the example of The Forest. There are no documents tying Weeks to it directly, but we know that the Dunbars were among his earliest friends in Natchez, that Harding was their attorney as well, and that no one else in the territory at the time, or for some time thereafter, was capable of taking such an extraordinary leap forward.

Architecture is a conservative art, especially amid the anxieties of the frontier. A full-tilt classical revival is radical in practice, however antiquarian it may seem in theory after the fact. A decade passed before another bold client, in this case a man, found reassurance in the presence of another experienced architect to reiterate the lesson of The Forest.

The client was an Irish-American horse breeder and cotton planter, James Jackson, who created the South's second fully peripteral (columns all around) house, Forks of Cypress, near Florence, Alabama, about 1828. The architect was probably William Nichols of Bath, in Somersetshire.

Nichols came to America around 1803 and practiced in North Carolina for nearly thirty years, experimenting in a variety of classical applications to American conditions. Then, after a sojourn in New Orleans, he received commissions to design most of the public buildings in the new capital cities of Alabama and Mississippi. In Montgomery he centered his work on a colonnaded rotunda for the University of Alabama and provided plans for neighboring planters to add colonnades to their hip-roofed houses.

Thereafter, thousands of upcountry, landlocked raised cottages were remodeled to gain classical dignity. Thousands more were newly and classically built, with an enthusiasm equal to that of the piazza craze of a century earlier. The readiness clearly was there. Apparently what was required was the presence of European architects to preside over this aspect of the last Renaissance, this final transition from Greek temples to American Free Classicism.

One of the Europeans effecting that transition was Charles Reichardt, who was trained at Potsdam by the celebrated Karl Friedrich Schinkel. Reichardt was in New York by 1834 and at the end of the decade had executed a series of projects in South Carolina for the Hampton family. He gave classical panache to two of their mansions, a new creation, Milford, and a remodeled Millwood, which was given the first of these fully peripteral colonnades *east* of the Appalachians.

The extended kinship of the Hamptons of South Carolina was essential to the popularizing of the classicized creole cottage. Before the War of 1812, the patriarch of the tribe, General Wade Hampton, was in Louisiana, putting down slave revolts, acquainting himself with the richness of delta soil, and acquiring plantations. He took an avid interest in the use of steam engines to operate cotton gins and in new methods of sugar refining brought there by refugees from other slave revolts in Saint Domingue, as the French called that part of Hispaniola which today is called Haiti.

The general's sons, daughters, and sons-in-law learned other things in the region: French formal garden design and the utility of the creole cottage as a residential form for hot, humid climates. And they set the social and equestrian standard for the parvenu planters of the cotton-growing new South. The Hamptons and John Jackson completed the work begun by Dinah Clark Dunbar, classicizing the creole cottage, with the assistance of the cosmopolitan training and adaptability to new conditions of Levi Weeks, William Nichols, and Charles Reichardt.

The Hamptons were the largest absentee landowners in Mississippi, and their tribe of cousins owned tens of thousands of acres in Alabama as well. Their lesson was irresistible; a thousand white-columned houses appeared after the flowering of Hampton mansions. Many of them were set amid French gardens like those of Houmas House, the chief Hampton mansion in Louisiana, and the Houmas-like garden at Millwood.

The Social Structure Beneath the Architecture

Though they owned plantations in Mississippi, Alabama, and Arkansas, the Hamptons were rooted in Charleston. The association of village life to the classicized cottage form was reinforced by their identity as Charlestonians. Their great houses were built in upland South Carolina beyond the reach of navigable rivers, but they sustained Charleston's urban bias. Wherever their overseers might live, *they* kept together, not quite in compounds but in clusters of great houses, almost as if they were living in a port city.

The houses they built and the creole cottages created by their friends along the Mississippi were characteristic of a different kind of agriculture and social structure from those represented by either of the Palladian forms. Most sugar and rice planters built classicized creole cottages, and most voted Whig because Whigs were for "protection," meaning heavy taxation of imported sugar and rice. It is also true that the members of the cotton- and sugar-growing "Natchez Junto" were famous for their staunch Federalism and later Whiggery. They tended to eschew the architectural symbols of Jacksonian Tennessee, though only subtle distinctions separate their porticoed forms from Tennessee Romanism. Natchez was an anthology of antebellum forms: beside its porticoed houses are enlarged cottages with verandas, evocations of its ties to the creole culture lying southward in the Delta.

Like most of the larger planters of the Georgia Piedmont, the builders of these raised cottages drew credit from branches of Nicholas Biddle's bank. And after the War of 1812, during which the New England Federalists had threatened secession once too many times, these southerners went over to the Whigs *because* they were Unionist. The richest among them feared the loss of their virtual monopoly of the best farmlands of Arkansas if the protection of the contracts clause of the federal Constitution were removed, so they regarded Jefferson Davis, who came from the backcountry, with horror. They were rich and content and therefore more conservative than planters living farther inland. Fertile land was getting scarce in upland Mississippi and Alabama, and even more scarce in Andrew Jackson's Tennessee. Sitting under their Jeffersonian porticoes amid the Mississippi sandhills and the Alabama wiregrass and pine barrens, the smaller and somewhat poorer planters rallied behind Davis, recalling the Kentucky and Virginia Resolutions and talking nullification and, ultimately, southern secession.

Louisianians might not think of Georgia as the first place to look for white cottagelike buildings with columns all around, but it is. In the 1940s and 1950s Wilbur Zelinsky drove every dusty road in Georgia, and the few paved ones, and noted on his map the location of every house with a columned façade. Nine out of ten of them were located in towns, not in the countryside. These were not plantation headquarters, as the villas of Palladio had been. They were the houses of investor-owners huddling in villages at a great distance from their plantations. In Georgia overseers, not owners, lived on the land among the slaves.

The same semiurban pattern is characteristic of several villages in Mississippi, of which Natchez and Columbus are the most famous. These towns, with their neat, suburban, columned villas within hailing distance of one another, were built by the new rich of the first new South. Though they spoke of themselves as if they were squires and dreamed of chivalry, they were, instead, agents of a system anticipating the multinationality of modern capitalism. Their markets and their prices were set in Liverpool, Manchester, and Lowell, and their work force was supplied by an international slave trade. Chivalry was made of other stuff.

These Georgia and Mississippi market villages, which seem so sweet today, represented a brash, upland stage in the life of the South, away from the old ways of the merchant-planters of Virginia, Maryland, and tidewater North Carolina, who sold tobacco grown on fields visible from their own bedroom windows, from their own wharves, directly to their buyers. The largest cotton growers of Georgia and Mississippi were absentee owners operating through overseers and selling their cotton indirectly and collectively. In their market ports, such as Natchez and New Orleans, their crop was entrusted to agents (factors), who were often more powerful than the planters themselves.

Though the absentee landowners and merchant princes of the Piedmont and of Natchez grew immensely rich during the cotton boom of the 1850s, their status was always fragile. Despite their brave talk of King Cotton, they were several stages removed from the places where their economic fate was negotiated. Natchez looked downriver to New Orleans for capital and commercial leadership. In the Crescent City, Yankee-born merchants, bankers, wholesalers, and factors created a sudden suburb of the newly rich, now known as the Upper Garden District. But they, too, lacked sufficient capital to assure their own fate; as early as the 1820s the failure of one factor, Vincent Nolte, to secure additional

European credit had plunged the whole system into a depression. In the 1850s they looked to Philadelphia, and over their shoulders to their clients and partners in Natchez.

Though Natchez, like New Orleans, had a broad river at its door, most Georgia towns and the centers where upland planters of Mississippi and Alabama traded were landlocked. It is important to note that even away from navigation, the great houses of the planters were not dispersed on their plantations; instead, they were concentrated in villages. This was possibly because their founders recalled the traditional significance of the fortress towns built by the French in the region: Mobile, New Orleans, and Natchez itself. But it is more likely that the crystallizing idea emerged from another, British, urban tradition. Most of these planters had emigrated from a region dominated by Charleston and Savannah, the only two compact fortified cities built by the British in the South.

These dense, powerful towns ruled the countryside. Their founders owned plantations beyond the city limits, but they seldom built plantation houses of any grandeur there; social life was town life, within the walls. The inhabitants of Charleston were described as huddled within "forts, half moons, platforms, entrenchments, flankers and parapets, sally ports, a gate and a drawbridge and blind."

We are not talking here of Charleston and Savannah as seats of Greek Revival architecture but of their role in setting an urban tone to the patterns of emigration, which went westward from Georgia and the Carolinas. The course of empire took Carolinians across central Georgia, where their memories of Charleston were reinforced by the peculiarly militant urbanism of Georgia. Oglethorpe's colony had been intended as a border province, laid out and settled by captains, those rectilineating "marchers" (see Chapter 13), some of whom had dreamt of rising to become suzerains of a domain such as Carolana or the margravate of Azilia (see Chapter 1).

Savannah was only the first of six early Georgia towns established by military engineers in the form of fortified camps like those of the ancient Romans. This Georgia-Carolina tradition of the *castrum* built around a central campus (see Chapter 13) was reinforced when the Anglo-Americans invaded the Mississippi Valley and found French and Spanish villages-as-encampments and garrison-towns-as-missions.

The sugar planters of Louisiana, like the indigo planters who preceded them, had settled into habits more European than American as their wealth grew under French and Spanish rule. They met frequently to concert their actions and were accustomed to the guidance of centralized authority. The technological devices that made them so rich had been provided by the state or by religious orders; the commercial manufacture of indigo and, forty years later, of sugar were Jesuit contribu-

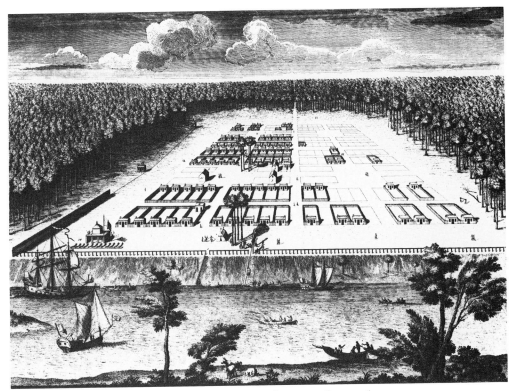

Peter Gordon's application of the *campus martius* format to Savannah, 1734.
Courtesy of the Georgia Department of Archives and History

tions to the Louisiana economy. They brought crops to market concert-edly in New Orleans through its factoring system.

Though their strings of plantation headquarters along the great river and the bayous do not at first glance seem urban, they were extended, upper-class, linear villages. The market was reached by water; visiting was done by water. Safety from slave revolts could be found by retreat-ing from the shore. Roads hardly existed, so the planters reinforced one another by boat.

The planters along the Teche or in the Feliciana parishes lived in attenuated villages more like Natchez or New Orleans than met the eye. Where these linear villages came together, residences could actually be seen in clusters.

The classicized creole cottage *is* more urban in outlook than the Roman designs of the planters of the upper South. The Tennesseans had emigrated from the Chesapeake region, where plantation headquarters of resident owner-managers were also strung out along navigable rivers, but with different results architecturally and psychologically from the creole culture along the bayous. I offer a hypothesis that this was because the planters of the James looked to the English *country* squire-archy as their paradigm.

However that may be, the distended — or expanded — Chesapeake pattern reappeared in the West where Virginia and Maryland emigration predominated. This observation may be confirmed by some current research on the location of the churches built by the delta and bayou planters who were also the most consistent builders of classicized creole cottages. They seem to have gone to church in their villages. Their peers of the Tidewater went to the crossroads, and so after them did their descendants in Tennessee and the colonies of Tennessee — Arkansas, red-dirt Louisiana, east Texas, Alabama north of Muscle Shoals, and north Florida.

The crossroads church, or the church built at the intersection of huge landholdings occupied by resident owner-managers, is a Chesapeake and Tennessee phenomenon, extending into the upland cotton lands where the wealthier planters built brick houses with porticoes in the Roman fashion. Saint John's in Maury County, Tennessee, built by the Polks where their plantations came together, recalls Christ Church, Lancaster County, Virginia, built a century earlier by "King" Carter at the intersection of Carter lands.

Finally we turn back northward, into the Bluegrass country of Tennessee and Kentucky, for one last look at the architectural consequences of the Chesapeake migration. We noted the transmission to this new, or second, South of the symmetrical plantation headquarters, descended by way of Thomas Jefferson from one of the forms of the Palladian villa. Between Andrea Palladio and Jefferson in the process of transmission, largely carried on through books, were such British Palladians as Inigo Jones and John Webb in the seventeenth century and such British and French neo-Palladians as Lord Burlington in the eighteenth. Jefferson and his circle might therefore be called neo-neo-Palladians.

The hallmark of this tradition is the ordering of a hierarchy of building blocks centered on an imperious, pedimented portico. The houses of the new South west of the Appalachians simplified the pattern — three neos now — and were generally of one block only. They are rectilinear, not square like creole cottages, with the portico on the long side.

A Palladian social structure accompanied this Palladian architectural structure. The Venetians ashore consciously re-created in the Veneto the latifundia, the huge, diversified plantations of the Romans, and two centuries after the Venetians, so did the great planters of Virginia and Maryland. Their kindest gift to their descendants of Tennessee was neither the Roman idea of the plantation nor the Roman idea of a "noble" portico. Instead it was acknowledging the lesson of excessive reliance on a single crop, to which I referred in Chapter 7. Though their crops had been diversified at the very beginning, by the end of the seventeenth century they were already drawn into excessive reliance on tobacco. Its pernicious effects were clear within seventy years, and the wisest among them strove to diversify into wheat and other crops.

That passion for diversification increased as the Chesapeake social structure, accompanied by the rectilinear, porticoed form, spread with successive waves of emigration across the Appalachians. This form came to dominate Kentucky and Tennessee, and by way of Tennessee the environs of Tallahassee, Florida, upper Alabama, and east Texas. There it became characterized as a large, highly diversified estate managed by the resident of the porticoed "big house." These plantation headquarters were widely separated, as their proprietors, unlike the citizens of Natchez or New Orleans or the villages of piedmont Georgia, lived in the midst of their field slaves. Many of the products of Greater Tennessee were grown for local consumption, not for sale into international markets. Corn, wheat, rye, cattle, and horses were (and are) raised along with some tobacco and cotton.

Though the architecture of the latifundiasts of Greater Tennessee was derived from that of their ancestors among the early tobacco growers of Maryland, their revenues were not so dependent on international pricing mechanisms, which still determined the fortunes of the cotton and rice planters of the lowland South and Georgia.

Those fortunes were, of course, determined by political factors that supervened all these interwoven but essentially evanescent considerations. The entire system that produced the southern Greek Revival was based upon racially based slavery and was therefore archaic. It became more and more obvious that this was the case, as slavery was bounded by laws representing the judgment of its contemporaries. It was forbidden to spread north of the Ohio River by the Northwest Ordinance in 1787. Though the hasty and tragic equivocation of the Kansas-Nebraska Act of 1854 abrogated the legal inhibitions on slavery's spread west of Missouri, it took no firm hold upon the plains. Southward the limits had already been set by the abolition of slavery in Mexico in 1829.

The southern Greek Revival existed for scarcely three decades, during which a bitterly divided nation lived in uneasy equipoise between fear and pride. The South consoled itself with an architecture that implied a permanence it knew it could not enjoy and a balance it did not feel.

15

....

The Search for the Source
The Heroism of Giacomo Beltrami

A PERSON who has no interest in the source of rivers is unlikely
to have an interest in the origin or cause of anything else. I do
not wish to know him, or even her. Give me life's plaintiffs,
not its perpetual respondents; give me those who in the 1820s
could be found sloshing up the headwaters of the Amazon, the Niger,
the Congo, the Blue and White Nile, the Volga, or the Mississippi. They
sought out mystery in bogs. They did not settle for mountain certainties,
as did the explorers of the headwaters of the Missouri, the Ganges, or the
Columbia, ascending with assurance that at the end of some box canyon
or in some well-defined glacial lake all would be made obvious.

Things are especially uncertain in Minnesota. It is by no means clear
which way is down or out. Northward the long swamps ooze toward
Hudson Bay. Eastward the St. Lawrence begins its erratic passage
through the rocks and muskeg toward the series of deep basins —
Superior, Huron, Michigan, Ontario, and Erie; finally, surging over
rapids, tearing at the sides of rocky islands, it pours out into the Atlantic.
Southward a thousand streams wander down the tilted prairie, finding
allies, joining under limestone bluffs, broadening and strengthening
until all are gathered into the onrush of the Mississippi-Missouri system.

The statesmen who wrote treaties among the great powers of Europe
seldom had experienced places like these. They had come to power on a
continent where the Alps and Pyrenees make sources clear and where
rivers are large by the time they divide nations. So when France, Spain,
and Britain came to argue for title in North America to the moose,
sphagnum, mosquitoes, water lilies, wild rice, and arrowroot found in

254

the land where its great rivers rise, they kept making mistakes, to which American statesmen succeeded.

The story I have to tell occurred while the ownership of the headwaters of the Mississippi was still as unclear as its hydrology. Treaties gave the United States a claim there as early as 1783, but the British did not withdraw their posts for thirty more years. The natives continued to converse in their own languages, perfectly at ease without European contributions, except perhaps for a little French. Sovereignty was not established with any certainty until 1842, when all natural divisions were abandoned and statesmanship returned to the arbitrariness of the straightedge. Then finally Alexander Baring, Lord Ashburton, agreed with Daniel Webster that the British and American governments should fuss no longer over "wild country . . . of little importance to either country," and a line was drawn along the forty-ninth parallel from Lake of the Woods to Puget Sound. This placed the Mississippi safely within the United States.

This essay recounts how one of its sources was located by an adventurer who was financed in his explorations by an account of mysterious origin in Baring's bank. It is only a coincidence that Baring had inherited from his American grandfather, William Bingham, two million acres of good pine land in Maine (see Chapter 5). Rendering that extremity of the Canadian-American border tranquil was of considerably greater importance to him than the bogs and rivulets beyond Lake Superior.

By the time of the Webster-Ashburton Treaty, Europeans had been trying to sort out the geography of northern Minnesota for two hundred years. The French were on Lake Superior by 1620. They knew the interior of Wisconsin before the men of Massachusetts Bay were certain of the contours of the Berkshires. The Mississippi and St. Lawrence rivers provided two invasion routes into the heart of the continent, converging at right angles in Minnesota, with a few stream-and-portage shortcuts through Wisconsin blunting the angle.

These systems alternated in importance to European-American relations until the last part of the nineteenth century. The east-west St. Lawrence route was most important while the fur trade drew pelts out of the vast region of the lakes for the markets of Montreal. Later, Indian and colonial wars obstructed this route, the flatland lakes were trapped out, and the prime pelts came from the upper Missouri. For two decades after the invention of the steamboat, New England politicians had good cause for anxiety: the Mississippi became the spine — or rather, the sluice — of the West. The compass needle of western attention slipped ninety degrees from east to south. The people of the upper valley looked to St. Louis and New Orleans, not to New York or Boston.

But in the 1820s the needle returned to its previous setting. The Erie Canal made it possible for New York to compete with New Orleans for western goods, and after the 1850s the railroads completed the link. The North was reunited as the rails reached the Mississippi and drew off its traffic eastward through Chicago to New York.

Railroads and highways have occupied our minds for fifty years as we pass high over the rivers on steel trestles. Most of us lack enough experience in canoes to know how powerful a rush of water can be. Only those with Francis Parkman's gift for imagining the heroic world in which man directly faced midwestern nature can see the rivers as the early explorers saw them:

> The Missouri . . . fierce, reckless, headstrong, exulting in its tumultuous force, it plays a thousand freaks of wanton power; bearing away forests from its shores, and planting them, with roots uppermost . . . sweeping off islands, and rebuilding them; frothing and raging in foam and whirlpool, and again, gliding, with dwindled current along its sandy channel. At length, dark with uncurbed fury, it pours its muddy tide into the reluctant Mississippi . . . the disturbing power prevails . . . and the united torrent bears onward in its might, boiling up from the bottom, whirling, in many a vortex, flooding its shores with a malign deluge fraught with pestilence and fever, and burying forests in its depths, to ensnare the heedless voyager.

The source of the Mississippi lies within what has always been a borderland. Before humankind came into the region, two frontiers already intersected there. One divides east from west and green from brown as the pine lands strike the prairie. The empire of the pine was the St. Lawrence watershed, extending into central Minnesota and an area covering the northern curlings of the Mississippi. Between it and the open grassland lay an intermediate zone of hardwood clumps, which ended on the shore of the vast dry lakebed that has become the Red River Valley, where the wind has to contend only with a few bedraggled cottonwoods.

Another ancient transition zone divides north from south, separating the deep brown soil of the central valley from the rock, swamp, and muskeg of the arctic littoral. In northern Minnesota farms and pastures abandon their effort, leaving the scene to wolves, moose, and migrating birds. It was not until the middle of the nineteenth century that the agricultural frontier was recognized to lie so far north. Previously it was assumed that the domain of the Arctic extended into central Minnesota and Wisconsin. Prairie du Chien in southwestern Wisconsin was believed to be the farthest possible outpost of farmers. Though the country was gentle in contour and well provided with water, it was also cold, remote, and exposed to vicious winds. Few observers before 1870 thought it hospitable to masses of settlers. As we shall see, for some this was one of the chief attractions of the region.

This forbidding region was brought within the grasp of the settlers-to-come by an uncomfortable alliance of scientific inquirers and roman-

Beltrami's Search for the Headwaters of the Mississippi

tic adventurers. The scientists — who mapped the region's geology, listed its landmarks, skinned and classified its birds and mammals, and carried home in their saddlebags the dried husks of its insects — were not disinterested. They were engaged in a great enterprise in preemption. They sought to deny the interior of the continent to the ambitions of the French and the Spaniards; they proceeded in defiance of that British power which brooded on the north and west. Meriwether Lewis and William Clark, Zebulon Pike, and Stephen Long were instruments of American imperial policy while they carried forward a broader process of occupation, the expansion of the known at the expense of mystery.

At the same time, the rivers of the upper valley were explored by adventurers who had no interest whatever in continental power relationships and only the most casual commitment to science. These romantics sought in the West a series of scenes upon which to display themselves. It was a concession by history to comedy that Stephen Long, the quintessential engineer, dour, drab, surly, and methodical, was accompanied on one of his most important explorations by the fantastic Giacomo Beltrami, playwright, producer, and protagonist of a pageant that took seventy-six years to perform.

Their meeting was a consequence of the geopolitics of John C. Calhoun. In the years after the War of 1812, President Monroe's ambitious secretary of war developed a grand design for calming the Indian tribes, protecting the fur trade, and obstructing British influence at the extremities of the Louisiana Purchase. The Lewis and Clark expedition had secured information about a narrow pathway to the Pacific, but, all about their illuminated corridor, there remained a vastness of rumor and potential peril. Calhoun determined to send explorations to extend American knowledge and plan American occupation of the upper reaches of the Missouri-Mississippi system. His primary agent for these endeavors was Major Stephen Harriman Long of the U.S. Army's Corps of Engineers.

Long was born in the Puritan village of Hopkinton, New Hampshire, in 1784 and graduated from Dartmouth College in 1809. After teaching for a few years, he entered the army during the War of 1812 but, displaying his lifelong penchant for avoiding glory, was assigned to administrative chores. In 1816 he became a teacher of mathematics at West Point. In the next year, however, he began a reconnaissance of the West that led him, according to his own account, to explore far more territory than had Lewis and Clark. But with far less fame.

He first traveled the southwestern area between the Arkansas and Red rivers, then in 1817 the valley of the upper Mississippi as far as the present sites of St. Paul and Minneapolis. In 1818 Calhoun instructed Long to investigate the headwaters of the Missouri's central tributaries, the Arkansas and the Platte. This expedition did its fieldwork in 1819 and 1820; he set out again two years later with a refreshed staff to assert the American presence in the region to the west and north of Fort Snelling, Minnesota. It was on this tour that Long was accompanied by Beltrami.

After his return from Minnesota and the publication of his report on his travels, Long undertook surveys for the Baltimore and Ohio railway. In 1829 he published the first American treatise on railroad engineering and in 1836 a pioneering text on bridge building. In 1861, as the Civil War broke out and younger colleagues went forth to heroic exploits, Long, at the age of seventy-seven, became chief of the Corps of Topographical Engineers. He spent the early years of the great conflict sending maps to field commanders. Mustered out in 1863, he died the following year in Alton, Illinois.

In all of Long's letters, reports, and the books written by his companions, it is difficult to find a single instance in which Long expressed rapture or even exhilaration. He was consistently unimpressed by the continent he explored and gloomy about its prospects. As a young man he toured the richest farming region on the eastern seaboard, Lancaster

County, Pennsylvania, and found it depressing; its villages were "sinks of dissipation and debauchery." When later he reached the site of Chicago, he pronounced it unfit for either commerce or agriculture. Long and his chronicler Edwin James achieved some notoriety in history as those most responsible for providing the American public with the idea that the Great Plains were a great American desert. They called the region "almost wholly unfit for cultivation, and of course uninhabitable by a people depending upon agriculture for their subsistence."

In his somber way, Long found encouraging words for the region now occupied by Denver, Colorado Springs, and Boulder. He saw it as so forbidding as to "serve as a barrier to prevent too great an extension of our population westward." James went on to say that as a barrier zone it was "an unfit residence for any but a nomad population. . . . The traveler who shall at any time have traversed its desolate sands will, we think, join us in the wish that this region may for ever remain the unmolested haunt of the native hunter, the bison and the jackal."

It has been said in defense of Long that he was not congenitally cheerless but instead was merely bereft of the imagination to conceive what irrigation and the railroad could do in the absence of navigable streams and supplies of native wood. Though water and wood aplenty were to be found in Minnesota, his glance withered its lush green prairie, blighted its groves of hardwoods, and ignored its borders bearing hundreds of millions of pine trees. West of Lake Superior, he said, was a "sterile dreary waste," and the valley of the Minnesota River (then thick with prairie grass and now lush with grain supporting a score of prosperous towns) was a desolation:

> [There are] no buffalo ranging across the prairies, no deer stalking through the forests, no birds interrupting the solemn stillness which uniformly reigns over the country. . . . Where game is scarce, the Indian of course finds no inducement to hunt, and hence the party frequently traveled for whole days without seeing a living object of any kind.

260

Giacomo Costantino Beltrami, on the other hand, was transported by the beauty of that landscape. Indeed, his response to the region was so rapturous that Minnesota's legislature (which has named not so much as a roadside rest stop for Long) has celebrated Beltrami with a county, a village, and a park known as Count Beltrami State Monument. Beltrami would have been delighted, for a lifelong aspiration was thereby posthumously fulfilled: although he was many things, he was not a count.

He was born in Bergamo, Italy, in 1779, the sixteenth child of a Venetian customs officer. The same dramatic genius displayed in opera by Gaetano Donizetti, born in Bergamo twenty years later, was expressed in autobiography by Beltrami.

Early in life he determined that a bureaucratic existence was not for him; he would become "a hero of romance." He enlisted in the cause of the arch-hero Napoleon in 1796 and was amply rewarded. He flew in the prop wash of Bonapartism, becoming a "vice-inspector of armies." Then, despite his sketchy knowledge of the law, he became chancellor of the Department of Justice of Parma when he was barely twenty-one and was presiding as a judge when Napoleon's empire began to crumble.

Beltrami was always fortunate in his choice of women. In 1813, pleading ill health, he retired from the bench to Florence and the salon of Louise Maximilienne Caroline, countess of Albany. This magnificent woman welcomed him along with Chateaubriand and Lamartine, Lords Byron and John Russell, poets, painters, and hungry artists of all sorts to her palace on the Arno. He must have had considerable charm, for he was not yet a literary lion but a mere cub — and a lawyer. Still, she was generous, living as she did on a pension from George III of England, or

Opposite: **This portrait, painted in 1931 by G. A. Micheli, accepts Giacomo Costantino Beltrami's view of himself.** *From the Collection of the Minnesota Historical Society*

Prince Charles Edward Stuart about 1785, no longer bonnie. *National Portrait Gallery, London*

262

that portion of it which she had not expended for a vast tomb by Canova for her lover, the poet Alfieri, in the nearby church of Santa Croce. Also nearby was the convent to which she had fled from the drunken violence of her husband, Charles Edward Stuart, once known as Bonnie Prince Charlie and, for forty pathetic years thereafter, as the Young Pretender.

Charles had died in 1788, Alfieri in 1803. The countess of Albany was coming to be an old lady, and the beautiful young men who now surrounded her were not there for all the reasons that drew those who had made her Queen of Hearts in Paris in the 1770s. Those were the first years after her forced marriage; she was to provide a legitimate heir for the Stuart claimants to the English Crown, but she proved to be barren. After the Stuart pretensions died with Charles, the British privy purse was opened to sustain her and her young friends like Beltrami.

It may seem ungracious to inject a pecuniary note at this point, but I must explain how Beltrami was able to finance his exile, which occurred after he became embroiled in a plot of the carabinieri and was banished in 1821. The Queen of Hearts opened hers to him, that is clear; she managed his successful retention of some church property purchased at distressed prices during Bonaparte's confiscations. Perhaps she also managed its timely sale, or perhaps it was she who created a fund for his use in the Baring Bank in London. All we know is that he was still able to turn to the Barings after her death in 1824.

By that time Beltrami was already in America, having walked into the White House uninvited and unannounced, having called out for a servant and having been answered instead by James Monroe. Monroe was alone, in leather riding boots with his crop in his hand, preparing for a ride. "I am the president," said Monroe, "at your service." It was merely the first of a succession of American shocks. Beltrami had learned his manners at the court of the countess of Albany, who became more and more royal as her claims upon a throne became more and more remote.

Beltrami was delighted with Monroe's squirely demeanor. On the other hand, he complained at the avarice of the merchants of Philadelphia, with whom he spent $1,000 of somebody's money on canes, six dozen umbrellas, books, and other insignia of civilization that he intended to sell in the frontier regions toward which he thereupon set out. In reaching Pittsburgh, he observed the formation of the Ohio River from two subsidiary streams and conceived the idea of capping the water-borne achievements of his countrymen, Columbus, the Cabots (Caboti), Vespucci, and Verrazano, by discovering the headwaters of the Mississippi.

The exiled hero encountered the very man he needed to lead him thence, an American of Italian descent who had been appointed by Monroe as an agent of the United States government commissioned to tend the Indian tribes of the upper Mississippi, Major Lawrence Taliaferro. The major was impressed by Beltrami: "Six feet high, of commanding appearance and some forty-five years of age; proud of bearing and quick of temper, high spirited, but always a gentleman. He expressed an earnest wish to explore the sources of the Mississippi. I gave him a passport to go where he pleases." Beltrami accompanied Taliaferro, aboard the steamship *Virginia,* to his post at Fort Snelling, where the Mississippi is joined by the Minnesota River.

His contemporaries were impressed by Taliaferro, the "uncorruptible and high-toned Virginian." The "Tolivers" of Virginia had somehow reached Jamestown as early as 1637, and this representative of the ancient clan is famous not only for his association with Beltrami but for being one of the few men in the history of Minnesota who can be said with literal truth to have given a woman in marriage. The bridegroom was Dred Scott, the bride Taliaferro's slave Harriet Robinson. Taliaferro probably introduced African-Americans to the upper Mississippi. His retinue of slaves were regarded with awe by the Indians, who called them black Frenchmen. He freed them all not long after he gave Mrs. Dred Scott away. (It seems likely to me that he was in correspondence with Edward Coles, another young Virginian friend of Monroe's who did likewise. Taliaferro attempted to establish, at his own expense, an agricultural community for Indians called Eatonville in something of the same spirit by which Coles not only freed his slaves but staked them out with farms in central Illinois.)

We must leave aside the later career of Lawrence Taliaferro to re-introduce Stephen Harriman Long. Shortly after Taliaferro and Beltrami reached Fort Snelling, Long's party arrived. Its official journal later marked the encounter that ensued in these words:

> An Italian whom we met at Fort St. Anthony [Snelling] attached himself to the expedition and accompanied us to Pembina. He has recently published a book . . . which we notice merely on account of the fictions and misrepresentations which it contains. S.H.L.

While Beltrami was with Long's party, they had no choice but to notice him. He was a poet in a pack of engineers, and his was the poetry of action. Beltrami would often wander from their encampment to spend the night transported with delight in one moon-drenched glade or another. They were intent upon maintaining scientific detachment; he sought to feel and record "every impression which so novel a scene is capable of producing." To them a landscape must be broken into its physical components; to him it was a stimulant for "feelings I cannot describe . . . feelings which perhaps no other scene could awaken." Often "in this remote and central wilderness, my heart and mind are filled with the most delightful emotions." One day, while recording the course of granite outcrops, they found him spread-eagled on a boulder and moist with "tears of gratitude and attachment." He luxuriated in the exquisite "emotions which . . . agitate my heart."

Not unexpectedly, Long and his associates regarded Beltrami with annoyance; Beltrami regarded Long as a clod:

> Major Long did not cut a very noble figure. . . . I foresaw all the disgusts and vexations I should have to experience. Nonetheless, I was obliged to sacrifice my pride and my feeling of what was due me . . . and to give myself up to all I foresaw I should have to endure from littleness and jealousy.

To Beltrami, Minnesota was a theater for "feelings of intense and new delight. The sublime traits of nature; phenomena which fill the soul with astonishment, and inspire it at the same time with almost heavenly ecstasy . . . sentiments of faith and piety, perfect and profound." To Long and his associates, Minnesota was merely terrain traversed by fauna, some of which ate each other. They did everything possible to induce Beltrami to experience his transports privately. Then they set about to make his life sufficiently grim to induce him to depart.

At the outset Long was courteous — barely; he learned only slowly that Taliaferro had made him tentmate to a dervish. He sought to discourage Beltrami by tales of the terrors of the country, which of course merely ignited the latter's heroic instincts.

They set out on July 7, 1823, turning away from the Mississippi itself and following instead the Minnesota River Valley southwesterly for a hundred miles or more before it turned northwestward again to proceed in parallel to the greater stream. His commission required Long to follow the Minnesota to its source, then to continue northward along the Red River until he located the Canadian border, and then to turn eastward to explore that border. Beltrami was content to join the expedition because he thought the Red, Minnesota, and Mississippi rivers might all have their origins in the same plateau.

On the second day out, Long's men tried a new method to discourage their companion. Beltrami reported that, crossing the river in a small boat, "my sailors were so deficient either in strength or skill, that they suffered it to be carried away by the current and dashed in pieces against a rock, upon which I remained perched." He does not report either how he escaped his perch or what happened to the "sailors," but it is difficult to regard this as an accident, especially in view of his trials of the night of July 11:

> Our tent being open on both sides . . . the major . . . had the attention to place me on one of the two sides of the tent, in order, no doubt, that I might observe the weather at my ease, and reap the glory of struggling valiantly against the fury of the wind, rain, hail, thunder, and lightning.

On July 13:

> We might have had some good shooting, and the savans among us might have gained new and valuable ornithological information, but the major was intent on making an expedition and consulted nothing but his compass: it was sufficient for him to say, "I have been there."

Beltrami seldom found it sufficient to say so little. At the mouth of a little stream sometimes called the Brandy River, he went to view the countryside and "went alone, that the delicious reverie it threw me into might not be broken by cold-heartedness or presumption." Later he had another romantic spell: "Tears filled my eyes. . . . I should have given myself up to its sweet influence had I not been with people who had no idea of stopping for anything but a broken saddle."

Beltrami refused to be deterred by marooning, exposure, or studied coldheartedness. Long resorted to mystification. He "carefully concealed . . . the exact geographical location" of the source of the Minnesota River when that point was reached, and farther along kept the findings of his instruments from Beltrami so that the latitude and longitude of Pembina, a settlement on the Red River, were husbanded "with more care than the priests of Tibet conceal their Grand Lama."

Beltrami responded by amassing evidence to disparage Long's professional reputation as an Indian negotiator. On July 17 "the major pronounced a speech, which appeared probably very good to his government, whose . . . generosity he greatly extolled, but very bad to the Indians, since it concluded with the information that he had nothing to give them, and accordingly neither the chiefs nor anybody else made the slightest answer."

To Beltrami each newly encountered Indian tribe might be the elusive exemplars of Rousseau's noble savage; what joy might ensue from joining them in their quaint native pastimes! "I begged the major to endeavor to induce the chief to give us the sight of a buffalo hunt with bows and arrows, but he replied, with his usual complaisance, that he could not stop." Long had information to gather and a report to deliver. Beltrami, in perpetual revolt against all forms of governmental authority except Napoleon's, and temperamentally averse to bureaucratic necessity, found the major's frequent writing of reports a constant irritation. To him the elaborate and painstaking process of scientific exploration was not only vexing to the free spirit but needless as well:

> A single individual, possessed of practical philosophy and genuine philanthropy, with a moderate knowledge of geography and astronomy, would . . . accomplish much more than an expedition fitted out at great expense. . . . The advantages which have been hitherto derived from these expeditions have not, I believe, answered the views of the government, or the expectations of the public. They have consisted of a few plants, with which perhaps all but the members of the expedition were acquainted, and which swell that mass of unintelligible hieroglyphics, that scientific but tasteless and terrifying nomenclature, unfortunately consecrated by a great name, serving merely to overlay the memory and to blot out the lovely picture of nature; a few gaudy butterflies and other insects, of which we have already too many everywhere; of birds, which can only satisfy curiosity and luxury; of stones, suggesting a thousand conjectures of their nature and origin, and which . . . serve as materials for the idle discussions of pretenders to science, but contribute little or nothing to the benefit of the public, such have been the principal results of these pompous and costly enterprises.

Finally, at Pembina, the break came. Beltrami is, for once, silent about the proximate cause. Long's diary carries an entry under August 7, 1823: "Mr. Beltrami, our Italian companion, having taken offense at the party, generally, and being highly provoked at my objecting to his turning an Indian out of our lodge, left the party in a very hasty and angry manner."

Major Taliaferro gives a brief version of the next part of the story, emphasizing the loss of a horse he had loaned Beltrami:

> At Pembina, a difficulty occurred between Major Long and Beltrami, when the latter sold his horse (my horse) and equipments [Long's

account book indicates that the price was $90], and in company with a half-breed passed near the line of 49 degrees to the sources of the Mississippi. His sufferings were of no agreeable nature.

Those sufferings began soon after Beltrami left Pembina and were increased by his refusal to demean himself by adapting too much to the requirements of survival in a swamp. He made his way over the prairie to a small stream, which he followed by canoe until the Chippewa guides who were willing to paddle him upstream were terrified by a Sioux war party and deserted him. They had given him ample opportunity to learn the simple technique of navigating a canoe with a paddle, but he scorned to learn an exercise perhaps associated in his mind with lower-class folk like gondoliers. So he proceeded up a wandering watercourse and across an interminable marsh, dragging the canoe by a rope. This is not today a pleasant countryside to traverse by road, in an automobile. It is infuriating to attempt it on foot even when protected by mosquito repellents. Only a true hero of romance would wade through fifty miles of it towing a canoe, grubbing for food, drenched by rainstorms, and unable to sleep because of the stinging of insects.

The river came into a wetland too deep to wade. Now, at last, Beltrami made an attempt to learn from an Indian "how to guide a canoe with an oar." It was not successful, so he propped up his bright red umbrella in the bottom of the canoe to cover his equipage and continued on alone, wading, splashing, slipping, and floundering upstream. After four days of such trials, he had the good fortune to meet another client of Taliaferro's, who reported the consequences and made it possible for Taliaferro to recount them to us:

> He fell in with a sub-chief, the "Cloudy Weather," most fortunately, who knew Mr. B., having seen him in one of my councils at the agency. The old man was given, by signs, to know that the white man wanted to descend the river. The chief took our Italian friend in his canoe, and turned down stream. Indians are proverbially slow, hunting and fishing on the way; Beltrami lost all patience, abused his Indian crew, made many menaces, etc. The "Cloud" tapped him on the hat with his pipe stem, as much as to say, "I will take you to my father safe, if you will be still." The old chief told of this temper of my friend, but Mr. B. never made allusion to it.

Taliaferro's friend "Mr. B.," with Cloudy Weather's aid, *almost* "discovered" the source of the Mississippi. The quotation marks are necessary because, like the discovery of America, a first viewing of something by someone who reports the event in a language intelligible to the historian is quite a different matter from the first viewing by any human eye. As Washington Irving remarked (a remark that will reappear in another context in Chapter 19), the Indians "discovered" by Columbus did not know they were lost. Likewise, the Indians had known the sources of the

Mississippi for a long time before the Europeans began searching; furthermore, the first group of Europeans to see those sources probably did not take the trouble to report their findings. At least one fur trader had been there as early as 1803.

Henry Schoolcraft is generally credited with the discovery of the true source of the Mississippi. As he was working his way across Sandy Portage some years after Beltrami's adventure, with only a vague sense of his destination, he met on the trail "a small company of Chippewa." One of them agreed to return to the region with which he was thoroughly familiar and point out the way to the discovery. Schoolcraft gave it a name provided him by a clergyman, a combination of the Latin words *veritas* and *caput* — meaning "true head" — and had the grace to make it into the bogus Indian Itasca.

Beltrami, who certainly had the Latin, did not have the luck. Source finding is a tricky, scientific business, and Beltrami was in a hurry. He did discover a small lake lying between the watersheds of the Red River and the Mississippi. The lake was, appropriately for him, heart-shaped; in its midst water boiled from an unfathomable depth. It had, he said, no visible issue and was therefore the source of both rivers, by filtration. He named it Lake Julia after a lady — "not my wife," he told Taliaferro, "but a lovely woman."

Meddlesome surveyors have since found the outlet of Lake Julia into the Red River chain through a neighboring pond named Puposky, or Mud Lake.

Such details were of little concern to Beltrami. For him the supreme moment was reached beside the little heart-shaped lake in the midst of a vast ooze. "I feel with pride, that I have been more than human in not trembling then . . . and the phenomenon of that lake, which is only surmounted by the Heavens! . . . Those enchanting situations! That silence! That somber solitude! My poor savage repast! My bark porringer! What an assemblage of wonders, of thoughts, and of feelings, surrounding the eyes, and the soul!"

Beltrami was then, as always, as conscious of the effect upon a future reader of an account-making event as the effect of that event upon himself at the time: "Let us only stop here a moment to allow some souls of sensibility to consecrate again their tears of regret and veneration to the most pure virtue."

Stop we should, to consider purity, a quality and condition important to Beltrami. He repeatedly assured his readers of his own, and extolled that of the women for whom he named North American landmarks. His relationship with women in general is too complex to record at this point (we will stop again to consider it), but it is worth noting that his adventures included surviving a drunken brawl among the Indians at Leech Lake through the timely intervention of an Indian woman.

She appears only briefly as "the beautiful Woascita." When recounting this part of the tale, Beltrami asserted that "the picture of the dreadful Bacchanals at Leech Lake is of a sorrow entirely new, and I believe that the terrible dangers from which I have escaped . . . may affect the reader of sensibility."

The effect upon Cloudy Weather and his Chippewa of encountering the water-logged hero under his red umbrella must have been deeply satisfying to Beltrami's theatrical instincts. It must also have satisfied that sense of humor which flickers through his prose.

Beltrami thought he had achieved his end, the discovery of the Mississippi's source. He continued down the Mississippi, admonished by Cloudy Weather's pipe stem. At the end of September he arrived at Fort Snelling to the amazement of the garrison, who had heard from the commandant's son that Beltrami had disappeared after leaving Pembina and was presumed to have died in the ooze.

After a few days at the fort giving his side of the story (the commandant and his family "were indignant against Major Long for acting toward me in the miserable manner that he did"), Beltrami took a keelboat to St. Louis and New Orleans. There he expanded his audience with a published account in French. In the next few years he crossed Mexico from east to west, returned to the United States, and then perched briefly in London to produce a two-volume, English-language version of his adventures in America. Two years later, in Paris, he brought out two more volumes on Mexico. After further wandering, he returned to Italy in his seventieth year and died at Filottrano in February 1855.

While he resented the repeated efforts of Long and the American critics sympathetic to Long to denigrate his accomplishments, Beltrami did not seem to mind very much the wholesale plagiarism of his account by Chateaubriand, his old friend from Florentine days. Chateaubriand's famous account of his voyage to America, published in 1828, explicitly quoted only three pages from Beltrami's account, but borrowed another fifty-six without acknowledgment. Further, modern scholars are emphatic that Chateaubriand never visited many of the places for which he borrowed descriptions in Beltrami's hyperbolic words. Beltrami *was* guilty of hyperbole but, unlike Chateaubriand, never of fraud.

The story seems so simple: Major Stephen Harriman Long and "Count" Giacomo Costantino Beltrami spent an exasperating summer together in 1823. Each did his duty as he saw it. It is not difficult to ascertain from what Long said of himself and what others reported of him that he saw his duty as any soldier might — to follow orders, to accept the policies established by other men, and to fulfill the description they provided of conduct proper to an officer. His interior plan or, to put it in a later jargon, his image of himself, did not transcend any directives he received from his superiors. Because we cannot detect any tension between his character and his circumstances, between his chores and his aspirations, Long emerges as a stolid personality. Perhaps that is why there remains as his cenotaph only the mountain peak he named for himself, which partakes in his own fate — though it looms nearly as large and as high as Pikes, no one has ever sworn to make *Longs* Peak "or bust." Even beyond ungrateful Minnesota, no national, state, or even county monument has ever been set aside for Long.

Honors went instead to the Italian romantic who failed to discover the source of the Mississippi River.

Beltrami survives even the most derisive descriptions of his contemporaries as a man whose requirements for himself were so intense that he could almost force others to take him seriously. His insistence upon his heroic role was so vehement that he could not be set down as a mere posturer.

Beltrami left no doubt about the man he meant to be. When he achieved the standard he had set, he said so with pride. "My constancy against difficulties perpetually increases. . . . The lists are always open; I feel as yet firm in the saddle, and shall sustain, be assured, many a shock and conflict before I surrender." When in his solitary encampment at Lake Julia he finally found a moment worthy of his dream, he imagined himself surrounded by a congratulatory assembly led by those countrymen, Columbus, the Cabots, Vespucci, and Verrazano, who had led him to America and then to the sources of the Mississippi.

Why America? It was distant from Italy and largely unknown. It was serviceable, therefore, for romantic exploits, attractive because Italian pride proclaimed it to be an Italian discovery, named by Italians. The requirements of romantic heroism always include distance from the audience — distance in time, distance in place, distance in culture. Beltrami's audience, like Lord Byron's, was literary Europe; what Byron said of Albania, Beltrami could have said of America: "The scene was savage — the scene was new." Distance and novelty were necessary, savagery a pleasant accessory. To an Italian who grew up amid moldering ruins and ancient, festering feuds, "strangeness" required a fresh and empty scene.

America was a popular candidate. Its novel republican experiment was very much in the minds of rebellious European intellectuals. Disappointed by the restoration of the "legitimacy," which placed again upon the thrones of Europe the inept lot Napoleon had sent waddling from their capitals, they looked to America for a new chance, a new race of heroes.

The frontiersmen, of whom Daniel Boone was the best known in Europe, seemed to be such a race. The chronicler of the Long expedition

The St. Croix River, between Minnesota and Wisconsin. In 1830 it was in Ultima Thule. *Photo by Robert Lautman*

Previous page: **A Minnesota bog, the sort of place Giacomo Beltrami explored.** *Photo by Robert Lautman*

Fort Snelling, Minnesota, the meeting place of Beltrami and Long and the military neighbor of Henry Sibley's trading post. *Photo by Dick Bancroft*

Next Page: **Skyscrapers and Ol' Man River: Minneapolis from the Mississippi.**
Photo by Robert Lautman

had reported after a visit to Boone in 1819 that the old man felt that it was time to move when he could no longer fell a tree for fuel so that its top would lie close to the door of his cabin: too broad a clearing meant too long a residence and too many neighbors. Long's report was published and widely read in 1823. The next year Lord Byron wrote into the Eighth Canto of *Don Juan* a digression on Boone's condition:

> The lust which stings, the splendour which encumbers,
> With the free forester divide no spoil;
> Serene, not sullen, were the solitudes
> Of this unsighing people of the woods.

Here was a bare stage. In America there was a chance for a hero to stand forth, in Tocqueville's words, as "man himself, taken aloof from his country and his age and standing in the presence of Nature and God." In such a place the sixteenth child of a minor bureaucrat might fulfill a dream.

Beltrami was not merely a European restless under legitimacy; he was also an intellectual deeply imbued with the philosophy of Jean-Jacques Rousseau. Romanticism invested old words and old ideas with colorful and delightfully vague new meanings merely by capitalizing them. When Rousseau spelled nature with a capital *N,* his disciples, such as Beltrami, knew that what was implied was something more wonderful than just an uninhabited place. Nature, even in Minnesota, was titillatingly savage. The rude delights this promised drew Beltrami onward through many a squalid scene and many a humiliation; as a disciple of Rousseau he expected that where there is Savagery there would be scope for Heroism. The confines of the library and drawing room were burst open; in America there was space, and one might find an arena free of the shackles that in Europe bound men to a dead past and a diseased present.

Beltrami's worst disappointment in America was not the treatment he received from Long and his associates; his joy was truly clouded by the degree to which the Indians failed to fulfill their assigned roles in the romantic scenario. They were not the noble figures he expected; instead they were "corrupt and degenerate . . . uncivilized, indolent and cruel." There was, of course, an explanation that could still preserve the purity of Rousseau's concept: these Indians had been corrupted by the presence of the traders among them. They had already caught the contagion of civilized life: the "red men who are most in contact with the whites are uniformly the worst."

Most European painters and writers who toured the Great Plains in the 1820s and 1830s did not record what they saw coldly, as anthropologists might. They mixed passion with their paint. They saw the ragged, proud, apparently simple, illiterate folk they found in America as somehow closer to a lost perfection than the people they left behind in Europe; they were not excited by "progress." Even after he returned from America, Beltrami was still persuaded that "civilized man is more barbarous than the savage."

Beltrami's ideal of primitive life established the background of his drama, and it instructed him as to his own role. It was not just that he had to deal with the Indians in ways he found in practice to be perilous. More than that was necessary, more than all that Rousseau, Byron, or de Toqueville might ask of him. He was moving into the gravitational force of an ideal even more ancient and more demanding than romantic self-dramatization. In the depths of his nature there was apparently something grander, of which we catch glimpses through the perfervid rhetoric of his subsequent account.

This view of life, that of the suffering hero, arises from what might be called the Lancelot syndrome. There is a tradition of courtly love in European literature that probably originated at the court of Eleanor of Aquitaine in the twelfth century. She had been married in her lusty youth to the pious Louis, king of France by birth and celibate by preference. She had, she said, "married a monk." When this alliance was finally dissolved, she was next married to an amply passionate husband, Henry II of England. But he was eleven years her junior, and as she became older he became distracted by several fresher companions. Ultimately she and he parted company. Thereafter, in her court in Aquitaine, she had a sort of literary revenge. A series of poets in her court evolved stories of heroes who abased themselves to please the whims of women. Lancelot was chief among these men with a pathological desire for humiliation, willing to undergo any disgrace to secure the smile of his lady. Out of some deep murk of masculine self-loathing comes Lancelot. We read of him riding through the mud in a farm cart or permitting himself to be besmirched or even unhorsed to prove his love.

Long after the death of the unappeasable Queen Eleanor, this strange cult of honor in dishonor, of ugliness made beautiful beneath the gaze of a lady, proliferated. One new tale told of three knights who received a blouse from a lady with the insane suggestion that the one who truly loved her would wear it, but no armor, in a tournament. Two "excused themselves"; the third was skewered. It is said that German knights drank their own bath water and cut off their hands to please women. If this behavior seems odd, one need recall only that Eleanor and Lancelot are with us still. Consider the words of Owen Wister describing the moment at which his Virginian finally broke through Molly Wood's defenses: "He was not now, as through his long courting he had been, her half-obeying, half-refractory worshipper. She was no longer his half-indulgent, half-scornful superior. Her better birth and schooling had been weapons to keep him at his distance."

The elements of the Virginian's ritual have been fairly fixed since Eleanor gave to Chrétien de Troyes the "matière et san," the content of his myth — Beltrami's myth. The hero suffers for the love of a woman of higher station (in America, as Wister indicated, birth and schooling will do, though in Europe a title is to be preferred). The lady is married to someone else who is unworthy of her (or at any rate, inattentive). And to complete the picture, suffering gains him no consummation. A pallid smile is vouchsafed, a perfumed handkerchief, a garter perhaps, or at best a tearful interview in a gazebo in which she takes his hand in hers and pledges that she loves him, but not, of course, in "that way."

Beltrami's American journals are full of echoes of the literature of courtly love. The very form of those journals, his report on the dangers and disasters of "a poor, solitary traveler constantly contending against obstacles," was a series of letters to a "countess" whose mailing address and full name are not given. Later the citizens of Bergamo in their memorial to him recounted that she was the Countess Compagnoni, born Passari. The "Lady Julia," after whom the heart-shaped lake was named, was the Countess Giulia Spada de Medici, a lady of wealth and some poetic talent who had given him sustenance during his judicial years in Macerata, before he met the munificent countess of Albany, "friend of Alfieri and Foscolo."

Which of these was the "lady of high station" whose image was before his eyes as the mosquitoes bit, the Indians threatened, the boggy footholds sank? For them all, probably, he endured his humiliations and his sufferings; for them all he remained celibate. If he lapsed, the courtier-queen relationship would suffer. "Love," said Beltrami, "may be as pure and irreproachable as it is ardent and elevated." He would have no dalliance with "the beautiful Woascita," the elusive heroine of the "dreadful Bacchanals at Leech Lake." He was constant, uncontaminated to the end.

Beltrami dedicated the English edition of his *Travels* to womankind. However ridiculous his critics might think courtly love to be in Minnesota in 1821, they "shall in nothing affect my worship for this adorable sex, nor even my last will. I bequeath my heart to woman; my soul to God; and the wicked to the D——."

Beltrami was not only an actor in a series of set pieces, nor was he merely his own historian. He was a true hero, insisting, as heroes do, that history should occur in certain ways, with himself as the central figure. And he created his own opportunities for heroic action. It is something to behave well accidentally or in sudden, unrepeated spasms of virtue. But the name of hero should be reserved to those who, like Beltrami, form an image of themselves and stick to it, forcing circumstances to accommodate their ideal. This is *heroic insistence,* the sustained performance of a self-chosen role.

Another exemplar of heroic insistence was Henry Hastings Sibley, the next subject of these essays. Sibley sent to the mayor of Bergamo an official copy of the naming of Beltrami County together with a letter from Major Taliaferro. In his covering communication the old statesman reflected upon the changes that had ensued since the three of them, Sibley, Taliaferro, and Beltrami, had known "the hospitality of the savages in their rude wigwams" and the prairies when they were "known only as the resort of countless herds of the bison and the elk." Sibley assured the mayor that Beltrami would be the "delighted spectator of the marvelous transformation" of that scene into "cities, towns and villages." I doubt this would have been true for Beltrami, and I am certain it was not true for Sibley himself.

16

....

The Self-Conscious Frontier

The Heroism of Henry Hastings Sibley

IN THE SPRING of 1849, at the same confluence of streams where
Giacomo Beltrami and Stephen Long had struck up an instant and
implacable antipathy, two of the most formidable public figures of
the first half of the nineteenth century in the American Middle
West met for the first time. They were Henry Hastings Sibley and Alexander Ramsey.

The fort on the top of the limestone bluff above the Mississippi and
Minnesota rivers was now much enlarged. Because its walls were hewn
of the same rock, it was impossible to distinguish the natural fortress, its
parapets cut over the ages by the great river, from the manmade complex
of defenses along the crest. The bastions and parapets of Fort Snelling,
then as now, gave the aspect of a walled town, like many in the Swiss
canton of Vaud and many others along the angry little rivers of the Dor-
dogne in southwestern France, where they are thought to be most picturesque.

It is difficult to think of Fort Snelling as picturesque; many of us
were mustered in and mustered out there and came to loathe its dusty,
hot, crowded barracks as we awaited our "papers." It has been amiably
restored in recent years, and in the right light and at the right season, it
does have its charm when seen from the floodplain, where the great
cottonwoods that sheltered Ramsey and Sibley still grow, protected
from the prairie wind by the bluffs. Ducks and geese still complain
as they circle for landings in the shallow meanderings left behind as the
conjoined rivers rush south and east on their long journey to the
Gulf. The little town of Mendota, Sibley's headquarters, can be seen

Painting (1888) by Alexis Fournier of Henry Sibley's house and trading post, built in 1834, in Mendota, Minnesota. *From the Collection of the Minnesota Historical Society*

through the trees, across the stream, up on a terrace, its buildings partaking of the limestone of the fort and of the bluffs. The church of the French-Canadian fur traders, Saint Peter's, where they worshiped with their Dakota and Ojibwa wives and their children of mixed blood, stands near the symmetrical, stately house of the greatest of these traders, Alexander Faribault, built in 1834 and just touched with the Greek Revival.

Now as then, the most imposing house in Mendota, this village under the hill, is the headquarters of the seigneur of the northwestern frontier, Henry Hastings Sibley. Though he was Faribault's partner and friend, he received Faribault's deference, for he was an educated man. When he came to Mendota early in the 1830s to take up his role he was magnificent: athletic, upright, and rebellious. He was still magnificent two decades later when he met his friend and nemesis "Bluff Alex" Ramsey, another sort of man: heavy, physically phlegmatic but quick and shrewd, unreflective, morally complaisant, and infinitely adaptable.

Though from another tradition than Beltrami's, Sibley was a romantic frontiersman. Alexander Ramsey was a spoilsman-politician who became a frontier capitalist. Sibley's happiest years were spent among the Indians in a wilderness; Ramsey was as content in the sordid politics and commerce of the 1860s and 1870s as a rhinoceros in a mud hole. Sibley was a Jeffersonian Democrat, Ramsey a Grant Republican.

Ramsey was Minnesota's first appointed territorial governor, Sibley its first congressional representative and first elected state governor. Ramsey became a powerful United States senator, then secretary of war; Sibley became, to his misfortune, a general. Ramsey was accounted by his contemporaries to be a great success; Sibley was thought a little strange, an eighteenth-century anachronism persisting into the Gilded Age.

There was a friendship between these two that survived many political confrontations and the reciprocal calumnies of their associates, a friendship that transcended dissimilarities of background, goals, and style and persisted for more than four decades, until Sibley's death in 1891. Every year when the two were both in residence, Sibley would call

Portrait of a romantic hero becoming an anachronism: Henry H. Sibley. *From the Collection of the Minnesota Historical Society*

278

on Ramsey on the anniversary of that first meeting in Mendota. Every year the arc widened between their divergent paths, but that friendship never snapped. On those annual visits they often sat together in heavy, high-backed, gray wicker chairs in the cavernous shadows of Ramsey's front porch, looking out on the carriages passing toward the fat, fashionable frame houses in the neighborhood, where in their youth clumps of oak trees had sheltered Indian ponies and the blackbirds had sung beside the ponds.

Ramsey's house is still there, too, but it is not hidden away on a limestone bench below Fort Snelling. Although it too is made of limestone, for some reason it has grown gray, whereas the buildings of Mendota retain their fresh buff color. Ramsey's mansarded mansion, now owned by the Minnesota Historical Society, has darker gray shutters, a gray-blue iron fence surrounding its ample grounds, and a gray carriage house behind. Urban renewal and gentrification have restored its surroundings; "downtown" is a quarter of a mile away and a vast hospital complex has filled the area to the north. A block away in the other direction, the great iron fountains play again in Irvine Park, and a nearby restaurant features violet-colored napery and nouvelle cuisine.

My last visit to the house while it was still in the family's hands was as escort for the Australian actress Zoe Caldwell. We were calling on Ramsey's granddaughter, Miss Anita Furness, who had changed very little in the house or on the front porch, including the wicker chairs. Our call

Ramsey's limestone mansion on Walnut Street in St. Paul as it appeared in 1890 and as it still appears today. *From the Collection of the Minnesota Historical Society*

was in the interest of the Guthrie Theater, of which I was chairman and Zoe was leading lady. Wearing a hat, pearls, and little white cotton gloves, she gave her best version of how Dame Edith Evans as Lady Bracknell would have gone calling. Miss Anita told me afterward she thought the whole thing wonderfully funny and gave us a very nice check.

The conversations between her grandfather and Mr. Sibley (whom she thought a little "outlandish") were private, and so were the views each held about the other. This is a little odd, because Sibley was given to writing character sketches of his old frontier friends, and Ramsey, who survived him by a decade, had ample opportunity to memorialize Sibley in the fashion of the times. Perhaps they had become so accustomed to each other that they had learned to overlook imperfections, or perhaps neither wanted to look at the other as directly as portraiture requires.

Sibley was described by another contemporary as being six feet tall, rangy, and muscular in build. His complexion was dark, "his eyes, with the iris rather small, of a dark lustrous brown, and of a kind, pleasing expression. . . . His hair was black, and in his earlier portraits he is represented as wearing a plain, black, closely trimmed mustache." He himself said that during his long hunts with the Indians, which sometimes took all winter, his beard grew shaggy. Clothed in rough buckskins stained with grease, blood, and sweat, with dogs at his heels, he looked like the frontiersman he was and wanted so much to be.

But he was no barbarian. At his headquarters at Mendota, this intellectual-as-athlete, conscious of his education, functioned as satrap for the American Fur Company over an area now occupied by large portions of five states. He came there for the first time from Prairie du Chien in southwestern Wisconsin up the Mississippi through wild country. He saw only one cabin in three hundred miles. It took two weeks to reach the cluster of huts that was to be his headquarters and home for thirty years.

The position of a trader in this period was unlike that of the vagrant mountain man of the Rocky Mountain fur trade. Sibley lived as a feudal baronet might, surrounded by whatever complements of civilization he wanted and could bring upriver from the outposts of civilization. He had his books, "his horses and dogs and retainers to do his bidding." Soon after he arrived he began the construction of the large stone building that is called the Sibley house today. It served as his warehouse, office, a dormitory for his voyageurs, and his fortress. Representing a company almost as powerful in his region as the government of the United States, he was also justice of the peace for a region radiating three hundred miles from Mendota. He became the arbiter of disputes among Indians and settlers, receiving more deference than the commander of the garrison at nearby Fort Snelling. As the territorial population grew toward five thousand at the end of the 1840s, the old traders and some of the new settlers turned to him to organize the territory. He was their inevitable choice to serve as their delegate to Congress.

Sibley's biography progresses with apparent seamlessness from this point through his governorship, his military exertions against the Sioux, and his gray years as a grand old man. But with his election as a delegate to Congress, that period in his life for which he had been prepared by training and inclination came to an end. Thereafter, civilization closed in on him and he entered a world to which he was a stranger, as he made clear again and again in his letters and speeches and reminiscences. That world was made for men like Ramsey, not for a romantic refugee from Puritanism.

Sibley wanted a life free of constraint, noble but uninhibited. The wilderness in which he wished to lead this life was the romantic wilderness. It was not Ramsey's arena for exploitation. Neither was it the Judaic-Puritan wilderness of Stephen Long or of Sibley's own father, Judge Solomon Sibley of Detroit. The Old Testament had taught the Puritans to think of wilderness as a desolation like unto Sinai, where a man could wander sun-crazed for days, seeking water, hearing the wings of the kites flapping closer and closer. This was the image of the Great American Desert that was so strong in Long's accounts: a Middle Eastern image of baked, cracking earth left after the primordial deluge had receded, a desert surrounding the oases of prideful man, a wasteland stretching forbidding and reproachful to the horizon. With Sinai in mind, a rabbinical commentator had said, "The earth . . . became mountainous as a punishment . . . and will not become level again until the Messiah comes." This view of wilderness was inherited from the rabbis by the men of the Middle Ages and from them by the Puritans.

In America the wilderness was the West, toward which some New England Puritans had not only biblical sanction for a gloomy view, but also good economic reason to fear too much mobility and the absence of discipline. Cotton Mather called the West "the wrong side of the hedge." Michael Wigglesworth thought of it as a "devil's den . . . inhabited [by] hellish fiends." Timothy Dwight conjured up a population of "foresters . . . impatient of the restraints of law, religion, and morality." Edmund Burke had used the same key word, for he too feared what might happen when men were free to "wander without the possibility of restraint." Even Washington Irving, in his conservative phase, feared to see such nomads appearing on the western horizon ready to descend upon the settlements of those who had "gotten cattle and goods."

This admixture of political conservatism, religious paternalism, and capitalist concern equally for a ready, cheap labor supply and for the protection of the already wealthy was succinctly stated in a lament of Cornelius Felton. Writing in the 1830s, Felton deplored the West as a place where there were "none of the restraints which fetter the characters of the working classes in other countries." The Puritan fathers, like English Tories, feared that beyond the "hedge" there would beckon a licentious life that parishioners and workingmen might be unable to resist.

Generations of young New Englanders did indeed set forth for the West to escape restraints, as others had left their villages for the city. Though western migration was also propelled by overpopulation and encouraged by the exhaustion of rocky soil, it was often an alternative to revolt (an "escape valve," in one of Frederick Jackson Turner's just phrases). Escape to the frontier resulted from an explosion of those energies which could not be confined within the suffocating Puritan climate.

This escape had to be remade in each generation as parents who had gone to the frontier were joined by Yankee peers and in their maturity reinstituted some of the same constrictions from which they had fled in their youth. Thus Henry Sibley, the son of Yankee pioneers, escaped from a new England those pioneers had re-created in Ohio and Michigan. He rebelled against the newly imposed constraints of which his father was the chief guardian.

Solomon Sibley was born in Sutton, Massachusetts, six years before the Revolutionary War. He studied law in Boston and went west in 1795. After settling in Detroit, he rose rapidly to eminence: mayor, auditor, Indian commissioner, bank director, congressman, justice, and finally Chief Justice of the Supreme Court of Michigan. His fourth child and second son was Henry Hastings Sibley. A biographer provides the awesome catalogue of this child's Puritan antecedents: the Sibleys arrived in the first shipments to New England, where

> in all matters of importance relating to the common weal, in church or state . . . [they] stand out as foremost figures. . . . Their name is "Legion." They swarm. Sutton is their hive. . . . And all are interlaced and intermingling in a network of intermarriages, crossing and recrossing . . . with . . . other influential families . . . ministers, elders, deacons, church wardens, rectors, canons, bankers. . . . How thoroughly Puritanic this celebrated stock was is seen in the names transmitted to the children . . . among the antediluvian Noah stands as prominent as ever . . . Abraham, Isaac, and Jacob . . . Reuben, Simeon, Levi, Joseph, and Benjamin . . . Moses, Elijah, Joel, Amos, Jonas, Nathan, Nahum, Heremiah, Isaiah, Ezekiel, and Daniel,

and so forth through Baarak, Zerubbabel, and Rufus to the ladies, who included Tamar and Vashti. Sister Mary Sibley, it seems, was suspected of witchcraft in 1692 but was freed, though she did admit to making cakes for the Indians. Her descendant Henry took up her task.

The credentials of Sarah Whipple Sproat, Solomon Sibley's spouse, were just as compelling. She was the daughter of Colonel Ebenezer Sproat, who built a new *Mayflower* at the headwaters of the Ohio, down which he and his family floated to the mouth of the Muskingum, where a new town was founded. There Sarah was born and, in 1802, was married.

Her son Henry was a wild, rebellious boy. Sixty years later he said of himself, "I was more given to mischief than my fellows. . . . My dear mother often declared me incorrigible, and the black sheep of the family." He was given the best that the academy in Detroit could provide, then put under a tutor in Latin and Greek for two years and abided with increasing impatience the study of law. After two years he gave it up, longing, as he said, "for a more active and stirring life."

William Watts Folwell, president of the University of Minnesota, historian, and friend of Sibley's in his later years, spoke of the young man as having "no stomach for the law or for scholastic or sedentary pursuits. His heart was with the Wild West."

Minnesota, Sibley thought, was unlikely ever to be anything but wild. Like most of his contemporaries, he assumed that he would find a permanent wilderness there. Congressmen would dismiss it as "that hyperborean region of the Northwest, fit only to be the home of savages and wild beasts." Francis Parkman would write of the "frozen northern springs" of the Mississippi, where "the fur-clad Indian shivers in the cold." And Sibley himself went there trusting that he had found a place beyond the reach of the civilized world: "I had no belief that Minnesota would become fairly well settled within fifty years. I had no faith in it as a farming country. I thought that the year 1900 would find it no better occupied than the country along the northern shore of Lake Superior."

Despite the sickness and loneliness he experienced at the time, later Sibley recalled his wilderness years as his best. He enjoyed both freedom and dignity; he was respected, powerful, but unburdened. It was precisely the life he wanted.

> It may seem strange that men of education and culture could be induced to endure the hardships, perils, and exposure incident to the life of an Indian trader; nevertheless many such could be found among that class. The love of money was not the incentive, for rarely could or did a trader accumulate or become wealthy. . . . What constituted the fascination, it would be difficult to describe, except upon the theory that the tendency of civilized men, when under no restraint, is toward savagery as the normal condition of the human race. There was a charm in the fact that in the wild region, inhabited only by savage beasts, and still more savage men, one was liberated from all the trammels of society, independent, and free to act according to his own pleasure.

The young Sibley was, in William James's words, "an unencumbered man." His childhood had been a long rebellion, and now he was free,

free among other things to be the exemplar of a rebellious generation, engaged in a revolt against Puritanism. Young Yankees rebelled against their ancestral burdens in a general passion for newness. Henry David Thoreau asked for "a spiritual molting season"; his friend Nathaniel Hawthorne asked for a "busk," a ceremony in which society's old forms and devices would be thrown upon a bonfire and destroyed so that men could start afresh. For many, escape to the frontier was in itself a form of busk. Sibley loved to quote "old Leatherstocking," James Fenimore Cooper's hero who found newness in nature, "where he could . . . open his heart to God without having to strip it of the cares of wickedness of the settlements." Nature was a place to start fresh, where Herman Melville could envisage his heroes emerging naked each day into the "golden, glorious, glad sun."

Some of the true heroes of the northwestern frontier so envisaged themselves. By the time Minnesota, Wisconsin, and the Dakotas were being invaded by European-Americans bent on settlement, it was no longer possible for educated men and women to escape an awareness of how they should think of themselves on the frontier, of what a proper stance upon it should be. A literature of the West had grown up; the ideals it set forth were a part of the intellectual inventory of them all. All in their own degree were watching themselves. It is possible, therefore, to find in their stories not only a sequence of events but also a pattern of intended action: there was a necessary history and a hoped-for history. Though for a few there was only a gray world of duty or a silver world of profit, for many others the Midwest offered an occasion to assert heroic character, brightly colored and proud.

Here is the romantic tradition in a new guise, Rousseau hybridized with German ideal philosophy. Jefferson had made the noble savage an honorary citizen of the new republic, and the New England transcendentalists set him "solitary in a wide, flat space" surrounded by the quiet humming of the oversoul. Transcendental Nature was noble: it partook of the nature of God. Rousseau's Man was noble so long as he was free of the vexations, seductions, and restraints of city life. Man was good. Cities were evil.

Sibley accepted this doctrine and adhered to it all his life. As a middle-aged statesman he lamented that the Congress had made preemption of land so expensive that "high rates of sale had forced thousands . . . to remain in the corrupting atmosphere of our large cities who otherwise would have become contented and happy tillers of the soil." He respected not only the happy yeoman on his farm but also men "who like Cooper's Leatherstocking are brought face-to-face with nature in her deepest solitudes." Daniel Boone joined Leatherstocking as the model for a whole race of frontier heroes, and Sibley could understand what lay behind James Perkins's description of Boone in 1846 as one who would have pined and died as a nabob in the midst of civilization. He wanted a frontier, and the perils and pleasures of a frontier life, not wealth; and he was happier in his log cabin, with a loin of venison and his ramrod for a spit, than he would have been amid the greatest profusion of modern luxuries.

There were, of course, few so heroic as to seek to live completely in accordance with the precepts of the Boone myth. The simple life was accepted by many out of necessity rather than conviction, and it became progressively less simple when money could be found for beguiling complexities. Yet the vigor of the myth persisted, to be expressed in its full fervor by William Jennings Bryan as late as 1920.

By then, of course, it had become nostalgic, and it is in this late and rather rancid form that it appears to most of us in Wild West novels and western films. In our day it is the program of a spectator sport. In Henry Sibley's day it was an exhortation to a life of adventure. J. Fletcher Williams gives us our first picture of Sibley as a young man sitting at the feet of frontiersmen of an older generation, already

disposed . . . to a life of close contact with the strange and romantic elements that have always given such a charm to frontier life in the eyes of the courageous and active. . . . His boyhood . . . was passed in a region where every one of the old inhabitants was a fireside bard, reciting those wonderful epics of hairbreadth escapes and "accidents by flood and field," perils and feats of the half mythical heroes of the frontier, legends full of poetry and romance, well calculated to stir the blood and excite the ambition of the youthful listener. This largely accounts for the life he subsequently led. . . . He listened to their stories of life in the great wilderness of the Northwest (so he once stated to the writer) like some tale of romance, filling him with a keen desire to see and traverse this wonderful land of lake, prairie and forest.

That Sibley was romantic does not mean that he was soft or impractical. He took the risks his code required, seeking out exploits and wild companions, and he also assumed the no less hazardous responsibilities of an Indian trader. It was said that he was the best bareknuckle fighter in Wisconsin Territory and that he once threw the wildest of the voyageurs at Mackinaw out the door of his store. Williams reports a little gingerly that "some of the early settlers used to say that Sibley preserved order and discipline among his rough voyageurs by the actual use of the lash and bludgeon."

But it is also true that he held so strongly to a romantic idea of "noble savagery" that his treatment of the Indians was thought by many of his contemporaries to be sentimental. When Charles Flandrau, another trader, read in a dispatch that Sibley had captured three hundred hostiles and was about to consign them to the tender mercies of the settlers, he turned the paper over and wrote on its back, "He won't do it." Why not?

Flandrau knew that Sibley (and a very few others) were incorrigible in the belief that Plains Indians could become "useful citizens." This is no place to debate what might have happened in the 1840s and 1850s had the tribes we (but not they) cluster as the Sioux been afforded means to make a dignified change from their full pride as hunters to become self-supporting farmers. Here we can only recall that many in Sibley's reforming generation were convinced that all humans are basically good (not, as the Puritans held, sinners perpetually seared by the wrath of an angry God). Therefore, by adjusting institutions, all, including Native Americans, could "progress" from a "natural" state of relative purity to a sophisticated, if rural, condition of dignity. As optimists, they were naturally reformers.

No one has ever told well the story of the effect of the reformers of the 1830s, 1840s, and 1850s upon the Indian policy of the United States. It is a story well worth telling. In a mere essay the best I can do is emphasize a part of it, in which men like Sibley brought reforming and transcendental romanticism to the Midwest. They applied its precepts to the least urbanized residents of the continent, the Indians of the Great Plains. Similarly, what they felt and said about the Indians tells us much about their view of themselves and how they wanted to live.

Many of the early Indian traders in Minnesota were well-educated men, convinced of the truth of Jefferson's ideals and of the doctrine of the goodness of "natural" humanity. They shared with Beltrami (see Chapter 15) a presumption that the Indian, uncorrupted, was likely to be noble. It is remarkable that a long and intimate acquaintance with real Indians failed to alter this view. After fifteen years of Indian trading, Sibley still spoke to the Congress of "the wild and noble savages who roam the western plains" and uttered a passionate plea for a humane Indian policy:

> The busy hum of civilized communities is already heard beyond the mighty Mississippi. . . . Your pioneers are encircling the last home of the red man, as with a wall of fire. Their encroachments are perceptible in the restlessness and belligerent demonstrations of the powerful bands who inhabit your remote Western Plains. You must approach these with terms of conciliation and friendship, or you must suffer the consequences of a bloody and remorseless Indian war. Sir, what is to become of the fifty or sixty thousand warriors and their families who line your frontier when the buffalo and other game upon which they now depend for subsistence are exhausted? Think you they will lie down and die without a struggle? No, sir; no! The time is not far distant when, pent in on all sides, and suffering from want, a Philip, or a Tecumseh, will arise to band themselves together for a last and desperate onset upon their white foes.

Sibley was no distant exponent of comfortable philanthropy, like some New England puppeteers of abolitionism. He lived among Indians for long periods and was the father of a half-breed daughter. He married a "fine New England woman" in 1843, but like Richard Mentor Johnson of Kentucky and Sam Houston of Texas, he cared for his child and never disavowed the fullness of his participation in earlier life. Even in the tight, inhibited world of late Victorian Minnesota, it was safe to *remember* sexuality, though not to speak of it directly. In a memoir Sibley, in a tone of yearning, recalled the experience of an Indian friend after a battle, when the two sides reconciled themselves physically: "The young and the Chippewa were by no means backward, in returning the compliment. . . . Old Leatherstocking would doubtless have been shocked. . . . Nevertheless, according to his old maxim, 'Human nature will be human nature the world over.' "

Sibley's own nature was an amalgam of romantic models. He drew these models not only from Cooper but from many of the same writers who contributed to Beltrami's imaginary world: Froissart, Sir Thomas Malory, Sir Walter Scott, and the romantic poets. Sibley read about heroes both medieval and contemporary, molded his life after them, and paid as much attention as Beltrami to his audience. He did not take false postures, but he was acutely self-conscious.

For years he reported his own adventures for magazines like *The Spirit of the Times* and *Wildwoods*. As late as 1841 he left his post for five months and went on a foray with the Indians, "remained with the hunters, one of their number, assuming their dress, copying their manners, entering into their sports," and keeping careful mental notes. Here is a sample of one of his reports:

> I rode carelessly along, with but one barrel of my gun loaded, when, nearing the buffalo, he turned quick as lightning to charge. At this critical instant I had risen in stirrups, and released my hold on the bridle-rein. The moment the buffalo turned, my horse, frightened out of his propriety, gave a tremendous bound sidewise, and alas! that I should tell it, threw Hal [his name for himself] clear out of the saddle, and within ten feet of the enraged monster . . . face to face with the brute, whose eyes glared through the long hair which garnished his frontlet like coals of fire, the blood streaming from his nostrils. . . . Holding my gun ready cocked to fire if he attempted a rush, I stood firmly, although I . . . thought my last hour had come! How long he remained there, pawing and bellowing, I have now not the least idea, but . . . at last he turned slowly away, and I gave him a parting salute. . . . The only one of the party within view now came up. I was so near the buffalo . . . that my companion asked me if I had struck the beast with the barrels of my gun.

That companion might well have been Sibley's partner of many expeditions, a half-breed hunter named Jack ("Iron Face") Frazer, with whom, it seems, Sibley identified. Frazer was the subject of Sibley's only long literary work, a biography in which Frazer's adventures are often almost identical with those "Hal" reported as his own in the earlier

Jack Frazer, trapper and friend of Henry Sibley. *From the Collection of the Minnesota Historical Society*

288

magazine reports. In his biography of Iron Face, the author and subject tend to merge. A reader of that biography who also found Freud's biographical work intriguing might savor Captain Frederick M. Marryat's horrified comment on Frazer, whom he met on his American travels. He said of Iron Face that his chief ambition was "[to add] the scalp of his father." Marryat supposes that Frazer's reason was revenge for "the father's not having brought him up a white man." At times Sibley seems to have been sorry that his own father had.

Sibley was not alone in sending to eastern readers tales of his exploits in the West and in keeping one eye on the audience while the other was on target. The same self-consciousness was reported of other western heroes. Daniel Boone, the father of them all, survived a first effusive biography by twenty-six years. He was not, it is said, altogether pleased with it. Kit Carson thought that *his* chronicler, DeWitt C. Peters, "laid it on a leetle too thick" and later was embarrassed when, leading a search party, he found a worshipful account of his own career among the plunder taken by the Apache from a wagon train. Davy Crockett of course

Minnesota Gothic: the William Gates Le Duc House in Hastings.
Photograph by Dick Bancroft

wallowed in the adulation of crowds. As Henry Nash Smith has pointed out in discussing "Buffalo Bill" Cody, "the persons created by the writers of popular fiction were so accurate an expression of the demands of the popular imagination that it proved powerful enough to shape an actual man in its own image."

In the 1830s and 1840s, scores of imitations of Cooper's forest romances were current and read along with the medieval romances of Sir Walter Scott. Mark Twain wryly complained that chivalry, which had been interred with *Don Quixote,* had been restored to life by Scott's *Ivanhoe.* It was the Louisiana state capitol, with its Gothic turrets and finials, that provoked Twain's remark, but all the way up the Mississippi to St. Anthony Falls, frontiersmen read "border ballads" and tales of chivalry and laid up Gothic Revival houses. Sibley's friend William Gates Le Duc, fur trader, piano salesman, and town site boomer, built the most ambitious castle in Minnesota and in its parlor read *Ivanhoe* over and over again to his daughters. Sibley himself kept a complete set of Scott beside his Cooper, Hallam's *Middle Ages,* and Froissart's *Chronicles.*

Edmund Burke's picture of bands of buckskinned condottieri sweeping across the Great Plains was confirmed in some degree by the exploits of western outlaws. The armed horseman, free from the restraints of church and tradition and set loose in a strange and savage scene, behaved in America as he had elsewhere, but after 1830 he was provided with a new stock of instructions in the form of tales of chivalrous knights. These instructions complicated the simpler processes of plunder and reciprocal slaughter. There was a brief, local, sporadic, and artificial reprise of the Age of Chivalry.

To take an extreme example: the propensity for dueling with weapons, which was part of the life of Andrew Jackson's old Southwest, did not penetrate into the colder regions of the Mississippi Valley, but dueling in a new guise was demanded of men who would be leaders. In Illinois, Abraham Lincoln "wrestled his way into the legislature," taking on all comers in each forest hamlet he canvassed. It was Lancelot and Gawain all over again, though without the armor; in Minnesota, Sibley went through the same test. His friend Folwell reports: "Endowed with a splendid athletic figure, he developed such skill and strength in the manly art of self-defense that, in the traditional words of a contemporary, 'there was but one man in the territory that dared stand up against him and that was Bully Wells.'"

It should not be thought that in the dust of a wrestling or boxing match Sibley abandoned his pride. He was no more an egalitarian in his direct relationships (whatever contemporary theory might have been) than was Andrew Jackson. Cooper, in his romances, always kept a clear distinction between the humble but heroic Leatherstocking type and the Oliver Effingham type, the gentleman disguised as hunter. Henry Nash Smith recognized the latter as "an indisputably upper-class hero." Sibley was the legitimate descendant of the disguised duke of Shakespeare's pastoral romances, of the hereditary lord of Locksley Hall amid the Merry Men, and of Sir Wilfred of Ivanhoe in the fellowship of the forest. But now the Merry Men were the Indian traders, "that bold and hardy class of men, who despising the comforts and seduction of civilized life . . . fascinated by the unrestrained liberty of action offered by the trade with Indians . . . who equally with honest Leatherstocking shunned the society of [their] fellow white men, and above all, despised the whole machinery of the law." And Sherwood Forest extended a thousand miles.

Major Thomas Newson, who knew Sibley for thirty years, spoke of him as "very jealous of his reputation." Folwell recorded the story of Sibley's election by the French-Canadian squatters, who had occupied the site of the future city of St. Paul, to represent them when the land was finally sold out from under them at auction. As he proceeded to bid for the land in his grave Yankee fashion, he was surrounded by a forest of clubs, as his clients stood by to dissuade any counterbidder. Thereafter, "Sibley conveyed to each person . . . his proper area. . . . It was only after long delay and much persuasion that he could induce them to take their deeds. Ignorant of American ways, they felt their home would be more secure in the hands of Monsieur Sibley, their ancient patron, than in their own."

This was not strange, since for many years he was the only civil magistrate in "a region . . . large as the Empire of France." While one biographer, Nathanael West, wrote so uncritically of Sibley that his truth cannot be fished out of his gush, he is probably right in saying that "the simple-minded people by whom [Sibley] became gradually surrounded . . . were verily persuaded he possessed . . . the high power of life and death. His word was the code imperial, his decisions unappealable."

Part of his magic was that he was a seigneur who went savage, as a sort of liturgy of renewal in nature. Often he left his castle at Mendota to join Iron Face and the Indians in their annual hunt. "I allowed my hair to grow very long . . . and being bearded like a pard, and dressed in Indian costume, with two enormous dogs at my heels [looked like] a wild man of the woods." When he returned, he cut his hair and resumed the seigneurial "dignity and grand manner," in Folwell's words. He almost failed to be reelected as the territorial representative to Congress because it was feared that, in his aristocratic phase, he would lack the heavy heartiness of congressional camaraderie required to secure the concessions the settlers desired.

"Bluff Alex" Ramsey possessed all those convenient qualities Sibley lacked. Ramsey became governor, senator, and a cabinet officer, while the surge of prosperity, settlement, and speculation that carried him upward were engulfing and destroying the frontier world. Meanwhile Sibley merely persevered, performing his tasks conscientiously and leading his constituents with dignity down the road which opened before him. It was Sibley who persuaded Congress to call the territory Minnesota and to select St. Paul as its capital. Counties and towns were named after him, and as soon as the territory became a state and the inhabitants could have their own way, he was elected the first governor.

But things began to go awry; his old Jacksonian-Houstonian principles were not easy to apply, and his preference for a simple life in a sparsely settled country did not comport well with the requirements of a state that was doubling and redoubling its population each decade. Nor did he truckle to the speculators and land promoters. His prickly honor led him, as governor, first to fight a powerful railroad lobby seeking state underwriting for its bonds, and then, when ordered by the state supreme court to support the bonds according to the legislature's requirements, he insisted upon honoring the state's obligations even after the legislature had changed its mind. He was not reelected. The Republicans, led by Ramsey, who had made a convenient switch from Whiggery, surged to victory in 1860.

To Ramsey the frontier was an invitation to exploitation, a vast tract of real estate which, when cleared of its wild animals, trees, and original inhabitants, would be ripe for development. To Sibley it was a lost Arcadia.

In August 1862, from Fort Abercrombie on the Red River to New Ulm around the crook of the Minnesota River, along a two-hundred-fifty-mile front, two thousand Sioux (the word is ours, not theirs) launched the first assault of their Thirty Years War against steam engines, broken promises, agriculture, usury, breech loaders, extortion, the telegraph, and the white man's "civilization." In forty days they killed nearly five hundred of their foes and drove the farmers and traders back within the walls of forts and towns. They also demonstrated conclusively that theirs was a losing battle (see Chapter 9).

The Sioux could not win even against the dregs of the forces of civilization left after thousands of men had been drained off to fight in the Civil War, civilization's own sort of fraternal warfare. They could not

A painting (1891) by Alex Schwendinger of the attack by the Sioux on New Ulm, Minnesota, in 1862. *From the Collection of the Minnesota Historical Society*

win despite their early success in effecting a surprise attack. (The biggest news in the local newspapers in the days *before* their assault was the appearance of new novels by Anthony Trollope and Victor Hugo.) They could not win even under the leadership of a great warrior like Little Crow. When the American Civil War was over and veteran armies were let loose on the Sioux, they still put up a good fight, but they never had a chance.

The task of defeating this first Indian effort was meted out to Sibley, who had been their friend and companion. But their true antagonist, the organizer of their disinheritance, the proponent of their extermination, was Alexander Ramsey. While Sibley had been hunting with the Sioux and playing out the game as frontier seigneur, Ramsey was learning the new politics in a tough school, Pennsylvania. Pennsylvania had changed much since William Penn said, "Oh, how sweet is the quiet of these parts, freed from the troubles and perplexities of woeful Europe." Two centuries of settlement and industrialism had created troubles and perplexities aplenty and battened on Penn's commonwealth a corrupt political system, of which Ramsey was a product.

He had been orphaned at nine, had struggled to learn the law, was admitted to the bar in 1839 and elected to Congress four years later, serving two terms. By then he was a thorough professional, ready for higher service to the Whig party. He could speak German to Pennsylvania Dutch farmers and talk tariffs with the local manufacturers. He became chairman of the State Central Committee, and after doing potent service to secure Zachary Taylor's victory in 1848, stood ready for his share of the spoils. Taylor was not slow in satisfying his friends; he replaced 540 of 929 presidential appointees and 6,200 of a total federal service of 17,780.

Ramsey aspired to be collector of the port of Philadelphia and was sorely disappointed when he was passed over for that potentially profitable post. He was given instead the governorship of Minnesota Territory.

When the new governor arrived, his province was a wilderness and his capital a squalid hamlet, "a dozen framed houses, not all completed, and some eight or ten small log buildings with bark roofs. . . . [It was] just emerging from a collection of Indian whiskey shops, and birch-roofed cabins of half-breed voyageurs." The population of St. Paul was about two hundred fifty, that of the whole territory less than five thousand.

To Sibley's eye the wilderness had been beautiful and, he hoped, permanent. Not to Ramsey. In his first message to a somewhat skeptical territorial legislature, he spoke of the vast country still under the control of the Sioux as "extensive, rich and salubrious . . . equal, in soil, to any portion of the valley of the Mississippi; and, in healthfulness . . . probably superior to any part of the American continent." Then, in the ringing words of a prospectus: "It is known to be rich in minerals as in soil; is sufficiently timbered . . . watered by some of the finest rivers . . . and is bespangled with beautiful lakes in every direction." He set about to secure that land for settlement.

By a shrewd stroke, Ramsey made allies of the Indian traders under Sibley's leadership. They might otherwise have opposed settlement, because it inevitably would bring the end of their already flagging business, dependent as that business was on the fruits of the wilderness. But Ramsey's timing was impeccable.

After the lush years of the early 1830s, fur-bearing animals were becoming scarce, the traders more numerous, and the fashion for fur hats and trim declining. The traders had borrowed their stock in goods from their companies, advanced those supplies to their best "producers" among the Indians, and hoped for a good hunting season in pelts to secure a return on their advances and pay off their loans. Hunting was increasingly difficult, the prices of pelts lower. The traders were in deeper and deeper trouble; since 1842, Sibley, by his own account, had lost ten thousand or more dollars a year. Their only hope was that frequent device of American capitalism, a government bailout. If the federal government would *buy* land from the Indians, the funds would flow through to pay off their accumulating obligations to the traders in a sort of terminal recoupment for the fur trade. Sibley admitted that this would be enough "to set me on my feet and pay all my heavy liabilities for losses." Thus, for the first time but not the last, traders whose influence with the tribes was great were used to advance the interests of land speculators (and, in fairness, of settlers generally).

While Sibley, of necessity, acquiesced in the outcome, he raised regular objections to the process. The acquisition of the Sioux lands in the treaties of 1851 was a sorry tale of extortion and undue influence. Ramsey presided over the whole affair, of which Sibley, it seems certain, was much ashamed. (His authorized biography, written under the eye of the old man, never mentions the matter.) One callous observer remarked that "they were as fair as any Indian treaties." It seems very unlikely that much of the money reached the Indians after the traders and their agents, intermediaries, and sponsors got their share. More than $400,000 went immediately to the traders. More than a million dollars was to be set aside as a trust fund to pay for the twenty-five million acres acquired, but the Indians themselves probably obtained no more than a cent or two an acre in cash.

At one stage Sibley was willing to forgo his portion to complete the process, believing that a failure to conclude treaties after so much gold had been promised to the Indians would lead to a bloody war. A more general attitude was that of another trader-politician, Henry M. Rice, who for a "bonus" induced the assent of his client Indians. Authorized

A contemporary image of a Sioux "outrage" as outraged Indians retaliated against settlers encroaching upon their land. *From the Collection of the Minnesota Historical Society*

by Ramsey, Rice expended $5,173 in bribes, and the amount was charged against the Indian funds for "removal and subsistence."

By the 1851 treaties, an empire of rich agricultural land was "liberated from the hand of red savagery" and made ready for settlement, town site promotion, railroad land grants, and speculation, in all of which Alexander Ramsey played a leading part. A second province of a million acres was added to this empire in 1858 when the Sioux were bilked again, this time receiving something less than $85,000 after the claims of the traders had been satisfied. Those who have studied these treaties agree that their effect was to strip the Sioux of their ability to support themselves and to crowd them onto a ribbon-thin reservation along the Minnesota River. There they existed at the mercy of Indian agents and rapacious traders, with little recourse except to the violence of which Sibley had warned. Bishop Henry Whipple wrote to President Abraham Lincoln that the Indians had been swindled and were certain to resort to bloodshed and that "as sure as there is a God, much of the guilt lies at the nation's door."

A painting from the 1890s of the Battle of Acton during the Sioux War of
1862. *From the Collection of the Minnesota Historical Society*

Humiliation and fraud worked to incite their counterattack. Failure
by the government to catch and punish outlaws who murdered isolated
settlers gave the impression not only of its injustice but also of its impo-
tence. Refusal by local Indian agents to provide food to starving women
and children detonated the eventual outbreak.

Sibley undertook a long, slow, underequipped campaign to drive the
hostile bands across the Missouri. In effect, he was used by Ramsey to
visit upon his old friends and hunting companions the wrath of those
forces of civilization which Sibley himself had distrusted, to carry out
the military necessities caused by a treaty and an extortionate system he
had resisted.

Sibley accepted from Ramsey the command of the tatterdemalion
troops which could be mustered to defend the frontier after most of
Minnesota's best men had gone to fight the Confederacy. The Sioux had
many hostages, the settlers were in panic, and Sibley's cautious prosecution of the war could gain him very few friends. Ramsey was constantly
prodding him along, and after a few months Sibley was further embarrassed by the orders received from General John Pope, a superior officer

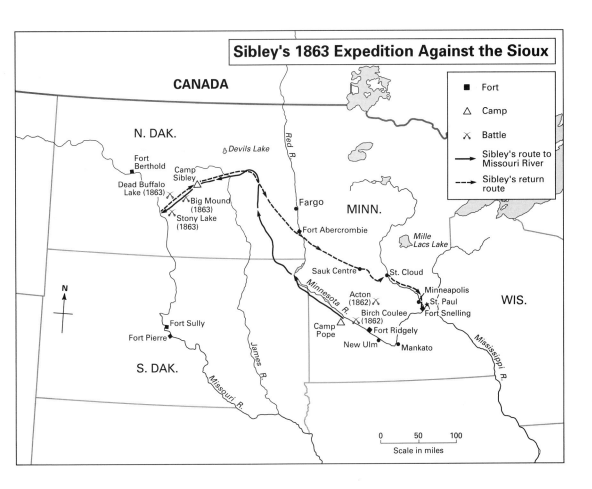

Sibley's 1863 Expedition Against the Sioux

CANADA

N. DAK.

Devils Lake

Fort Berthold

Camp Sibley

Dead Buffalo Lake (1863)

Big Mound (1863)

Stony Lake (1863)

Red R.

Fargo

MINN.

Fort Abercrombie

Mille Lacs Lake

Sauk Centre

St. Cloud

Minneapolis

St. Paul

WIS.

Acton (1862)

Birch Coulee (1862)

Fort Snelling

Minnesota R.

Camp Pope

Fort Ridgely

New Ulm

Mankato

Fort Sully

Fort Pierre

S. DAK.

James R.

Missouri R.

Mississippi R.

N

Legend:
- ■ Fort
- △ Camp
- ✗ Battle
- → Sibley's route to Missouri River
- ⇢ Sibley's return route

0   50   100
Scale in miles

sent from Washington. Pope, whose titanic ego had been bruised by defeats on Civil War battlefields, was desperately seeking a quick and dramatic success to restore his reputation. Both he and Ramsey insisted upon an extermination policy. It was not only beyond Sibley's means, but less effective than his process of keeping down the number of hostiles by weaning away Indians who could be induced to seek peace. Sibley, at the front, tried to save the lives of hostages held by his opponents by avoiding a precipitate attack and to minimize his own casualties by wooing defections among his opponents.

After the first summer's successful campaign to drive the Sioux from the settlements, Ramsey told Sibley that "a feverish apprehension exists that you may be unable . . . to protect our border settlements from the stealthy encroachments of the wily foe . . . with a repetition of the dangers and horror from which it was fortunately rescued last fall." Ramsey's rhetoric clouded another objective: to hold on to the lucrative trade with the British colonies along the Red River. The routes to those settle-

General John Pope, searching for glory in Minnesota in 1862. *From the Collection of the Minnesota Historical Society*

ments lay just behind Sibley's advance posts. Perhaps, the governor suggested, a little more attention might be paid to them and a little less to the exposed and frantic settlements. He wrote Sibley that "the gold regions of the Saskatchewan and other portions of British America" were rapidly developing, and the Hudson's Bay Company "have for a few years past been shipping to a great extent their annual supplies" by the exposed route. He asked that Sibley dispose his forces with an eye to "the profitable trade which it will furnish our people, and our national pride." Sibley responded a little wanly, saying he was overextended already but would "open the communication referred to by you as speedily as I have the means to do so."

Ramsey affably assured Pope that Sibley would terminate the unpleasantness with the Sioux quickly and neatly. The great man from Washington arrived as the first summer's campaign was nearing an end. He set a tone at once by dismissing a small victory by Sibley's men as a mere skirmish and expressing chagrin when Sibley addressed one of his dispatches to Ramsey instead of himself. From his comfortable head-quarters in St. Paul, Pope wrote the exhausted commander in the field, who was seeking to effect agreements with some Sioux bands:

> It is idle and wicked, in view of the atrocious murders these Indians have committed, in the face of treaties and without provocation, to make treaties or talk about keeping faith with them. The horrible massacres of women and children, and the outrageous abuse of female prisoners still alive, call for punishment beyond human power to inflict. There will be no peace in this region by virtue of treaties and Indian faith. It is my pur-pose utterly to exterminate the Sioux . . . destroy everything belonging to them and force them out into the plains. . . . They are to be treated as maniacs or wild beasts, and by no means as people with whom treaties or compromises can be made.

Sibley replied, patiently, that he was endeavoring by delicate negoti-ation to detach those Indians who

> had abandoned the fortunes of Little Crow . . . to state to them that their friendly conduct in refusing to countenance or harbor Little Crow would be appreciated. . . . It would not do to precipitate matters now, for fear of alarming those who are coming forward to take their chances. . . . It has been clearly proven that some of them even risked their lives in defense of the whites.

Despite increasing pressure from Ramsey, Pope, and the growing vigilante spirit on the frontier, Sibley persisted in seeking to distinguish between hostile and friendly Indians and between those who had mur-dered isolated settlers and those who had participated in open warfare. Even after Pope's rebuke, he ordered his subordinates to "assure the Indians that it is not the purpose of the government to punish innocent persons. . . . You will of course prevent the men under your command from using any undue or unnecessary violence toward the Indians, should you take any of the latter, and especially do not permit any insult to the female."

Pope assured Ramsey that he was executing a policy in which they had agreed to place the Indians

> where they can no longer impede the progress of the settlements nor endanger the settlers. To treat all Indians (as the late outrages and many previous outrages have demonstrated to be the only safe and humane method) as irresponsible persons. . . . By this mode of treatment a great barrier . . . will be at once removed, and the whole region to the Rocky Mountains will, in a very short time, be opened to emigration, travel and settlement.

By such pronouncements, it seems, despite the difficulties of the field commanders such as Sibley, Pope was confident that he could quickly do his chores on this side show campaign and return to glory in the war against the Confederacy. In October 1862 he announced happily to Major General Henry Halleck at the War Department that "the Sioux War is at an end."

Charles Flandrau, who was serving under Sibley on the frontier, knew better and wrote Ramsey a month later that Pope was "fatally mistaken." There were tens of thousands of angry Indians. Little Crow was, it was feared, busily recruiting and might return

> from the west with reinforcements sufficient to reenact all the horrors of the past summer. . . . These fears . . . may be regarded by General Pope and yourself as foolish . . . [but] there is no peace. The whole country outside the lines of the troops is in the possession of the Indians. You, nor General Pope, dare not go 20 miles from St. Cloud without an escort of at least a company.

When spring came in the following year, Sibley wrote Ramsey that he was still short of men and supplies and that "we are in a state of war with the Sioux nation." Sibley spent the summer of 1863 leading an expedition against the Sioux across the Dakota badlands:

> If the devil were permitted to select a residence upon the earth, he would probably choose this particular district for an abode, with the redskins' murdering and plundering bands as his ready ministers. . . . Through this vast desert, lakes fair to the eye abound, but generally their waters are strongly alkaline or intensely bitter and brackish. The valleys between them frequently reek with sulfurous and other disagreeable vapors. The heat was so intolerable that the earth was like a heated furnace. . . . Yet through all these difficulties men and animals toiled on until the objects of the expedition were accomplished.

Pope was in Milwaukee, where he had set up a new general headquarters. The food was excellent, accompanied by string quartets.

Sibley had to contend with other difficulties, among the worst of which were mobs of settlers attacking his camps. Encouraged by politicians, these vigilantes wanted to execute all the Indian prisoners Sibley had captured. Ramsey was counseling President Lincoln (in jest, his daughter thought) to hang a few more Indians and increase Republican votes in Minnesota. Though Lincoln courageously insisted upon due process before hanging *any* prisoners, Sibley was charged with their protection and had to bear the wrath of the settlers. Twice he had to fight off lynch mobs, and his political career was at an end. In the South in the 1890s, the cry would be "nigger lover." In Minnesota in the 1850s, as in Wyoming or Montana in the 1870s, once the epithet "Indian lover" was fixed upon a man, he was beyond redemption at the polls.

The end of the Minnesota phase of the "Sioux War" was reached when Sibley and General Alfred Sully drove the hostiles west to the Missouri and an uneasy truce was reached. (The war was to be resumed

A photograph of Little Crow at the time of the Sioux War of 1862. *From the Collection of the Minnesota Historical Society*

301

again, farther west, when Civil War heroes like George Armstrong Custer had an opportunity to seek further bloody exploits there.) Sibley returned to private life.

Though Ramsey was demonstrably fond of him, that fondness grew only after Sibley ceased to be a potent political rival. Ramsey had been quick to deploy Sibley in Indian emergencies; Sibley had made his attitude toward the Indians very well known. Possibly Ramsey was just lucky; he had a friend and rival competent in achieving his ends at that rival's expense. But Ramsey was usually unwilling to permit history to evolve unaided. His training had occurred in Pennsylvania, where luck in politics was customarily arranged. On two occasions his lieutenants wrote him, "We have Sibley where we want him," and "We have succeeded in making a regular Sibley and Rice affair of it, with the Sibley party on our side."

It may not have been necessary for Ramsey to be so full of guile. Sibley had little appetite for public life in Ramsey's world. As early as 1850, when Ramsey had just arrived in the territory, the new politics had begun to replace the more seigneurial style of the old frontier days. A friend noted that year that Sibley, upright and proud, had barely won a congressional contest in which his opponents had used "hope, fear, avarice, ambition, personal obligations, money, whiskey, oysters, patronage, contracts, champagne, loans, the promise of favors, jealousy, personal prejudice, envy — everything that could be tortured into a motive." That was "Bluff Alex" Ramsey's stock in trade.

302

In his last years Henry Hastings Sibley, honorable and anachronistic, walked to his office down Summit Avenue every weekday morning, talking with my grandfather about the old days.

A temple-form church, drawn in 1794 or 1795 by Pierre Pharoux for the
Livingston family's Speranza (now Athens, New York). The drawing was
discovered in 1990. *The Huntington Library*

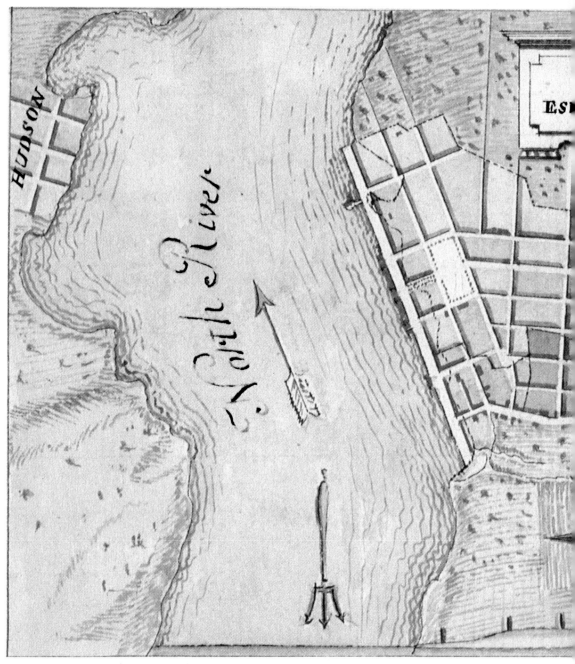

French neoclassical speculation in the 1790s: a map of Speranza on the Hudson, drawn by Pharoux and never before published. *The Huntington Library*

A PLAN of ...ANZA TOWN

Scale, 16 chains to an Inche

2 4 6 8 10 12 14 16 ch.

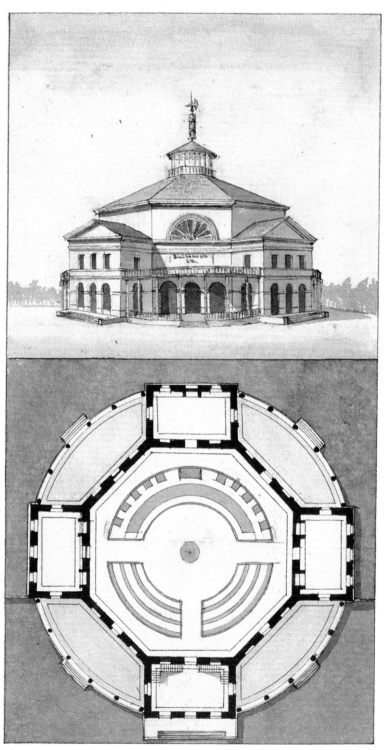

The original grand-scale cruciform courthouse designed by Pharoux
for Speranza about 1794. The plan was later reduced but was still
too ambitious to be built. The drawing was found in 1990.
The Huntington Library

17

The Wild Jackass of the Prairie
The Heroism of Ignatius Donnelly

I T MUST HAVE BEEN when we were fifteen or so, in 1940 or 1941. We decided to ride our bicycles from St. Paul down to Hastings, about seventeen miles, and follow the Mississippi downstream along Highway 61 until we came to the sign pointing to Nininger. Then we would head across the flat fields of wheat and corn to try to find the old Donnelly place, where, we had heard, the crazy old man's library was lying open to the weather, with books and papers strewn all about. It sounded like great foraging to us. As I recall, we traveled only about ten miles before somebody — perhaps me, perhaps Jimmy Turner — developed simultaneously a serious blister and a recognition that we would have to bicycle back the same distance to get home again. We never got to Nininger. That was the first time I tried to do some research on Ignatius Donnelly.

I did a little more in college, and was encouraged to undertake a serious perusal of his papers by an event some nearly forty years after the aborted assault upon Nininger. I was at an interminable investment conference in London, attending as chief financial officer of the Ford Foundation. People were droning on about beta coefficients and R-squares and covariances. I noted that the old gentleman across from me was setting the right tone; his head was held in his hand, his hand propped on a forearm stabilized by an elbow placed in his lap, and his eyes were closed. Had the head not been nodding slightly, the impression of rapt concentration would have been convincing.

I whispered to a neighbor, though I could not expect to be understood, "What this meeting needs is Ignatius Donnelly." My neighbor looked puzzled, but the old gentleman trembled; one of his eyelids quivered and opened slightly. He reached for his pad — "S. G. Warburg and Company" was at its top, with his name as chairman. He wrote: "Did you say Ignatius Donnelly?"

He was then Sir Eric Roll, formulator of many of the economic policies of the Western Alliance in the immediate postwar years and one of the most distinguished economic historians of our century. He is now (1990) Lord Roll of Ipsden, leader of the Labour party in the House of Lords on economic matters. He has been generous with friendship to me ever since our common enthusiasm for Donnelly permitted us to pass notes back and forth that day, and thereafter to dine. Donnelly has been for both of us a representative of the intellectual as politician, the ebullient warrior for good causes in the face of economic power and the conventional opinions power can sponsor. A little nutty, perhaps, suffering somewhat from the isolation brought on him by his location and his opinions, but a great man, nonetheless.

The career of Ignatius Donnelly began as the settlement and exploitation of the Mississippi Valley presented for the reaping a harvest mankind had not planted. The trees had grown high and thick; the prairie was deep with the accumulated loam of the ages; the prairie animals bore hides that the Indians were prepared to collect and supply to traders. After the harvest of furs came the harvest of lumber and then the harvest of wheat. Riches poured forth from the land. Hard labor was needed to gather up its offerings, but a man with a flair for managing his fellow men could organize and discipline that labor. Extraction could proceed, retarded only by the occasional depressions that ensued after the capacity of the earth to pour forth bounty outran the capacity of civilization to absorb it.

In the 1880s a territory larger than that of the thirteen original states was put under European-American settlement. As Frederick Jackson Turner noted, there was added to the farms of the nation an area equal to the combined territories of France, Germany, England, and Wales. The population of the six wheat-growing counties in the Red River Valley of the North jumped from 21,123 to 71,190 in the decade. St. Paul doubled its population between 1880 and 1883, and doubled it again by 1888 as it profited from its position as a railroad and jobbing center. The lines it fed were reaching out into the Dakotas, Kansas, and Nebraska while the population of parts of those states quadrupled. Railroad mileage in the Dakotas grew from 399 in 1880 to 4,726 in 1890, in Nebraska from 1,634 to 5,407. The Great Northern and the Northern Pacific were pushed through to the West Coast; the range cattle industry moved northward into the trade territory of Minneapolis and St. Paul; then, accumulating profusion upon profusion, another natural outpouring was added to lumber and burgeoning agriculture: iron ore was found, millions of tons of it, on the escarpments of the Lake Superior basin.

In 1884 the first ore was shipped out of Two Harbors from the Vermilion Range, bound for Andrew Carnegie's furnaces. James J. Hill and John D. Rockefeller joined forces thereafter to seize control of thousands of additional acres of red oxidized earth, and by 1891 the Mesabi Range was producing. The population of the lumber and ore port of Duluth leapt from three thousand in 1880 to thirty-three thousand in 1890. Farther south, Minneapolis used six million board feet of lumber to lay sixty-seven miles of boardwalk in a single year (1887).

Yet amid this profusion there arose a sense of injustice. It was not just that the bonanza was unequally shared — that is the way of bonanzas. It was not only that there grew up, in Donnelly's famous words, "two classes . . . tramps and millionaires." There had always been poor people struggling to survive on the bare, windswept, shelterless prairie, amid blizzards, drifts, and a temperature of 40 degrees below zero Fahrenheit in winter, and as the summer dust swirled, watching the thermometer (if they had one) reach 104 degrees. The Dakota, Santee, and Ojibway had lived in relative equanimity in the face of the climate. On the upper Missouri the Arikara, Ree, and Mandan, like some of the sodbusters who succeeded them, lived in agricultural villages over many decades (most of them died of European diseases). Others moved from place to place seeking food, as the later migrant workers — "tramps" —moved about seeking work.

What was different now was that power over the day-to-day conditions of life was known to be held by a relatively few people located far away. These absentees demonstrated little interest in the struggles of the inhabitants of the region and squeezed them, like Irish tenants or Hungarian peasants, for profits drawn from their last drops of sweat and tears. The owners of the railroads and the grain elevators and the slaughterhouses controlled the prices they would vouchsafe to the farmers. The managers of the seed, salt, and machinery trusts controlled the costs of the means to produce. The bankers controlled the price of credit. Legislatures were bought and paid for by the same manipulators and extractors; if democracy functioned at all, it was because some few voices loud enough to be heard in its defense were still left in the land. Ignatius Donnelly was one of those who kept democracy alive, and with it hope. He had a loud voice. Those in parlors and paneled offices who conspired in well-modulated tones to rig prices and corner food supplies spoke of him as "braying." He was known among them as "the wild jackass of the prairie."

They tried to silence him, perhaps to silence their own residual consciousness that he was right. They succeeded for a time, and he fell in with them. But with the passion of a reformed sinner, he rose up again to

Ignatius Donnelly in his prime: "And are you sure of that?" *From the Collection of the Minnesota Historical Society*

306

make them uncomfortable. At the end they seemed to have done him in with derision. His corpulent red Irish body, which had survived so many blizzards and dust storms and endless haggling conventions and caucuses, sustained him until 1901, when he died of a heart attack in his seventieth year, two months after he lost his twenty-third election campaign. Nor did his spirit die even then; it animated the reforms of two Progressive decades built upon his forty years of agitation, and it went marching on into the agriculture policies of the New Deal.

But his reputation, that part of him we first encounter, was buried under the ridicule of respectable politicians and journalists during his lifetime and of respectable historians thereafter. Even during the New Deal years, Ignatius Donnelly, like William Jennings Bryan, was thought to be too much the hayseed Gracchus, too much the product of the pre-deodorant era to please fastidious urban intellectuals.

The Minnesota Don Quixote.

A contemporary cartoon of Ignatius Donnelly: someone so upsetting could not be treated seriously. *From the Collection of the Minnesota Historical Society*

"Ignominious" Donnelly he was called. He had led the Anti-Monopolists and the Greenbackers and the Grangers and the Populists, had lost so many campaigns for the House and the Senate and the governorship and the presidency that he had become a figure of fun. William Watts Folwell, the establishment historian of Minnesota, called his life a "dreary record." Latter-day critics agreed. Richard Hofstadter said he had been a leader of "country cranks"; Eric Goldman said he had a reputation for theories produced by too many nights on the prairie.

During Donnelly's lifetime Folwell set him down as "discredited . . . a mountebank politician," and the pamphleteers of the right and left were no kinder. Socialists disliked him: Everett Fish called him a "fat brute," and Sidney Owen called him the "Benedict Arnold of Populism." The merchants' editorialists disliked him as well: the *St. Paul Pioneer Press* said he was "like Judas Iscariot . . . a dictator [and] a dog," and the *Mississippi Valley Lumberman* called him a "dishonest political juggler." During a famous exchange of invective, the stately Elihu Washburn of Illinois accused him of taking bribes, of being an "office beggar," a coward, a liar, and a criminal "whose record is stained with every fraud . . . a man who has proved false alike to his friends, his constituents, his country, his religion, and his God."

Donnelly was quite capable of sustaining this sort of discourse. He replied to Washburn seriatim, pausing on the matter of office begging to note that four Washburn brothers had sat in the House of Representatives (Folwell piously notes "with honorable records") and that "out of office they are miserable, wretched . . . as the famous stump-tailed bull in fly time — every young male of the gentleman's family is born into the world with 'M.C.' [Member of Congress] franked across his broadest part. The great calamity seems to be that God, in his infinite wisdom, did not make any of them broad enough for the letters 'U.S.S.' [U.S. Senate]." Donnelly gave his valedictory to Washburn in these words:

> And if there be in our midst one low, sordid, vulgar soul; one barren, mediocre intelligence; one heart callous to every sentiment and every generous impulse, one tongue leprous with slander; one mouth which like unto a den of the foul beast giving forth deadly odors; if there be one character which, while blotched and spotted all over, yet raves and rants and blackguards like a prostitute; if there be here one bold, bad, empty, bellowing demagogue, it is the gentleman from Illinois.

Donnelly's words were thought to have been so intemperate as to cast him beyond the pale of parliamentary discourse. He was censured, while Washburn was not. Why the difference? Their language was equally sulfurous. But Washburn, according to Folwell, was "distinguished"; he was rich and related to other rich and distinguished men. Much could be forgiven him. Donnelly was poor and reluctant to acknowledge any man to be his better. Major Thomas Newson, reviewing Donnelly's career, concluded:

> Had his sense of propriety or even policy enabled him to have endured the slings of his enemies quietly . . . it is possible he would have saved himself the opposition he has since encountered, but that would not have been Donnelly. . . . He resented what he felt was a wrong. . . . The combative elements of the man have kept him in political hot water for nearly twenty years.

Newson was writing in 1884. Actually, the water had been hot for *thirty* years and remained at a slow boil for sixteen more. One of his allies, Wilford L. Wilson, said that Donnelly had "fallen in the esteem of the cultivated, refined, and religious people who largely make up the Republican party," while Washburn and his brothers went on to greater eminence among these same people. Even Folwell admitted that if Donnelly had omitted the olfactory references and the word "prostitute" in his excoriation of Washburn, "his own future and that of Minnesota politics would have been different from the dreary record."

What was that record? Was it really so dreary? Now that the tempers have cooled, can the man Ignatius Donnelly be described without either patronage or billingsgate?

Ignatius Donnelly was never a member of the House of Lords or lesser clubs in which status is secure and peers exchange esteem and reassurance. There does exist, from time to time, an "establishment," but not in his time and place and not for him. From the outset he was an outsider. His father was an anticlerical Irish immigrant who had barely begun the practice of medicine in Philadelphia when he contracted typhus from a patient and died. The education of the children, like the medical schooling of the father, was financed by the pawnshop kept by the proud, stiff, domineering mother.

The city was aglow at night, but not with brotherly love. Long afterward Donnelly recalled that "Philadelphia was afflicted by many riots; riots between whites and blacks, between natives and foreigners, between the different churches and different fire companies." Especially after the panic of 1837, there were riots with the members of the Native American party. These Know-Nothings would have been mystified by today's use of "Native American" to describe those they called red Indians or savages. Their politics were grounded in their proprietary residence in America, in racial hatred, and in the fear of competition for jobs from the Irish newcomers. The Irish, in response, made ample use of their tradition of civil disorder. They had a long inheritance of suspicion and resentment of authority, and authority in Philadelphia adopted the same ethnic antipathies as authority in Ireland: "If an Irishman is hanged for murder, his nativity is freely admitted," Donnelly commented, "but if he distinguishes himself in an honorable walk of life, then it is discovered that he is Scotch-Irish."

Ignatius Donnelly was proud of his heritage, although the signs DOGS AND IRISH KEEP OUT were constant reminders of a bitter welcome. Nor was he a member of the "club of Irish," for he was not a Roman Catholic and attended public schools. A half century later, after he had written *The Great Cryptogram,* he remembered his pride in his father's love of literature and his own encouragement by the great Oliver Wendell Holmes (to whom he had sent a youthful poem):

> A good many people believe that the proper occupation for a person of Irish blood is digging a ditch or flourishing a shillelagh. They are presumed to know nothing about literature and ultimately lack those qualities of patience and perseverance which are held to be the birthright of the Anglo-Saxon. . . . I think I have done something to dispel that prejudice.

American Prices and Wages 1840–1900

1900 = 1.00

estimated

- - - Retail prices—cost of living
——— Average hourly wages in manufacturing

310

After high school he studied law with Benjamin Harris Brewster, who was to become the attorney general of Pennsylvania and later of the United States. Brewster and his clerks were courteous, correct, but distant. "I lived with them, as it were, per gratia. The bond of connection has never been a pleasant one — I sever it without regret," he said after three years. Then Donnelly began his political career as he would end it, indifferent to party but vehement in his identification with the underdog. His maiden speech was for the Democrats in Independence Square, supporting an open immigration policy. He ran for the state legislature as a Democrat, but came to support the Whig candidate, who took a strong anti-nativist position. In June of 1856 he was back with the Democrats, attacking the Republicans and their nativist allies as "holding midnight council over the Irish and the Dutchmen [German immigrants]."

Two years earlier he had married Kate McCaffrey, the daughter of a shopowner, despite the opposition of his family. It was, he later recalled, "the most ludicrous affair imaginable . . . the pawnshop broker's shop and the market stall holding a heraldic disputation." His stern, ambitious mother resisted the match, and he resisted her, finally deciding in 1856 to make a new start in the West. She never forgave Kate, although she did admit in later years that Ignatius could not have prospered so well in Philadelphia as he did, for a while, in Minnesota.

The young Irishman went west on the make. He told a high school friend that "money makes the man, the want of it the fellow." He had seen enough of poverty. "Seneca praised the beauties of poverty, but Seneca had a large income. The beauties of poverty! . . . Nothing but unsatisfied wants, restricted capabilities, undeveloped virtues." One way to wealth was through real estate speculation. As a young lawyer in Philadelphia he had learned about land promotion, serving as an officer of five emigrant aid associations. He toured the new states of the Northwest and settled on Minnesota as the place to make his fortune: "What a beautiful land has the red man lost and the white man won!"

Despite his awareness of its beauty, Donnelly was not sentimental about the West in its primitive state. He had read his James Fenimore Cooper, but land to him was real estate. His was a dream of golden prairies producing a crop of dollar bills as settlers would come, ready to pay the man well who had gotten there first. Donnelly saw the peaceful land "waiting for the crowding numbers and the clamorous competition of the human animal to flow in." He arrived during the great land rush of the 1850s. Emigration spilled out upon the land. In six years, 140,000 people came flooding in where only 4,000 had been. A St. Paul newspaper admitted that "a very subordinate attention was paid to farming, the interest of the community being principally absorbed in projects of speculation." Major Newson said, "Almost everybody went into the business of buying and selling real estate, procuring acres and laying them out into cities and selling corner lots at fabulous prices. It became a mania."

Donnelly entered a partnership with John Nininger, brother-in-law of Alexander Ramsey, territorial governor of Minnesota. They bought a thousand or more acres along the Mississippi southeast of St. Paul, attracted investors, and sold land to the emigrants on the Mississippi packet boats. It was said that the settlers were equally at risk from "Bill Mallen . . . with his marked cards, and Ingenious Doemly [*sic*], with his city lots on paper selling for a thousand dollars each."

But this was unfair, for Donnelly believed his own propaganda. Mortgage debt in the territory grew from $22,553 in 1853 to $2,124,071 in 1854, and he borrowed with the rest to improve his cloud city. Among a hundred houses built on a platted but largely unsettled scene, he commenced the mansion for himself which was the destination of our bicycle expedition almost a century later. In his fever he thought himself a millionaire. After all, tax valuations in Minnesota had grown from $3.5 million in 1854 to nearly $50 million in 1857. Everybody was getting rich.

Then the bubble broke. In the summer of 1857 the credit system of the West collapsed. It was said that half the population of St. Paul retreated to the East. Hundreds of town sites returned to weeds, and Donnelly, in September of that black year, failed to pay his creditors. The collapse of 1857 had three crucial consequences for him: it repelled him back from prosperity into the arms of the debtors and the poor; it forced him into farming (for he had to do something with land that would never, now, contain a city); and it propelled him into full-time politics.

Donnelly, the disappointed land shark struggling to pay his own debts, refused to join in Nininger's squeezing of payments from those on his town site who could not produce the full price asked before the collapse of the land boom. Donnelly's partner was no more disposed toward idealism than before. "Self-defense is the first instinct of nature and the first duty to ourselves. A man who would take the clothes off his back to give his creditors would only be kicked for his pains." The partnership broke up. Donnelly was left with the land, the debts, and the friendship of his neighbors.

He became even more dependent on the patronage of Alexander Ramsey, who supplied him with legal work and political opportunity. After two unsuccessful races for the state senate as an organization Republican, he became Ramsey's hand-picked lieutenant governor in 1859 and remained a janissary of the Ramsey machine for nearly a decade. It sent him to the U.S. Congress in 1862, accommodating the urging of his wife ("Money to live on and glory to die on," she said) and his creditors ("If I am [elected] I will be able to do something for you," he said.)

His career reached its nadir during his three terms in Congress, when he was most "successful." He lobbied for railroads and speculated in the same roads personally, covering his tracks with patriotic forensics.

In 1864 he sold information about government commodities dealings to speculators, taking railroad stock in exchange for supporting land grants. In 1867 he took more stock for delaying the passage of a land grant until promoters could buy ripe town sites. In 1869 he was involved with General John C. Frémont in fraud and bankruptcy resulting from the unsuccessful promotion of the Atlantic and Pacific Railroad. Throughout the period he was one of the chief congressional agents of the promoter of the Northern Pacific, Jay Cooke.

There were important exceptions to this unprepossessing record, as we shall see, and all the while the instincts of the outsider were growing stronger. He differed with Ramsey and the "dynasty" over the tariff issue, believing that high tariffs were penalizing consumers. The bitterness that burst out in his reply to Washburn indicates that he felt himself increasingly isolated from the millers, lumbermen, and railroad builders who supported Washburn. Through the *St. Paul Globe*, he called them a "cold-blooded, purse-proud aristocracy." Finally he broke openly with Ramsey's machine in both the congressional and the Senate campaigns of 1868, which he lost. He was slower to break his ties to Cooke, but when he ran for Congress in 1870, supported by the Democrats and an organization he called the People's party, he lost again as Cooke's contractors organized against him. Though he told crowds during the campaign that "railroads . . . were created to transport the commerce of the country, not to rule its politics or corrupt its laws," he did not yet have the strength of will to resist Ramsey and Cooke and, to his shame, returned to the Republican fold "like a drowned gopher." Even more shamefully, he told the Republican convention that he had committed no sin in his flirtation with the Democrats for, like a boy caught fishing on the Sabbath, he said, "I hain't ketched nuthin."

Even then, at the bottom, Donnelly was lovable; his generous spirit illuminated even the dark corners of his years as a spoilsman. He never forgot what it had been to be "poor and powerless" in Philadelphia; and he was not too proud to recall "the people of my blood, my ancestors, [who] for generations led lives of savages and peasants, in mud hovels, without comfort, pleasure, or enlightenment." While antipathy to slavery might have been expected from a northwestern Republican, Donnelly went beyond the convenience and conventions of his place and time. He knew education and decent jobs were necessary to the advancement of the poor and distressed of the world; he espoused them for the Blacks and, remarkably for his time, for the Indians.

Indeed, it was his insistence that the Sioux be treated justly during and after the outbreak of 1862–1864 that put him in conflict not only with Ramsey's Republicans but also with the wing of the Democratic party led by former Senator Henry M. Rice. While in the Congress, Donnelly unflinchingly supported the unpopular views of Henry H. Sibley and another old Indian trader, Joseph R. Brown, at a time when his constituents were howling for more dead Indians and for the political scalps of "Indian lovers."

A year after the outbreak, Donnelly ripped into the Indian agents' exploitation of the Chippewa. Those agents included Rice, who dominated St. Paul politics, and several associates of the unimpeachable John S. Pillsbury, who was becoming the most powerful citizen in Minneapolis. Donnelly's persistence in espousing a humane Indian policy has been dismissed by some recent critics as utopian, but it won the praise of old Joe Brown, who reviewed it carefully and said, "It breathes the true spirit of Indian improvement."

His reconciliation with Ramsey in 1870 was temporary, the last of the vain expedients of a period when Donnelly's compass spun. Donnelly was not trusted by Ramsey's regulars; they knew him to be "sanguine . . . pugnacious." He was both, and he was, at this time, noisily inconsistent; as a result, it was for many years conventional to dismiss him as a bumpkin and an ignoramus.

Urbane inconsistency in an Edmund Burke may be forgiven, especially under aristocratic patronage, but bumptious country politicians are not so easily pardoned. Furthermore, their country manners may mislead some observers to dismiss them too quickly. Larzer Ziff, an otherwise respectable literary historian, was wont to speak of Donnelly's "rural upbringing," of his "principles instilled on the farm," of his living as though "the artifacts of civilization, unknown on the farm, were equated with viciousness." Whose farm? Not Ignatius Donnelly's farm, as we shall see. The artifacts about which he was thoroughly comfortable were the works of Shakespeare, of modern and ancient archaeology, linguistics, the Icelandic sagas, and modern economic theory. Though he was a city-bred intellectual driven to agriculture by the failure of his efforts to build cities, he became accustomed to the use of country language and was always a steadfast friend to farmers.

At first there was in him more of the physiocrat than the agriculturist, for of course he knew little about country realities. Only after he found himself forced to find another use for land that had been intended for the metropolis of Nininger did he resort to farming. Then his first self-definition was as the supervisor of his tenants. He started an agricultural society and advised his neighbors to set aside an acre as "Mind's acre" for the cultivation of the intellect. This was Minnesota in 1860, not Virginia in 1780, and he had no slaves to support his theorizing.

He was still using the rhythms of his Philadelphia speeches, invoking the image of a golden bridge between the hungry masses of Europe and "a billion empty acres" on this side of the Atlantic. But he was learning other rhythms and other lessons. Though he was in favor of filling those acres with farmers, he had few of the agrarian illusions of the eighteenth century. Dumping millions of unprepared townsmen upon the land would not make them into free and independent yeomen, no matter how many congressional incantations were made over their heads. Nor was cheap land enough without tools and money and education. "A human being on 80 acres of unimproved land is as helpless as if he were on 80 acres of water — in fact more so, for he could get a fishing line and probably catch something to eat." Land was a commodity like any other. "Hang on to your land to the last gasp," he told the farmers; "there are no more Minnesotas on the planet; and every day the battle of life will grow fiercer."

It is odd how urban liberals love to put Donnelly down as a dreamer of impractical dreams. Eric Goldman, for example, wrote, without evidence, that Nininger was to be "a community where everybody was to love everybody else," as if Donnelly was intending Brook Farm or New Harmony. He was not so sentimental; Nininger was a promotion. In the 1870s his physiocratic period came to an end along with his dependence on Ramsey. Reduced "to his fists and his backbone," he borrowed money and took his sons to farm an unbroken prairie in treeless Stevens County. No glade, no sheltering oak or pine, broke the wind sweeping down from the Arctic. The land cost one dollar an acre, but three times as much was required to turn the sod with a steel plow.

His recourse to full-time farming opened him to the ridicule of his urban enemies. Said the *St. Paul Pioneer Press*: "Woe to the usurer, the wheat-scalper, or the grasshopper that tries to pitch his tent" on Donnelly's land. Grasshoppers were no joke to the farmer that year. The Rocky Mountain locust fell upon Stevens County. In the towns "the very lawns [were] eaten bare by them"; the wheat fields were ravaged. Farmers desperately tried to drive off the locusts by dragging ropes across their fields or catching the insects with coal tar and sheet iron scoops.

Remembering those days, Kate Donnelly wrote her husband, "When I think of farming — I get almost sick. Think how hard they work — and they invariably come out in debt — and then [more] borrowing . . . and then misery — life is scarcely worth having."

Even at his most miserable, Donnelly remained a man of letters who drew upon his reading to write very well indeed — better than most of his critics. Like his father, he was widely acquainted with the literature of the Elizabethan period. Out of this reading, not out of "too many lonely nights on the prairie," came his enormous volumes asserting that Francis Bacon, not Shakespeare, was the author of the plays and sonnets. No critic has demonstrated that Donnelly's conclusions were hasty or his knowledge of Shakespeare's time superficial. William Ewart Gladstone, prime minister of England, and many others wrote Donnelly to commend him on *The Great Cryptogram,* and there are some who are still persuaded that Donnelly was right.

Out of his admiration of Francis Bacon's *New Atlantis* probably arose his own *Atlantis,* requiring researches in the Platonic literature, in Greek and Roman myth. He was groping toward a sort of pioneering comparative anthropology. Though he did not produce *The Golden Bough* (he was writing in the 1880s and 1890s), he did produce *The Golden Bottle,* an admirable political fable, and *Doctor Huguet,* an anthropological treatise in the form of a novel, describing the experiences of a White man who awoke one morning to find himself Black. William Styron's *Confessions of Nat Turner,* itself a remarkable work of the imagination, attempted less. *Ragnarok,* Donnelly's exercise in astronomy and geology, may be no more than a fascinating failure, but his apocalyptic novel *Caesar's Column* is a masterpiece of despair. It was written when he feared that the just resentments of the farmers and workers would find no redress, that the cities would become ungovernable, and that mobs, gang warfare, and military rule would ensue. It was a call to conscience in the 1890s; appallingly prescient, it remains a call to conscience a century later.

In 1873 the experience of 1857 was repeated; another panic deposited on humble folk the debris of speculators' overreaching and the subsequent failure of credit in general. (Donnelly was correct at the time, as we will note, that it settled into depression as the result, in part at least, of the federal government's deliberate reduction of the money supply.) In this case the bubble had been blown by Donnelly's old patron, Jay Cooke.

Jay Gould: the face of a buccaneer gone ashore and gone (fairly) respectable. *From the Collection of the Minnesota Historical Society*

316

Cooke's failure had its most dramatic effects on Duluth, the town where the Northern Pacific Railroad touched Lake Superior, which he, with Donnelly's aid, had "boomed." Within sixty days after Cooke's fall, half the businesses in the city went bankrupt; thousands of people went hungry and cold; the population dwindled from five thousand to thirteen hundred. The driver of the town's fire engine quit because there were no funds to fuel it, and in 1877 the city government simply resigned its charter.

It was not strange that many midwesterners thought eastern financial manipulators had undue influence on the life of the region. Jay Cooke's fortunes recovered, but it took the development of the Iron Range to bring Duluth back to life. Panics and booms were dramatic, but it was the drab daily evidence of concentrated power that slowly drove Don-

317

nelly into open opposition to the railroads. Rates were rigged so that
one third of the price of a shipment of wheat in Chicago was the cost of
conveying it there from Minnesota. Systems were built with bonds, then
stock was floated for a promoter's profit "to go home with."

Cooke, Jay Gould, Jim Fisk, William Vanderbilt, E. H. Harriman,
and James J. Hill grew immensely rich buying and selling the transportation systems upon which the agricultural West depended. Their methods
were not identical; Cooke, Fisk, and Gould encouraged the settlement
of desert regions with false promises, bilked their stockholders with false
accounting, built extravagantly in complicity with fraudulent contractors, and then sought to repay their bondholders with the proceeds of
excessive rates. They bought and sold legislators (as Donnelly knew
at first hand) and judges too. Hill, on the other hand, had little use for

such devices. He introduced "clean" books; it is likely that he actually believed that breaking the prairie sod was good for it and that plowing actually brought rainfall. Alone among the railroad promoters, he was seriously interested in agriculture and the breeding of cattle.

But even in the hands of a benign despot like Hill, the power of these railroad magnates was greater than that of many European princes. This was the era before a national income tax; the magnates' personal expenditures were more than princely, they were regal. They built palaces while the country people who paid their fares died of malnutrition, overwork, and debt. All the while the variegated colors of the upper Midwest were reduced to few, as the sodbusters replaced the perennials that had composed the natural sod of the prairie with annual, domesticated grasses — wheat, corn, oats, and rye.

The railroad fares were paid — then. The full *price* of overplanting and overgrazing was deferred until the droughts and blizzards of the 1880s and early 1890s. It is infuriating to read modern historians, writing in tenured complacency from sweet little New England villages, sustained by endowments and the remittances of trust companies, attacking Populists such as Donnelly as "nostalgic for an imaginary Eden." The farmers' and ranchers' sufferings were real. They did not hanker for some vanished past; they wanted justice in their own time and did their best to obtain it through the democratic process.

Donnelly's rhetoric may be excessive by monographic standards; let us concede that if his audiences had been faculty committees rather than sweaty farmers, he would have been unlikely to land an endowed chair. But though he was ambitious, after 1870 he commenced thirty years of agitation in which his own interest was sacrificed again and again to that of his neighbors. He was no dreamer; he was a successful legislator and could build alliances when he had to do so to find remedies for the midwesterners' grievances.

He offered a series of specific remedies, and he was often successful. As early as 1871 he persuaded the Republicans to adopt a platform calling for a graduated income tax to lighten the property tax load on the farmers. Through his exertions debtors received protection against usurious interest rates and quick foreclosures of their farm machinery. Farmers' children were given fair prices on schoolbooks because of his textbook law and his exposure of the publishers' ring. Though he was seldom credited with them, many of his proposals during the Granger period became law, including a commission to regulate the rates charged by railroads. His persistent efforts to secure electoral reforms during the Populist period led to their adoption during the ensuing Progressive era. As early as the 1880s he scored victories over the machines and succeeded in reducing corporate control of state legislatures.

Later critics have sought to depict Donnelly as an inept windbag, but bruised opponents did not complain of his ineptitude as, after many a

**Advertisement for a lecture
by Ignatius Donnelly in
Winona, Minnesota, in
1875.** *From the Collection of the
Minnesota Historical Society*

legislative session, they gathered themselves up out of the dust. He was
not always successful, but during one of his ascendent phases the *St. Paul
Daily Press* said, "Donnelly rules the Senate with lawless license of dema-
gogic deviltry, as the commune ruled Paris." In 1887, well after his prime,
he introduced fifty-seven measures into the Minnesota legislature, eighteen of which were accepted either entirely or in amended form.

This effort of the *Daily Press* to color Donnelly "red" by references to
the Paris commune of 1871 was to be expected, but in fact, he was careful
to avoid provocations to violence. If the message of *Caesar's Column* was
too subtle, he put into political practice his aversion to the devices of
the commune, which only thirty years later became the devices of the
Fascists.

After the depression of 1873 came decades of violence in the West when grievances exploded in terrorism. There were pitched battles between strikers and militia, between farmers and ranchers, and between sheriffs' posses, bent on foreclosure, and both farmers and ranchers. As revolutionary tensions rose in 1877 and again in 1894, he sought legislative remedies skillfully and patiently.

After the Granger movement died like a tired warhorse beneath him, he went slogging along with the foot soldiers of the threadbare Farmers Alliance. Russell Nye to the contrary, Donnelly did not "climb aboard" any Alliance "bandwagon." It was a hay wagon, and he pulled it right into the Republican convention. Buried in the hay was a set of very sensible proposals, most of which became law a little later. These measures are now so conventional that it is amusing to hear them decried as absurd by the hostile William Watts Folwell: "The Republican convention listened to the overture and to Donnelly's delicious blarney and straightway lifted into their platform substantially all the 'demands' of the Alliance and its associates."

Donnelly's objectives were frequently achieved by advancing the ambitions of others. He encouraged the entrance into politics of Cushman K. Davis, who became governor and then senator by adopting Donnelly's reforms at a prudent distance in time. Davis set a pattern of unacknowledged acquiescence that was followed by later statesmen such as John Lind, Knute Nelson, and Frank B. Kellogg. In the 1890s Donnelly himself was still a contender for the governorship and the vice presidency, but as a state legislator he went about his work of uncredited achievement. It became the practice of statesmen to deride him in public and seek his counsel in private.

Donnelly brought a new vitality to legislative investigation as a means of social change. In the decade following his Indian Bureau exposures of the 1860s, he demonstrated the overcharges made on books for the school system and the depredations of the lumbermen on state lands. For this, of course, he was not beloved by the publishers' or timbermen's lobbies. Folwell charged at the time that Donnelly's investigations were "leading nowhere," but they led in the 1880s to the exposure of lumber and iron ore frauds. In the 1890s Donnelly investigated the monopolistic fixing of prices on hard coal and tax evasion by some of Minnesota and Wisconsin's leading lumbermen. Folwell excised from his *History* the names of most of the plunderers because "by making liberal benefactions to churches, communities and colleges [they] have brought forth fruit meant for repentance."

Donnelly brought to Populism the eloquence and discipline learned from his years of oratory, pamphleteering, composition of novels, and scientific work. He wrote the most pungent documents of the Populist revolt. He animated the councils of that party, and his oratory could still rouse a crowd. Though John Hicks, Populism's historian, scored him for "florid rhetoric" and Larzer Ziff sniffed at "Donnelly's preamble to the Populist platform of 1892 . . . familiar high-flown changes on biblical rhetoric . . . the romantic lyrics of the cardboard motto, written to be sung to the accompaniment of the melodeon," the test of rhetoric is whether or not it convinces, and Donnelly's did.

The abuses against which it was directed would not have yielded to sweet diffidence. The call for initiative, referendum, and direct primaries was heeded, and Hicks himself acknowledged Donnelly's achievement; after 1902 Theodore Roosevelt's presidential messages "read like the preamble to the Populist platform" written fifteen years earlier.

In his last years Ignatius Donnelly was poor, exhausted, and powerless. But after a squalid start, he had achieved dignity through standing by his principles in a remarkably unprincipled era. In 1895 Donnelly stepped down as leader of the Farmers' Alliance. He returned from the last session of its annual meeting to sit alone in the dining room of the Brunswick Hotel in Minneapolis. He was too fat, too scarred, too shabby, to be an impressive figure. Then L. C. Long, the new chief of the Alliance, came into the room and asked him to join many of his old friends and antagonists in the hotel parlor. There they presented him with a pen. Long said, "May it be used unhesitatingly against the enemies of your cause." As Martin Ridge described the scene: "Before Donnelly could reply, Major J. M. Bowler, who had known him as a political friend and foe for thirty-seven years, also presented him with a gold-headed cane. Donnelly was deeply touched. 'I assure you that I have always tried to do right,' he responded. 'I know I am not infallible. . . . I am not used to a cane.'"

During the previous year Donnelly had privately received evidence of the personal esteem of a frequent butt of his polemics against the railroads, James J. Hill, and of Hill's political agent in the Democratic party, Michael Doran. Kate Donnelly, who had been ill for a long time, died in June. Donnelly himself was crippled with rheumatism. His eldest son, Stan, who had cared for his mother to the point of exhaustion, now required medical care. These illnesses drained the old man's small reserve. Both Hill and Doran offered to help Donnelly in his extremity. Hard men like these, who had learned contempt for most office seekers and knew that Donnelly was beyond the reach of their influence even in his extremity, would not have volunteered to aid him unless he had had their respect.

In the summer of 1900, after fifty years on the stump, Donnelly was having trouble getting through his speeches in support of the Democratic presidential ticket headed by Bryan. He noted that though "my hair is not yet gray . . . my legs are weak." Just as the new year began, on the morning of January 1, 1901, he died. His pallbearers were "some of the most distinguished business and political leaders of Minnesota — some of whom had been his bitterest political enemies." Chief among them were Senator Moses E. Clapp and Governor John Lind.

It is well to remember him as he was at the peak of his career, in the 1880s, as described by Major Newson:

> Mr. Donnelly looks and acts like a young Falstaff, with a round, chubby face, a round, well-developed body, and round, chubby hands. . . . One not knowing him would take him to be a jolly bishop. . . . As a man he is very social . . . bubbling over with good humor and anecdote . . . his hearty laugh is like the cholera, very contagious. . . . In debate he is a stubborn, able, political opponent; fearless . . . and decided in his convictions; remarkably ready in repartee and inexhaustible in resources.

Donnelly's hopes for wealth and eminence within the emerging establishment of the upper Midwest had long before died. In the cities, other speculators waxed rich, along with the brokers and millers who reaped the chief returns from bonanza years. But on the farm Donnelly had seen crops turn brown and shrivel in drought years and ripe wheat consumed by locusts. His insistence that the winners share more with the losers had made him a hero to the farmers he led. Donnelly spent the last decades of his life insisting on what he believed to be the truth, and insisting as well that those with the power to rectify injustice should do so.

From time to time his compliance with their desires was solicited to the accompaniment of their good wines and their exquisite sauces — the rewards of going along. Yet loving luxury and equipped with the taste to savor what they merely owned, he refused their blandishments and held them to a standard of behavior nearly all of them found too radical, too unsettling.

Those of us who find history more real when we can find ourselves in the places where it was made, and those of us who cannot deny an admiration for the unrepentant opulence of the architectural taste of these hearty nabobs of the 1880s and 1890s, would be happier if, in an architectural sense, Donnelly had not ultimately won. The reforms he espoused were nearly all adopted, though some took fifty years, but the prelude to victory was the collapse of the old freebooting system into depressions so deep that its infirmities could not be denied. Those depressions, in the 1890s, in 1907, and especially in the 1930s, destroyed the red-stone castles that once lined the slopes of Lowry Hill in Minneapolis and Summit Avenue, Dayton's Bluff, Capitol Hill, and Crocus Hill in St. Paul. Once there were dozens of Richardsonian fortresses, turreted and orieled,* laid up of boulders of granite and blocks of Portage Entry sandstone, their perfumed interiors lit by flaring stained glass of ocher, moss green, indigo, and gold, filled with an abundance of rich stuffs, marvelously carved woods, and silken hangings.

*An oriel window is like a small bay, generally on an upper story.

The fruits of the frontier: mansions on the hill behind the Minnesota State Capitol in St. Paul in the 1880s. The John L. Merriam House, by Harvey Ellis for J. Walter Stevens, is in the foreground. Merriam made his fortune as a hardware merchant. *From the Collection of the Minnesota Historical Society*

The traveler of the 1990s can find only a few isolated survivors of their great number, and even these have been sacked of their furniture and textiles. Yet we may be grateful for the surviving reminders of the world of Ignatius Donnelly's antagonists. The Minnesota Historical Society has been restoring James J. Hill's mansion on Summit Avenue, though Hill's three-story art gallery will seem a little nude with the Courbets and Corots gone. There is nothing like it left where once there were a score; in Minneapolis and even in St. Joseph, Missouri, the nation's chief museum of the style, none of the great mansions are still complete. It is odd that we have a hundred reasonably intact historic house museums to show us the 1780s, and even a handful, completely furnished, of the 1680s, but it is difficult to list more than two of equivalent importance for the effulgent 1880s in the midwest.

Perhaps we would prefer to forget the "tramps" that were as representative of that decade as its millionaires. "Tramps and millionaires . . . One man proclaiming truth year after year . . . One man clothed in the armor of a righteous cause . . . All the hosts of error." The cool Progressives did not use biblical phrases like these. Plays like *Inherit the Wind* have sought to make those who used them, and believed in them, seem silly. But William Jennings Bryan and Ignatius Donnelly in their prime *did* contend for justice against the hosts of error — and the larger hosts of indifference. Well-fed urban playwrights may chortle over rural reformers grown old. But in the days of their long, sweaty struggle to bring justice to the Middle West, these men were giants.

Some of the contributions made by hot Populism to cool Progressivism are now accepted even among those who persist in treating Ignatius Donnelly as a joke. But there lingers still from the older historians a derisory opinion of his views on "the money question." Was he a crank, leading other cranks, Greenbackers, Alliancemen, and Populists? I think not.

Donnelly's opinions on the manipulation of the national money supply were sophisticated — and correct. He was not a free silverite; his monetary policy was not limited, as was that of William Jennings Bryan, to the simple thought that "remonetizing" silver would cure all the ills of the world. Indeed, the victory of the Bryan silverites was Donnelly's last great defeat.

This was his position:

> If silver was remonetized, there are still vastly important questions of government paper money, of an abundant currency, of land, and of transportation. . . . We all believe that metallic currency is a temporary expedient — a relic of barbarism, but so long as either metal is to be used, because both constitute a larger and more abundant currency . . . [we must] divorce the idea of money totally from any metallic commodity; to make the measure of values rest entirely upon the . . . power of government. . . . We do not believe in commodity money [whether based on] gold, silver, brass, lead, wheat, or potatoes, but as long as gold is continued to be used, we insist that its ancient colleague, silver, shall be used with it as a matter of justice to the debtor class.

Donnelly perceived that the slowed growth of the money supply after 1871 was the cause of a deflation lasting three decades. He helped the farmers, its chief victims, to understand that fact. The bankers were its chief beneficiaries, as they quite clearly intended.

The gold standard was a weapon of economic warfare deployed by creditors against debtors. This was clear enough to Donnelly, who called the gold standard a relic of barbarism. Walter Heller, chief economic adviser to President John F. Kennedy, picked up the phrase nearly eighty years later, calling gold a barbarous metal. Donnelly campaigned for the abandonment of a gold standard, the use of both silver and gold to support the currency, and a slow, steady reduction of "fiat money" such as the greenbacks of the Civil War. Though Milton Friedman, Barry Goldwater's chief economic adviser, agreed on little with

324

Heller, after reviewing the evidence of the deflationary period he did conclude, as Heller and Donnelly had, that

> on the whole the adoption of silver would have been preferable [to a commitment to gold]. . . . Adoption of silver by the United States would certainly have moderated or eliminated deflationary tendencies here. It would also have moderated and might have eliminated deflation in the world at large. . . . If one regards the deflationary price trend as an evil and a horizontal price trend as preferable, as we do, though with some doubts, silver would on this account and for that period have been preferable to gold.

The long deflation penalized the debtor class and favored creditors. A midwestern farmer who borrowed "100-cent dollars" in 1870 was forced to repay in dollars worth 150 cents, 200 cents, or if his note could be imagined to come due as late as 1890, even 300 cents. Ignatius Donnelly foresaw this and protested against national monetary policies that artificially increased the value of the dollar. The stock of money *was* subject to Treasury Department influence, and the Treasury *was* subject to persuasion from bankers, domestic and foreign. There *was* a "goldbug" plot behind both the deflationary legislation of 1873 and the veto by President Ulysses S. Grant of an act to continue the issuance of a limited supply of irredeemable (paper) currency. Thereafter the farmer in debt paid the price for a national policy of shrinking the money supply.

Throughout the post–Civil War period, western farmers were heavy borrowers. In 1890, for example, the census showed that though it was relatively poor, Kansas had the highest ratio of mortgage debt to true value of taxed real estate of any state except prosperous New York. Nebraska, the Dakotas, and Minnesota were all within the top nine states in these ratios. In Kansas and North Dakota there was a mortgage for every two people, and in South Dakota, Nebraska, and Minnesota there was one for every three. In many wheat-growing counties total mortgage debt was close to three quarters of true valuation.

During the same period the dollar was appreciating in value against a cost index made up largely of farm products. If the dollar's "commodity value" were set at a base of 100 in 1865, it reached 200 in 1876, 250 in 1885, and 300 in 1894. Friedman's survey of the years of Donnelly's career as a Greenbacker yielded the conclusion that "in no other period did wholesale prices fall so continuously at so high a rate . . . over 1 percent a year from 1879 to 1897." The farmer felt the consequences in two ways. The weight of his debts doubled and redoubled, and the value of his crops shriveled; commensurately, the rate of return for his labor diminished.

The government of the United States wanted it that way.

In 1865, Treasury Secretary Hugh McCulloch deliberately set in motion a return to "constitutional currency," meaning a gold standard.

The farming West had expanded rapidly to meet the needs of wartime and had borrowed greenbacks to do so; McCulloch was using pious words to espouse a tax on debtors. The government had issued paper money, not redeemable in gold, to finance the Civil War. The chief business of the states east of the Rockies was being done in that currency. The money stock fell precipitously from 1867 to 1879; not until the 1931–1939 period, reflected Friedman, "was there anything like it." Then, after a deflation of 50 percent, the farmer-debtors led by Donnelly abandoned their wary acceptance of a moderate deflation through a gradual return to prewar prices and came out fighting.

Talk of constitutional currency or other patriotic pieties to cloak extortion did not impress them. They found no deflation clause in the Constitution, no independence from silver-based money in the Declaration of Independence (the dollar was tied to the silver peso during the first decades of American independence), and no mention of the gold standard in the Bill of Rights. They wanted debts to be repaid in the same currency that had been obtained from the lender. "Can you keep a room warm next winter, with the thermometer at 30 below zero, by reciting the Declaration of Independence?" Donnelly asked.

Scholars are in dispute about all the causes of the long deflation. But Friedman and Anna Schwartz found that the Greenbackers' contemporary discussion

> attributed falling prices and depressed conditions largely to the behavior of the stock of money — and rightly so in the sense that, given a rapid rate of economic growth, the price decline would have been avoided only by a more rapid rise in the stock of money. . . . An unusually rapid rise in output converted an unusually slow rate of rise in stock of money into a rapid decline in prices.

This was about what was said in 1887 by a farm journalist:

> There is something wrong in our . . . system. The railroads have never been so prosperous, and yet agriculture languishes. Manufacturing enterprises never made more money . . . and yet agriculture languishes. Towns and cities flourish and "boom" . . . and yet agriculture languishes.

The Greenbackers and Donnelly Populists were early monetarists in that they were intensely interested in the supply of money. Unfortunately, their focus on that issue became blurred with the side show over free silver. "Bimetallism" was ultimately fatal to the farmers' fight for a growing or at least a steady money supply. Donnelly resisted to the end the reduction of the reformers' platform from a dozen or more specific measures to the narrow question of the free coinage of silver. But the financial pressure of the silver magnates of Colorado and the urge of politics toward simplification were too great for him.

PUCK

POPULIST PARTY

DEMOCRATIC PARTY

SWALLOWED!

Donnelly was no enthusiast for nostrums such as free silver. Like many Populists, he resented the absorption of the complex Populist program by single-issue silver Democrats. Then, as now, cartoonists often got things reversed. *Courtesy of the Library of Congress*

Then, ironically, in the 1890s gold suddenly became cheaper and the whole effort to assure a congruence of economic growth with growth in the currency supply was put to sleep. The formal return to the gold standard in 1900 was given a "soft landing" by fresh discoveries of gold in South Africa, Colorado, and the Klondike and by such new ways of extracting gold from ore as the cyanide process. With cheaper gold came higher prices. Thus the issue to which Donnelly demanded attention seemed, for a decade or two, moot.

It has been argued that Donnelly saw the monetary policies of the government too much in terms of conspiracies of bankers and international financial speculators. Some critics have sniggered at his fear of the power of such conspiracies. Yet he knew more than they of the power over courts and legislatures of a small number of men with a large supply of dollars. Like a reformed drunkard, a reformed machine politician and a reformed agent of commodity speculators can be unusually conscious of the temptations of sin. He knew the potency of money and the pliancy of policy to its requirements. He had watched the government of the United States twice go begging to private bankers to support its credit, first during the Civil War when his patron Jay Cooke managed the national bond issues for a substantial profit, and again in 1895 when J. P. Morgan and August Belmont helped Grover Cleveland survive a gold crisis, also for a substantial profit. He knew, too, that international gold brokers and the holders of gold securities had influenced national policy year in and year out. Even the locally based silver interests of the mountain states were occasionally capable of using their strength in Congress to secure fat speculative profits, as they did for a few weeks during and after the passage of the Sherman Silver Purchase Act of 1890. The monetary policy of the United States was manipulated during the Grant and Cleveland administrations and in between by small groups of powerful men who may have been wise but were certainly not disinterested.

It is not strange that Ignatius Donnelly did not endear himself to these men or to their western representatives. He rejoiced in pouncing on the porous platitudes they employed to justify their manipulations. But they controlled the magazines and newspapers of large circulation, and they saw to it that he was depicted as a crank. It has taken a century to restore something of his reputation.

18

···

Bluegrass Chivalry

Margaret Johnson, Richard Mentor Johnson,
and Julia Chinn

THE BLUEGRASS REGION of Kentucky is known chiefly as horse country. White wooden fences trimly border the ample acres owned by heirs of traction magnates, hog butchers, department store operators, and steel makers. Fine thoroughbreds are led from stalls more comfortable than many a cottage to be gently walked about private racecourses; jockeys wearing "colors" recall for us the brilliant banners and caparisons of Agincourt and Crécy. Chivalry is dead, it is often said, but horsemanship is very much alive in Kentucky, and riders in bright red or green coats provide even muggy midwestern afternoons with a final feudal reminiscence. In one corner of the Bluegrass, as we shall see, are recollections of chivalry much closer to our own time, of a cavalier who led the Kentucky Rifles in heroic charges, winning victories for his country — and who was chivalric in other, more difficult and uncelebrated ways. And of his lady, "fair" in many ways, though not in complexion.

Horses are latecomers to this turf. Once its tall grass provided forage for great herds of elk, deer, and bison. Carrier pigeons flew in innumerable, murmuring herds overhead, and the rivers were crowded with fish. It does not appear that the medieval Indians built large cities there, as they did between A.D. 1000 and 1350 along the Mississippi and above the Ohio; perhaps this enormous pasture was kept for hunting grounds. When the first Europeans, the Spaniards and French, came upon this

329

land they thought it a very Eden, luxuriant beyond their imaginings, so fertile and well watered as to make them laugh when they thought of the Pyrenean rock lands and the barren plateau of Castile. There were just enough trees to provide shelter, but not so many as to require clearing.

When the first Virginian traders arrived there in search of furs, they could scarcely credit the testimony of their eyes and nostrils. In the warmth of spring the grassland was a garden stretching for two hundred miles.

These first Virginians of the seventeenth century were followed by a rush of settlers just before the Revolutionary War. One of the reasons for that war was this wondrous land into which their settlement had come. The British government had tried mightily to deny it to the colonists, preferring to leave some space at their colony's western border to make it less expensive to conduct further wars of conquest against the Indians. But the Americans would have none of such restrictions. They ignored the Parliament's inhibitions and proceeded into Kentucky to conquer and settle, and conquer and settle again.

The Virginians brought their Englishness with them, but they acquired New World customs as well, especially the custom of having their hardest work done by Black slaves. This was not the practice of the gentry back home, and it was not how Virginia began. In northern Europe, as in earliest America, there had been conditions like slavery — serfdom and indentured servitude — but they were not hereditary. Slavery by race and inheritance was a new creation, with much to commend it from the point of view of the slave owner, who otherwise might have had to work considerably harder. As the eighteenth century bore on, New World slavery became a habit.

In frontier regions like Kentucky, however, in a culture in which slavery was based upon race, and most Blacks were slaves, the rules of behavior were not quickly established. There was considerable "play" in the system, much uncertainty in the application of those rules, and wide variety among the practices of slave owners.

Some places in the Bluegrass can remind us of those variations and of the fluid and flexible society that kept Kentucky unpredictable. The antebellum South was far from uniform, in any case, and Kentucky's interests were unlike those of slave-importing states such as South Carolina, or slave-selling states like Virginia, or new, raw, slave-buying states such as Texas, Missouri, and Arkansas. Nor were its interests like those of the free states north of the Ohio. The mountain country of eastern Kentucky and western Virginia was antipathetic to slavery. Even in the Bluegrass, Henry Clay and his cousin Cassius Marcellus Clay opposed slavery. And Kentucky stayed with the Union during the Civil War — barely.

In Lexington, capital of this ambiguous region, the most romantic residence is the curious Greek and Gothic amalgam called Botherum

Botherum, the idiosyncratic villa of Madison Conyers Johnson in Lexington, Kentucky.

(now 341 Madison Street), built by Major Madison Conyers Johnson in 1851. It defies description and baffles photographers. Defiance was a Johnson family tradition, as the name of the place suggests; it was probably meant to "bother" the neighbors. It bothers architectural historians today, as well. John McMurtry, the architect who worked on it with Major Johnson, was quite capable of delivering structures in accordance with the rules, but he and Johnson broke them all for this one. The interior is Gothic, with vaults, bosses, and Tudor arches, polygonal bay windows, and mysterious spaces lit dimly by pinkish purply stained glass. The exterior has a Corinthian portico, as underscaled as most Bluegrass classicism is overscaled. Atop the mixture, like a maraschino cherry on a complex ice cream sundae, is an octagonal ironwork watchtower.

Madison Johnson was thought to be an eccentric because he had a close friend who was Black; a novel, James Lane Allen's *Two Gentlemen from Kentucky,* was written about them. It makes lively reading but not as lively as the most celebrated novel about the Johnsons, John Seymour Erwin's *Like Some Green Laurel.* Erwin's book does not confess that it is fiction, and it is frequently cited as history.

Its chief character is given the name and some, but not all, of the biography of Margaret Johnson, first cousin of Madison. This redoubtable lady built Mount Holly, a mansion that is now a bed and breakfast, in Washington County, Mississippi. She was married to James Erwin, who had earlier been married to the daughter of Henry Clay. The house

Mount Holly, the home of Margaret Johnson. *Mississippi Department of Archives and History*

is not what one expects in the Delta country. It is brick and flamboyantly Italianate, brackets, arcades, and all. Like Ammadele in Oxford, Mississippi, it is based upon a design — number 27 — in a pattern book by Calvert Vaux, who was the partner of Frederick Law Olmsted in designing New York's Central Park.

That much is clear enough, but Margaret Johnson, controversial in her lifetime, became controversial again in the 1980s, when a furious scholarly controversy erupted about the publication of *Like Some Green Laurel* by Erwin, her great-grandson, and the Louisiana State University Press. Erwin told of having seen in 1937 a packet of Margaret's letters in the hands of the Philadelphia antiquarian A. S. W. Rosenbach. The letters subsequently and mysteriously disappeared, but Erwin claimed to have retained shorthand notes he had taken of items he read. These he filled out with recollections of family members, some of whom, he said, had lived until "nearly 100 years old . . . clear in mind, memories unimpaired." The resulting "correspondence" between Margaret and various family members is erratic as to dates, names, and places. (For example, it describes Felix Mendelssohn performing a concert two years after his death and a Kentucky friendship with Stephen Foster, who resided in Pittsburgh though he did write "My Old Kentucky Home.")

After savage attacks on the book, as if it were a work of history, and on Erwin and the LSU Press for failing to warn their readers that it was not, Erwin counterattacked. The book, he said, was meant to be "an incomplete vignette of a woman unique for a South of mealy-mouths and battle-axes. It was never meant to be taken as gospel by 'historians,' semi-professionals and dilettantes for fuel for Ladies Study Club mentalities resulting in an auto-da-fé." "Ladies Study Club," indeed! What would Margaret Johnson have said to that? Perhaps that it was a good thing somebody was studying something. And what would have been said by Julia Chinn, her kinswoman, it seems, by marriage? We will have to think about that; we will come to Julia Chinn in a moment.

Whatever Erwin's book *was* meant to be, his tale of Margaret Johnson has crept into the historiography of innumerable pamphlets and guides, and her story is part of our folklore. Among other items, on the strength of "Margaret's" letters Mount Holly is frequently attributed to Samuel Sloan. He was the Philadelphia architect who had brought another kind of fantasy to Natchez with an immense oriental octagon for Haller Nutt about a year after Margaret Johnson Erwin Dudley herself began work.

All this would be less important if John Erwin's second-stage denial of an intention to write history as it was, and his insistence that he meant only to suggest how it might have been, had not confused matters, making it even more difficult for us to rescue the true story of Margaret's Johnsonian independence of mind. Perhaps, as Erwin insisted, this Mississippi matron freed her slaves in 1858, despite Mississippi's rigorous laws to the contrary. Perhaps she did, in fact, have a lifelong admiration for William Tecumseh Sherman and Abraham Lincoln. It is probable that she shared with other members of the family a point of view toward slavery and racial oppression that was unusual in the 1850s along the lower Mississippi. But it is certain that such a view could be found in Kentucky in the 1820s and 1830s among the Johnsons and their circle.

It is also likely that Margaret and her cousin Madison were reassured in their views by the most famous of the Johnson-Erwin-Ward clan, another first cousin, Richard Mentor Johnson, the vice president of the United States.

Mount Holly is not the family's proudest architectural achievement, nor would it have been the place to which the cousins repaired for family conferences at the peak of their power. Their "power house," like the Clays' Ashland and the Polks' Rattle-and-Snap, was Ward Hall. A visit to this chief monument to the architectural aspirations of the Johnson family is a good way to enter the world of Richard Mentor Johnson.

Ward Hall and Mount Holly are open to the public; Botherum is not. Ward Hall, a very large brick house behind Corinthian columns forty feet tall, stands one mile west of Georgetown, Kentucky, on the Frankfort Road. It is almost a cube, very stately and stable upon its fossil-laced coquina foundations. Its silver hardware is unscathed by the passage of decades, and the plaster work in the interior is much as it was when the house was completed in 1855, unique in America in retaining its original, unrepentant, flamboyant color. It is the supreme symbol of the trans-Appalachian explosion of American idiosyncrasy, political courage, and personal bravado.

Ward Hall has been restored in recent years, its magnificent rooms scrubbed and brightened by its chatelaine, Frances Susong Jenkins. Because Mrs. Jenkins "does right" by Ward Hall, she and her neighbors are fighting off the promiscuous development that threatens the surrounding landscape. Kentucky's women still display that steely determination which glints from beneath their graciousness as it did with Margaret Johnson — and Julia Chinn.

The restoration of Ward Hall has presented twin gifts — a magnificent physical object and a vastly enlarged understanding of the people and the culture that produced it. The house reposes in a landscape that will itself benefit from restoration, but even as it is, one can observe the legacy of Capability Brown and Humphrey Repton in the little lakes created by the Wards and Johnsons as they carefully diverted and dammed the creeks. This may have been a romantic "Chinese" landscape plan like that at Chaumière du Prairie, not far away. We will have to wait for garden archaeologists to tell us about that.

The big, cubic, red brick mansion stands today as it has for a hundred thirty years, more Roman than Greek, its proportions tall but not attenuated, muscular but not clumsy, grandiloquent but without that bullying anxiety which often accompanies the merely ostentatious. It is a house built by people who were rich, proud, powerful, physically strenuous, aesthetically alert, rejoicing in their capacity to make large and beautiful things where only lately they had been happy merely to survive. The original log cabins they had first occupied were not swept away but were left on the property and are still in use. The Wards and Johnsons did not pretend to be other than what they were. Like Andrew Jackson at the Hermitage, the builders of Ward Hall integrated their past and their present without scrubbing either to please the neighbors.

These were not the sort of people who commended themselves to some of their own grandchildren, however. They were too hearty; they chewed tobacco and fought Indians, put their own hands to the plow, hammered nails, and loved those they loved whatever might be said of them by others, no matter how politically expedient it might have been to select more "appropriate" objects of affection.

Ward Hall, the greatest of the Ward and Johnson mansions. *Courtesy of Ann Bolton Bevins*

The Johnsons went west in 1779, settling on Beargrass Creek, then moving onto the Big Buffalo Crossing area of the Elkhorn Valley in Scott County, Kentucky. There were battles with the Shawnee, meetings of the territorial assembly, and camp meetings as the Johnsons laid the foundations for the Baptist church during the first rush of evangelism into Kentucky. Robert Johnson (1745–1815) helped to draw Kentucky's border with Virginia and establish Transylvania University. As his fortunes rose he became the satrap of Scott County, putting thousands of acres under tobacco, beans, and corn. His wife, Jemima Suggett, gave him eleven children. After she died, he married again just before his seventieth birthday and founded yet one more new community, on the Ohio River, the town now called Warsaw.

Two of Robert Johnson's sons were serving in the United States Congress at the moment one of his grandsons, Richard Mentor Johnson, took his seat in the Senate. Another son was a justice of the Arkansas Supreme Court, and his daughter Sallie was leading the clan to join the Erwins and the Carolina Hamptons in the conquest and development of the cotton lands of Mississippi's Washington County, with soil as black and rich as the delta of the Nile.

Johnsons Station -1783-4-

An imaginative drawing of Robert Johnson's frontier station. *Courtesy of Ann Bolton Bevins*

Sallie (1778–1816) was married to William Ward; her son Junius was the builder of Ward Hall. The house is the chief physical monument to the family, as the career of Richard Mentor Johnson (1780–1850) is its chief political achievement. The house is nearly restored; the reputation of Richard Johnson is not. And the story of the most interesting person to know that house well, Julia Chinn, has been so nearly lost that we can reconstruct it only from wisps. We can search out something of the life of this deliberately forgotten woman if we begin with the background of her consort's political career.

At twenty-three, Richard Johnson was elected to the Kentucky legislature, and three years later to the Congress of the United States. Still serving while sojourning in the Kentucky Rifles, he returned to receive a resolution and a ceremonial sword from his colleagues. The postwar depression of 1819 caught him exposed, but he commenced rebuilding his fortunes and was sent to the Senate to fill a vacancy later that year. The era of good feelings was coming to an end, and modern political parties were beginning to form. Johnson was a Jeffersonian during the administration of John Quincy Adams (1824–1828) and under Andrew Jackson (1828–1836). In 1836 he was the Jacksonian vice-presidential candidate on the winning ticket headed by Martin Van Buren, but he went down to defeat with Van Buren in 1840.

John Neagle's heroic image of Richard Mentor Johnson. *In the Collection of the Corcoran Galley of Art, Bequest of Mrs. B. O. Tayloe*

337

There were two party slogans in the campaign of 1840: "Tippecanoe and Tyler too" and "Rumpsey Dumpsey, Colonial Johnson killed Tecumsey." The former prevailed. The Whigs under William Henry Harrison defeated the Jacksonians under Van Buren and Johnson. Twenty-nine years earlier Harrison had been the general in command at the Battle of Tippecanoe, a victory over Tecumseh, the Shawnee chief whose confederacy was in league with the British. Johnson was the Jacksonians' alternative to Harrison, for at Thames River two years after Tippecanoe he had shot a Shawnee chief who was (probably) Tecumseh himself.

"Rumpsey Dumpsey" had worked well, set to music, when Van Buren and Johnson had been elected in 1836. But by 1840 Johnson was suffering from three infirmities. The first was his old-fashioned frontier political views, which were by then coming to seem unfashionably fervent: too strenuously in favor of religious liberty, too committed to the abolition of imprisonment for debt, too devoted to public education, even for Indians and Blacks.

His public views, namely, his friendliness for Blacks, were a second cause for embarrassment. Not only did he associate with them as friends and propose to educate them, but he also lived openly as husband with one of them, Julia Chinn. He had a third infirmity, now difficult to diagnose, but it was probably Alzheimer's disease; by the end of the 1830s he was becoming less and less able to present his ideas coherently on the stump. In private, it was noted in the press, his dress was becoming untidy. (Alcoholism would seem another possibility, but in that contumacious age it is unlikely that if he had been a heavy drinker it would have gone without comment; nothing he did was spared an ugly interpretation.)

338

That was at the end; the beginning was glorious. Along with five of his uncles, Johnson served as an officer in the War of 1812, and it was he who developed the tactical system for the Kentucky Mounted Infantry that led to the victory at the Battle of the Thames in 1813. Wounded five times, he may well have administered the coup de grâce to Tecumseh, though he never personally claimed to have done so. In any event, he was certainly the only chairman of the Committee on Military Affairs of the Congress of the United States to get that close to an enemy. He summoned almost equal courage on his return to propose raising congressional pay to a level that would permit poor men to serve, an error of political calculation which then, as now, went unthanked.

Johnson was a tall, stately man with military bearing though sloping shoulders, a splendid cavalry leader, brave and generous. When he was in his forties his face began to acquire some flesh at the chin and neck. He did not take himself too seriously, for even in formal portraits he seems about to burst into a grin. He was immensely likable; historians of variegated prejudices have liked him, applying to him descriptions drawn from their own lexicons of likability. For example, Thomas P. Abernethy, who was drawn to cavaliers and aristocrats, said that he was "possessed of . . . dash, and military bearing . . . and of the clear-cut, classic features which one associates with patrician blood." Arthur Schlesinger Jr. depicted him as if he might have lived at Hyde Park rather than White Sulphur Springs, reaching out from his estate toward the masses. He was a hero among "mechanics . . . while Andrew Jackson was still a vague figure in the minds of the urban working classes."

Schlesinger, almost alone, has given Johnson a measure of his due and helps us see him as he was in his prime: "burly, genial, very good-looking . . . with a jovial face and wandering, curly light-auburn hair, turning to silver-gray; in public he was conspicuous in a flaming-scarlet waistcoat. He was, above all, a man of the utmost sweetness of nature." Margaret B. Smith, the often acrid chronicler of social life in Washington during the Jacksonian years, found him "the most tender-hearted, mild, affectionate and benevolent of men."

Mrs. Smith had nothing to say of the character of Julia Chinn, to whom Johnson turned his affections and who was the mother of his children. But then, while everyone in Mrs. Smith's Washington knew, or

An imaginative depiction of the battle in which Tecumseh was killed, perhaps by Richard Johnson. *Courtesy of the Library of Congress*

knew of, Julia, it was not good form to acknowledge her presence. This was not because Richard Johnson kept her hidden; he was a courageous man, and not only in battle. He took five musket balls in the body at the Battle of the Thames but fought on; some said he suffered more from wounds administered to him and Julia metaphorically, later.

After the War of 1812 there was some effort to create "a new sort of union . . . a Christian party in politics." It was not, in fact, based upon the teachings of Christ, for it had little interest in the poor and the oppressed. Quite the contrary, it was contrived to deploy sectarian tracts to keep unruly workingmen docile and to impose on working-class immigrants a set of national sumptuary laws. Thomas Jefferson roused himself in his old age to ring the alarm bell, and Richard Mentor Johnson took up the fight after Jefferson's death. In a report of the House of Representatives written by Johnson, the separation of church and state was asserted once again: "It is not the legitimate province of the legislature to determine what religion is true, or what is false. . . . Our government is a civil, not a religious institution."

This was not wholly popular in the face of a rising tide of evangelism that sometimes slopped over into politics, but it gained Johnson a worldwide reputation. In London the report was called "the noblest political plea for the rights of conscience produced in modern times."

Johnson was popular, but he was not adept at organizing that popularity into a disciplined following. Martin Van Buren consistently outmaneuvered him. He probably lacked the capacity to adapt what he had learned in the politics of clan and region to the politics of class and commercial interest. He was both friend and rival to Henry Clay and friend and lieutenant to Andrew Jackson. His loyalty to Old Hickory led him into positions inconsistent with his generally humanitarian stance, for in the House he alone of the Military Affairs Committee supported the general's depredations against Florida while opposing Clay's call for support to South America and Greek rebels against tyranny. In the Senate, where he served ten years, he supported Jackson over Clay, lost his seat, and went back to the House. There he acted as personal agent for Jackson, often in political matters and sometimes in such delicate affairs as rounding up support among Washington's ladies for Peggy O'Neill, who was raised in a tavern and married another Jacksonian stalwart,

Peggy O'Neill Eaton as a matron. Earlier she was a source of contention in Andrew Jackson's cabinet, quite possibly for religious as much as class reasons. *The Hermitage: Home of Andrew Jackson*

John C. Eaton, the secretary of war. Such a reminder of the rapidity of American social escalation was unacceptable to some of the more refined females married to other members of Jackson's cabinet circle, especially to Mrs. John C. Calhoun.

Feminine politics was exceedingly important in those years, though so little of it was recorded that we can only glimpse its effects. The breach opened by Mrs. Calhoun widened the differences between her husband and the president into an open feud and may explain some of the fervor of Jackson's opposition to Calhoun's nullification policies.

Johnson's own domestic life, which centered on Julia Chinn and their daughters, was even less conventional than Eaton's. As if to show how little Andrew Jackson cared for gossip, especially that directed against women (his own Rachel suffered so much from malicious talk that some felt she lost her will to survive her final illness), Jackson saw to it that Johnson was rewarded with the vice presidency. This was despite a chorus of criticism that Johnson was far too friendly to Blacks.

The obliteration of Julia Chinn from conventional histories of the period was so complete that we possess no painted or photographic images of her, though she was a prominent figure of Kentucky and Washington life. This may seem odd until we note as well that the attacks on Johnson for his friendship to Blacks generally have been omitted from standard texts of the period, which content themselves with assertions that he was thought to be eccentric.

It is true that throughout his career, Johnson did take independent stands, relying on his immense personal following to offset the consequences of political risks. It is also true that he was bored with the chiefly ceremonial functions of the vice presidency. When he was not delightedly breaking ties in Senate votes, which he did as often as three times a day when that body was in session, he and Julia went off to Kentucky to manage the hotel he built upon his property at White Sulphur Springs, affronting Virginia gentlemen who thought it strange that he would "give his personal superintendence to the chicken and egg purchasing and water-melon selling."

It was not, however, his attention to his private business affairs, to chickens, eggs, and watermelons, as it was thought, that disqualified Johnson for high office. It was that he was living with, and probably married to, a woman who had a Black great-grandmother. It was this which, as recently as 1974, led one historian of the vice presidency to call Johnson's occupancy of the post "astonishing. . . . His private affairs . . . evidenced a total disregard for propriety." His conduct, says this writer, "many in the country, particularly in the South, considered outrageous."

What was so outrageous? Not that Johnson was a southern gentleman who had children by a woman who had been a slave, but that he treated his consort, Julia Chinn, as his wife. This she probably was, though no one had the temerity to ask them to produce a marriage

license. She served as the vice president's official hostess in Washington and at White Sulphur Springs. Furthermore, Johnson left large endowments to their daughters, whom he educated as Kentucky ladies and saw married into the local gentry.

It is not easy to discover the traces of this shadowy side of a man and a woman living in the glare of public life, but occasionally one comes upon a notice such as this in *Kentucky Marriages,* a genealogical work published in Baltimore in 1965:

> Thomas W. Scott, a white man, to Miss Adeline J. Johnson, a mulatto girl, reputed to be the daughter of the Hon. Richard M. Johnson, Representative in Congress. M. Nov. 8, 1832, in Scott County. A few days after this marriage Thomas W. Scott was presented by his wife's father a fine tract of land known as the "Blue Spring Farm." Daniel Pence married Imogene, Colonel Johnson's eldest daughter, in 1829 or 1830.

The progeny of Adeline and Imogene Johnson, now living respectably in Scott County, must find it amusing that one historian provided Johnson with this epitaph: "He left no widow, children, father or mother living."

Perhaps they are not amused. Julia Chinn was a beautiful, intelligent, well-educated person who deserves better than obliteration. Her great-grandmother was Black; so, in the logic of the times, she was Black and a slave. Johnson inherited her from his father, rejected an "appropriate" match to a local belle, and chose to make his life with Julia. The ineffable Duff Green, a turncoat Jacksonian who wrote campaign literature for the Whigs, told the world that she was "a jet-black, thick-lipped, odiferous negro wench" and that Johnson's "astonishing" behavior was that he "reared a family of children whom he endeavored to force upon society as equals."

In fact, their two daughters, Imogene and Adeline, were educated by tutors in the Johnsons' magnificent house on E Street, were given the Johnson name, and were welcomed at Ward Hall. They traveled as a family in the segregated railroad and coach systems, and not only Whig pamphleteers noticed. In 1842 Charles Lenox Remond, a cosmopolitan leader of Black Americans, returned from Europe and remonstrated with the Massachusetts legislature over continued segregation.[1]

It was, as Remond noted, absurd. "Color is made to obscure the brightest endowments, to degrade the fairest character, and to check the highest and most praiseworthy aspirations." Unless, of course, the person seeking to breach the line between the "complexions" was rich enough or powerful enough. What would happen, Remond asked, "if

Opposite: **Andrew Jackson, political sponsor of Richard Mentor Johnson.**
Courtesy of The Historic New Orleans Collection, Museum/Research Center

some few West or East India planters or merchants should visit our liberty-loving country with their colored wives — how would we manage? Or, if R. M. Johnson, the gentleman who has been elected to the second office in the gift of the people, should be travelling from Boston to Salem, if he was prepared to separate him from his wife or daughters." The reporter noted an "involuntary burst of applause, immediately restrained."

After Imogene Johnson married Daniel Pence she was listed in subsequent censuses as White, though the Pence descendants of today proudly recall the remarkable Julia Chinn. And the descendants of Adeline Scott of Scott County do not seem to be embarrassed by the memory of Richard M. Johnson.

Even after his health began to fail, Johnson continued to receive electoral votes for the presidency and was a serious presidential possibility, because of his wide popularity in the West, until 1844. Despite the derision with which later historians treated him, he was consistently supported and reelected by the people who knew him best, the voters of Kentucky. They kept him in office until a fortnight before his death in 1850. His support for education never wavered; the "national seminary" he envisaged in Washington led to the creation of Columbian College, now the George Washington University. Besides his benefactions to Transylvania University, he was a founder of Georgetown College and the primary source of support for the Choctaw Academy (equally "outrageous" in the eyes of some).

Here are two great characters, only now beginning to receive their due. Richard Johnson's "private behavior" rendered him unacceptable to historians for a time, though we know something of his private character and possess a number of fine portraits of him. Of Julia we know very, very little, and we can only imagine how she looked, especially how she looked *at* Mrs. John C. Calhoun. As late as 1894 respectable opinion in Kentucky was baffled as to the appropriate response to their lives together. In a congressional campaign that year, one candidate, W. C. P. Breckinridge, referred to their case in responding to a charge of having kept as a mistress a woman journalist who had borne him two children. That, according to Breckinridge, was as scarlet a sin as his own, though, he pointed out, Johnson had not been denied public office. Breckinridge failed to point out that he was married to another woman and had exploited his mistress. Johnson had not married anyone else and was never accused of promiscuity while Julia lived.

The women of Kentucky, who were not easily fooled, rallied against Breckinridge. In a long, solemn letter to a newspaper on August 15, 1894, L. L. Bristow, the historian of the legal profession of Kentucky, joined them. The shroud of genteelism still hung over the discourse, with its careful avoidance of the matter of race, but the sentiment was at least candid. Julia Chinn, of course, remained a nonperson:

The Choctaw Academy, one of Richard Mentor Johnson's philanthropies.
He saw no irony in being famous for both killing Indians and educating
them. *Courtesy of Ann Bolton Bevins*

No one justified Colonel Johnson's course, least of all his family, but all
admit that his honest effort to rectify his mistake was, if not saintlike,
certainly most honorable. . . . In spite of prejudice and loss of friends, he
stood by those he loved — though the law gave them no claim — and
was faithful until death. The generous, noble-hearted Kentuckian of
today will take off his hat and pause with reverent tread before the grave
of this honorable old statesman and soldier, this courtly old-time hero,
Richard M. Johnson.

Johnson's name is associated with the greatest surviving mansion of
the Johnson and Ward families, Ward Hall. As visitors explore that
amazing building, they may consider the possibilities of further archaeology in the social history of the antebellum South. Like the biographies
of Richard Mentor Johnson and Julia Chinn, another Johnson mansion
remains under the mud: their plantation headquarters, under construction near Princeton Landing, Mississippi, in the 1850s. The banks of the
river crumbled in 1885, it is said, and the house was submerged. When the
river is low, you can see the outlines of its foundations. And when our
energy to relearn our history is high, we may discern, as well, the outlines of the lives of two great Kentuckians.[2]

19

....

Francis Parkman and
the Evidence of France

France . . . toujours France, belle France, is our best and true connection
abroad, and must be for years to come.

— RICHARD RUSH, 1821[1]

FREDERICK JACKSON TURNER delivered his manifesto "The
Significance of the Frontier in American History" in 1893, during the Chicago Columbian Exposition. In that year Americans
gave an unusual amount of attention to their sense of themselves, taken as a group. Explanations of how they had come to be as they
were appeared in the daily press and were much bruited in barber shops,
at feed stores, and at other places of assembly.

Four of these hypotheses had reached the public in unusually dramatic fashion. Even today, even amid the readily disposable wisdom of
the 1990s, these same four are still in competition, though seldom explicitly identified. Secretly they continue to vie with one another in scholarly papers, in street corner conversation, and in the clichés of political
discourse.

There is truth in each, though none of us is equally persuaded by
them all. Unconsciously, we are drawn to one central idea or another,
and any reader who has come this far with me knows which of the four
predominates here. The four great themes are Turner's frontier; the
germ history, also known as the prepotency of Europe; the centrality to
American life of racially based slavery and its aftermath; and the contest
between French and Catholic absolutism and English Puritan individu-
alism. In 1893 an American interested in understanding himself and his
country could go to the mailbox and find there ample reason to ponder
all four of these organizing ideas.

Turner gained immediate fame and wide reprinting by encouraging Americans to think of their history from the inside out, not as a mere extension of events in Europe. He managed to convince his colleagues to abandon their earlier fascination with the germ theory, which held that American institutions had been carried aboard European ships along with European diseases, awaiting only revolutionary circumstances to emerge. Indeed, the Columbian Exposition itself was a celebration of that view. It was probably the last occasion at which a sizable number of respectable historians concurred in the view that Columbus discovered America, as if no one had been here to receive him in 1492. (David Levin of the University of Virginia interjected in a copy of this manuscript that as early as 1809 Washington Irving had noted that the Indians did not know they were lost.)

By the 1990s European prepotency has been reduced to a contributing, not the dominant, force in our affairs. The point of view against which Turner contended is today more likely to be found among Ku Klux remnants invoking the ghosts of anonymous Anglo-Saxons rather than among historians overemphasizing the baggage of Genoese seafarers.

Turner prevailed, though he was not an eloquent writer nor did he possess the storyteller's gift. He was not much interested in stories, much less so in tales of individual lives. He thought and wrote most comfortably of groups; had he possessed a computer, he would have been the first social historian.

But not with quite the same comprehensiveness that would be expected of him today. Turner was a product of a midwestern experience that had not yet had much acquaintance with darker-skinned people. He did not devote much of his energy to questions of race and the legacy of slavery. Those were not popular themes in 1892 or 1893. The generous passions of the Civil War had faded; Jim Crow was settling in. Nonetheless, out of the prairie came a familiar voice of conscience; from his library at Nininger, Ignatius Donnelly launched *The Golden Bottle*, the second of his two novels intended to provoke a fresh acquaintance with racism as a central fact in the life of his country. Two years earlier, in *Doctor Huguet*, he had depicted the life of a young White southern physician whose refusal to speak out on the subject resulted in heavenly retribution: Huguet awoke one morning encased within the body of a Black man, and he came to a violent end.

Doctor Huguet was not a novel likely to enhance the prospects of its writer for national office. Even less politic was *The Golden Bottle*. Donnelly created the fable of Ephraim Benezet of Kansas, who, making use of a magic bottle having the property of turning base metals into gold, accumulates the resources to contend with the "money power" controlling America. Installed as president, he leads a fraternal army of Blacks and Whites to liberate Europe from despotism, humbling the

Pencil sketch of Francis Parkman in 1889. *Courtesy of the Hood Museum of Art, Dartmouth College, Hanover New Hampshire; Gift of Oswald D. Reich*

348

Francis Parkman
27 Feb. 1889

kaiser and the czar. He goes on to establish a Jewish national state in Palestine and a United Nations (called a Universal Republic).

I have already attempted to give Donnelly something like his due. So we must leave him, doffing our hats to Doctor Huguet and Ephraim Benezet, and press on to Francis Parkman, who would have been most unlikely to approve of the juxtaposition, and to the fourth of the organizing ideas prominent in 1893.

Parkman died in 1893, celebrated and widely read, having convinced many that "the most momentous and far-reaching question ever brought to issue on this continent was: Shall France remain here or shall she not?"[2]

That question was important. Had one answer not been given in 1763, had Britain not suddenly surged to victory in its worldwide contest with France, and had a French *empire* remained in North America, the streams of history thereafter would not have flowed as they did. But how momentous was the political issue of the Seven Years War, and how final? Dynastic claims over vast areas inhabited by other nations quite unresponsive to those claims are not the same as actual political control; terms such as "French Louisiana" would not have meant much to the Kiowa or Cheyenne. And the concerns of kings failed to determine the behavior even of people whom they thought to be their subjects, but who declined to be subject to anyone. The most important of these people were artists and merchants, to whom, by his nature and training, Parkman was indifferent.

France did "remain," despite its loss of that imperial contest of the eighteenth century which Parkman described with incomparable eloquence. It remained indelibly a part of the language and life of Louisiana and Quebec, two radically distinct cultures, but both French. It remained artifactually in many other places, in architecture, city planning, and garden design.

Parkman's bitter anticlericalism and his passionate New England patriotism required him to associate all but a handful of Frenchmen with the Bourbon dynasty and the Roman Catholic Church. The result was his presenting a cosmic drama of light and darkness contending for empire, a drama leaving little space for people whose lives proceeded in the interstices of politics. They were not petty men, creeping about the huge legs of generals and statesmen; they simply lived by other laws, and answered other questions.

Parkman ignored them, for they could not find roles in his saga of noble, freedom-loving, individualistic New Englanders contending against "Feudalism, Monarchy, and Rome . . . Feudalism still strong in life, though enveloped and overborne by new-born Centralization; Monarchy in the flush of triumphant power; Rome, nerved by disaster, springing with renewed vitality from ashes and corruption, and ranging the earth to reconquer abroad what she had lost at home."[3]

Nonconforming biographies passed unobserved by Parkman, though the American-constructed landscape was profoundly altered by them even before 1763, his momentous date. The pace of their work quickened thereafter. The distractions of warfare were out of the way between 1763 and 1778, and these artistic and commercial aberrants throve even more during the long romance between France and the early republic, roughly from 1778 to 1798. Americans embraced French ideas and French craftsmanship throughout the eighteenth century and well into the nineteenth. Affairs of state had never much affected affairs of the heart, and as we shall see, even after political relations cooled, art and architecture proceeded warmly.

Parkman's question was "brought to issue" in 1763, but we shall also observe in some detail how it refused to be settled until 1867, with the withdrawal of French troops from Mexico. Nonetheless, Parkman reemphasized the "momentous" date, as it had been earlier asserted by George

Bancroft, and added to it a set of rigid political categories that took hold in New England and among genteel Americans who took their cultural cues from Boston and Cambridge. Many of us can certify that this was the case even in the South and West; it required some contortion to put one's head in Boston and one's feet in Milwaukee or St. Paul, but it was done.

This was before Turner placed the spotlight on the frontier and while men like Donnelly were still derided as cranks. Parkman's tale of a continent disputed by a despotic and Catholic France and an individualistic and Puritan New England seems much too simple even if it were convincing, which it is not. But we have lost much value in repudiating it, for today we pay too little heed to how important the French have been to us. Why should that be? It seems to me that the best explanation is Parkman's very power. He stands between us and that recognition. Like a dark knight of myth, he awaits us; we must contend with him before we are free to look about the garden to which he might have served as guide had he been so disposed.

Already we can glimpse what lies beyond his huge figure. The evidence of France is apparent to anyone who approaches our shores by

Broadway as a French neoclassical vista, culminating in City Hall, the work of Mangin and McComb. *Courtesy of the Museum of the City of New York*

water from the south or east. A French-designed fortress guards every significant means of entry. The French presence is more subtly to be seen in those of our cities where remnants remain of the taste of the early republic, a taste deeply tinctured by French neoclassicism.

In New York, for example, the City Hall, the first Saint Patrick's Cathedral, and the once elegant residential area along lower Broadway were brightened and clarified by French designers between 1790 and 1810. The skyline of booming Baltimore was dominated by the domes of architects who were or called themselves French; the capital cities of colonial Virginia, Williamsburg, and of the new nation, Washington, D.C., together with the first of our company towns, Paterson, New Jersey, were laid out on French principles. So too were the central sections of Detroit, St. Louis, and New Orleans a half century earlier.

As the new seaports expanded, French surveyors and planners were at hand; a Parisian guided the expansion of New York above the City Hall; northwest of the old city of New Orleans, the Garden District was laid out by the same piratic hand that conveyed one set of Alsatian ideas (from Nancy) to Donaldsonville, Louisiana. Another set had come from Strasbourg and was applied to a score of towns along the North Carolina coast. French-designed villages still line the Hudson River and dominate sections of the interior of Georgia. In North Carolina, Maryland, and New York, French garden planners created the first American estate plans, and French architects gave the American villa its first elegance in Massachusetts, New York, and Maryland. (This list could be much extended if we were to take Benjamin Henry Latrobe, our greatest architect-engineer of the nineteenth century, at his word. Latrobe said he was more French than English, calling himself sometimes B. H. Latrobe Boneval and sometimes Latrobe de Boneval.)

We will return to these buildings, gardens, and plans for towns as we follow the careers of some of those who built them. Now let us contend with Francis Parkman.

How strange it is to find his momentous question placed foremost in an epic treatment of our national experience written in the midst of the Civil War. "At this hour, half a million bayonets are vindicating the ascendancy of a regulated freedom."[4] In these cool words Parkman expressed as much as he was able to feel about the events of his time, at the pivot of American history. Was this the moral lesson of the war? As the fighting went on, other and larger themes emerged, though not, apparently, for him. Abraham Lincoln, who began his presidency by insisting that it was a war to preserve the Union, came through suffering to understand something Parkman never did (perhaps that is why he never fully approved of Lincoln).

Lincoln came to believe that something more demanding was required of him and of his countrymen than a mere reassertion of "the

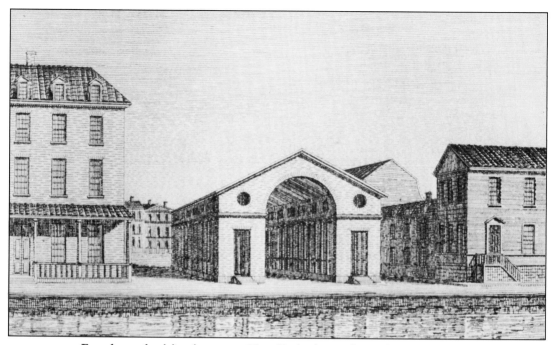

French neoclassicism in upstate New York: the market at Speranza (now Athens), New York, by Pierre Pharoux (1794). *The Corcoran Gallery of Art*

ascendancy of a regulated freedom." That phrase, after all, might have covered the enforcement of the fugitive slave act. Lincoln sought "a new birth of freedom," not merely a restitution of the old. That flawed polity must be repudiated, for the central question had become race and slavery.

The source of the war could be found in sin, a sin shared by the Puritans themselves, the central and original sin of the American experiment in freedom. Lincoln understood the war to have arisen from the ownership of "colored slaves." That ownership "contributed a peculiar and powerful interest. All knew the interest would somehow cause war. To strengthen, perpetuate and extend this interest was the object for which the insurgents would rend the union by war."

Out of his own agony of conscience, Lincoln set forth in his Second Inaugural Address a larger question, as profound as that posed by Job:

> If we shall suppose American slavery one of those offenses which, in the providence of God, needs must come, but which, having continued through his appointed time, He now wills to remove, and that He gives to both North and South this terrible war, as was due to those by whom this offense came, shall we discern that there is any departure from those divine attributes which believers in the living God always ascribe to Him?

Benjamin Henry Latrobe: dramatist, diarist, carica-turist, poet, engineer, and architect. *Architect of the Capitol*

353

And he gave his answer:

> If it be God's will that it [the war] continue until the wealth piled by bondsmen by two hundred years' unrequited toil shall be sunk, and every drop of blood drawn by the lash shall be paid by another drawn by the sword . . . so it still must be said that the judgments of the Lord are true and righteous altogether.

Some New Englanders spoke this way, and some southerners, too, but Francis Parkman was not among them. Though a patriot of New England, he was a Puritan without religion, without compassion, and without a generous spirit. It did not trouble him that the founders of Plymouth and Boston had themselves imposed slavery on Native Americans and imported Africans as slaves as well. He was willing to admit that slavery had been "a tremendous national evil," but even his friend and biographer Charles Haight Farnham admitted that "the anti-slavery question was by no means a burning one with him."⁵

Why was this so? Perhaps because Parkman carried snobbery into the realm of ideas, refusing to be interested in aspects of history associated with people he found distasteful. He was disinclined to pay attention to those to whom he might not have been introduced. Parkman deplored universal manhood suffrage and predicted that hideous consequences would follow the bestowing of the franchise on women. Though a master of biography of males of European descent, as long as they did not descend to take part in commerce, he was capable of compressing millions of diverse people into a fabricated uniformity, even of appearance. He could write of "nature [having] stamped the Indian with a hard and stern physiognomy," and place within that description (unrecognizable in most pueblos) a synthetic character having only four "ruling passions . . . ambition, revenge, envy, jealousy."

There were exceptions to Parkman's round categories: Pontiac and a few Iroquois statesmen, but they were, shall we say, untutored gentlemen. Dismissing the Native American masses as savages confirmed his preconceptions and permitted him, and people like him, to escape the necessity to assess the behavior of those heroes of the Puritan wars who behaved savagely toward them. Parkman sustained his great myth of American history by such devices, deriding William Penn's "benevolent and philanthropic view of the American savage" in the colonial period and describing as "a mistake" the thought that "blandishments" or "kind treatment" might alter the behavior of the Indians of his own time, to whom "robbery and murder have become . . . a second nature." For such savages, "attempts at conciliation will be worse than useless," he said, leaving the alternative undescribed. For a man of the library, he was very bloody minded.[6]

If Parkman seems to us to be more a man of the eighteenth or seventeenth century than a contemporary of Jay Gould, that is because he thought of himself so. He was "not at all enthusiastic about the nineteenth . . . it is too democratic and too much given to the pursuit of material interests." There is the key to another of his blind spots, and so convincing is he that an unwary reader may fall into thinking that what he did not see was not there. Commerce, of course, leads to art. To Parkman, however, it merely gives rise to "vulgarity, crudeness, pretentiousness . . . ignorance and complacency." We would not know how important it is to pursue merchants home, to find there the artists they employed, if we agreed with him that they would have no energy for anything other than their "overstrained and morbid activity, and incessant tension of nerves." (Seventeenth-century entrepreneurs such as Le Sieur de La Salle might be "bold" in their pursuit of furs, even "noble" in their capacity to serve public ends while growing rich, but not Parkman's contemporaries.)

It is doubtful that, even if Parkman had bent to examine the patterns of trade, he would have detected its consequences for architecture, art, or engineering. His mind was more fully developed than his eyes or ears.

A man of enormous physical courage and stamina, though prone to ailments, he was determined not to permit himself to become a "milksop." He honored "the warlike instinct and the military point of view." Farnham tells us that "Parkman cannot be called an artist born . . . nature . . . [denied] him . . . much interest in the fine arts. . . . The stage had no deep interest for him. . . . Music was an unknown world to him."[7]

It is no wonder that Parkman is a poor guide to the artifactual evidence of France in America. His greatness was deficient in qualities necessary to its study, for much of it was not created by soldiers or statesmen. He could permit himself admiration for such gentlemen as Montcalm and Frontenac, though they were agents of the Catholic king, and for the bravery of individual Jesuit missionaries, though they owed fealty to the pope of Rome. But the creation in French Canada and French Louisiana of a culture that has lasted into our own time as the result of the exertions of women, of artisans, and of innumerable anonymities was beneath his notice.

This was especially true if they were Catholic and anonymous. Parkman was, it is sad to say, a paranoiac, as that word is used clinically. He was prone to theories about Roman conspiracies, believing himself beset by "ultramontane catholics" as well as the "ultra democrats, and woman suffragists" who had been offended by his remarks about "promiscuous suffrage," his opposition even to the granting of degrees by Harvard to women, and his tendency to dismiss the working class as "boors" and "barbarians." (There was something called Cahenslyism among American Catholics in Parkman's time, which sought to keep immigrants Catholic; it was encouraged by the sentimental Catholic rulers of Bavaria and by a few recalcitrant archbishops. But it was not directed at Francis Parkman, and it quickly dissipated as the pope heeded the counsel of Archbishop John Ireland, leader of the "Americanizers.")

Furthermore, Parkman could not understand that sometimes economic forces do determine large historical outcomes, and he was astigmatic in his reading of artifactual evidence. Statecraft he could understand, but he avoided the intersection of art and economics, where the French were very active indeed.

(It would stretch this essay into a monograph if we were to try to compensate here for another of his blind spots: the differing ways in which French and English travelers treated the architecture they found as they explored the continent. His blanket term for Native Americans was "savages"; he could not think of them as architects and builders, so even his fierce intellectual curiosity — unlike Thomas Jefferson's — was not strong enough to permit him to examine Native American architecture. Therefore he could not discern how Europeans brought their own preconceptions to the mute evidence of a past they did not understand. As each of them interpreted what they found — as we do — to confirm what they already knew, they told as much about themselves as about the evidence they were trying to place in its proper boxes. Some other time . . .)

Parkman's stance toward African-Americans can be understood in the light of his other debilitating snobberies. He was not much stirred by the condition of slaves when they were not Europeans, and thus was able to pose Puritan New England as a noble alternative to cruel and despotic New France. Parkman was not distressed by the necessity to integrate into that simple picture servants of the British Crown such as Edward Randolph. In 1676 Randolph's regret at the slaughter of three thousand Indians, men, women, and children, in the Second Puritan War of Conquest did not arise from compassion but from a more practical emotion. A labor force had been lost. "If well managed [those people] would have been very serviceable to the English." They were dead and could not be enslaved, "which makes all manner of labour dear."[8]

As the battle clouds rose from the South, Parkman did not find reason to expand his theme of the antagonism of "Liberty and Absolutism, New England and New France" to set it in the broader context of transatlantic ambitions and migrations willing and unwilling. In the midst of a devastating war for liberty, it did not seem to occur to him that some reference might be made to the ironies implicit in his terms. (Parkman's terms did *not* imply that he was uncritical of "liberty." He thought too much of it a bad thing — too much free coming and going and voting and complaining and bargaining on the part of the lower orders who failed to know their place — but it had the virtue of energy which, in himself, was a quality Parkman admired as much as he deplored its possession on the part of the vulgar.)

We may ask: What was liberty to slaves taken in battle by the Puritans and sold in exchange for Blacks brought from Africa? What was freedom of the seas for the seventeenth- and eighteenth-century slave traders? Why was it of no importance that liberty for the Europeans meant freedom to enrich themselves by a commerce in persons? Did the history of this period have nothing to do with the slave trade of the Dutch, the French, and the British? What were the varying attitudes toward racial intermarriage held by the British of Virginia, the British of New England, the French of Canada, and the Spanish of Florida? (For some thoughts on these matters, see Chapters 1–4.)

Though we must recognize that Parkman chose to limit his history largely to events north of the Mason-Dixon Line — the first part of which was drawn in his "momentous" year of 1763 — and thus to areas in which African-Americans were not present in large numbers, the pivot of New World history in the period he was chronicling was the West Indies: Canada was a side show. It was the side show he chose to describe, and he did it with such immense skill that we may be grateful to him, though these questions remain in our minds.

They have been in some minds since 1763 and were forcibly brought to everyone's attention by the Civil War. Parkman had no obligation to address them, but it is passing strange that he did not.

Liberty never was compatible with slavery. New England's war against New France was never a contest about personal liberty. It was a conflict between systems of economic organization and ways of responding to the expansion of Europe during the revolutions of the seventeenth century. Parkman's political and religious distinctions do not help us much. The civil wars among the sects no longer have much nobility in them, nor do the slogans of the time explain much. The seventeenth- and eighteenth-century superpowers shrouded their struggles for market share and for hegemony in the vestments of religion. Even as restated by Parkman with his inimitable verve a century later, their rhetoric is unconvincing. These old words have lost their power to move us, except to feel sorrow for the dead, the maimed, and the mourning. As our own history has become conspicuously engaged with that of the peoples of Asia, Africa, and Europe, we have come to think of the intermittent struggles between New England and New France as the raids and counterraids of outposts on the distant fringe of larger contests.

As Parkman's categories fall from focus, they may still remain before our eyes, fuzzily obtruding before the spectacle of Frenchmen coming and going, in and out of British colonies, throughout the colonial period. Not all these Frenchmen were Roman Catholic, though many were. Not all Catholics served the Bourbons, though many had or did. And Parkman helps us not at all in understanding that quadrilateral relationship among Britain, France, America, and Ireland that has meant so much to this continent, perhaps especially to Boston.

In the Irish wards of that city there must be few schoolchildren who have not heard of the Battle of the Boyne. Green comes forth on Saint Patrick's Day, and woe to him who wears the orange. In a half-million households of Parkman's own city, the tale may be told that the Boyne was the contest in which the very *prince* of Orange, William, king of England he claimed to be, defeated his father-in-law, the true king of England and Ireland, James II, and at the same time brought to an end the remaining hopes of the old Catholic nobility of Ireland.

At the Boyne, on July 1, 1690, William and his Huguenot, Danish, and German mercenaries, stiffened by a few Protestant Englishmen and Dutch, defeated King James and the Catholic Irish under Richard Talbot, earl of Tyrconnel. The Protestant victory sentenced Catholic Ireland to the penal laws and drove James from his throne to France. In America the Boyne had another consequence; it was, in effect, the first great battle of the French and Indian Wars. It terminated three hundred years in which England and France were more often allies than enemies, and sixty during which the Puritans of New England had been left undistracted to complete their two wars of conquest against the Native

Americans. William, Protestant prince of Holland, now rallied against France his three new kingdoms, Ireland, Scotland, and England, and required of Britain's American colonies that they join in the fray.

This would fit neatly into Parkmanian drama but for the addition to the greens and oranges at the Boyne of the white and blue of seven thousand French regulars led by Marshal Lauzun. They implied certain religious confusions that were observed in Vienna. In Saint Stephen's Cathedral the triumph of William over James and Lauzun was celebrated by the court of the Holy Roman Emperor in a solemn *Te Deum*. And what are we to make of the joy expressed by the pope himself, Innocent XI, and of his subsequent approval of the displacement of the Catholic king of England by the Protestant? Rome, in this case, did not accommodate Francis Parkman, for Louis XIV of France had stolen Avignon from the pope and was threatening schism. The "most Christian king" of France threatened as well the Hapsburg family lands of the Holy Roman Emperor, who was also emperor of Austria, by whom all "momentous" questions were decided on the continent of Europe and to whom both Ireland and America were side shows. So the pope, the emperor, and the good Puritans of New England rejoiced concurrently, if not together, and prepared for war against Catholic and Absolute France.

Already Governor Thomas Dongan of New York had begun attacks on French trading posts. As readers of Chapter 6 may recall, he led to the placement of "feudalism" on both sides of the North American drama by garrisoning manors along the Hudson. Dongan was an Irish Catholic, nephew of Tyrconnel, trained in France. He counted many of the French noblesse among his friends — they took more seriously his claim on the earldom of Limerick than did the English. Yet he anticipated the policies of William while serving James, his Catholic king. It seems likely that the schoolchildren of Boston would expect that he would do so, and expect as much of his kinsmen, the other Catholic royal governors of an English colony, the Lords Baltimore. They were proprietors of Maryland, descendants of George Calvert, who had been given the title for his Irish services to James I.

Having observed the complexities of how "Feudalism," "Monarchy," and "Rome" were brought to play in 1688, we should now look more closely at why these forces had not, in fact, been earlier arrayed against the Puritans of New England. What restraint was removed, finally, at the Boyne? That restraint was the extension of the realpolitik of Puritanism in the person of Oliver Cromwell. Cromwell brought his godly commonwealth into league with Rome — with the "most Christian king of France," to be more exact — against the Puritans of Holland.

Cromwell's First Dutch War, in 1652, had no hint of nobility in its origins; it was "a watershed in English history . . . the first war waged for purely commercial ends."⁹ Commercial rivalry with Holland in the West and East Indies, on the Chesapeake and along the slave coasts, dictated amity with Holland's enemy, with little room for consideration of abstractions such as Despotism, Feudalism, or Rome. That rivalry led Cromwell into an otherwise inexplicable alliance with Louis XIV, the foe of Holland. After the death of Cromwell, Charles II returned from his exile in Holland. Without permitting the fires of Dutch hospitality to cool, he sent British shells to add warmth to the hearths where he had so recently been made welcome. Charles was adaptable and quickly sustained the mode of dialogue Cromwell had employed with his fellow Puritans of Holland.

New England was sheltered from New France as an incidental consequence of the fattening of the privy purse of Charles II of England by bribes received from Louis XIV of France. It was not until the merry monarch was replaced by the dour James II and he by the utterly humorless prince who became William III (of the firm of William and Mary) that Feudalism, Rome, et al., were turned loose on New England. The depredations of the French and Indians, and of the British and Indians, upon each other provide much of New England's history over the next seventy-three years. But in the main theater of contention, William's wars were impoverishing his native country and soon it was no longer out of loyalty to their king that British heroes went to war with France. Holland was no longer a threat to British trade, and from the rivulets carrying furs from Hudson Bay to the islands of the Caribbean, France could be attacked wholeheartedly.

It is worthy of note that even in this period, when dynastic, religious, and pecuniary passions were synchronous, there were many in America who were not so ardent. The role of religion in these conflicts was complicated, especially when it conflicted with the role of commerce. The merchants of New York and Albany seldom ceased their trade with France, confusing their Iroquois allies, and a lively commerce was sustained between the Carolinas and the colonies of Catholic Spain. Ultimately, however, the lucrative opportunities for such clandestine profits, for privateering, and for heroism in the forests came to an end. Canada and the Mississippi Valley became parts of the British Empire under the treaties of 1763. France was not, of course, removed from the continent; French *political power* was removed, but French culture and language remained dominant in the regions where that continent's two great river systems, the Mississippi and the St. Lawrence, issued into the ocean.¹⁰

Soon after 1763 the imperial contests between Britain and France were renewed. After twenty years there was a new participant, the United States, which appeared now on one side and now on another. A first consortium with Feudalism, Monarchy, and Rome produced victory in the Revolutionary War. To memories of expeditions against Louisburg and Quebec and of "massacre" at Deerfield, new recollections were added: the French were once again visible in New England, supplying George Washington's troops around Boston and garrisoning Newport, forming there the great amphibious force that secured the allied victory at Yorktown. French supply contracts built the fortune that endowed the Wadsworth Atheneum in Hartford.

During the War of 1812 the French monarchy, now the military dictatorship of Napoleon, diverted British energies that might otherwise have been sufficient to crush Andrew Jackson's forces at New Orleans. That victory redeemed a number of embarrassments that had occurred during the second Franco-American cobelligerency, from 1812 to 1815. Only a few months earlier the British had captured the capital of France and burned the capital of the United States. Though the Americans kept up the fight, the French abandoned it. Napoleon went off to exile on Elba, while the British occupied the coast of Maine and New England took a position approaching neutrality. The cattlemen of Maine and Vermont supplied most of the needs of the British forces in the northern sector, as southern New England had profitably supplied the French thirty years earlier.

One might say with Parkman that his momentous question was "brought to issue" in 1763. But France did not abandon her dream of empire in the Western Hemisphere. After the first cobelligerency and throughout the second the ardor of the Franco-American romance was receding. Though the American Revolution had been very violent, the king of England was not close at hand to feel it, and in 1793 the French decapitated their king. The British had done as much in 1649, and the rhetoric of some Americans during the revolutionary years carried the implication that they might have as well, had George III been unlucky enough to be marooned on their shores. But the French were so ungentlemanly about it.

Between 1798 and 1800 the American government of John Adams and the Federalists combined conservative apprehensions about regicidal Jacobinism, the Bolshevism of its day, with mercantile policy, in a remarkable indifference to racial antipathies. The United States went into a quasi alliance *against* France with the second independent nation in the hemisphere, the Black republic of Toussaint Louverture on Saint Domingue. Though the ensuing quasi war was not quite declared, it produced ample bloodshed and reawakened French aspirations to a New World empire.

As the warships issued their broadsides, trading vessels bickered as well in a fierce competition for the trade of the Negro republic. American merchants were protected by the West Indies squadron, and French merchants, in league with dispossessed slave-holding planters, stoked the fires of Bonaparte's ambitions. In 1800 Napoleon extorted Louisiana from Spain in the secret treaty of San Ildefonso and proceeded to assemble two great armadas. One was to take back Saint Domingue; that base achieved, it was to join the other armada in garrisoning Louisiana.

The invasion of Saint Domingue failed, the invasion of Louisiana was aborted, and the American empire placed in abeyance. In Chapter 8, I discussed the adventures of the Bonapartist expeditionary force in Texas in 1818 and the proposal for a buffer zone garrisoned by Frenchmen across that then independent country in 1839. But these cannot be contended to have been imperial in intention or in scope. Parkman's momentous issue was reopened along the southern, not the northern or western borders of the United States, but not until the end of the 1830s. A French expedition under Admiral Baudin and the prince de Joinville seized Vera Cruz in 1838, leaving many scars of their occupation to be found by the American army, which came upon the scene nine years later.

Louis Philippe, king of the French at the time, had had his own American sojourn in 1797–1799, together with his artist-brother the duc de Montpensier. But he was no more impressed with the obligations of a former guest than Charles II had been. The occupation of Vera Cruz strengthened his intentions to install his brother's heir as emperor of Mexico, but when the time became ripe, the throne of Mexico went to a designee of the Bonapartes, not the Bourbons.

The American nephews and nieces of Napoleon did not attempt to become emperors or empresses. Neither his sister Caroline's Murat princes, of Florida and Louisiana, nor the Baltimore Bonapartes, the offspring of his brother Jerome, did so. The Adirondack daughter of Joseph, the former king of Spain, who was not born to his wife, was made legitimate only by action of the nephew who did make that attempt, and that was late in their lives, after he had become the Emperor Napoleon III. Louis Napoleon, who assumed that title in 1852, had long dreamt of a French empire in Central America, presiding over a canal between the oceans. Two years after he took the throne, French filibusters under Count Raousset de Boulbon made an effort to seize Sonora. They failed, but a petty squabble over the debts of a failed Swiss banker in Mexico created the pretext for the last French imperial adventure in the New World. In 1860 the banker was given French citizenship and the "rights" of his creditors enforced by thirty thousand French bayonets. The sorry tale of the Emperor Maximilian began.

It ended when French troops were withdrawn under the glowering gaze of Ulysses S. Grant, whose battle-tested forces appeared along the Rio Grande in 1866. Maximilian went to his death in 1867; I have been unable to find a comment by Parkman on the matter.

With this in mind it may become easier to perceive the motivation of the gifted Frenchmen who, unaware of Francis Parkman's thundering cate-

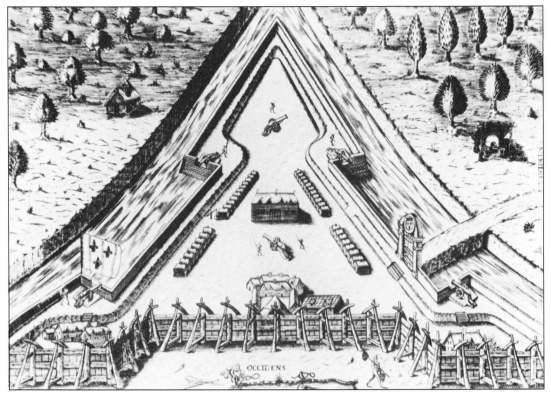

Fort Caroline, built by the French Protestants on the coast of South Carolina and destroyed by the Spanish. It later served as a model for English forts on the James River of Virginia. *Courtesy of the Library of Congress*

gories, came to the colonies of British North America and effected large changes on its landscape. The first of them came by sea, and it is on the seacoast that the largest of their consequences are still to be seen.

Fort Caroline, the triangular stronghold Jean Ribault's Huguenots built in 1564, has been overcome by four hundred and thirty Florida rainy seasons and hemmed in of late by developers extending the sprawl of Jacksonville's northern suburbs. At the other extreme of the Atlantic seaboard, the gardens laid out forty years later by Pierre du Guast amid the huge cedar trees within the walls of his garrison on the Isle of St. Croix in Maine have gone as well, though they have pride of place in being established before the English reached Jamestown, Virginia. In one of many instances in which he *does,* in fact, point to useful evidence, Parkman tells us that the foundations of the St. Croix settlement could still be discerned as late as 1798 "among the sand, the sedge, and the matted whortleberry bushes. . . . The wilderness had resumed its sway, and silence and solitude brooded once more over this ancient resting-place of civilization."[11]

Gone as well is the triangular fortress derived from a published image of Ribault's fort and erected by Nicholas Martieu at Yorktown, Virginia. This underappreciated French engineer received a sixteen-hundred-acre patent in recompense for providing those Jamestown settlers with the benefits of French military engineering. Among the other accomplishments of Martieu was providing the gene of military competence that reappeared in his descendant George Washington. Washington's most famous victory was achieved in 1781 — by a combined force including more Frenchmen than Americans — on land once owned and fortified by his French ancestor.

Gone as well are once famous French fortresses in Alabama, Mississippi, Texas, Louisiana, Arkansas, Missouri, Michigan, Wisconsin, Indiana, Pennsylvania, New York, and Tennessee, gone with the seigneuries of Vermont. But some recognition of their importance to our history may arise from visiting two reproductions of them, recently built where we might not at first expect them. Twelve miles northeast of Montgomery, the park rangers of the state of Alabama have re-created the stockade of Fort Toulouse, first established by a lieutenant named La Tour in 1717, when this was the territory of the Creek. It requires some force of imagination to press so early into the history of the European invasion of Alabama, but we are propelled to do by the words of the

An imaginary scene, engraved in the 1820s, of the Bonapartist colony at Aigleville, Alabama. It hangs in the French Room of the State History Museum, Archives Building, Montgomery, Alabama.

great historian of the oldest South, Verner Crane, that "until the establishment of Georgia, and for many years after, the diplomacy of the southern frontier largely revolved around this pivot."

Fort Loudoun can be found partially reconstructed on the shores of Lake Tellico, now in East Tennessee, then in Cherokee country. Many British fortifications were laid out by French military engineers during the French and Indian Wars; this one came as the culmination of a sequence of ever more ambitious contending strongholds lining the rivers draining the Cumberland plateau.

La Salle had begun the process in 1684 when he built a stockade on Chickasaw Bluffs on the Mississippi near the present site of Memphis (three years later he built another in Victoria County, Texas). It was succeeded by Fort Assumption, a larger work with three bastions facing inland and two on the river. Its designer, Ignace-François Broutin, was one of the grandfathers of the Greek Revival. Broutin was also the designer of the classical fortress St. Jean Baptiste at Natchitoches ("Natch-it-tush"), Louisiana.

Fort Loudoun was designed by Guillaume-Gérard de Brahm (1710?–1799), probably a Huguenot, who had learned his trade serving with the Austrians against Louis XIV on one front and against the allies of the "most Christian king," the Turks, on the other. James Oglethorpe, while similarly occupied, may have induced Brahm to come to Georgia. He came in 1751, to complete work left undone at Oglethorpe's own departure and to design garrison towns for Protestant German and French-Swiss refugees. Brahm knew his business and was soon in charge of all the fortifications of the southern colonies of Britain. He completed the walls of Charleston and Savannah and planned such towns as Ebenezer and Frederica on good Franco-Roman lines. "After Monsieur Vauban's method," Oglethorpe put it admiringly.[12]

"Monsieur Vauban," Sébastien Le Prestre, Marquis de Vauban, marshal of France (1633–1707), was an architect of churches, a town planner, a hydraulic engineer, and an expert in sieges who gained his chief fame as the designer of defenses for the cities along the frontiers of France. Some of them he had just captured for Louis XIV, whose favorite military engineer he was until he stepped beyond the already wide swath of his skills to criticize the Sun King's tax policies. Vauban brought together ideas in fortress design developed by the blind theoretician Blaise François de Pagan and by the Florentines, including Leonardo da Vinci. By 1750 his lessons had become widely followed. Vaubanesque fortresses had been laid out from the upper Volga to the headwaters of the Tennessee, most of them by Protestant French engineers.

Brahm's Fort Loudoun was one of those. It was intended to abash the Cherokee and to withstand any attack by the forces of Louis XIV. It displayed the full Vaubanian repertory: "A Rhombus with two . . . bastions . . . a hornwork, Cavalier, and Lunettes before the Courtain."[13] The Catholic French responded by creating a system of fortress-towns downstream on the Tennessee and stiffened their garrisons across the wide area where the Ohio, Missouri, Mississippi, and Tennessee rivers converged. There, at St. Louis, as at Detroit and New Orleans, another device of Vauban's appeared — a drill field in the middle of the city, the *place d'armes,* which could also serve as a market — or merely as a breath of green, as it does in New Orleans to this day.

Fort Loudoun was never completed. After a siege by the Cherokee, its garrison surrendered and it slowly sank into desuetude. The site has benefited by responsible archaeology, displayed in 1990 in a good interpretive center.

We have come a little distance from Parkman, but that is because he was not drawn to the nonconforming presence of Protestant Frenchmen doing important work within the English colonies. A pity, for his love of literature might otherwise have given us full-length portraits of two engineers, one of whom had extraordinary claims upon any literary historian. He was Gabriel Bernard of Geneva (1690?–1747), uncle and guardian of Jean-Jacques Rousseau. The other was an engineer-architect who anticipated the freeway system (for the same reasons later asserted by another general, Dwight David Eisenhower), laid out most of the important canals to be built in America, and left a larger imprint upon our land than any other designer in our history.

I have thought hard about that final clause. Daniel Burnham? The composite of Skidmore, Owings and Merrill? Frederick Law Olmsted? Gifford Pinchot? Not by the most generous extensions of the term "designer" can we stretch these others to the amplitude necessary to match the accomplishments of the modest marshal of France, Simon Bernard (1779–1839).

Let us take the two Bernards in chronological order. Rousseau could not have been especially fond of his mother's brother, who was also the husband of his father's sister. Bernard became his unwilling guardian after returning to Geneva from serving beside Oglethorpe in the Turkish wars. All of the information about Gabriel Bernard in *The Confessions* is false except that he went to America and died there. He did not design or build Charleston (Rousseau's version); that city was already in place. It was probably Savannah; "Oglethorpe's" plan bears a close relationship to other French-Swiss plans and ultimately to Roman garrison towns. Savannah also might have been drawn from Irish "establishments," but we know that from the late 1720s until his death in 1747 Bernard created towns for Oglethorpe and for the philanthropists of Neuchâtel who established villages around Purrysburg on the Savannah River.

After Gabriel Bernard passed his baton to Brahm, French control of the planning for the coastal defenses of the southern British colonies remained constant. Brahm was in charge of them until the brink of the Revolution, with the assistance of Claude-Joseph Sauthier, primarily a garden designer. (Though the two disciplines were then, and are now, closely related, we will come back to Sauthier after we are done with fortresses.) Thereafter a series of French engineers assisted the growing officer corps of the United States, trained under Le Chevalier de Roche-fontaine at West Point, until the need for a first-rate, French-trained organizing genius for coastal defenses was made painfully obvious by the charred remains of the Capitol and the White House after the War of

1812.

That genius was Simon Bernard, and genius he was — and his timing was right; or is that a tautology? In any case, at the end of his advancement as an artillery officer and builder of military roads for the salient of the French empire reaching into the Balkans, a new career opened. He did not resign as a general in the service of France (he had been a *maréchal de camp* and baron of Napoleon). He took a leave that lasted from 1816 to 1831, when he returned to France. He twice became the minister of war, though he was a diffident fellow, inept at politics, and was sometimes derided as a "mere engineer."

The southernmost of Bernard's American creations is also the largest of American fortresses, Fort Jefferson, seventy miles west of Key West. It occupies an entire island but has an interior body of water, a moat teeming with sharks and barracuda. With ports for 450 guns, it is probably the largest fortress anywhere which does not surround a town. It is desolate, dry, and utterly without the neoclassical charm of Bernard's masterwork, Fort Pulaski, off Savannah. Fortress Monroe was his first American creation; it is still in use, I believe, as the headquarters of CONARC, the Continental Army Command. From Fort Gorges in Maine, around the coast to Fort Jefferson, and on to the batteries guarding the Mississippi and Mobile Bay, the fortresses we see today are largely Bernard's work.

At Mobile, a reconstruction of Fort Condé reminds a visitor that French architecture arrived there long before Bernard. In 1711 Jean-Baptiste le Moyne began presiding as governor of Louisiana in that turreted brick stronghold in the old Vaubanesque mode. Beyond the city, at the mouth of the bay, Fort Morgan shows how much Napoleon's engineers had learned about massing artillery. Bernard's design placed three tiers of guns atop one another — and still Admiral David Farragut was able to get his fleet past in 1861. Fort Morgan was preserved because Farragut did not yet possess the rifled cannon that brought Fort Pulaski and another Bernard stronghold in Confederate hands, Fort Macon, North Carolina, to surrender. It did not matter how many old-fashioned guns a fort might have if the new, long-range cannon could send their shells spinning through the walls, boring holes through each stack of masonry in turn until they could reach the magazines.

Fort Pulaski, Georgia, a neoclassical fortress designed by Simon Bernard about 1820. The Confederates who held it in 1862 found that it had been rendered obsolete by the invention of the rifled cannon.

The Bernard fortresses remain, beautiful in baleful efficiency, though pathetic expressions of a period in which Americans had every reason to feel exposed. Maine had been occupied in the War of 1812, Washington burned, Baltimore and New Orleans assaulted; in the 1780s the villages of the Virginia and Connecticut shore had been burned out, so Americans turned once again to the friends of their nation's youth, the French. And not merely in the training of their armies and the engineering of their coastal defenses. Napoleon was a specialist in the use of a strategy of "interior lines," rapid movement across the inside of a region while holding enemies at bay on the periphery. He had used men like Bernard to create hard-surfaced highways to facilitate that strategy. Some Napoleonic roads overlaid earlier demonstrations of the same concept by the Romans; between 1933 and 1939 a third layer was created in a few instances by Adolf Hitler's autobahns.

General of the Army Dwight David Eisenhower admired the autobahn system and, when he became president of the United States in 1952, undertook the creation of the most extensive network of military highways in American history. As the freeway system, it also served as an employment stimulus to deter the anticipated postwar depression. In 1816 James Monroe, who had much in common with Eisenhower, had seen both the economic and military virtues of such a system. So, under Monroe's orders, Bernard was asked about his highway from Ragusa to Zara and Trieste. (Perhaps he was also asked about the story in which the emperor of Austria expressed regret that the French had not stayed a little longer — to get the road finished.) Thereafter, when Bernard was not laying up fortresses he was laying out macadamized roads. One was to anticipate Route 1, going from Washington along the Atlantic coast and west to New Orleans, where it would meet another that had gone overland by way of Knoxville. Others were to connect Washington to Buffalo and St. Louis.

Bernard was also to work on a breakwater across the mouth of Delaware Bay and new methods of combining railroads, inclined planes, and canal locks to cross mountains. These were to be parts of a canal system to shorten communication and diminish freight costs for the nation's rising industries. Bernard sloshed through swamps, tore through brush, dodged rattlesnakes, and fought off black flies and mosquitoes over fifteen years of exploration. To these exertions we owe comprehensive designs for the following waterways, most of which have been built along the lines he suggested: the Florida Canal, the Dismal Swamp Canal, the Chesapeake and Ohio (no success there); the Susquehanna and Schuylkill; the Delaware and Raritan; the Cape Cod Canal, and the waterway between Narragansett Bay and Boston Harbor.

Having completed his work, Bernard went back to France. Back too, at about the same time, went the Napoleonic generals and colonels who had taken shelter in the United States, building houses and colonies in Alabama (Demopolis and Aigleville) and Texas (Le Champ d'Asile). Point Breeze, the mansion in New Jersey of Napoleon's brother Joseph, lately king of Naples and Spain, is gone, as are all but one of his houses in the Adirondacks. Gone, too, is the Florida plantation house of Napoleon's nephew, the Murat crown prince of Naples (Naples went to the emperor's sister, Caroline Murat, after Joseph was sent off to Spain), but Murat's other establishment remains, in Baton Rouge, Louisiana.

Joseph Bonaparte's famous gardens have disappeared, but two earlier estates remain, evidencing French planning in quite different ways. These are to be found at the Governors' Palace at Williamsburg and the Governor's Palace of North Carolina. Both were re-created in the 1930s and 1940s as parts of that intriguing phenomenon, the celebration of dependency, otherwise known as the Colonial Revival. Why Americans of the Depression years chose to revive the architecture and gardens of a period in which they still deferred to European guidance, rather than of a later period in which Americans were giving guidance to Europe, is not the subject before us. But recognizing that this *is* a question presses us once again to look beneath the surface of the Colonial Revival itself. One difference between the glorious flowering geometry of Williamsburg and that beside Tryon's Palace is that Governor William Tryon of North Carolina had a French designer at hand, while the governors of Virginia had only one in mind.

Claude-Joseph Sauthier (1736–1802) was the first professional landscape architect of European training to find major commissions in America. (It is certain that the elaborate gardens of the Aztec and Inca required professional designers, but we do not know who they were.) After a distinguished career in Strasbourg, producing gardens and estate plans on a grand scale, he was convinced by Tryon to come to North Carolina. There he produced the designs for the garden we see today, together with those for two nearby plantations, Hayes and Chowan. Sauthier also laid out (or merely mapped) ten or more North Carolina villages. When Tryon was transferred to New York in 1773, Sauthier accompanied him and, as surveyor for New York (a post equivalent to that filled by Brahm for the southern colonies), produced a military map sufficiently inaccurate to confuse first the British invasion forces and then the French investors in western New York, who relied on it after independence. Sauthier remained in the city of New York during the Revolutionary War and there met Lord Percy, who served with the occupying forces. Percy had estates of his own in the north of England, and after the British withdrew, Sauthier went along to continue his career as Percy's planner.

One of the victims of Sauthier's deficiencies as a mapmaker was his successor as America's preeminent estate planner, Pierre Pharoux. Pharoux also abandoned a successful architectural and engineering practice in France and joined two partners appropriately named Desjardins in providing garden, estate, and city planning and hydraulic engineering for a syndicate of French investors who thronged to New York as the American Revolution was succeeded by disturbances in France.

Pharoux and the Desjardins were engaged by the Castorland Company, which bought what Sauthier's map indicated to be four hundred thousand acres between the Adirondacks and Lake Ontario. Actually, the tract was only a little more than half as large, but in the process of finding this out and laying out the towns of Castorland and Basle, Pharoux encountered Baron von Steuben, who was living close by in a log house, awaiting a rush of settlers to a speculation of his own at the intersection of the Moose and Black rivers. In 1794 Pharoux provided Steuben with the first extensive estate plan to be created for the northern colonies since that of Pierre du Guast in Maine nearly two centuries earlier. It showed a small formal garden like that Sauthier had given Tryon and sweeping romantic walks through an idyllic countryside.

Before he drowned in the Black River the following year, Pharoux also provided plans for villages now known as Rome, Athens, and Tivoli, New York, and delivered other estate plans and designs for houses for two clans of merchants, the Le Rays of Nantes, Paris, and Watertown, New York, and the Livingstons of the island of Jamaica, of New York, and for all intents and purposes of Paris, to which they provided ambassadors for forty years. (I offered some hypotheses about Pharoux in *Orders from France* four years ago. Bits of confirming evidence have dribbled in subsequently, and as this text went to press, his sketchbook was discovered at the Huntington Library. It provided final confirmation — to my immense relief!)

The Livingstons were one of a number of Hudson River families who sprang from fiercely anti-English, Francophilic, seventeenth-century founders and persistently thereafter carried their cultural affinities into architecture and politics. They also employed Pharoux, creating a series of mansions along the river around the turn of the nineteenth century and constituting the northern anchor of Thomas Jefferson's set of alliances of Francophile gentry. (As noted, their ally in politics and art, Aaron Burr, received from a student of Pharoux, Marc Isambard Brunel, a house design that was as splendid an example of *retardataire* French taste as the one Major Pierre-Charles L'Enfant gave Robert Morris of Philadelphia.)

Before the overt cobelligerency of France and the United States commenced in 1778 — indeed, before the French and Indian Wars came to an end in 1763 — many holders of New York manors, Parishes, De Lanceys, Beekmans, and Livingstons, were not only doing an active business with French Canada, they were importing French furniture and house designs. Because many of them were Scottish in origin and had spent time fuming in Dutch exile (the Parishes and Livingstons especially), it is impossible to distinguish the Franco-Scottish in their taste from the Franco-Dutch. But it is not really necessary to do so since the same celebrated French models were followed in both Scottish and Dutch practice and found their way to America in such houses as the Livingstons' Teviotdale. Dutch and Scottish architects had already reduced the scale of their French models to accommodate their own necessities (space in the first instance and purse in the second), thereby accomplishing work Americans might have had to do.

We may expect evidence of France along the Hudson or the St. Lawrence, so we are not surprised even at rediscovering the most important remaining work of Pharoux, the villa of James Le Ray, now the residence of the commanding general of the Special Forces Unit at Camp Drum outside Watertown, New York. We are less accustomed to noting the French qualities in the red brick, high-roofed mansions along the James River, such as Westover or Carter's Grove. But French they are, for reasons arising from the political confusions recited earlier, from the residence of an Italian guidebook writer in France, and from the intricacies of the tobacco trade.

The Pilgrims, Parishes, and Livingstons were not alone in having sojourned in Holland. For architecture it was far more important that Charles II had done so, for he returned to Britain with a retinue of architects who had observed earlier reductions of French prototypes and were prepared to apply them in red brick with white trim.

By the end of the Stuart period a few American houses were already manifesting the Franco-Dutch style transmitted to England by Hugh May and Christopher Wren. Then, when the Dutch William of Orange became king of England and commenced his own building campaign, this style came fully into its own. Williamsburg, William's capital in Virginia, was laid out upon the "footprint" of Versailles (as was Washington, D.C., later), and its principal buildings were all built in the Franco-Dutch "Wrenaissance" fashion, giving it the aspect of a market town on the Scheldt or the Rhine Delta. The architectural accent along the James was largely Franco-Dutch, though at some places, such as Shirley Plantation, it was Franco-Caledonian. Dynasties might come and go, but the Chesapeake swarmed with traders, at first Dutch and later Scottish. Tobacco went in one direction, architectural ideas in the other. Shirley exemplifies even better than Westover the merger of French influences brought from Holland to England with Charles and William, and then to America, with those taken into American practice the result of Scottish assimilation of French prototypes.

When these houses were built (with advice so far unidentified) by Virginians having close commercial ties to Glasgow and Edinburgh, Scotland's memories of its "auld alliance" with France was still intense. Lowland lairds and lowland merchants were themselves building residences derived from the study by lowland architects like William Bruce of the châteaux at Blérencourt and Balleroy. Though Bruce's mansions were much larger than anything built in America, one can see his work clearly at second hand either at Shirley or at Mount Pleasant in Philadelphia, the transatlantic obeisance of Captain James MacPherson to his lowland youth.

MacPherson's gesture toward Scotland was clear enough, and if we know Bruce, we can extend it to France beyond. Those of the tidewater merchant gentry such as the Byrds and Carters were somewhat more circuitous. They deferred to France not only by way of the Scottish and the Dutch, but also through the books of an Italian who worked in France and learned from French practice. Sebastiano Serlio (1475–1554), a Bolognese, completed his career in France and was, it seems to me, at least as important to the American landscape as his more celebrated contemporary, Andrea Palladio.

Serlio's influence can be seen on the James, in the Wentworth mansions of Portsmouth, New Hampshire, and in the Livingston villas along the Hudson. They are French in aspect not only because of their Scottish and Dutch ties but because Serlio, not Palladio, brought to print their basic form. This was a firmly symmetrical brick house of five or seven bays under a tall roof. Serlio made provision for snow, as Palladio did not. More important, Serlio provided for middle-class housing, which, by European standards, was what colonial America required.

According to his own notations, the middle class entered Serlio's clientele, imaginary or real, in France. Through his widely distributed builder's guides, he gave his readers in Holland and Great Britain, and thus to the New World, a bourgeois element to be merged with derivations from French château building.

All this flowed into American practice while the imperial wars were being fought. It was as if Americans took into their homes a steady succession of French contraband. To put the matter a little differently: art cheerfully went on about its transforming and enlivening work while politics sputtered and declaimed over its head.

We come now to the great romance. From 1778 to 1783 French officers and men joined in alliance with Americans upon American soil. Many sustained that romance after Yorktown; they not only created the coastal defenses of the United States but, as Aaron Burr gratefully reminded his countrymen twenty years later, continued to command them. That was the period when Major L'Enfant was applying the outline of Versailles to Washington and to something almost as ambitious to be built around the falls of the Passaic River for the industrial town at Paterson. He had already designed our first capitol, Federal Hall in New York, a greater success than his huge preliminary plans for the Capitol and White House in Washington. L'Enfant had little sense of scale, and thereby botched his opportunities for the largest residential commissions offered any architect of the time. He did commence a château in Philadelphia for Robert Morris, but it exceeded his client's resources. So grand was L'Enfant that he did not even respond to a request from Stephen Girard, the city's coming young man and still a French citizen.

New York City had residences and a hotel by Pierre Pharoux. Its first cathedral, grand-scale theater, City Hall, and penitentiary were designed by the brothers Charles and François Mangin, and its Merchant's Exchange (called Tavern) by Étienne Hallet, who also won the first competition for the Capitol in Washington.

As for Benjamin Henry Latrobe de Boneval, he was neither French nor English. His taste was as international as his parentage: he was born of Irish, French, German, American, and English antecedents while his parents were resident in Yorkshire. He studied in Germany, France, and Italy and wrote, practiced, and spoke in French as much as in English. Many of his draftsmen were French, and when he was not complet-

George Washington taking the oath of office as president at Federal Hall, New York, the first Capitol of the United States, remodeled by Major Pierre-Charles L'Enfant. *The New-York Historical Society, New York City*

ing Hallet's work on the Capitol, he was competing in Baltimore with two eminent French architects, Joseph-Jacques Ramée and Maximilian Godefroy. The most important buildings of that city — its cathedral, Masonic Hall, Unitarian church, Saint Mary's Chapel, and finest neoclassical country house, Calverton — came from them.

Ramée is the last figure whose American career we will attend, for this recital must, by this time, have made its point: France did not disappear from the American landscape merely because nominal title to

Joseph-Jacques Ramée's competition design for a Washington Monument for Baltimore (he lost). Compare it to Pierre Pharoux's market.
Peale Museum, Baltimore

Canada and Louisiana was transferred in 1763 to the king of England from the king of France. This is evident in the vernacular practices we associate with tall roofs and galleries, cottages raised from the ground on stilts in Louisiana, carried on platforms in Missouri and Illinois, and half buried in hillsides in Canada, but it is easiest to pinpoint in architecture marked with the signature of an individual, especially an individual with so distinct a touch as Ramée.

Ramée was competent in all those occupations required of a French architect, and unlike the others, he had opportunity to display them all, though his American career lasted only from midwinter 1811–1812 to 1816. Ramée left us the first campus plan built around a rotunda, Union College in Schenectady, which is four years older than that of the University of Virginia. He laid out gardens and estates from Baltimore to the shores of the St. Lawrence, villas and country houses, barns and ironworks. His Saint Michael's Church in Antwerp, New York, was the first convincing Gothic Revival building in America, and his Fort Oswagatchie on the St. Lawrence antedated some of the methods of Simon Bernard.

In the life of Ramée a number of our themes came together: he succeeded to the northern New York practice of Pierre Pharoux, made use of the military map of Claude-Joseph Sauthier, and was sponsored by David Parish, of the other Scottish-Dutch family of Francophile taste, which for a time vied with the Livingstons.

France was present in North America before and after 1763. Its political activities were not brought to final issue in 1763, though its governance *was* reduced to the islands of St. Pierre and Miquelon. The lives of most French-speaking people on the continent were not much affected by politics. Even on those two fishing stations, which are still held by France, the inhabitants have gone about their business very much as if they were among their cousins in the villages along the Gaspé Peninsula or the Cajun communities of Louisiana.

Of course it matters that France lost Canada and Louisiana, but an exclusively political view of history flattens the landscape to treaty lines and to those colors, such as paint-can red for English and green for French, which bear no relationship to the real colors of gardens or of fortresses or of buildings.

The evidence of France is all about us. Once it is decontaminated of Francis Parkman's insistence that it serve to illustrate Rome, Absolutism, or Feudalism, it can be seen as the triumph of art and commerce over sectarianism and politics. Still, we would not know it was there at all if he had not insisted that we give France its due as a potent and continuing force in our national life, though not of the kind that interested him.

Notes

Preface

1. Jefferson's account is to be found as the answer to Query XI in his *Notes on the State of Virginia*, available in countless editions. I have used that of the Library of America (New York, 1986).
2. I am grateful to John Julius Norwich for bringing to my attention, in his *Christmas Cracker* for 1989, this passage from Jefferson's letter to the Reverend Isaac Story on December 5, 1801.
3. See my *American Churches* (New York: Stewart, Tabori & Chang, 1982).
4. "A Field Guide to the American Greek Revival" (Chapter 14) is a shrinking down of *Greek Revival America* into a few dozen pages to describe American Free Classicism. This was the final phase of the late Renaissance (1825–1860), succeeding Franco-American neoclassicism as the dominant force in the construction of the American intentional landscape, including architecture.
5. See my *Men on the Moving Frontier* (Palo Alto: American West Publishers, 1969).

Chapter 3

1. Downing quoted in Francis Jennings, *The Invasion of America* (New York: Norton Library, paperback, 1976), 275.
2. The quotations are taken from Gary B. Nash, *Red, White and Black* (Englewood Cliffs, N.J.: Prentice-Hall, paperback, 1974), 106.
3. Quoted in Carl H. Moneyhon, *Republicanism in Reconstruction Texas* (Austin: University of Texas Press, 1980), 18.

Chapter 5

1. My favorites among Upjohn's churches are Saint John Chrysostom in Delafield, Wisconsin; Calvary Church in Stonington, Connecticut; Saint Andrew's in Prairieville, Alabama; and Saint Mary's, built in

Burlington, New Jersey, for Bishop George Washington Doane, who wrote the hymn "Fling Out the Banner" and, somewhat later, had himself shipped parcel post — or was it Railway Express? — from Burlington to New York.

2. I am quoting the account of Upjohn's employment found in a wonderful family memoir, *Early Recollections of Robert Hallowell Gardiner,* printed in 1936 in Hallowell, Maine, which I obtained from the Ohio University Library.

3. *New York Herald,* July 7, 1847, 3.

4. Gardiner, *Early Recollections,* 179.

5. Ibid., 107.

6. Arnold Sakolski, *The Great American Land Bubble* (New York: Harper and Bros., 1932), 241.

Chapter 6

1. Historians seem to enjoy bludgeoning each other for misusing the term "feudal," which is derived from the medieval Latin *feudalis.* The term came into currency at the time the institution it described was passing from the scene; "feudalism" was used by political theorists such as Baron de Montesquieu to mean a system "of parcelling out sovereignty among a host of petty princes, or even lords of villages." These theorists were somewhat vague as to whether they meant true sovereignty, as in a principality, or merely the holding of a manor. But as we are reminded by the greatest of French scholars of feudalism, Marc Bloch, "Words, like well-worn coins, in the course of constant circulation lose their clear outline. . . . Provided that he treats these expressions merely as labels sanctioned by modern usage for something he has yet to define, the historian may use them without compunction. In this he is like the physicist who, in disregard of Greek, persists in calling an 'atom' (the irreducible and indivisible core of matter) something he spends his time dividing." (Francis Jennings, *The Invasion of North America* [New York: Norton Library edition, 1976], 327.)

2. Parkman, in his *The Old Regime in Canada,* Part Four of his *France and England in North America* (Boston: Little, Brown, 1905), 325.

3. The Dutch had no similar experience. They constituted a hard little granule of independence between great powers. The Irish, from time to time, unsuccessfully sought to imitate that status, having thrown off the rule of England to become a granule that papal, Scottish, Spanish, and French alliances against the English could gather around.

Chapter 7

1. James Sterling Young, "The Washington Community, 1800–1828," in *The City in American Life: A Historical Anthology,* ed. Paul Kramer and Frederick L. Holborn (New York: Capricorn Books, 1971), 57.

Chapter 10

1. Douglas D. Scott, et al., *Archaeological Perspectives on the Battle of the Little Big Horn: The Final Report* (Norman: University of Oklahoma Press, 1989), 328.
2. In the 1870s Missouri rustling was as great a risk as the equestrian predations of the Kiowa and Comanche out on the plains. Charlie Goodnight and Oliver Loving took their cattle out of Texas to the mining camps of Colorado around the other side of the hostile Indians, on a long western detour by the way of the Pecos and the Purgatory. The gauntlet, formed by the Kiowa and Comanche on the west and the good yeomen of Missouri who obtained cattle in the dead of night on the east, constrained the drivers of Texas beef and breed stock to pay their way through another kind of Indian territory in the middle.

   Awaiting them with a smile in Oklahoma were the Cherokee, Choctaw, Chickasaw, Creek, and Seminole, inconveniently put there by treaty. Having survived their own civil war, which was contemporaneous with the American Civil War, they had made peace among themselves and were settled astride the safest cattle trail to the railheads, smugly situated upon the unfenced prairie on the way to Dodge City and ultimately Chicago. Old Cherokee survivors of the Trail of Tears of the 1830s collected cattle-trail fees on the Chisholm Trail in the 1870s. Some of their customers were so ignorant of history as to wonder at their obvious satisfaction.

Chapter 13

1. Jefferson in his letter to Hugh L. White and others, May 6, 1810.
2. William L. MacDonald, *The Pantheon* (Cambridge: Harvard University Press, 1976), 88.
3. Quoted ibid., 92.
4. Ibid.
5. Ibid., 88.
6. Ibid., 111.
7. Jefferson quoted in Louis Wright, "Thomas Jefferson and the Classics," paper read before the American Philosophical Society, midwinter and autumn meeting, Philadelphia, 1942–1943, 230.
8. Quoted in Fani-Maria Tsigatou, *The Rediscovering of Greece* (New Rochelle: Carataz Bros., 1981), 152.
9. Quoted in Michael Kammen, *Spheres of Liberty* (Madison: University of Wisconsin Press, 1986), 83.

Chapter 14

1. The emphasis is mine. Carol Rifkind, *A Field Guide to American Architecture* (New York: New American Library, 1980), 39.
2. Again the emphasis is mine. Wayne Flynt, *Dixie's Forgotten People* (Bloomington: Indiana University Press, 1980), 16.

3. Wilbur Zelinsky reported that "the pillared mansion was quantitatively an insignificant element" in its cultural landscape. "The Greek Revival House in Georgia," *Journal of the Society of Architectural Historians* 13, no. 2 (May 1954): 11. It is not necessary that all symbols be significant "quantitatively." But if there were only one or two cathedrals, would we think of them as we do, as the most incandescent symbols of the Middle Ages? Would Rheims and Durham impart to us a sense of their epoch if they stood as isolated and exceptional as do the handful of southern houses of Greek Revival design?

380

4. Let us rejoice in their infinite variety, as recorded in local guidebooks: *Majestic Middle Tennessee* depicts two tall red brick mansions with Roman porticoes, Bethel Place and Tulip Grove. The first, it says, is "pure Greek Revival" and the second "Greek Revival perfection." Another tall Roman portico, imposed upon the middle of the red brick façade, is described in *Ante-bellum Mansions of Alabama* as a "tremendous Greek temple facade . . . architecturally perfect." A hip-roofed frame house in Tuscaloosa with colonnades around three sides is said to be "high perfection of Greek Revival architecture," while another hip-roofed frame dwelling in Forkland, this time with a pleasant, unpedimented front portico, adheres "in every respect to the finest points of Greek architecture."

According to *Old Homes of Mississippi*, D'Evereux has become "the official Natchez example of classic Greek architecture." It is hip-roofed and white frame, with a monumental two-story colonnade all across its front. Sure enough, the Spring Pilgrimage tour book dubs it "pure Greek Revival." But on the next page this honor is diluted by being bestowed as well upon Dixie, a red brick, one-story cottage with a small, four-columned porch amidships: "This charming townhouse is pure Greek Revival." And not far away, in Louisiana, a Palladian two-tiered, pedimented, balcony-over-loggia is described as a "fine example of the Greek Revival style." Textbook writers have generally refused to permit this format to work its way under our umbrella term, but the history of the Renaissance in Europe and America gives it as much right to be there, historically, as others that are admitted to the canon.

(Helen Kerr Kempe, *Old Homes of Mississippi: Natchez and the South*, vol. 1 [Gretna: Pelican Publishing, 1979], 36. The Spring Pilgrimage Tour Guide in my possession is for 1985. My Louisiana reference is to Nancy Harris Calhoun and James Calhoun, eds., *Plantation Homes of Louisiana* [Gretna: Pelican Publishing, 1977], 112.)

5. As a final demonstration of the capaciousness of American usage of the term "Greek Revival" and even of the subspecies "pure Greek Revival," one can observe Palladian porticoes, derived from Roman prototypes and without Greek antecedents, in Kentucky and note this descriptive passage from the work of a distinguished and very sophisticated architectural historian, Rexford Newcomb, FAIA.

In motoring through the Kentucky countryside, perhaps nothing so captivates the eye as do the white-columned mansions, which set in deep groves or atop the gently sloping hills . . . with their deep hospitable porticoes . . .

give tangible evidence of the culture of those pioneers . . . coming over the mountains from Virginia. . . . They are, for the most part, pure Greek Revival in style. (Rexford Newcomb, *Architecture in Old Kentucky* [Urbana: University of Illinois Press, 1953], 131.)

6. Palladio popularized Venetian boldness in portico building through the use of printed books, employing the movable type that became available during his career. The architecture of the Renaissance was as much a literary as a masonry achievement, and the final, American Renaissance of the eighteenth century was even more so. Thomas Jefferson, its most celebrated practitioner, drew upon books *about* books; his taste was drawn from Palladio only indirectly. He never saw a building by Palladio, a drawing by Palladio, or more than quotations from Palladio's own prose. What Jefferson and his contemporaries knew of such matters came to them through intermediaries, and often by way of two sets of intermediaries.

7. America's first Palladian synthesis did not treat monumentality too seriously. The Redwood Library was based upon a casino by Kent for Sir Charles Hotham.

8. Another was built in the 1770s for a now lost house called Teddington, about the time that Thomas Jefferson began devising his biloggial plan for the first Monticello. See my *Orders from France* (New York: Alfred A. Knopf, 1989).

9. Custis became a personal follower of Andrew Jackson, though not a Jacksonian, drawn to him for the psychological reasons discussed at length in my *Architecture, Men, Women, and Money* (New York: Random House, 1985).

10. This essay is not intended for architectural historians, but some general readers may wish to pursue family resemblances among American Greek Revival houses. Here are some suggestions:

Doric Greek Revival is extremely rare in residential form: Arlington House is unique in the gravity of its portico, though it has un-Greek wings. It is really a Hellenic Regency villa.

For examples of the four-columned Ionic derived from the Temple on the Illisus as depicted in Stuart and Revett (1796), see the Governor's Palace and New Chapel in Raleigh, North Carolina (1820–1824 — Wm. Nichols); Powelton, near Philadelphia, Pennsylvania (1825 — Wm. Strickland); J. C. Perry House, Brooklyn, New York (1832 — James Dakin); Matthew Newkirk House, Philadelphia (1835 — T. U. Walter); and the Commercial Bank, Natchez, Mississippi (1839 — James and Charles Dakin?). An example of the same format in Doric is the Joel Hayden House, Haydenville, Massachusetts (1828 — Ithiel Town or his contractor?).

Examples of the six-columned Ionic derived from the Erechtheum include the War Department Building, Washington, D.C. (1796–1797 — G. Hadfield); Washington City Hall, Washington, D.C. (1817–1821 — G. Hadfield); Bowers House, Northampton, Massachusetts (1826 — I. Town); J. A. Parker House, New Bedford, Massachusetts (1833 — R. Warren); Phil-Ellena, Philadelphia (1844 — ?); Elias Baker House,

Altoona, Pennsylvania (1845 — R. C. Long); Fatlands, Valley Forge, Pennsylvania (1845 — J. Haviland?); Madewood, Napoleonville, Louisiana (1846 — H. Howard); and Magnolia Hall, Greensboro, Alabama (1855 — B. F. Parsons).

11. There are always inexplicable exceptions to any rule: one villa of the Veneto, the Villa Morosini Capello, built at the end of the sixteenth century at Cartigliano, near Vicenza, bears a striking resemblance to Jefferson College, built in 1831 just upriver from New Orleans in Convent, Louisiana, which is now the Manresa Retreat House. The villa has twenty columns across the front, and the college twenty-two. Both have a pedimented central section, and both are essentially classicized raised cottages on a vast scale. But there is little likelihood that anyone in Louisiana had ever seen the villa.

Nor, though it would be delightful to think otherwise, is there any evidence that any of the architects of the classicized cottages knew anything about the *villa maritima,* a Roman form of colonnaded building stretched along a cliff or raised above a high basement, as depicted in the frescoes buried under volcanic ash at Pompeii and Herculaneum.

12. Palladio's contemporary, Sebastiano Serlio, depicted similar structures in a book of designs for small houses, which began to circulate soon after European explorers first returned from the New World. It may be significant that Serlio produced those drawings in France, not in Italy; it is possible that, like the Regency balcony, this was a European adaptation of an American idea.

13. The best summary of the current evidence, and the best purge of preceding misconceptions about The Forest, is "A Note on the History of the Forest Plantation, Natchez," by Alma Carpenter, in the *Journal of Mississippi History* 46, no. 2 (May 1984), from which come my quotations. A letter from the Dunbars' son, Archibald, to his mother, written in 1817 and printed in Carpenter's article, suggests that the new house was not quite complete in that year, so it seems best to fudge between 1816 and 1817 on the completion date.

This squares with the entry for January 13, 1852, in the journal of Dr. John C. Jenkins, grandson-in-law of the builder, stating that "the family mansion house at the Forest caught fire this morning . . . and burned to the cellars. . . . The Forest mansion was erected by my wife's grandmother . . . soon after the late war and has consequently been built about 36 years." "The late war" might be taken to be that with Mexico in 1848, but the rest of the evidence makes it clear that the good doctor was talking about the War of 1812, which squares with his "36 years."

14. Those Tuscan columns were illustrated in each of the five builder's guides listed in the inventory of Weeks's estate. Other works are listed, but five was enough for me to be quite confident that Weeks had the references at hand to do the work. For the inventory, see Milly McGehee, "Auburn in Natchez," *Antiques,* March 1977, 553, n. 14.

The scrutiny of Weeks's inventory was a useful inquiry because without it one might have thought that those Tuscan columns could have been derived not from Anglo-American practice but from the French.

Pierre-Denis de la Ronde is said to have built a magnificent plantation house about 1805, the ruins of which are still to be seen in New Orleans. It had a double gallery, with one set of columns above and the lower gallery being composed of an arcade of Tuscan columns. Samuel Wilson Jr. has noted that de la Ronde's grandfather, the architect-engineer Ignace-François Broutin, was probably the architect of the previous house on that site, built by Sieur Balthasar Ponfrac, chevalier de Masan. Broutin had proposed (but had not built) such a double gallery, with Tuscan columns below, for the Intendance in New Orleans as early as 1749. Masan's house may have had such an arrangement too. See Wilson's essay "Architecture of Early Sugar Plantations" in *Greek Fields,* a catalogue of an exhibition at the University of Southwestern Louisiana (1980), 55 ff.

My favorite New Orleans pirate-architect, Barthélemy Lafon (see Chapter 1 and *Orders from France*), proposed a set of monumental Tuscan columns for his public baths project for that city in the first decade of the nineteenth century. While Lafon was notorious, his designs were not famous, so with regret I must relinquish a claim for him as the great precursor for The Forest.

15. Weeks, on his client, to Ep Hoyt, September 27, 1812, Weeks Papers, Mississippi Department of Archives and History.

In my *Greek Revival America* I followed the "hearsay" embedded in local histories of Natchez to assert that before Lyman Harding gave him the commission for Auburn, Weeks did some classical remodeling for Winthrop Sargent, a Massachusetts Federalist who sheltered Weeks after Burr passed from the scene, adding a Roman portico of the Monticello style to Gloucester. But Ron and Mimi Miller, the preeminent historians of Natchez, have investigated that house and report that the evidence is quite clear that its portico dates from after Weeks's death, as does that for Cherokee, previously thought likely to be Weeks's work. Another house in Natchez, Monmouth, built for John Hankinson, has been attributed to Weeks, but Samuel Wilson Jr. informs me that the present portico was added in the 1840s or 1850s. It replaced a smaller one, which might have been the work of Weeks.

Chapter 18

1. I am indebted to my colleague James O. Horton for pointing out Remond's speech, printed in *Liberator,* February 25, 1842, to be found in the Black Abolitionist Papers, Library of Congress, microfilm reel 4.

2. The only biography of Richard Mentor Johnson is Leland W. Meyer's *The Life and Times of Colonel Richard Mentor Johnson of Kentucky,* Columbia University Studies no. 559, New York, 1932. There is *A Biographical Sketch of Col. Richard M. Johnson* "by a Kentuckian" (New York: Saxton and Miles, 1843).

The popular histories of the vice presidency cannot be recommended. On the other hand, Arthur Schlesinger Jr. deals respectfully with Johnson in *The Age of Jackson* (Boston: Little, Brown, 1945, and many subsequent editions), and Thomas Perkins Abernethy does so in briefer compass in his entry in the *Dictionary of American Biography*.

Like Some Green Laurel was published by the Louisiana State University Press in 1981. The subsequent controversy can be sampled in the *Journal of American History* 69, no. 4 (March 1983): 932–945, and no. 5 (June 1983): 224–226.

Chapter 19

1. Rush served as secretary of the treasury, attorney general, and ambassador to Great Britain.
2. Parkman's momentous question was posed in the introduction to his *Montcalm and Wolfe* (New York: Library of America, 1983), 844.
3. Parkman presented "Feudalism, Monarchy and Rome" in the introduction to *Pioneers of France in the New World*, the first volume of *France and England in North America* (Boston: Little, Brown, 1905), xix. The volume is dedicated to three of Parkman's kinsmen who were "slain in battle"; one of them was Robert Gould Shaw, a central figure in the film *Glory*. Even so close as that came the question!
4. "Half a million bayonets" appears in Parkman's introduction to *Pioneers of France*.
5. Charles Haight Farnham, *A Life of Francis Parkman* (Boston: Little, Brown, 1905), 191 ff., 281, 283–284, 287.
6. Francis Parkman, *The Conspiracy of Pontiac*, vol. 1 (Boston: Little, Brown, 1880), 45.
7. See note 5, above.
8. Quoted in Wilcomb Washburn, "Seventeenth Century Indian Wars," in *Handbook of American Indians*, vol. 15 (Washington, D.C.: Smithsonian Institution Press, 1978), 94.
9. Lawrence Stone, "Results of the English Revolution," in J. G. A. Pocock, ed., *Three British Revolutions: 1641, 1688, 1776* (Princeton: Princeton University Press, 1980), 47.
10. It is salutary to be reminded periodically of the unimportance of the North American possessions of Britain, Holland, and France relative to their holdings in the East and West Indies. In the Treaty of Breda, when the Dutch turned over New York to the English, it was exchanged for the nutmeg island of Pulo Run. In 1783, after the alliance of France, Spain, Holland, and the United States had beaten Great Britain to its knees, the French preferred to accept the island of Tobago and a slaving station in Senegal rather than Canada — which Voltaire dismissed as "a few acres of snow."
11. Parkman, *Pioneers of France*, 254.
12. Quoted in F. D. Nichols, *The Early Architecture of Georgia* (Chapel Hill: University of North Carolina Press, 1957), 234.
13. Brahm's account of Fort Loudoun is in a manuscript in the Harvard University Library. I have used James Patrick's version in his *Architecture in Tennessee* (Knoxville: University of Tennessee Press, 1981), 57.

Index

386

388

398